Programming Parallel Processors

Programming Parallel Processors

EDITED BY **Robert G. Babb II**
Oregon Graduate Center

ADDISON-WESLEY PUBLISHING COMPANY, INC.
Reading, Massachusetts • Menlo Park, California • New York
Don Mills, Ontario • Wokingham, England • Amsterdam • Bonn • Sydney
Singapore • Tokyo • Madrid • Bogotá • Santiago • San Juan

This book is in the Addison-Wesley Series in Computer Science.

Library of Congress Cataloging-in-Publication Data

```
Programming Parallel Processors.

   Includes index.
   1. Parallel programming (Computer science)   I. Babb,
Robert G.
QA76.6.P75168   1988   004'.35                  87-18833
ISBN 0-201-11721-5
```

Diagrams in this book were prepared by David C. DiNucci using gremlin and ditroff under Berkeley UNIX 4.3BSD on an Imagen 8/300 Laser Printer at Oregon Graduate Center, Beaverton, OR.
The text was typeset by ETP Services, Portland, Oregon, in Times Roman and Courier on a Linotronic 100 from troff source prepared by the editor.

BCDEFGHIJ-DO-898

Contents

Contents

Preface

This book reports practical experiences with programming commercially available scientific parallel processors. The intended audience is programmers, managers, and students in computer science and other disciplines with an interest in understanding the state of the art in software tools for programming the current generation of parallel processors. This record of our adventures should also prove of interest to the large number of software engineering researchers and system builders working actively today to develop better parallel programming languages and environments for the next generation of parallel processing computer systems.

This book developed from class projects in a graduate software engineering seminar that I taught at the Oregon Graduate Center in Spring 1986. Most of the students in the seminar had little or no experience with real parallel programming, although a few of the students had run parallel programs on the Department of Computer Science and Engineering's 32-node Intel iPSC Hypercube.

Although parallel computers are becoming increasingly available to the programming community today, the fraction of people (whether in industry or academia) who have actually run a parallel program is still small. Our experiences are probably representative of what any programmer might experience when first confronted with the brave new world of parallel programming. Some details reported in the chapters on programming the various machines are actually composites of some of the more interesting things that occurred during the course of our programming experiments, although they are written as if they all happened to the chapter author.

Since, by one recent count, there are currently over thirty companies worldwide that are building various flavors of parallel computers, we have been able to include only a small subset of machines in this compilation. The choice of machines was determined by the following criteria:

1. The machines had to be commercially available, rather than one-of-a-kind research testbeds.

2. The machines had to be accessible by the class. Generally, this meant that we needed either remote access via dial-up phone lines or travel support to gain

physical access to remote machines. Several machines (BBN Butterfly, Loral LDF-100, IBM 3090, and FPS T Series) were added to the list by class members after the class ended.

3. We wanted to include a wide range of machines, from supermini class (Sequent and Intel) to minisupercomputers (Alliant) to parallel vector supercomputers (CRAY, IBM).

4. We wanted experience with a variety of architectures and programming models, including both shared memory (Alliant, CRAY, IBM, and Sequent) and message-passing machines (BBN Butterfly, Intel iPSC, FPS T series, and Loral).

Since several of the machines that we worked on during the writing of this book were still quite new, the half-life for some of the implementation details discussed is quite short. In fact, it has been difficult for us to keep chapters up to date during the nine month period over which this book was written! However, some of the parallel programming environments have been fairly stable, and many of our more general observations about the nature of parallel programming should prove less perishable.

This book is not intended as a handbook on parallel computer architecture, although parallel architectural aspects are included for each machine where necessary to provide a basis for discussing various parallel programming issues.

In addition to the people who provided technical help with specific chapters, the editor would like to acknowledge the following people who read and commented on earlier drafts of the entire manuscript: Dan Hammerstrom, James Hardy, Ian Kaplan, Alan Karp, Richard Kieburtz, Kim Korner, and Alaine Warfield. The editor would also like to thank the reviewers of this work: Jack Dongarra, Argonne National Laboratory; Robert Hiromoto, Los Alamos National Laboratory; Harry Jordan, University of Colorado; and David Klappholz, Stevens Institute of Technology; for their suggestions and support for this project.

Beaverton, Oregon   R.G.B. II

Disclaimer:

Although we include examples showing how parallel execution performance can be measured for most of the machines, and we describe various ways in which this performance data for our tiny Pi Program example could be interpreted, these results should not be interpreted as definitive, formal performance benchmarks. It would be a serious misuse of our data to draw general conclusions regarding the relative performance of the various processors based on our limited experiments with a single small parallel program.

Contributors

Timothy S. Axelrod, Lawrence Livermore National Laboratory

Timothy S. Axelrod received the B.S. degree in physics from California Institute of Technology in 1969, the M.S. degree in applied physics from Stanford University in 1971, and the Ph.D. degree in physics from the University of California, Santa Cruz, in 1980.

Currently he is Group Leader for Parallel Processing in the Computational Physics Division of Lawrence Livermore National Laboratory. His interests include radiative transfer and numerical modeling of supernovae, as well as performance issues in parallel computing. He has published widely in these and other areas.

Robert G. Babb II, Oregon Graduate Center

Robert Babb is an Associate Professor of Computer Science and Engineering at the Oregon Graduate Center. He received the B.S. degree in astrophysics and mathematics from the University of New Mexico in 1969. In 1974 he received the M.Math. degree in computer science from the University of Waterloo, Ontario, Canada, and the Ph.D. degree in electrical engineering and computer science from the University of New Mexico.

From 1974 to 1976 he was an Assistant Professor in the Computer Science and Statistics Department at California Polytechnic State University, San Luis Obispo. From 1976 to 1978, he was a Visiting Assistant Professor of Computer Science at New Mexico State University. From 1978 to 1982, he was a Software Research Engineer with Boeing Computer Services Company, Seattle, developing methods and tools for large-scale software engineering.

His current research interests center on the application of Large-Grain Data Flow (LGDF) methods to software engineering, data-driven parallel processing, and super-computer system architecture.

Dr. Babb is a member of ACM and the IEEE Computer Society.

Contributors

Michael S. Beckerman, Tektronix

Michael Beckerman received the B.S. degree in computer science from Portland State University in 1984 and is working toward his M.S. in the Department of Computer Science and Engineering at the Oregon Graduate Center.

He is a Software Design Engineer working for Tektronix, Inc., and president of Dialectic Software Technologies, Inc., a software consulting firm.

His research interests include languages, specifications, programming environments, code generation, and Large-Grain Data Flow.

Frederica Darema-Rogers, IBM Hawthorne Research Laboratory

Frederica Darema-Rogers received the B.S. degree in physics and mathematics from the University of Athens, Greece, in 1969, the M.S. degree from the Illinois Institute of Technology in 1972, and the Ph.D. degree from the University of California at Davis in 1976, both in theoretical physics.

She was a Research Associate at the University of Pittsburg and Brookhaven National Laboratory and a Technical Staff Member at Schlumberger-Doll Research before joining IBM Research in 1982 as a Research Staff Member.

Her research interests are in the areas of parallel algorithms and techniques and tools for the development and performance analysis of parallel applications.

David C. DiNucci, Oregon Graduate Center

David DiNucci is a full-time graduate student in the Department of Computer Science and Engineering at the Oregon Graduate Center working towards an M.S. degree in computer science. He received the B.S. degree in computer science from Portland State University in 1983.

He has worked as a System Programmer at Portland State University and a Data Systems Coordinator for the Portland Public School District.

His current interests are in the fields of Large-Grain Data Flow and formal specifications.

Stuart W. Hawkinson, Floating Point Systems

Stuart Hawkinson received his B.S. degree in chemistry from Washington State University in 1965 and his Ph.D. in chemical physics from the University of Chicago in 1968. He performed post-doctoral research at Chicago under an NIH fellowship and was an NSF Post-Doctoral Investigator at Oak Ridge National Laboratory.

He is a Staff Scientist in the Product Definition Group at Floating Point Systems, where he has been actively involved in the development of parallel algorithms and architectures. Previously, he was a manager of the programming staff responsible for verification and performance enhancement of Floating Point Systems Math Libraries.

Before joining FPS, he was an Associate Professor of biochemistry and biophysics at the University of Tennessee, Knoxville, for ten years. He also held a Guest Scientist position at Oak Ridge National Laboratory in the Chemistry Division.

His current professional interests include numerical mathematics, parallel processing algorithms, and scientific computing applications.

Richard K. Helm, Floating Point Systems

Kent Helm is a graduate of Evergreen State College, Olympia, Washington, where he received his Bachelor's degree in computer science in 1982.

He is employed by Floating Point Systems as a Software Design Engineer specializing in parallel operating systems implementation.

Allan R. Larrabee, Boeing Computer Services

Allan Larrabee received a B.S. degree in biology and chemistry in 1957 from Bucknell University, Lewisburg, Pennsylvania. He received the Ph.D. degree in biochemistry with a minor in organic chemistry in 1962 from the Massachusetts Institute of Technology.

After two years in the Medical Service Corps, US Army, he did post-doctoral work at the National Institutes of Health, Bethesda, Maryland. In 1966 he became an Assistant Professor of Chemistry at the University of Oregon and in 1972 became an Associate Professor at Memphis State University, Memphis, Tennessee. He became a Full Professor at Memphis State in 1978.

He completed an M.S. degree in 1986 in the Department of Computer Science and Engineering at the Oregon Graduate Center. His thesis research was on adaptation of a large-scale computational chemistry program to the Intel iPSC Concurrent Computer. He is currently a Parallel Application Specialist for Boeing Computer Services, Bellevue, Washington.

James R. McGraw, Lawrence Livermore National Laboratory

Jim McGraw received the B.S. degree in computer science from Purdue University in 1972 and the Ph.D. degree in computer science from Cornell University in 1977. His thesis topic was "Language Features for Process Interaction and Access Control".

Dr. McGraw then became an Assistant Professor at the University of California, Davis, and a researcher for Lawrence Livermore National Laboratory (LLNL). During this time he became heavily involved in the design and use of applicative languages for multiprocessors. He is one of the principal designers of the SISAL language, which is now being implemented on a variety of multiprocessors by different research groups. Currently, he works for LLNL in the Computation Department. His administrative assignment is to organize, evaluate, and promote research projects in computer science for the laboratory.

His current research activities focus on the problem of writing highly parallel programs for multi-processor computers and automatically partitioning them for high system utilization.

Phillip C. Miller, Floating Point Systems

Phil Miller is a graduate of Purdue University, where he received his B.S.E.E. in 1978. He is currently pursuing an M.S. degree in computer science and engineering at the Oregon Graduate Center.

He is employed by Floating Point Systems as a Senior Software Engineer specializing in compiler design.

Contributors

Kurt B. Modahl, Oregon Graduate Center

Kurt Modahl is a part-time student pursuing an M.S. degree in computer science and engineering at the Oregon Graduate Center. He received his B.S. in natural science from the University of North Dakota in 1971.

He was a Research Associate at the Oregon Regional Primate Research Center from 1972 to 1982. From 1983 to 1984 he served as a Computer Consultant for Infotec Development, Inc.

His research interests are in parallel processing, program visualization, and object-oriented programming languages.

V. Alan Norton, IBM Yorktown Research Laboratory

Alan Norton received the B.A. degree from the University of Utah in 1968 and the Ph.D. degree from Princeton University in 1976, both in mathematics.

He was an Instructor at the University of Utah from 1976 to 1979 and an Assistant Professor at Hamilton College from 1979 to 1980. Currently he is a Research Staff Member at IBM, Yorktown Heights, New York, managing the parallel applications and architecture group of the Research Parallel Processing Project (RP3).

His research interests include the performance analysis and architecture of parallel computer systems, parallel algorithms, fractals, and computer graphics.

Douglas M. Pase, Oregon Graduate Center

Doug Pase received a B.S. degree in computer science and mathematics from Northern Arizona University, Flagstaff, Arizona. He is currently a full-time graduate student in the Department of Computer Science and Engineering at the Oregon Graduate Center.

He has designed and assisted in the design of compilers and parallel languages at Floating Point Systems and the Oregon Graduate Center.

His current research interests are in parallel language design, compilers, and advanced (parallel) computer architectures.

Keith E. Pennick, Boeing Computer Services

Keith Pennick received the B.S. degree in computer science from Washington State University in 1980. Currently he is a Systems Programmer for the High Speed Computing Center of Boeing Computer Services.

His primary interests are in parallel processing, networking, operating system design, and knowledge-based systems.

Gregory F. Pfister, IBM Research

Gregory Pfister received the S.B., S.M., and Ph.D. degrees in electrical engineering from MIT in 1967, 1969, and 1974, respectively.

He joined IBM in 1974, and from 1975 to 1976 was on the faculty of the Electrical Engineering and Computer Science Department of the University of California at Berkeley. In the IBM Research Division, he was Manager of Software Support for the Yorktown Simulation Engine (YSE) and is presently Principal Scientist of the RP3 project.

He has been elected to Eta Kappa Nu, Tau Beta Pi, and Sigma Xi, and is a senior member of the IEEE.

Charles E. St. John, Floating Point Systems

Chuck St. John is a graduate of Youngstown State University, Youngstown, Ohio, where he received his B.S.E.E. in 1977. He is currently pursuing an M.S. degree in electrical engineering from Oregon State University.

He is employed by Floating Point Systems as a Hardware Design Engineer specializing in the design of VLSI floating point arithmetic hardware. He is a member of IEEE and the IEEE Computer Society. His interests include parallel and high-performance architectures.

Stuart M. Stern, Boeing Computer Services Company

Stuart M. Stern received his B.S. degree in mathematics from Fairleigh Dickinson University in 1963.

He worked for The Boeing Company from 1964 to 1967, performing operating system support. From 1967 to 1972 he worked for Informatics, Inc., on several contracts, including IBM systems development, CBS News Presidential Election forecasting, and Air Force Intelligence graphics retrieval.

Mr. Stern was one of the founders of *CP/M Review* and *UNIX Review* magazines. He has been working for Boeing Computer Services since 1972. During this period, he was one of the principal designers of the original EXCHANGE ATM message switching system, designed a multitasking operating system for the MOSLER Corporation, and supported the AI Center's UNIX environment. Currently, he is working as an AI Specialist with Boeing Computer Services High Speed Computing Center.

Janice M. Stone, IBM Research

Janice Stone received the A.B. degree in mathematics from Duke University in 1962 and pursued graduate studies in mathematics at Georgetown University, and in logic and the philosophy of science at Stanford University.

She joined IBM research in 1984, where her research interests focus on parallel algorithms and tools for development and analysis of parallel programs.

Lise Storc, Oregon Graduate Center

Lise Storc is a part-time graduate student in the Department of Computer Science and Engineering at the Oregon Graduate Center working on her master's thesis. She received a B.S. in mathematics from the University of Texas at Austin in 1977 and attended graduate school in mathematics at the University of North Carolina at Chapel Hill.

She is currently employed as a Computer Scientist in the Medical Computing Research Laboratory at Emanuel Hospital and Health Center in Portland, Oregon, working on expert and graphics systems for a wide variety of medical applications.

Her current research interests are in parallel processing, medical expert systems, and the graphical display of complex mathematical objects.

1
Introduction

Robert G. Babb II

> *...WANTED for Hazardous Journey. Small wages, bitter cold, long months of complete darkness, constant danger, safe return doubtful. Honor and recognition in case of success.*
> — Ernest Shackleton[†]

Programming parallel processors is different. In 1984, when I ran my first parallel programs on the then brand-new Denelcor Heterogenous Element Processor (HEP) at Los Alamos National Laboratory, it quickly became apparent to me that parallel programming led to a higher "astonishment factor" than anything I had experienced in computing since my undergraduate days doing battle with PL/I.

The HEP had a very elegant and simple way of specifying synchronization operations in Fortran by reference to special *dollar-sign variables* (e.g., `$I`). The dollar-sign variables were shared via ordinary Fortran `COMMON`[‡] blocks between subroutines that could execute in parallel. Each dollar-sign variable had, in addition to its ordinary Fortran value (real or integer), a special bit that indicated whether the variable was *empty* or *full*. Attempting to assign a value to a full variable would cause a process to suspend until another process *emptied* the variable by reading a value from it. Similarly, a process that attempted to access the value of an empty variable (usually on the right side of an assignment statement) would be suspended automatically by efficient hardware

---

[†]From a newspaper advertisement for an Antarctic Expedition.

[‡]Throughout this book, including the reprinted material in the Appendices, we have used this font only for program text and machine values, and for characters typed on terminals. Words like *subroutine* (that are used by programmers as if they were normal English words) are generally not put in the special font unless they refer to a particular line of code containing the word `SUBROUTINE`. On the other hand, Fortran program elements such as `COMMON`, `IF`, and `DO` are usually set in this special font because their meaning in programs differs from their English meanings.

mechanisms, to come back to life after another process had written a value into the variable, with the side effect of *filling* it. To get more than one Fortran subroutine running, the CREATE statement, a parallel version of the ordinary Fortran CALL, allowed start up of separate, parallel *threads* of execution.

These two seemingly innocuous extensions to Fortran let loose the parallel genie on the world. One could now (in safe, old-fashioned Fortran, no less) create *semaphores*, *locks*, *processes* or *tasks*, *busy waits*, *barriers*, *critical sections*, and *monitors*. On the down side, programmers now had to deal with unpredictable and usually nonrepeatable situations of *deadlock*, *livelock*, *race conditions*, and *nondeterminism*. Suddenly, even very simple tasks, programmed by experienced programmers who were dedicated to the idea of making parallel programming a practical reality, seemed to lead inevitably to upsetting, unpredictable, and totally mystifying bugs. The difficulties we parallel pioneers experienced on the HEP seemed a lot worse than could be explained by the hardware and system software bugs that are common features with any very new computer system.

Since the coming (and, sad to say, passing) of the HEP, a large number of companies around the world have built a whole menagerie of commercial parallel machines. Some of them were built as special projects by established computer companies, but many have been built by startups that were able to convince venture capitalists that parallel processing was an idea whose time (and money) had come.

This book attempts to capture, at least at a tutorial level, the state of the art in programming commercially available scientific parallel computers. A number of other parallel machines that are specialized for such tasks as pattern matching [1] and signal processing have also appeared recently, but they are beyond the scope of this book. The machines we have included range in power from minicomputers to supercomputers. Their unifying feature is that they are all examples of commercially available scientific parallel machines that support *user-visible* parallel programming.

1.1 A BRIEF HISTORY OF PARALLEL PROCESSING

Parallel processing is not new. Operating systems have relied upon simulated and actual parallel operation of computers for at least twenty years. Hardware designers have dealt with the problems and rewards of parallelism at least since the days of von Neumann. In fact, early paper designs for what we know today as the von Neumann machine included consideration of a variety of parallel features. These parallel designs were rejected mainly because of the poor reliability of the components available for building machines. The designers' lack of experience in building any kind of computing engine also argued for adoption of the simplest possible design.

What *is* new is that computer manufacturers have begun to provide ways for application designers and programmers to control and exploit multiple CPUs directly to cooperate in solving a problem.

Some of the current confusion in the field of parallel programming is due to the wide variety of different computing cultures that have given us the terminology in common use among parallel programming afficionados. This also leads frequently to situations in which one basic concept can be described with three or four different words or phrases that have almost, but not quite, identical connotations.

An even larger discrepancy in terminology arises in the difference between *shared-memory* and *message-passing* machines. Each type of machine can simulate the other, but there seems to be a clear dividing line between the two camps, which of course is reflected in two overlapping but not identical sets of terms for related concepts.

1.2   PARALLEL PROCESSING TERMINOLOGY

When a particular instance of a code is executed on a machine, all of the work needed to execute that program is referred to as a single *task* or *process*. When a task executes on a multiprocessor, it can divide into several (possibly many) different and independent *threads* of execution. in the absence of other constraints, each of these threads of execution can execute simultaneously on different processors.

Each independent thread of execution is known as a *process*. It is often necessary for two or more processes to share information. For example, one process may compute some values that are used by another. If these values are stored in memory that is accessible to both processes, we describe it as being *shared data*. Shared data must always be accessed carefully to ensure correct program operation. We would not want one process writing the data while another is trying to read it.

A *critical region* refers to a section of code that must be executed with exclusive access to the shared data referenced within that code. A process preparing to enter a critical region may be delayed if any other process is currently executing inside a similar region. *Semaphores* or *locks* are one type of programming tool that can be used by programmers or compilers to implement critical regions safely.

On distributed memory machines (such as the Intel Hypercube), *messages* are used in much the same way that locks or semaphores are used on shared memory machines to *synchronize* computations. Of course, locks and messages are not mutually exclusive, since it is possible to conceive of hybrid machines which could make use of both kinds of synchronization simultaneously.

One way to coordinate multiple threads of computation periodically is to create a *barrier*. Several types of barriers have proven useful in scientific application programming. In one type, all processes in a group must arrive at a certain point in their code (the barrier) before any are allowed to proceed. A variant is to have a *single-thread* section following the barrier that any one (but only one) of the processes executes. A variant of this latter type of barrier is to allow only the *last* process to arrive to execute the single-thread critical region.

When a process attempts to *lock* (acquire) a lock, the act of getting the lock must be *atomic*. That is, only one of a set of processes should be capable of obtaining the lock. Processes that fail to get the lock can choose to *suspend* (when another suspended process is available to use the CPU), or can *busy wait* (sometimes called *spinning*) and keep trying repeatedly to obtain the lock. (This last strategy is obviously unattractive if it is possible that the lock will never be released!)

Deadlock refers to a situation in which each member of a group of processes is waiting for another member of the group to do something (typically, to unlock or release a lock). *Livelock* is more active but no more productive. It refers to a situation in which each member of a group of processes is busy signaling (passing messages) to other members of the group, but doing nothing to advance the progress of a computation.

In real life, things are sometimes very complicated. It is possible for some parts of a parallel program to be deadlocked, some parts to be livelocked, while another running process manages to compute the desired answer. It is even possible for sequential program bugs to masquerade as parallel errors [2].

1.3   SOFTWARE ENGINEERING ISSUES

Parallel programming can be even more frustrating than is regular programming. In addition to the usual software engineering problems common to all forms of program development, an additional set of problems must be avoided, and additional criteria must be met for a parallel program to be judged successful. Software engineering problems directly related to the introduction of parallelism include:

- Avoiding deadlock and livelock;

- Preventing unwanted race conditions;

- Avoiding the creation of too many parallel processes; and

- Detecting program termination (no longer a trivial matter!).

New evaluation criteria for parallel programs include:

- Program speedup versus number of processors;

- Size of synchronization overhead;

- Effect of problem size on speedup;

- Maximum number of processors that can be kept busy; and

- Determinism of program execution.

In addition, new software design issues arise, such as:

- What size program "chunks" should be used?

- How many parallel processes should be created?

- What form of process synchronization should be adopted?

- How should access to shared data be managed?

- How can deterministic program execution be guaranteed?

- How should processing tasks be subdivided to make the most effective use of available parallel hardware?

Debugging parallel programs is notoriously difficult. Race conditions can masquerade as program logic errors. When deadlock occurred on the HEP, for example, the addresses where the various parallel processes were hung (waiting for each other) could, after some effort, be determined. However, figuring out the sequence of events that got the program *into* the deadlock situation was usually much more difficult. Attempts at traditional debug tracing can drastically affect the parallel behavior of a program. Non-deterministic programs often "fix themselves" when tracing is added, since the tracing serializes a portion of the execution.

1.4 EXAMPLE PROBLEM

The contributors to this book were asked to implement the same very small problem on each of the parallel processors. The Pi Program[†] computes an approximation to π by using the rectangle rule to compute an approximation to the definite integral:

$$\int_0^1 f(x)\,dx$$

where

$$f(x) = \frac{4}{(1+x^2)}$$

and the rectangle rule states:

$$R_n(f) = h \sum_{i=1}^n f(x_i)$$

where:

$$h = 1/n$$

$$x_i = (i - 1/2)h$$

Since this is such a small parallel program, some of the parallel programming pitfalls mentioned previously did not occur. However, even this very tiny benchmark problem was useful in exposing the "flavor" of the various parallel programming environments, and also led to some interesting experiences on the various machines. Note that the Pi Program is compute-intensive. It does not address other important issues in parallel processing, for example, the effect of I/O bottlenecks.

Outline of a Typical Chapter

The write-up for each machine in Chapters 3–10 is intended to characterize each machine with respect to:

- Hardware:

    Described only in enough detail to support the programmer's view of the various parallel features, and then just enough to explain the example — other, more detailed information on each system can be found in the Appendices.

[†]This problem was suggested by Cleve Moler, Intel Scientific Computers.

- Software:

  An introduction to the parallel software environment provided by the machine, the operating system, and how the parallel hardware mechanisms appear in software. We have also described how program development typically proceeds, including a brief description of the steps necessary to develop, debug, and time parallel programs.

- Parallel Program Example:

  A discussion of the parallel programming strategy for (sometimes several versions of) the Pi Program, along with a listing of the program interspersed with detailed explanations highlighting various parallel features and explaining what they do. The intention is to provide enough explanation, in small enough chunks, to understand the parallel highlights of the program. Readers desiring more in-depth information on the parallel mechanisms involved can find details in the Appendices.

- Performance:

  Including aspects of how timing was done, if not covered with the explanation of the example program.

- Pitfalls and Problems:

  Experience, including both parallel and non-parallel pitfalls/problems encountered, as well as positive experiences.

- Conclusions

- Acknowledgments

- References

The Appendices contain program listings for the example problem, selected excerpts from manufacturers' parallel programming documentation, and other information supporting Chapters 3–10.

Chapter 2, which was written in 1984, describes some early experiences with parallel processing on the Denelcor HEP and the CRAY X-MP by two researchers at Lawrence Livermore National Laboratory. The chapter examines problems involved in moving applications programs to multiprocessors and outlines possible strategies to resolve these problems. A preprint of this paper was one of the main inspirations for this book.

1.5 REFERENCES

[1]   W. Danny Hillis, "The Connection Machine", Cambridge, MA: MIT Press, 1985.

[2]   Robert E. Hiromoto, Los Alamos National Laboratory, private communication.

2
Exploiting Multiprocessors: Issues and Options

James R. McGraw and Timothy S. Axelrod

> *The behavior of even quite short parallel programs can be astonishingly complex. The fact that a program functions correctly once, or even one hundred times, with some particular set of inputs, is no guarantee that it will not fail tomorrow with the same inputs.*

2.1 INTRODUCTION

The time is very close at hand when the next generation of supercomputers will be upon us. Manufacturers, unable to provide sufficient speed solely through faster hardware components, now propose multiprocessors as the new direction that computers must take. As in the case of the arrival of the first vector processors, we now face the need to move into yet another form of high-speed computing. Our purpose in this paper is to examine the issues and options facing us as we prepare to make this transition.

We make two basic assumptions about the ways that we ultimately will use multiprocessors. First, we assume that all of the resources of a computing system should be applied to the execution of one program at a time. Second, we assume that programs must exploit more general forms of concurrency than is available simply through vectorization.

The first point addresses the issue of usability. Certainly we can choose to use multiprocessors by partitioning the available machine resources (e.g., memory) among the processors and run separate job streams through each one. In the near term, this option will almost certainly be used. To use multiprocessors effectively, however, we must be able to solve the largest possible problems in the shortest amount of time. Therefore, we focus on the issue of partitioning one problem at a time across all available processors.

The second point addresses the inherent weakness in vectorization. Although extremely useful, vectorization fails to include many forms of concurrency that we will need to use in the future. We cannot afford to give up vectorization, but we must look beyond it.

The thought of parallel processing immediately raises many difficult questions. Consider the following ones as examples:

- What means can we use to express various forms of concurrency in programs?

- How can we describe necessary forms of synchronization?

- What effects will concurrency have on the types of algorithms that best exploit multiprocessors?

- Will the various forms of concurrency lead to nonrepeatable results in programs?

- How can we debug concurrent programs?

- How will we know when a concurrent program is finally correct?

This paper begins to address many of these questions in two ways. The next section describes four recent and representative encounters that we have had in our attempts to program multiprocessors. For each case, we begin by describing the basic problem that we were trying to execute on the machine. We then describe the results we observed and the debugging strategies employed to try to remove errors. We conclude each case by identifying the ultimate causes for our problems and the lessons we drew from each experience. Following this section we highlight four basic strategies for programming multiprocessors that have received the most attention in the computer science literature. For each one we try to assess their future potential and applicability to large-scale scientific computing in places like Livermore and Los Alamos.

2.2   EXPERIENCES WITH FORTRAN EXTENSIONS

This section describes some of our efforts in parallel processing using several different types of Fortran extensions. Our objective is to convey a relatively high-level view of the issues and problems facing programmers who want to use this strategy for exploiting parallel machines. Fortran presents a well-defined approach to algorithm design and programming. However, parallel processing also has its own set of constraints that must be imposed. In this section we hope to demonstrate that the interface between these two sides is awkward at best. Most notable are the following problems:

- Non-repeatable errors will occur often;

- Correct answers *do not* necessarily imply a correct program;

- Conventional debugging techniques can yield misleading information; and

- Moving existing programs to parallel systems requires almost complete reexamination of every aspect of the program.

Some of the work reported here was carried out on the Denelcor HEP system, and the rest was done on the CRAY X-MP. These two systems extend Fortran in slightly different ways, but, for purposes of our discussion, they are very close. Both provide a basic mechanism for initiating parallel processes. For example, on the HEP a subroutine can be either `CALL`ed or `CREATE`d. In the latter case, the caller continues to execute, and the subroutine becomes a separately executing process. The key point is that programmers have full responsibility for deciding which operations will proceed in parallel. Communication between processes takes place in both systems through shared data. Both systems provide tools that allow programmers to establish critical regions. Here the key point is that programmers have full responsibility for making sure that every use of these tools actually provides safe access to the shared data.

With this quick overview, we now present several cases of parallel processing problems that we have encountered.

Case 1: Assigning Work

This program was written to compute the integral of a one-input function over a specified interval from `A` to `B`. The simplest parallel algorithm for this problem divides the interval into `N` different subintervals and gives each subinterval to a different process. Each process can then work independently, using some algorithm like the trapezoidal rule for computing the integral for its subinterval. As each finishes, a critical region can be used to have each process add its portion of the area into a global shared variable. The program begins by creating all of the processes and giving each one a unique identification number that can be used to determine which subinterval it should process. For that part, we use the following Fortran code:

```
        DO 100 I = 1 , N
            CREATE CALC (I)
100     CONTINUE
```

Each `CALC` process uses the formula:

$$(B - A) / N * (I - 1) + A$$

to find the left boundary of the interval to be processed. Details of the remaining portions of the program turn out not to be relevant for our discussion here.

Observed Results

The first phase of program testing executed the program with one process (substituting `CALL` for `CREATE` in the preceding loop). Once this phase was completed, it was assumed that the body of the function was operating correctly (given that it did no further `CREATE`s and accessed no shared variables other than in the final critical region). Parallel testing produced wildly differing behavior. No two test runs produced the same answer, and none matched the known correct answer. Even repeated tests of the same value for `N` produced different results. First, checks were made on the critical region that summed the results to make sure that only one answer at a time was being added into the total. That code was indeed correct.

The next step was to circumvent the critical region by having each process report its partial results separately into an array (using the value of `I` as the place where each result was to be stored). The next set of runs showed that several positions in the array were not receiving any value (or if they were, their answer was zero). Each run showed different intervals being left out, but most were concentrated toward the left side of the A-to-B interval. Furthermore, the sum of the values stored in the array was significantly less that the total reported by the processes when they added all of the values together in the shared variable.

Further tests showed that each process was doing some interval processing and reporting its results into the array. It was then determined that while some subintervals were being ignored, other subintervals were being processed more than once. Again, the distribution of repeated intervals changed with each run, and there seemed to be no correlation about how many times a specific interval was processed. Finally, we discovered that somehow each process was not getting a different value for I. Some processes got the same number, whereas other I values were not picked up by any process.

Problem Cause

The problem cause was finally identified as an unintended (and undesired) form of data sharing that arose in the CREATE statement shown earlier. Fortran passes all parameters by reference, which means that the address of the variable I was passed to each CALC and thus became shared by all N processes and by the initial process that created everyone else. As each process was created, it would access I to compute its interval of responsibility, but at the same time the initial process would be changing I as a part of the DO loop. Depending on the exact timing and scheduling of the processes, any one process could get either the value of I intended for it or some arbitrary later value of I.

One further point is worth noting here. A simple fix for this error, a solution based on years of experience with Fortran, is often proposed. By turning the parameter passed to CALC into some expression (something like I*1 will suffice), experience tells us that actions of the subroutine will not alter the value of I for the main program. This solution would seem to break the unwanted shared variable. It does not. Fortran simply creates a temporary variable to hold the value of I*1, and the address of that temporary variable is then passed to CALC. Now, instead of everyone sharing the address of I, they share the address of the temporary variable! The simplest correct solution is to create an array that contains the arguments for each task. In this case, the code appears as follows:

```
    DO  100   I = 1 , N
        IARG(I)  =  I
        CREATE CALC  (IARG(I))
100 CONTINUE
```

Post Mortem

This simple example shows some of the basic problems commonly encountered in parallel processing. Each time a program is run, different answers can appear—even with identical input. The nature of the errors do not help point out the section of the program that causes the different actions to occur. Note that using the array to store the result of each process helps, but it still caused confusion because we assumed that using I would store each process's result in a different location. In fact, since several processes had the same value of I, they processed the same interval and overwrote the same answer in the array. It simply looked like several processes were not doing any work, and the quite reasonable debugging step introduced yet another unintended shared variable (several processes accessed the same array positions). Admittedly, the error in the program was an extremely simple one. Our frustration arose out of the fact that such a simple error took so much energy and time to identify.

Case 2: Dual Algorithms

The next programming problem focuses on a more sophisticated form of parallel processing. The objective was a *divide-and-conquer* implementation of integration using an algorithm called adaptive quadrature [1]. The assumption in this algorithm is that the cost of function calls is extremely high. Therefore, we want to decide at run time where best within the interval the evaluations should be done. Divide-and-conquer means that we try to break the problem into independent intervals, use some test to decide if each one has a good approximation, and then make independent decisions on which intervals need to be divided further. As a result, some subintervals receive very little processing and others are broken up further and further.

The one catch to our implementation was that we wanted to ensure that the program did not create too much concurrency. In an uncontrolled situation, such a program could easily create a deadlock (various portions of the program need other portions to make progress before they can continue, but a circularity of need allows no process to go). For example, you might want to keep a list of all intervals needing further processing. What happens if the list is full, and all active processes need to put more intervals on the list? We wanted to absolutely safeguard our program against any possible deadlock.

We accomplished this goal by writing two versions of the algorithm for adaptive quadrature. The first (and main one) was the parallel form. It spawned more processes as it found more work to be done. However, if any machine limits were near (such as no more memory in the list) the algorithm dropped into the second version of the algorithm. This version made progress toward completion of the algorithm without spawning new work—but it did so sequentially. It also periodically checked to see if more work could be spawned, and if so, returned control to the parallel version.

Observed Results

This program created several different levels of problems. Initially, the program deadlocked quite frequently, in spite of our efforts to prevent this outcome. Fortunately, we could determine at which statement each process became stalled, and it took only several hours of work to discover and correct our errors. Those problems were caused by incorrectly writing a critical region around the list of intervals needing more work so that *no* process could access the list.

Once beyond that problem, the program always ran to completion and produced some answers. Unlike the other integration problem, however, we could not check out all of the code in serial mode because one of the two algorithms depended heavily on parallel processing, so the sequential algorithm was checked out.

In parallel execution, we again produced different answers each time we ran the program. This time they were usually close to the right answer, but still visibly wrong. Our first guess was that the two algorithms were somehow making different divide decisions when it came time to split work. Since different executions can allow different processes to proceed at different rates, such problems cause them to compute different answers. We first tried to trace the patterns of divide decisions (via print statements) and determine which version of the algorithm was making each decision. The resulting mass of data was too overwhelming to analyze.

The next tack was to find a smaller integration problem that exhibited the same execution characteristics so we could manage the output data. Very small problems produced correct results. Fortunately, by accident we stumbled onto one problem that was big enough to cause the problems, but small enough for us to manage the outpouring of intermediate divide decisions. Indeed, we did have such a problem in our two divide routines. It turned out that the divide routine in the sequential version (the one we thought we had checked out) was in error. It did work fine if it was the only one running, but not if it ever had to deal with subintervals of a region.

Unfortunately, fixing that mistake did not change the program behavior; it still produced nonrepeatable numbers. The answers were close, but still wrong. What was worse, we had finally discovered a way to make a sufficiently small problem use either one or the other of the two algorithms exclusively (they were small enough to avoid deadlock just by their size). Running with either algorithm inhibited produced the correct result!

Problem Cause

The core of the problem in this program was in a little-used section of code that allowed switching between the two versions of the algorithm. The following sequence of events had to occur for any computational problems to arise:

1. The queue of intervals on the list had to become full so that the sequential version of the integration went into use.

2. At least two of the intervals currently being examined had to complete with no further dividing so that some space on the queue could be freed up.

3. At least one of the intervals being processed under sequential integration had to discover the free space and try to deal off its excess work.

Once this sequence of events took place, the new intervals put on the list did not have exactly the same endpoint values as they were originally calculated. The likelihood of this set of events occurring turned out to be far smaller than we originally thought possible. Furthermore, it was nearly impossible to force this sequence of events to occur so that we could systematically check out that code ahead of time.

Post Mortem

The lesson we learned from this experience is difficult to explain. Divide-and-conquer is a very powerful technique for creating concurrency and achieving high processor utilization. Our tests were able to keep all available processing power active over 95% of the time. From a user's view, deadlock prevention is also essential. We cannot imagine trying to explain that a user's program fits on the machine but sometimes creates so much concurrency that the machine chokes on it. (I think the user would argue, "Well, use less concurrency.")

We believe that the problem is inherent in the nature of the language and the primitive features for describing concurrency and critical regions. The basic divide-and-conquer algorithm is clearly determinate, yet the tools that we use to describe that algorithm allow us to express indeterminate calculations routinely. Any errors in programming, whether in or out of critical regions, can lead to nonrepeatable results. In this case, by moving between two different versions of the same algorithm, we risk inconsistencies in processing—like the exact bounds of an interval changing slightly.

It seems natural to allow a programmer to identify the portions of a program that can operate simultaneously. But if the programmer has sole responsibility for the correctness of that information, we must be certain the programmer is correct. As the base language from which such analysis must begin, Fortran prevents compilers from making any such determination automatically. We know of no tools that can be added to Fortran to guarantee both concurrency and determinate behavior in all programs.

One final footnote to this problem deserves mention. We recently translated this program to run on a four-processor VAX cluster (after running over fifty tests on the HEP). After the program appeared to be running correctly, we began some simple timing tests. During those tests we began to get slightly incorrect answers in about one in every ten runs. The cause: yet another bug in the same section of code. This error was in the "final" HEP version, but it never made its presence known. The moral of the story: as long as programmers are responsible for managing all synchronization, it will be extremely difficult (if not impossible) to know that all possible timing errors have been eliminated.

Case 3: Unintentional Sharing

This problem arose during the conversion of a radiative transfer code running on the CRAY-1 into a multitasking code for the HEP. The problem being solved is time dependent, and the calculation for each timestep has three sequential stages. The code is restricted to spherical symmetry, and the heart of the algorithm, which is the second of the three stages, proceeds by stepping along a series of rays, each ray being tangent to a spherical shell. The integration along each ray can proceed independently of all the others, offering a natural partitioning of the problem. Therefore, for the HEP version, we created a group of parallel processes, each of which was to proceed by finding a ray that needed to be calculated, doing this calculation, and once again looking for a new ray. The first and third stages of the calculation also had simple partitionings, basically consisting of doubly nested DO loops with independent outer iterations.

There were clearly several places where synchronization of the parallel processes was required:

1. It was necessary to separate each of the three sequential stages by synchronization barriers so that no process could proceed to the next stage until all processes had completed the current stage.

2. Care was needed to ensure that no two processes ever picked the same ray to work on and that no ray would be left uncalculated.

3. During the process of stepping along a ray, it is necessary to update some shared arrays, and this update clearly had to be done within a critical section.

Observed Results

The conversion seemed to go smoothly at first. After only a day of work, the parallel version of the code had been written and successfully compiled. An initial bug, involving the synchronization barrier code, was rapidly found and corrected. The resulting code was tested with 1 and then 10 active processes, and both cases gave results identical to the original CRAY code. We were through! All that remained was to run the code for varying numbers of processes to get speedup information. This was rapidly accomplished, but in the course of examining the results, it was found that the run with 5 active processes did not give the same answer as the other cases. The differences were small, typically in the fourth or fifth decimal place, and showed up only after a number of timesteps had been run. Furthermore, successive runs of the 5-process case with identical input did not give identical results, with differences again showing up in the fourth or fifth decimal place.

An intensive debugging effort began. It was very difficult to make progress, mainly due to the lack of debugging tools that would not perturb the execution of the code. We found, for example, that it was useless to insert `WRITE` statements into the code for debugging purposes. The problem would simply disappear. Clearly, the presence of the `WRITE` statements significantly perturbed the timing of some critical events, masking the problem we were looking for. In the hope of isolating the difficulty to a single one of the three sequential stages, we made a version of the code that allowed any set of the stages to be run with only a single active process, whereas the remainder were run with all processes active, as originally intended. We ran all 8 possible combinations. The results were confusing, but seemed to point to "leakage" through the synchronization barriers. Intensive examination of this part of the code turned up nothing, however. After two days and nights of this, it began to appear that our difficulties could be caused only by a hardware problem. We ran out of time and went home discouraged.

Problem Cause

The real cause of the problem was found a few weeks later. The ray integration routine made use of several small arrays for storing intermediate results. In the original CRAY version of the code, it was convenient to keep these arrays in a `COMMON` block, and they remained in `COMMON` for the HEP code. But now, with multiple processes performing ray integrations simultaneously, each process needed its own private copies of these arrays. Instead, a single copy of each array was being unintentionally shared by all processes. Each process made use of these arrays for a very brief part of the calculation, however, so the probability was good that no two processes would use them simultaneously. The code therefore performed properly most of the time. Once this problem was corrected, the code ran properly for all cases we tried.

Post Mortem

There are clearly several lessons to be learned here:

1. It is especially hazardous to convert an existing code to run in a parallel environment. Since the changes that will be made are usually small, at least as measured in lines of code changed, it is rare to make the kind of thorough analysis that would happen as a matter of course if the code were being written from scratch. As a result, it is too easy to retain a structure that will be incorrect in the new environment.

2. In general, data structures should be shared between processes only after careful consideration. Unintentional sharing should be one of the first possibilities considered when debugging.

3. The prospects for finding a timing-dependent bug with the usual debugging techniques are bleak. With our current lack of debugging tools, the most profitable approach is often careful analysis of the code with paper, pencil, and listing.

Case 4: Races and Deadlocks

Nearly all of the parallel codes we have written share the need for synchronization barriers, a construct that forces each process arriving at the barrier to wait until all others have arrived. Barriers are most commonly needed when an algorithm consists of several stages to be performed in sequence, each of which has internal parallelism but which must not overlap their execution.

For the CRAY X-MP we wrote a subroutine called SYNCAL to implement the barrier and have used it in a variety of codes. The manner in which SYNCAL functions is very simple. When a process calls SYNCAL, a counter is incremented and compared with the number of processes that will eventually arrive at the barrier (which must be known in advance). If not all processes have arrived, the calling process waits for an EVENT to be posted. If the process is the last to arrive, it posts the EVENT, allowing all waiting processes to proceed, resets the counter to zero, and proceeds with its own execution. There is an obvious danger, however. Unless the increment of the shared counter is protected with a critical region, two or more processes can attempt the increment simultaneously, leading to incorrect behavior. We were careful to avoid this danger by using a LOCK to protect the counter.

Observed Results

We had SYNCAL working very quickly. It was, after all, less than 20 lines of Fortran. After the initial tests were passed successfully, we began to use SYNCAL within several codes. Problems immediately arose. Some significant fraction of the time, a code would terminate with deadlock, with one or more processes waiting forever for the EVENT to be posted. Again results were not repeatable, and again conventional debugging techniques were useless.

Problem Cause

A bit of thought turned up at least two ways that SYNCAL could malfunction, both of which occurred only when more than one barrier was present. In both cases the problem arose because the programmer had in mind a particular ordering of events when he wrote the program, but a great variety of orderings was in fact possible. To illustrate, SYNCAL consisted of the following code:

```
        SUBROUTINE SYNCAL
        COMMON /SYNCCOM/ NPR, NSYNCD, SYNCLOK, SYNCEV
C
        CALL LOCKON (SYNCLOK)
        NSYNCD=NSYNCD+1
        LNSYNCD=NSYNCD
        CALL LOCKOFF (SYNCLOK)

        IF (LNSYNCD .LT. NPR) THEN
            CALL EVWAIT(SYNCEV)
            CALL EVCLEAR(SYNCEV)
        ELSE
            CALL EVPOST(SYNCEV)
            CALL LOCKON (SYNCLOK)
            NSYNCD=0
            CALL LOCKOFF (SYNCLOK)
        ENDIF
C
        RETURN
        END
```

The programmer's tacit assumption was that all the code following the ELSE statement would be executed *at once* by the last process to arrive at the barrier. But there is no guarantee of this. What happens, for example, if that process "goes to sleep" for a while after executing "CALL EVPOST ..." but before resetting the counter? In that case, some other process can arrive at the *next* barrier while the counter still has its final value from the *previous* barrier. It then erroneously decides it is the last process to arrive and proceed on its way. We found another, similar, problem with the preceding code. With these problems fixed, SYNCAL worked reliably.

We then began running some of our codes on a much more lightly loaded X-MP, on which we almost always had both CPUs to ourselves. Codes again began dying with deadlock! The cause was nearly the same as before. Again there was a possible sequence of events that we had not considered and that would result in improper functioning. As it happened, the fix this time required major changes to SYNCAL which increased its length by over a factor of two. SYNCAL, has now been functioning without error for a long period of time, and we will be surprised (at least a little) if further problems arise.

Post Mortem

Again there are some useful lessons from this experience:

1. In a parallel environment, very small pieces of code are capable of a surprisingly great variety of behavior if they involve interprocess interaction.

2. It is therefore valuable to encapsulate such pieces of code as completely as possible and, once they are functioning correctly, share them as widely as possible.

2.3 OPTIONS ON THE HORIZON

Realistically, we see four different ways that applications software can be written for multiprocessors during the next five to ten years. Each of these currently has some severe drawbacks that limit their desirability. The four can be briefly described as follows:

1. Extend existing languages, such as Fortran, with new operations that allow users to express concurrency and synchronization.

2. Extend existing compilers to identify concurrent operations where possible and add the necessary synchronization to maintain program correctness.

3. Add a new *language layer* on top of an existing language to describe the desired concurrency and necessary synchronization, while allowing the basic applications program to remain relatively unaltered.

4. Define a totally new language and compiler system that integrates the concepts of concurrency and synchronization with all of our existing views of describing computational algorithms.

This section examines each of these options in a little more detail. For each option, we identify the primary motivations behind pursuing such an approach and the critical unsolved issues that limit its acceptance at this time. It should be pointed out that these options do not represent totally orthogonal approaches, and therefore there can be no hard lines drawn between them. Each involves some language and compiler changes. To some extent these four options can be combined to create other possibilities with improved advantages; however, they also tend to exacerbate the problems.

Language Extensions

Most experience to date with multiprocessors has been gained by using an existing programming language (usually Fortran) minimally extended to permit use of the multiprocessor. This approach typically requires changes in some or all of the following areas:

- Support of reentrancy;

- Creation and termination of parallel processes;

- Synchronization of parallel processes; and

- Distinguishing between process-private and process-shared data.

There are a number of successful language extensions that demonstrate differing approaches to providing what is needed [2] [3] [4]. Each of these language extensions has been used successfully to write and debug multiprocessing application programs. There are additional language extension efforts at earlier stages of development [5].

In addition to the obvious attraction of expediency, the language extension approach, when properly implemented, has some other advantages:

1. In many cases, the extensions can be added solely through the addition of new library routines, leaving the original language and its compiler untouched. This makes it relatively easy and inexpensive to experiment with alternative extensions. Extensions that prove valuable may eventually be incorporated into a new language.

2. An existing application code can be converted to multitasking with minimal changes, at least if the degree of change is measured by the number of code lines changed. Most of the changes are to the skeleton of the code that manages the parallel processes and their data, leaving the computational "guts" of the code unchanged.

There are also difficulties associated with the language extension approach. Most of these arise from the compiler's lack of knowledge about how parallelism is being used in the program. This makes it impossible to analyze how data is being shared between processes, for example, which eliminates a potentially valuable source of information for optimization and debugging. Similarly, the compiler may perform optimizations that are actually *incorrect* in the parallel environment. For example, the compiler, knowing nothing of synchronization primitives, may cause disaster by moving code outside of a critical region. This has actually occurred with Cray Research's CFT compiler.

A related difficulty (or perhaps feature) is that the programmer is only weakly restricted in the ways that synchronization constructs and shared data can be used. It is therefore very easy to write incorrect code, as our examples in Section 2.2 should amply demonstrate. A language designed from the beginning to support parallelism might reduce the incidence of incorrect code by enforcing more strict rules. Only experience will tell where an acceptable balance between freedom and restrictiveness lies. Clearly, much of this experience will be gained from experimenting with language extensions.

Compiler Analysis

From the perspective of the applications code developers, undoubtedly the hope is that they need to make no changes to use multiprocessors. The National Laboratories rely heavily on a tremendous amount of existing code. Any strategy that permits these codes to run unchanged on new multiprocessors must be considered superior to almost any other options because of the savings in recoding time. Furthermore, since current programs have repeatable behavior, any timing problems would not be the responsibility of the programmer.

This approach essentially requires an extremely sophisticated compiler. In this section we examine the current possibilities and limitations for building such a compiler. Not surprisingly, the evaluation partially depends on the structure of the target multiprocessor. Many basic compiler issues, however, tend to be independent of the target machine. Fortunately, much of the research on vectorizing compilers applies directly to the more general problem of multiprocessors. In this area, probably the most advanced work has been done by Kuck et al. [6]. To date, almost all of their emphasis has been on the analysis of loops to determine the maximum amount of concurrency available there. Multiprocessors have the advantage over vector machines in that conditional branching and subroutine calls inside loops do not require halting concurrency. Furthermore, any vector loops can obviously be mapped onto the more general multiprocessors with little effort. It seems quite reasonable to believe that this approach can be extended to identify more forms of concurrency within loops that can be systematically translated onto many different types of multiprocessors [7].
Two major questions regarding this approach remain unanswered:

1. If the compiler efforts remain focused primarily on loops as the source of concurrency, how much usable concurrency can they find?

2. If compilers must look to more dynamic program features, such as subroutine calls, how effectively can they continue to identify and use the available concurrency?

In both of these questions, "usable concurrency" causes problems. For many multiprocessors, such as the CRAY X-MP, we must find large-grain concurrency to ensure that expensive processors do not waste large amounts of time in system calls and busy-waiting for synchronization.

The first question depends on both compiler technology and the nature of the programs being analyzed. Rather than focusing on inner-loop analysis (as in the vector case), compilers for multiprocessors should focus on outer loops for concurrency because outer loops reduce the amount of interaction required by processors. The interesting aspect of the question is in what such efforts will find. Programmers using vector machines have been organizing calculations to expose inner-loop, not outer-loop, concurrency. It is impossible to determine the return until a major investment of resources is made to upgrade a compiler for this task.

If smart compilers need to look beyond loops, prospects for success are further clouded. The success of loop analysis is closely tied to the fact that the static loop definition corresponds closely to its dynamic execution structure. More dynamic features, such as subroutine calls, do not act the same. Concurrency depends on avoiding data dependencies. However, in subroutines, data dependencies are harder to calculate because static program analysis cannot always determine which variables will be passed to various subroutines.

Some efforts have begun in this direction. Ken Kennedy at Rice University is looking into global data analysis, and he may find ways of enhancing concurrency identification via subroutines. One aspect of the problem will still remain. Loops provide a rather straightforward way to approximate load balancing on multiprocessors (to ensure that every processor is kept busy). With the introduction of subroutines into the picture, balancing becomes much more difficult. Right now the general problem of load balancing is extremely expensive to compute, and we know of no good approximating heuristics.

Returning to the purpose of this general strategy (saving dusty decks), one further comment needs to be made. All of the compiler tools being developed by Kuck and others rely heavily on the precise adherence of programs to Fortran standards. Codes that use assembly language routines, access array elements beyond the defined bounds of the array, or rely on a particular scheme for loading COMMON blocks in memory, for example, will totally invalidate the correctness of the compiler tools. Such programs would need to be rewritten to conform to the standard language definition.

Language Layering for Concurrency

Most of the errors that we have observed in parallel programs are largely independent of the actual computations being performed. For example, errors are made in synchronization-related code or in partitioning data. These errors concern the parallel structure, or skeleton of the code rather than the details of the "guts" of the computation. Perhaps we should use a new language form for specifying this skeleton and rely on an existing programming language (Fortran or C, for example) to specify the "guts". The hope is that the incidence of errors could be greatly reduced while still making it easy to convert existing codes to a parallel environment and reuse existing modules. Some initial work has been done in this area [8] [9].

One attractive approach is to use a graphical language for the skeleton while retaining an existing textual language for the guts. The motivation for this is simply that it is natural to express parallelism graphically in a two-dimensional medium, generally with one dimension used for time and the orthogonal dimension for breadth of parallelism. In fact, when designing a parallel code, many sheets of paper are generally covered with such diagrams. It is often the case that errors arise and clarity is lost in the translation of the diagrams to text. On the other hand, graphics cannot compare to text for efficiency and clarity in representing the kind of algebraic manipulations that our codes use heavily. The information density per unit of display area is simply too low.

A layered approach could be implemented as a preprocessor to the compiler for some target language supporting concurrency. The skeleton specification would automatically be translated into concurrency primitives of the target programming language and integrated with the guts of the code, already specified in that language. There are clearly some unsolved problems associated with the layered approach:

1. For the skeleton language to be useful, it must be possible to specify not only synchronization interactions between processes, but also data partitioning. It is not clear how best to do this.

2. As is always the case with preprocessor implementations, debugging becomes more difficult. How does one debug in terms of the objects one originally used when programming?

We hope to have some experience with this approach in the near future.

New Language/Compiler System Design

The most radical approach to using multiprocessors rebuilds our entire software base from the ground up. Obviously, this strategy is extremely expensive and potentially very labor intensive. Given our tremendous investment in existing applications codes, this option must be viewed as either a last resort or a means for developing ideas on how we could gradually evolve our existing systems into a structure more amenable to parallel processing.

Probably the most fertile area for language and compiler designs specifically targeted for multiprocessors currently resides in the domain of applicative languages (e.g., SISAL [10], FP [11], and KRC [12]). These languages are designed to enhance the visibility of concurrency without requiring programmer management of synchronization. They also de-emphasize any particular model of parallel architecture. Hence, with intelligent compilers we may be able to exploit different machines with significantly less effort in tuning source codes.

An obvious question needs to be asked: Why even consider such a radical solution now? We see several important reasons:

1. In spite of our best efforts, it appears that a significant amount of applications recoding must take place regardless of the options, so why not pick a good source language? The situation we face is quite akin to our experiences in moving to vector machines several years ago. How much recoding effort was done to move programs onto the CDC Star so that it performed well?

2. Options that put responsibility for synchronization control in the hands of programmers require better methods of helping identify and/or prevent time-dependent results. Unfortunately, this problem is not new—operating systems writers have faced this one for years, and they have few good answers. We have no debuggers and no program analyzers to help find errors in these kinds of programs. Right now, all we have is time-consuming guesswork.

3. We are embarking on the use of a new architectural technology that is certain to be prevalent for decades. By starting with a clean slate, we can improve our chances for long-term code survivability and high system utilization.

Once you accept the possibility of moving to a new language/compiler system, applicative languages offer some unique advantages. Three of the most important ones include:

1. Concurrency is the general execution rule; sequencing of operations occurs only to satisfy data dependencies in a program.

2. Additional language features, such as recursion, enhance possibilities for expressing algorithms that contain more concurrency.

3. All program concurrency is sufficiently controlled by the language definition to ensure determinate behavior (or, if some indeterminacy is permitted, it is confined to well-identified modules).

Applicative languages present a cohesive strategy for addressing the problems posed by multiprocessor usage. Concurrency derives from one basic source—simultaneous evaluation of all input arguments to a function. In an applicative language, *every* executable action is a mathematical function, and many functions can be in the process of simultaneously evaluating their input arguments. In fact, any two functions can execute simultaneously so long as their input arguments do not depend upon each other. Furthermore, recursion enhances possibilities for concurrency because it encourages use of highly parallel algorithms such as divide-and-conquer.

Even though this style of concurrency definition may seem chaotic, the mathematical nature of the language ensures an orderly evaluation of the function that produces determinate results. Therefore, programmers can focus on the mathematical structure of the solution and the concurrency implied by that structure. They need not focus on the details of how tasks are divided or assigned to processors, and they do not need to express the details of the synchronization necessary to make the program work properly. These responsibilities fall on the compiler and/or architecture. In some specific cases we know that such a division of responsibility can be extremely effective. For example, the `SIMPLE` code has been written in an applicative language and executed on the Manchester data flow prototype machine. A 4-by-4 problem ran on that ten-processor system with 97.5% utilization. This program had no partitioning information from the programmer and to date has produced no time-dependent results.

Repeatability of results is a major benefit of the applicative language strategy, particularly as it relates to debugging. Almost all applicative languages impose a strict philosophy of writing determinate programs. Given our experiences in trying to debug parallel programs, the advantages should be obvious. If programs are repeatable, then we can apply current debugging techniques (such as they are) to determine how erroneous programs strayed. From the perspective of programmers, we cannot overstress the value of being freed from having to chase down intermittent errors.

Unfortunately, the applicative language approach still faces some unresolved problems. In general, the compilers in this approach require a significant amount of sophistication because they are responsible for partitioning, mapping, and synchronization. Since the target architectures may vary dramatically, each one will require specialized attention to ensure high performance. The expectation is that the form of the language will allow more effective solutions to the aforementioned problems than is possible through complete analysis of programs written in Fortran. Right now, efforts are in progress to implement SISAL on several vastly different architectures by different organizations. The target machines include the HEP, CRAY-1S, VAX 11/780, and the

Manchester data flow machine. Possible future targets include a four-processor VAX cluster and the CRAY X-MP.

The worst unresolved issue for applicative languages, however, affects all of these target machines. That problem is dynamic memory management. Simplistic implementations of applicative languages tend to require tremendous amounts of extra memory over and above that needed for concurrency. Such excessive demands for memory can be reduced by further compiler analysis techniques, but as yet they are still in the process of being developed. At this time we cannot determine how effective these techniques will be at reducing the amounts of memory needed to execute a program.

2.4   CONCLUSION

We have attempted in this chapter to distill several years of experience with real multiprocessors into a small quantity of information that will be useful to those writing codes for these machines. Our principal focus is on the difficulties encountered in creating parallel programs that function correctly, and on future options for alleviating these difficulties. We do not have the space to address a wide range of issues that affect the *performance*, as opposed to the *logical correctness*, of multiprocessor programs. We hope to cover these in a future paper.

To summarize our experiences, we want first to emphasize that we have been able to make effective use of multiprocessors for solving a wide range of problems. This is comforting, since we believe that increasing levels of parallelism offer the best hope of large speed improvements for future supercomputers. We have encountered significant difficulties in creating programs that function correctly, however, and we do not want to minimize them. They can be briefly summarized as follows:

1. The behavior of even quite short parallel programs can be astonishingly complex. The fact that a program functions correctly once, or even one hundred times, with some particular set of input values, is no guarantee that it will not fail tomorrow with the same input.

2. Tracking down a bug in a parallel program can be exceedingly difficult. This results from the combination of logical complexity, nonrepeatable behavior, and our present lack of tools.

No completely satisfactory solutions to these difficulties are on the horizon—only partial solutions can be expected. As we have tried to indicate, each of the possibilities has its own drawbacks. For those who must work with the tools currently available, we offer the following advice:

1. The process of converting a sequential program to run on a multiprocessor seems particularly likely to result in trouble. When possible, rewrite at least the skeleton of the new program from scratch.

2. Given the great difficulty of finding bugs, *much* greater emphasis must be placed on writing code that is correct from the beginning. In this regard, organizing programs in terms of pure mathematical functions (with clearly identified input

arguments and a disjoint set of outputs) enhances possibilities for correctness and automatic compiler checking.

3. Another technique that helps reduce bugs is to use standard synchronization patterns where possible and encapsulate them as completely as possible. In addition to localizing bugs and limiting the complexity of programs, this approach makes it easy to share code with other programmers.

4. When, in spite of the above preceding techniques, one is faced with the inevitable timing-dependent bug, the best approach to finding it is often to sit down with pencil, paper, and listing. It usually helps to enlist the assistance of someone who is unfamiliar with the program.

In considering longer-range strategies for alleviating our problems, it is more difficult to give advice. The number of alternatives is large, and our experience is still very incomplete. We suggest, however, that:

1. A wide variety of programming language alternatives, covering all of the approaches we outline, should be vigorously explored.

2. High priority should be placed on creating new tools to assist in the debugging process. Some of these tools may require special hardware support to function. This may impose important requirements on new supercomputers.

3. Solution of the problems associated with creating logically correct parallel programs is crucial to the successful use of future supercomputers.

4. Finally, we believe that acquisition of and transition to multiprocessors must be planned more carefully. We must balance the need for continued development of better physics algorithms in our codes with the need for development of an effective strategy for using multiprocessors.

2.5   ACKNOWLEDGMENTS

This work was supported (in part) by the Applied Mathematical Sciences subprogram of the Office of Energy Research, U.S. Department of Energy, under Lawrence Livermore National Laboratory contract #W-7405-ENG-48.

2.6   REFERENCES

[1]   D. H. Grit and J. R. McGraw, "Programming Divide and Conquer on a Multiprocessor", UCRL–88710, Lawrence Livermore National Laboratory, May 1983.

[2]   E. D. Brooks III, "A Multitasking Kernel for the C and Fortran Programming Languages", UCID–20167, Lawrence Livermore National Laboratory, Sept. 1984.

[3]   Cray Research, Inc., "Multitasking User Guide", SN–0222, Feb. 1984.

[4]   Denelcor, Inc., "HEP FORTRAN User's Guide", Publication Number 9000006, Feb. 1982.

[5]   Myrias Research Corporation, "Myrias 4000 System Description", Dec. 1983.

[6]   D. J. Kuck et al., "Dependence Graphs and Compiler Optimizations", *Proceedings of the 8th ACM Symposium on the Principles of Programming Languages*, Jan. 1981.

[7]   J. R. McGraw, D. H. Kuck, and M. Wolfe, "A debate : Retire Fortran ?", *Physics Today*, May 1984.

[8]   C. Fraboul and N. Hifdi, "LESTAP: A Language for Expression and Synchronization of Tasks on a Multi-Array Processor Architecture", *Experiences in Applying Parallel Processors to Scientific Computation*, March 1984.

[9]   P. F. Reynolds, "Parallel Processing Structures: Languages, Schedules, and Performance Results", Ph.D. Thesis, University of Texas at Austin, Dec. 1979.

[10]   J. R. McGraw et al., "SISAL : Streams and Iteration in a Single Assignment Language", Language Reference Manual, M-126, Version 1.1, Lawrence Livermore National Laboratory, July 1983.

[11]   J. Backus, "Can Programming Be Liberated from the von Neumann Style? A Functional Style and Its Algebra of Programs", *Communications of the ACM* vol. 21, no. 8, Aug. 1978.

[12]   D. A. Turner, "The Semantic Elegance of Applicative Languages", *Proceedings of the 1981 ACM Conference on Functional Programming Languages and Computer Architectures*, Oct. 1981.

3
Alliant FX/8

David C. DiNucci

Machine/Model:	Alliant FX/8
Location:	Argonne National Laboratory, Argonne, IL
Processors:	8 Computational Elements (CEs)
	6 Interactive Processors (IPs)
	32 Mbytes shared memory
	128 Kbyte cache shared by the CEs
	64 Kbyte cache for IPs
	(32 Kbytes shared by each set of 3 IPs)
Operating System:	Concentrix Version 2.0
Language:	Fortran 77 plus Fortran 8X array extensions
Compiler:	FX/Fortran Version 2.0.18

The Alliant FX/8 was designed to exploit parallelism found in scientific programs automatically. The intent was allow parallel processing on existing dusty-deck Fortran programs with minimal or no changes to the source code. Although the Alliant FX/8 is a fast parallel scientific processor in its own right, an even more powerful supercomputer, based on the Alliant FX/8, is being developed at the University of Illinois as part of the Cedar Project [1].

3.1 HARDWARE

The Alliant FX/8 consists of up to eight processors called Computational Elements (CEs), and up to 12 Interactive Processors (IPs). The CEs, IPs, and shared global memory of up to 256 Mbytes are connected through a common memory bus, as shown in Fig. 3.1. All access by the CEs and IPs to the bus occurs through cache memory (up to 512 Kbytes of cache shared by the CEs, and up to another 128 Kbytes for the IPs, with 32 Kbytes for every three IPs). The CEs are also connected directly to each other via a concurrency control bus.

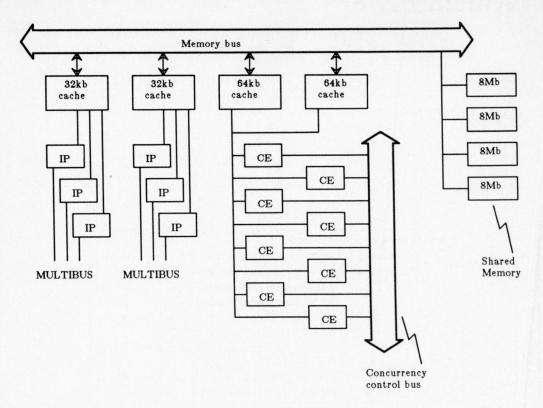

Figure 3.1   Architecture of the Alliant FX/8 (Argonne configuration).

Each IP contains a Motorola 68000 series CPU. The Computational Element CPUs use custom chips that support the M68020 instruction set augmented with instructions for supporting floating point arithmetic, vector arithmetic (32 elements, integer and floating point), and concurrency. Floating point operations from the CE processors are performed using Weitek floating point chips. In general, the CEs are used to perform computation-intensive processes that can benefit from vectorization or loop-level concurrency (as described in this chapter), whereas the IPs are used to perform interactive processes and handle I/O between the memory and peripherals.

3.2   SOFTWARE

The FX/8 operating system, Concentrix, is a version of Berkeley UNIX 4.2. Concurrent programming on the machine can be done in Fortran using a compiler specifically designed to support concurrency, or in C by explicitly calling routines to perform concurrency. This chapter discusses Fortran exclusively.

Program Development

Whereas many parallel processors require the user to define explicitly where concurrency is to occur within a program, the Alliant FX/Fortran compiler actively searches out concurrency within ordinary sequential programs. Even though these programs typically are not written with concurrency in mind, the compiler automatically produces object code that runs efficiently in the multiprocessor environment. The compiler technology is based on the work of Kuck and his students at the University of Illinois at Urbana-Champaign [2]. This approach should prove attractive to many scientists with shelves of dusty-deck programs, who would prefer to avoid having to rewrite their code to take advantage of the speedup offered by parallel processing.

There are two primary facilities within the hardware that support concurrency. The eight CEs allow entire sections of code to run concurrently (one on each processor). In addition, the pipelined vector units present in each CE allow pairs of operands to overlap in their use of the floating point adder and multiplier. This pipelining can result in a much higher computational rate, but it requires the availability of long enough vectors of operands. To use both of these forms of parallelism, the compiler tries to find code segments that can be executed concurrently (to be run on the eight processors) and vectors of operands that require the same pattern of arithmetic operations to be performed on them. Since both of these forms of parallelism are found within DO loops in Fortran, this is where the compiler concentrates [†].

When the compiler recognizes an opportunity for concurrency, it generates concurrent code only as long as it can guarantee that this will not change the outcome of the program. In most cases, the compiler is very conservative in this regard. It bases its decisions on the types of statements within a loop and the way variables are used, since the latter often affects the degree to which the iterations of the loop can be overlapped.

Concurrency is applied to DO loops by executing the different iterations on different CEs. Since there are eight processors, up to eight iterations can be active at one time. If necessary, the compiler inserts synchronization points into the object code to ensure that variables within a loop are updated and accessed in the correct order and to guarantee that the program statements following a loop do not execute until all iterations of the loop are finished.

If the compiler diagnoses a definite problem with executing a loop in this parallel fashion or just suspects one due to its inability to trace global program interactions, it produces an "informational message" to tell the user what it was trying to do and why it couldn't do it. If the user determines that there is really no problem with invoking concurrency at that point, he/she can place a *compiler directive* in the code, usually just before the DO loop in question, and recompile. With the directive in place, the compiler will perform the desired the optimization. The compiler directives and informational messages can be thought of as forming a dialogue between the compiler and the user.

[†]The compiler can also generate vector code outside of DO loops if the user specifies vector operations explicitly using Fortran 8X array features.

Note that if the user makes a mistake and inserts a compiler directive telling the compiler to "go ahead and make it parallel" when it is not safe to do so, the program is likely to exhibit the unexpected behaviors (such as nondeterminism) characteristic of buggy parallel programs. The bright point here is that the user can see if this is indeed the reason that the program is acting strangely by turning off all optimization and rerunning in sequential mode. If the program still misbehaves, a normal program bug is present. If it doesn't, concurrency can be turned off selectively (by commenting out compiler directives) until the problem is found. These debugging techniques are effective only because the concurrent program is still a valid sequential program.

Another advantage of this method for parallel programming over supplying a library of explicitly called routines is that the compiler knows where concurrency is taking place, thereby allowing it to prevent program optimizations that would not work correctly in parallel programs. In other words, the compiler is optimizing *for* parallel execution rather than in spite of it.

Mechanics

On the Alliant, concurrency is considered a form of optimization, and no optimization at all is attempted unless the −O option is present on the command invoking the compiler. Optimization can be limited (to only vectorizing, for example) by adding special letters after the −O. Omitting the −O option causes all compiler directives to be ignored.

Compiler directives are embedded within the program and begin in column 1 with CVD$. This means that they are treated as comments by other compilers, increasing the portability of code. The letter immediately following the $ tells whether this directive is to apply only to the DO loop following (in which case the letter L is used) or to the rest of the source file (in which case a G is used). A keyword, starting in column 7, specifies the optimization being allowed or forbidden.

By default, a subroutine call within a loop inhibits concurrency of the loop contents, starting at the call. The CVD$L CNCALL directive overrides this rule, allowing such a loop to execute concurrently. The directive is effective only up to the end of the loop, due to the L following the $. This directive is the programmer's assertion that the subroutine can run in parallel with other executions of itself and/or other subroutines called within the same loop.

Concurrent tasks can be created by calling a subroutine within a DO loop that is immediately preceded by the previously described CNCALL directive. The subroutine can be passed the loop index, from which it can determine which occurrence of the call it is, allowing each iteration to behave differently if necessary through the use of computed GOTO or IF statements. The subroutine can even call other subroutines, which will continue to run in parallel.

We also made use of the CVD$G NOCONCUR directive to inhibit all concurrent loop execution through the end of the source file.

Data is shared among the main program and subroutines through COMMON statements or subroutine parameters, as in sequential Fortran. The Alliant does not have problems passing a loop index to a concurrent subroutine as a subroutine parameter (see Chapter 2) since the loop index doesn't really change after calling the subroutine. Each iteration of the concurrent loop from which the subroutine is called has its own copy of the loop index. As with other shared memory parallel machines, care must still be taken, however, when passing other parameters that are modified by the concurrent subroutine.

Even when a subroutine is invoked concurrently, there is only one copy of the subroutine code and local variables. This causes problems, since different invocations of the subroutine must be able to work with different values concurrently. To remedy this, the subroutine should be made recursive, either by compiling it with the `-recursive` option or by inserting the keyword `RECURSIVE` before the name of the routine in the code. Either method causes each invocation of the routine to allocate new space for its local variables on a runtime stack.

For more details on the Alliant approach to parallel processing in Fortran, see Appendix A3.

3.3   PARALLEL PROGRAM EXAMPLES

Pi Program with Automatic Parallelization

Implementing the sample program is trivial if we let the compiler do all of the work. We start by writing the program as we would write a sequential program to perform the same task, then compile it, paying attention to any of its informational messages.

```
 1    C
 2    C - - Pi - Program loops over slices in interval, summing
 3    C - -  area of each slice
 4    C
 5          real tt1(2), tt2(2)
 6          integer*4 intrvls, cut
 7          double precision sumall, width, f, x
 8    C
 9          f(x) = 4d0 / (1d0 + x * x)
10    C
11          read(*,*) intrvls
12          t2 = etime(tt1)
13    C
14    C - - Compute width of cuts
15    C
16          width = 1.d0 / intrvls
17          sumall = 0.0d0
```

The program is a straightforward translation of the problem definition. Lines 1–17 set up the problem and define the function `f(x)` to be integrated.

```
18   C
19   C - - Loop over interval, summing areas.
20   C
21         do 100 cut = 1, intrvls
22             sumall = sumall + width * f((cut - .5D0) * width)
23    100  continue
24   C
25   C - - Finish overall timing and write results
26   C
27         t1 = etime(tt2)
28         write(6, *) 'Time in main =', t1 - t2,', sum =', sumall
29         write(6, *) 'Error = ', sumall - 3.14159265358979323846d0
30         stop
31         end
```

From our knowledge of the workings of the compiler, we would expect it to concentrate its efforts on the DO loop at Lines 21–23. Invoking the compiler with the command

```
        fortran -O pi.f
```

confirms this by producing the following messages:

```
Start of Unnamed Program Unit
  Line 22   Informational message # 1219
            Concurrent and vector loop optimization inhibited by
            carry-around scalar -- SUMALL
  Line 22   Informational message # 1308
            Concurrent and vector loop optimization inhibited by
            not allowing associative transform (i.e., SUM or
            DOTPRODUCT) -- SUMALL
```

The first message says that the DO loop will not be executed in parallel because of the way the variable sumall is used. The compiler terms this type of usage a *carry-around scalar*, which means a scalar variable that is used on both the left and right sides of an assignment statement within a loop. This causes a data dependency between each iteration of the loop and the preceding and following iterations, meaning that only one iteration can be executed at a time.

The second message is closely related to the first, but it pertains to the operation that we are repetitively performing on sumall. Theoretically, it should not matter in what order the loop iterations add their portion (i.e., area of a slice) to the sum, since it should all come out the same by the time all the loop iterations have finished anyway. The same would be true if we had been multiplying sumall by a different number in each iteration and storing the result back to sumall. The compiler knows about these associative properties of addition and multiplication and is telling us that it can handle the concurrent execution of this loop (the carry-around scalar notwithstanding) if we just allow it, by including either the −AS option on the fortran command line or a CVD$L ASSOC compiler directive just before the loop beginning.

It may seem puzzling that the compiler would "ask" about such a thing rather than just act on its knowledge. This is an example of the caution we mentioned earlier. Although running the loop concurrently would not (theoretically) cause any problems, summing the slices in different orders can cause variations in the answer due to floating point round-off effects.

When we ran this program in its original form, it worked fine, but did not take advantage of any concurrency. We then recompiled the program with the −AS (associative) option:

```
fortran −O −AS pi.f
```

The program compiled with no informational messages, and we now had a concurrent program. The timing from the program produced by the second compilation was more than 14 times faster, running at about 17 Mflops (more timing details are given under "Performance" below). The answers produced by the two programs were just slightly different (by about 3.3×10^{-14}), showing that the use of the −AS can cause minor round-off differences. As often seems to be the case, the faster (parallel) program gives the better answer.

Pi Program with Explicit Parallelization

Although this example shows the ease with which a program can be converted to run in parallel, it does not show some of the complications that can arise. We therefore describe another implementation of the same program that makes the concurrency more visible. This version also allows us to control the amount of parallelism to make more meaningful timings. Note that although this style of programming is not encouraged by Alliant, the user must be aware of the problems and techniques outlined here when he or she uses the CNCALL compiler directive.

The new main program accepts the initial input, calls a summing routine (in a DO loop) and prints the results. Each instance of the summing routine forms a sum of its set of slices of the integral, then adds its local sum into a global sum. By forcing the summing loop within the subroutine to execute sequentially and the loop that calls the subroutine to run concurrently, we can experiment with starting up different numbers of concurrent work routines. This algorithm works just as well whether the summing routines are called in parallel or the entire program is run sequentially. The only difference is that locking must be performed in the parallel case.

```
 1    C
 2    C - - Main - This program starts the workers and writes out the
 3    C       final answer as well as the times for all workers
 4    C
 5          double precision sumall, time(50)
 6          real tt1(2), tt2(2)
 7          integer*4 prcnum, nprocs, intrvls
 8          common /comm/ sumall, time
```

The named COMMON /comm/ at Line 8 contains the overall sum sumall and a time vector to record how long each process takes.

```
 9    C
10          read(*,*) nprocs, intrvls
11          t2 = etime(tt1)
12    C
13    C - - Call subroutine concurrently to do work
14    C
15    CVD$L CNCALL
16          do 100 prcnum = 1, nprocs
17             call work(prcnum, intrvls, nprocs)
18    100   continue
```

Although this loop is normally prohibited from running in parallel since it contains a CALL statement, the compiler directive at Line 15 overrides this rule. This allows all nprocs copies of subroutine work to execute concurrently. Actually, since the hardware had eight processors, at most eight copies of work could execute at once. Note that one of the parameters in the call is prcnum. It is important that this be supplied as a call parameter rather than placed in COMMON since it must be different for each instance of the subroutine when multiple instances are executing simultaneously.

```
19          t1 = etime(tt2)
20          write(6, *) 'Time in main =', t1 - t2,', sum =', sumall
21          write(6, *) 'Error = ', sumall - 3.14159265358979323846d0
22          do 200 i = 1, nprocs
23             write(6, *) 'Process ', i, ' Time = ', time(i)
24    200   continue
25          stop
26          end
```

The remainder of the main program prints the results and quits. This portion of the program does not execute until all previous loop iterations (Lines 16-18) are completed, even if that loop executes concurrently.

```
27            subroutine work(idproc, intrvls, nprocs)
28   CVD$R NOCONCUR
29   c
30   c - Computes integral for every nprocs-th slice, using a
31   c - rectangular approximation.  Number of slices is passed
32   c - to routine as integer * 4 message.
33   c
```

The NOCONCUR directive in subroutine work at Line 28 prevents any of the loops within the subroutine from executing in parallel. This allows us to keep strict control over concurrency within the program. Since the compiler cannot tell whether or not a particular subroutine will be executed concurrently, the compiler cannot detect and account for possible timing problems created by simultaneous referencing of shared variables. This task is relegated to the programmer, who must handle this problem in much the same way as on other machines through the use of *lock* variables. The lock is locked before accessing the shared variable, and then unlocked afterwards.

```
34         Integer * 4 cut, intrvls, idproc, nprocs
35         Real dummy(2)
36         Double precision sum, sumall, width, f, x, time(50)
37         common /comm/ sumall, time
38         common /synch/ lock
```

We declare such a lock, called lock, in Line 38. It is shared among all copies of the subroutine (since they all have COMMON /synch/). Its purpose is to prevent simultaneous updates of the sumall variable. It is not necessary to use the lock in the main program since there is no possibility that the sumall variable will be accessed in the main program at the same time that it is being accessed by a subroutine.

On the Alliant, the lock can be any integer variable, and it does not need to be specially declared as a lock. Since the locking and unlocking are performed by modifying the value in the lock variable, that variable should not be used for any other purpose. Locking and unlocking is performed by calling the lockon and lockoff routines respectively. These routines were available at Argonne, but were not supplied by Alliant. Each consists of only a few lines of assembly code that perform test-and-set machine instructions on the locks.

The lock and the shared variable being accessed must both in COMMON. Attempting to obtain a lock that is already locked by another process causes the routine to spin (i.e., wait in an idle loop) until another process (typically the process that locked the variable) unlocks it.

The compiler itself uses implicit synchronization, resembling locks, in code that it has parallelized. Whereas this may not seem important, it is important to note that the compiler's locks are suppressed when optimization is turned off, but these explicit calls to lockon and lockoff are not suppressed. Therefore, the compiler's locks can cause the same program to execute differently with concurrency enabled than with it disabled.

```
39              f(x) = 4d0 / (1d0 + x * x)
40      c
41              t1 = etime(dummy)
42      c
43      c - - Get number of cuts and compute width of cuts
44      c
45              width = 1.d0 / intrvls
46      c
47      c - - Calculate area in every "nprcss" cuts and sum
48      c - - (This is the WORK part)
49      c
50              sum = 0.0d0
51              do 100 cut = idproc, intrvls, nprocs
52                  sum = sum + width * f((cut - .5D0) * width)
53      100     continue
54              time(idproc) = etime(dummy) - t1
```

Lines 39–54 form the body of the `work` routine. The `DO` loop at Lines 51–53 does not execute in parallel due to the `NOCONCUR` directive at Line 28. There is no need to prevent simultaneous access to the `time` array at Line 54 since each process accesses a different location in it. Also, the main program does not attempt to access `time` until all instances of the subroutine are finished.

```
55      c
56      c - - - Return answer to the base node
57      c
58              call lockon(lock)
59              sumall = sumall + sum
60              call lockoff(lock)
61              return
62              end
```

As mentioned previously, two copies of the work routine cannot be allowed to change the overall sum `sumall` simultaneously (causing a write-write conflict). To ensure that this doesn't occur, a variable (in this case `lock`) is locked at Line 58 before the access and unlocked afterwards, at Line 60. Since this variable is also shared by all copies of the work routine, and since it is guaranteed by the hardware that only one process can lock this memory location at once, the access to `sumall` is safe.

Upon compiling (without −AS), the following informational messages result:

```
Start of Unnamed Program Unit
  Line 23   Informational message # 1297
              Concurrent and vector loop optimization inhibited by
              restricted statement
Start of Program Unit WORK
  Line 52   Informational message # 1219
              Concurrent and vector loop optimization inhibited by
              carry-around scalar -- SUM
  Line 52   Informational message # 1308
              Concurrent and vector loop optimization inhibited by
              not allowing associative transform (i.e., SUM or
              DOTPRODUCT) -- SUM
```

The first message applies to the write loop in the main program, since a `write` statement within a loop inhibits the compiler from breaking the loop into parallel sub-loops. This doesn't bother us, since parallel execution of this loop serves no useful purpose.

The second and third messages are the same as for the previous implementation. We do not want to make this loop concurrent for the time being since we would like to strictly control the concurrency utilizing only the loop in the main program. (Later, for experimentation, we did recompile it with the `-AS` option and found that it ran nearly as fast as the first program with the same option as long as the number of processors given was a multiple of 8).

The program ran correctly the first time. We were able to run it in serial and parallel mode with no difference in results.

3.4 PERFORMANCE

Timings for the first and second versions of the program were very different, so they are discussed separately and then compared. In each case, timing was done with both `etime` and the UNIX `time` function.

Timing was done internally with the `etime` subroutine, which is supplied by Alliant and returns the CPU time in seconds as a floating point number, with a resolution of 0.01 seconds. For the second version of the program, we called `etime` from both the main program and each of the subroutines.

The UNIX `time` command breaks down the time into user time (`utime`), system time (`stime`), and wall-clock time (`ctime`). Although the latter is somewhat inaccurate since it includes the time taken to enter the input for the program and is affected by system load, our tests were performed on a mostly unloaded system and our input time was consistently 2 to 3 seconds.

First Program

With no optimization, the timing of the first program behaved as one would expect it to on any sequential machine. System time remained at zero, `utime` and `etime` were always equal to each other, and wall-clock time was always 2 to 3 seconds more.

Mflop rate (based on `etime` or, identically, `ctime` $-$ `3.0`) remained constant at about 0.59 for all inputs (number of slices) from 100,000 to 4,000,000.

We then optimized with the $-$`O` option but not the $-$`AS` option. For all inputs between 1,000,000 and 2,870,000, the system time became non-zero, but `etime` was still approximately equal to user time plus system time, and wall-clock time was about 2 to 3 seconds more than `etime`. Mflop rate (based on `etime` or `ctime` $-$ `3.0`) remained constant at about 1.16 Mflops.

However, for inputs between 2,871,000 to 3,120,000, the clock time rose sharply, whereas the other times remained largely on track. (At first, we thought that someone had started a large job, but this was not the case, since we were able to repeat these results.) Although the Mflop rate based on `etime` declined only slightly to about 1.06, Mflop rate based on wall-clock time (minus 3) dropped to about 0.45 Mflops. (See Fig. 3.2 for an illustration of this effect.)

For input values above 3,120,000, the program immediately aborted with a `bus error` message, sometimes accompanied by `segmentation violation` and `core dumped` messages. This was especially puzzling because it seemed clear that this program was not attempting to perform any out-of-bounds array references or other illegal memory accesses, which is the usual explanation for this error message. This effect is discussed in Section 3.5.

When both the $-$`O` and the $-$`AS` option were included, the timings reverted to the same pattern as in the unoptimized version, except of course that they were much faster. The bus errors did not materialize in this mode, even when we ran with inputs up to 200,000,000. Mflop rate (computed with either `etime` or wall-clock time minus 3) was now steady at about 17.5 Mflops.

Second Program

Our intention in writing the second version of the program was to gain some control over the amount of concurrency within our application. However, our timings revealed that we did not have as much control as we thought.

Since the machine had eight CEs, we expected to increase the program speed by breaking the total number of loop iterations into separate processes, up to eight processes. For a larger number of processes, we expected the time to level off since the additional processes would not be able to run while the first eight were running, or perhaps decrease since the overhead for loading a process into a processor was likely to be incurred more times for the same amount of concurrency.

The timings in this case are especially hard to interpret. When more than eight processes were run, the `etime` figures for the first eight to finish were usually about four to five times slower than for all subsequently finishing processes. This might be explained by instruction cache effects.

In addition, the `etime` figure reported from the main program seems to be the sum of the `etime` figures reported from process 1, 9, 17, and so forth. The system time and user time figures from the UNIX `time` command also add up to this number. It therefore seems probable that the `etime` and UNIX `time` figures are computed as the sum of all processes that execute on the same processor as the main program, rather than from the sum of all processes on all processors.

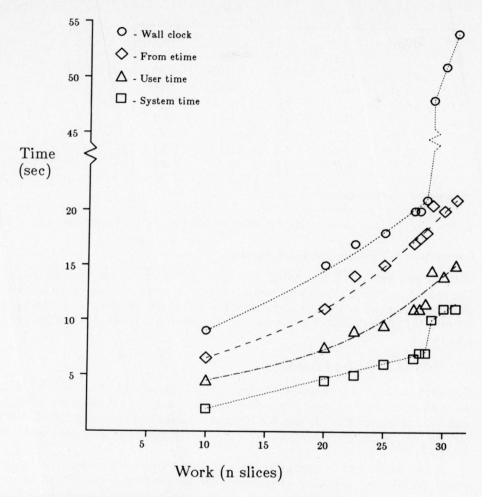

Figure 3.2 Timing relationships for Program 1, no −AS option.

The bus error problem returned. If any one process was required to compute more than about 50,000 loop iterations, the program aborted instantly. This kept wall-clock times for almost all runs below 10 seconds. Since this time was reported in seconds and was strongly affected by typing speed, it was relatively useless for computing Mflop rate. However, with 5,000,000 intervals, some behavior of both wall-clock time and system time could be observed when the number of processes was varied, as shown in Fig. 3.3. This table shows that both the system time and wall-clock time take a dramatic, non-linear leap with fewer than 13 processes.

procs	etime	utime	stime	ctime	Mflops[*]
10	37.94	14.3	24.1	3:04	0.19
11	25.78	14.0	12.3	1:18	0.47
12	16.31	10.2	12.0	0:56	0.66
13	14.45	7.3	7.6	0:18	2.3
14	13.33	7.0	6.7	0:17	2.5
15	12.76	6.2	6.9	0:16	2.7
16	12.57	6.7	6.4	0:17	2.5
40	7.2	5.1	2.6	0:11	4.4

[*] Mflops are based on `ctime - 3.0`

Figure 3.3. Timings for the explicit parallel version for 5,000,000 intervals.

Comparison of First and Second Programs

The first program, which was by far the easiest to implement, was also much faster. The second program computed for a given number of intervals faster when it divided them between more processes, but the speed of the second program never approached the first. A further discussion of performance measurements on the Alliant FX/8 can be found in [3].

3.5   PITFALLS AND PROBLEMS

Compiling with certain optimizations (or lack thereof) caused `bus error` aborts when too many loop iterations were attempted. This was not a problem when the program was optimized to its fullest, but if our application had been slightly different so that the `-AS` option could not have been used safely, this could have been quite troublesome.

Alliant has offered an explanation for this. When a program is vectorized, computations (in this case additions) are performed on one set of elements (32) at one time. When the `-AS` option is used, once such a partial sum is formed, it can be immediately added to the running sum, and no extra storage is incurred.

However, when the `-AS` option is not used in this case, the partial results cannot be added directly to the running sum since the vector computations may not finish in the proper order. Therefore, as the partial results are computed, they are stored into a temporary array, which is kept on the run-time stack with the routine's other local variables. When all of these partial results are computed, the elements of the array are added in order.

In our case, this temporary array is simply too big for the stack. Some obvious solutions are:

- Increase the stack (which is a site-selectable parameter);

- Keep vectorized loops within a reasonable range when not able to use the `-AS` option (i.e. less than our rather ridiculous values);

- Break these loops up into smaller loops; or

- Suppress vectorization.

The last choice should be used only in extreme cases, as can be seen by the difference in performance of our benchmarks.

This long temporary vector also explains some of the timings, since running back through the vector to add all of the elements can cause a great many cache misses and page faults.

The operating system does not behave exactly like other versions of UNIX. For example, when running our second program with a large number of subroutine calls, a fair amount of output is generated. It seemed to be impossible to stop the output once it had started. Apparently the program had finished executing, and the output was simply being spooled to the terminal, so entering a `control-C` (abort signal) had no effect. In other cases, an abort request took several seconds to be recognized when a program was in a tight, computation-bound loop.

There are some drawbacks that stem directly from Alliant's whole approach to parallel programming. The method of having the compiler automatically detect the places where concurrency can be applied to Fortran programs is the only means currently supported for executing parallel programs on the Alliant. This is certainly helpful when the user has sequential algorithms that need to be converted to work in a parallel environment. Although it may at first seem that the user can just sit back and allow the compiler to transform a sequential program into a parallel one, it is clear that at times the user must give the compiler explicit instructions on how to perform the transformation. The differences between this and a more conventional approach, in which the user explicitly adds the required constructs to make the program run in parallel, is less clear than it might seem at first glance.

One factor in the Alliant's favor is that its approach gives the user direct hints of the possibilities that exist within the program for concurrency. On the other hand, the compiler allows a process to execute concurrently only if it can find the concurrency using its `DO` loop analyses. If a programmer has ideas about concurrency or wants to implement a well-known concurrent algorithm, the only way to force concurrency is to restructure the program so that the concurrent part fits within a `DO` loop. This can sometimes be very awkward, as we found when implementing a parallel version of quicksort. It is possible, of course, to create preprocessors to convert other models of parallelism into Alliant's model, and this is being investigated by organizations both inside and outside of Alliant.

3.6   CONCLUSIONS

The Alliant FX/8 computer designers seemed to have had a very clear goal in mind, and to a large extent they have accomplished it. The Alliant parallel programming approach ensures that most of the programs written for the Alliant are both fast and portable. It also allows scientific programmers to make effective use of the machine practically immediately, without extensive training. Users can experiment with adding to their programs different amounts of concurrency, from none at all to significant amounts.

Programs that are already written to run in a parallel environment, are not, however, easily ported to the Alliant. It could be argued that this is difficult in any case, lacking any standardization for parallel program constructions, and that the Alliant FX/Fortran does support many Fortran 8X extensions and almost all of the concurrency mechanisms described by Kuck et al. [1] [2]. But the Alliant does not currently offer any tools other than those already mentioned for converting an already explicitly parallel program or algorithm to the machine. It seems that these capabilities could be easily added; the hardware can certainly support it, and perhaps the rest could be done via runtime library calls, macros, and/or preprocessors.

Perhaps this view is similar to an assembly language programmer moving to a higher level language: "It's certainly powerful, but where is all the control that I've been accustomed to?" That control is later found to have been mostly unnecessary, and the extra power (without the headaches) is welcomed.

3.7   ACKNOWLEDGMENTS

Our work on the Alliant would not have been possible without the help of Jack Dongarra of Argonne National Laboratory. We would also like to acknowledge the assistance of Danny Sorenson and Rick Stevens at Argonne, and Richard Swift and Mary Beth Schultze at Alliant.

3.8   REFERENCES

[1]   David J. Kuck, Edward S. Davidson, Duncan H. Lawrie, and Ahmed H. Sameh, "Parallel supercomputing today and the Cedar approach," *Science*, vol. 231, no. 4741, 28 Feb 1986, pp. 967-978.

[2]   David A. Padua, David J. Kuck, and Duncan H. Lawrie, "High-speed multiprocessors and compilation techniques," *IEEE Trans. Computers*, vol. C-29, no. 9, Sept. 1980, pp. 763-776.

[3]   Walid Abu-Sufah and Allen D. Malony, "Vector Processing on the Alliant FX/8 multiprocessor", in *Proceedings of the 1986 International Conference on Parallel Processing*, Aug. 1986, pp. 559-566.

4

BBN Butterfly Parallel Processor

Allan R. Larrabee, Keith E. Pennick, and Stuart M. Stern

Machine/Model:	BBN Butterfly Parallel Processor
Location:	Boeing Computer Services Company
	Advanced Technology Center, Bellevue, Washington
Processors:	32
	4 Mbytes memory per processor node
Operating System:	Chrysalis Version 2.3.1
Language:	C
Compiler:	Green Hills C Version 1.8.0

The Butterfly Parallel Processor was developed by Bolt Beranek and Newman Inc., (BBN) with funding from the Defense Advanced Research Projects Agency (DARPA) as part of the Strategic Computing Initiative. BBN Advanced Computers is responsible for further development and marketing of the Butterfly system. Initially developed as a high-speed network switch, the Butterfly has been used in a variety of applications, including complex simulations, fluid dynamics, image understanding, and data communications. Network applications have all used the small configurations of th. Butterfly (up to 16 nodes). Since then the Butterfly has evolved into a general-purpose parallel processing computer.

4.1 HARDWARE

A Butterfly system is a tightly coupled, shared memory, MIMD machine consisting of three major components:

1. Processor Nodes;

2. The Butterfly Switch; and

3. I/O Hardware.

The Butterfly consists of a variable number of identical processing nodes that are independent of each other and are connected through a high speed switching network. As shown in Fig. 4.1, each processor node consists of:

- A Motorola MC68020 CPU and MC68881 floating point coprocessor;
- 1 or 4 Mbytes of local memory (1 Mbyte on the motherboard, 3 Mbytes on an optional daughterboard);
- Memory management hardware;
- A Process Node Controller (PNC) coprocessor;
- An I/O bus; and
- A Butterfly Switching interface.

Butterfly systems can be configured with up to 256 processor nodes, although a 128-node Butterfly is the largest configuration currently in use. As processor nodes are added to a Butterfly configuration, each node contributes additional processing power,

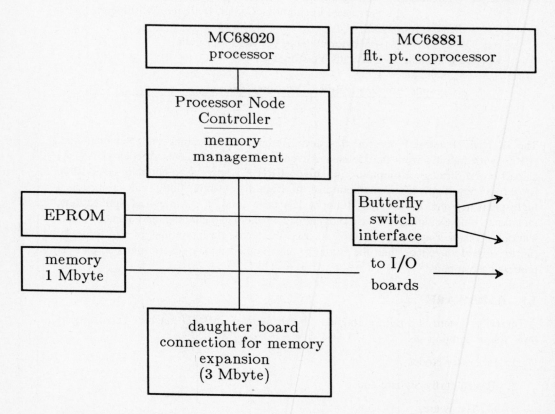

Figure 4.1   Block diagram of a Butterfly Processor Node.

memory, I/O capacity, and switch bandwidth, allowing the Butterfly's memory, switch, and I/O to scale in size with the number of processor nodes.

All memory is local to some processor node (each processor node has 1 or 4 Mbytes of memory). However, any processor in the system can directly reference any other processor's memory through the Butterfly Switch. The control of each processor's memory is handled by that node's PNC. The PNC determines if a memory reference is local or remote and sends and receives packets over the switch. From the programmer's point of view, memory is a single large shared memory in which remote references take somewhat longer than local references (approximately 6 microseconds versus 2 microseconds).

The Butterfly Switch is a collection of nodes arranged as a serial decision network. It has a topology similar to that of the Fast Fourier Transform Butterfly, hence the name. The Butterfly Switch uses packet switching to implement interprocessor communication.

Processor Nodes

User application software runs on the 68020/68881 processor combination. All code executed by the processor resides in local memory. The 68020/68881 processors are clocked at 16 MHz, and the rest of the Processor Node runs at 8 MHz.

The PNC is responsible for a variety of tasks. It sends and receives messages from the Butterfly Switch and uses the memory management hardware to map virtual addresses into physical addresses. The PNC is involved in all memory references by the processor, thus all memory references by application software appear the same, whether they access local or remote memory. In addition, the PNC implements operations necessary for parallel processing via microcode. These operations include test and set and queuing operations, as well as operations implementing an event mechanism and a process scheduler. The operations ensure that only one processor can access data at a time, as well as provide efficient communication and synchronization primitives. The PNC can ensure that these operations occur atomically because it monitors all local memory references, whether by the local processors or by a remote processor, through the Butterfly Switch.

The Butterfly Switch

The Butterfly Switch uses packet-switching techniques to provide high performance, reliable and cost effective interprocessor communication. The switch is a collection of serial switching nodes with a topology similar to the Fast Fourier Transform Butterfly. Each processor to processor path is capable of data rates of 32 Mbits/sec. The bandwidth of the switch grows linearly with the number of processor nodes. For example, a 32-processor system has an aggregate Butterfly Switch bandwidth of 1 Gbit/sec.

Fig. 4.2 shows the connection scheme for a 16-node Butterfly. Each node has 4 input and 4 output data paths and is implemented as a custom VLSI chip. A 16 input, 16 output switch is implemented by 8 of the custom VLSI chips on a single printed circuit board.

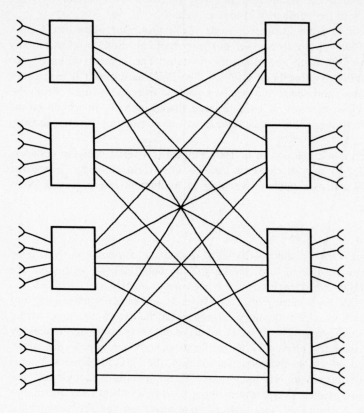

Figure 4.2   Switch connections for a 16-node Butterfly.

There is at least one path through the switch from each Processor Node to every other Processor Node. The switch operates much like a packet switching network. A packet is constructed by appending the data to be sent to the destination node address. The packet's address bits are used to route the packet through the switch. Each switching node strips off the two least-significant bits of the packet and uses them to select one of its four output lines. The remainder of the packet is transmitted over the selected line. There is not a dedicated path between each pair of Processor Nodes. Therefore, it is possible that a switching node will simultaneously receive two messages that require the same output port. In this case, one message is sent immediately to its destination, and the other is retransmitted after a short delay.

The complexity of the Butterfly Switch grows manageably with the number of Processor Nodes. A 64-processor switch can be constructed from a 16-processor switch by adding another column of switching nodes and enough rows to handle the 48 additional processors (see Fig. 4.3). The number of switching elements for an n-processor system

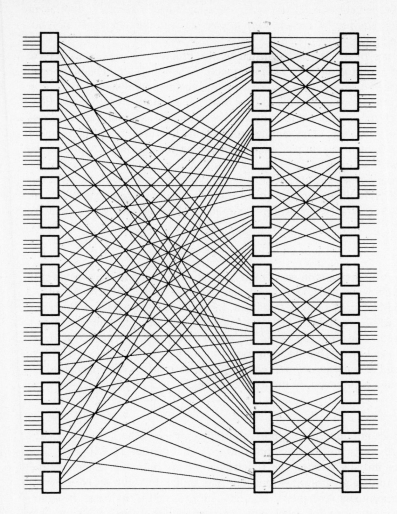

Figure 4.3 Switch for a 64-Processor Butterfly system.

increases at a rate of $n \log_4 n$. This is significantly better than the n^2 complexity of a crossbar switch.

By adding extra switching nodes, an extra path between every pair of Processor Nodes can be created. This is done in large configurations to increase reliability in the event of switch component failures. In addition, the alternate paths reduce contention within the switch. When a message must be retransmitted because of contention for a switching element's output port, the alternate path is used immediately. Machines are configured so that the probability of contention within the switch is relatively unlikely. Although the amount of contention is application dependent, the contention overhead typically is one to five percent of total run time. Message time is normally dominated by the amount of time required for the message to pass through the switch serially, not by contention for switching paths.

To illustrate the use of the Butterfly Switch by the Processor Nodes, consider the following example of a remote memory read reference. When the CPU makes the read reference, the PNC takes over and uses its memory management hardware to transform the virtual address into a physical address. To read the memory location, the PNC sends a packet through the switch to the remote processor node requesting the contents of the physical memory location. The remote processor node's PNC reads the memory location and uses the switch to return a packet containing the location's value to the local PNC. The local PNC then makes the value available to the CPU, satisfying the read request. Total round trip time for a remote memory reference through the switch is about 4 microseconds. The PNC can also transfer blocks of data larger than one word between any pair of Processor Nodes at the maximum 32 Mbit/sec transfer rate of the switch.

I/O Architecture

Each processor node is equipped with an I/O interface. Currently there are two types of boards available, the Butterfly MULTIBUS Adapter (BMA) and the Butterfly Serial I/O (BIO) board. The BMA board provides efficient communication between a Processor Node and a MULTIBUS. Any MULTIBUS compatible I/O device, memory or processor may be attached. The Butterfly Serial I/O board supports four RS-232 interfaces and four RS-422 connections. The machine used for the benchmarks uses a BMA to support serial lines and an Ethernet board. Currently, no disk drives are attached to the BMA. All mass storage is provided by the front-end host.

4.2   SOFTWARE

Since the Butterfly does not currently support a hard disk, it uses a host front-end. The Butterfly is connected to its host via a serial port and an Ethernet TCP/IP link. The serial line is used for initially booting the Butterfly from the host. Once the Ethernet software is in place, further program downloading may utilize the high speed Ethernet. The development environment (compilers, libraries, etc.) reside on the host. Programs for the Butterfly are written on the front-end computer, either a DEC VAX or SUN Workstation, running under UNIX 4.2BSD (see Fig. 4.4). These programs are then cross-compiled on the front-end computer and downloaded over the Ethernet to be executed on the Butterfly.

The Chrysalis Operating System

The Chrysalis Operating System is a UNIX-like, single-user system, consisting of several levels of support:

Shell   The shell that provides for program loading and execution. To an experienced UNIX user, the current Butterfly shell can seem limiting. For example, I/O redirection is not supported. The shell environment is similar to the UNIX Bourne Shell.

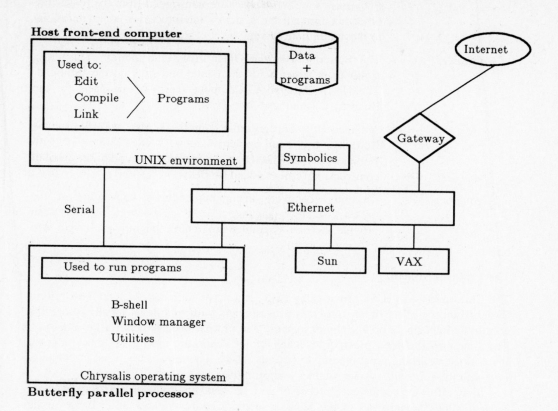

Figure 4.4   Butterfly software development configuration.

Window Manager	The window manager supports console I/O facilities to multiple processes. Its capabilities include window creation, deletion, switching, and resizing. In addition to screen editing facilities, the abilities to kill, freeze, and thaw processes are supported.
Kernel	The Chrysalis kernel consists of many microcoded segments and resides on each processor. Each processor's scheduler provides fast context switching, typically 120 microseconds.
Memory	The Butterfly's 68000 virtual memory system is controlled by memory map registers called Segment Attribute Registers (SARs), each accessing up to 64 Kbytes. Applications can directly control the memory mapping through system primitives.
I/O	Each processor has the ability to handle its own I/O. However, I/O is usually handled by just one of the processors, which is directly connected to the MULTIBUS. As various processor

Languages

I/O requests are made, they are transmitted from the requesting processor through the system's interprocessor communications to the appropriate server.

The Butterfly uses the Green Hills C compiler. This cross compiler is targeted for the 68000 and runs on the front-end. The UNIX Portable C Compiler (pcc) is the basis for the Butterfly C language.

A Green Hills Fortran cross compiler is also available for the Butterfly. It is a full implementation of ANSI Fortran 77, with Berkeley UNIX 4.2BSD f77 extensions. In addition, parallel constructs have been added by BBN.

Debugging

Currently, complete debugging requires knowledge of the 68000 assembler language. "Ddt" procedures, however, can provide the non-assembler programmer significant insight into existing problems.

The Uniform System

The Uniform System (US), provided by BBN, is a set of subroutines called the Uniform System Library. This library provides programmers with high-level parallel processor control by imposing a philosophy of memory and process management for the Butterfly. The functions provided incorporate many of the Chrysalis primitives, thus reducing much system-specific programming overhead. These functions can be used in conjunction with the Chrysalis system routines and primitives.

In an effort to provide each processor with an equal environment, memory management facilities organize all of the separate memory address spaces into a large single block of common memory shared by all processors. This provides a uniprocessor-like programming environment that reduces the need to deal directly with the Butterfly memory map registers, and it allows all cooperating processors to share data in an equal manner.

Due to the nature of the Butterfly Switch, memory contention can occur if multiple simultaneous accesses are attempted to the same memory. The US attempts to prevent this situation by providing functions that allocate memory uniformly across its shared memory space. Although remote memory access requires 6 microseconds as opposed to 2 microseconds for local processor memory, the simplicity achieved through the US is desirable for many applications.

Process management provides the programmer with the ability to support dynamic processor load balancing, using any number of processors. This philosophy treats all processors as a pool of available workers, each sharing a common memory segment. The programmer must identify the parallel aspects of the program and segment them into subroutines (tasks). Through the use of a generator, tasks are logically controlled and allocated to processors as they become available.

A Uniform System Emulator resides on the host and provides the programmer the ability to do initial partial debugging on the host workstation.

Future Developments

At this writing, BBN is about to release several enhancements to the Butterfly domain that will provide significant improvements. Chrysalis 3.0 will support a multi-user environment. Each user, at login, will be able to pre-allocate the full set or a subset (cluster) of the Butterfly's nodes. In addition, the user-host interface will provide a more logical approach to users' access and control of the Butterfly. A user will log onto the host workstation, do cross-program development, and access the Butterfly from the host's shell. System loading and initialization will be significantly enhanced through the implementation of a MULTIBUS RAM card, which contains a copy of the system. This should yield a great improvement in speed over current serial and Ethernet links.

A Butterfly disk driver will be implemented for an Storage Module Drive (SMD-type) disk. The initial disk software will support a flat file system. In addition, a VME bus Adapter is being tested and should provide high bandwidth I/O. A new subroutine library called the RamFile has been implemented. Its function is to provide the programmer a UNIX-style file system using unallocated Butterfly memory, which can be quite extensive.

Our 32-floating point processor system contains 4 Mbytes per node, for a system total of 128 Mbytes. The RamFile capability will facilitate the use of data structures that are currently too large to fit within a process's addressing space. Parallel access to the resident RamFile by various processors is supported. In addition to the current languages (C and Fortran), complete multiprocessor Common Lisp will be provided. Lisp will support a shared memory environment and incorporate the *future* construct developed at MIT.

An overview of the Butterfly parallel processing system is given in [1]. Details on strategies for effective use of the Uniform System for programming the Butterfly can be found in [2], a portion of which is reproduced in Appendix B2.

Timing

Program executions can be timed by successive calls to the system routine `GetRtc`. The time between the two calls can be output using `printf`, as shown in the Pi Program example in Section 4.3.

4.3   PARALLEL PROGRAM EXAMPLE

To calculate the integral for the Pi Program, each processor computes an equal portion of the integral. When the partial sum calculation is complete, each processor adds its contribution to a global variable named `tpi`. A shared lock variable is used to ensure that these additions are done atomically.

```
1   #include <us.h>      /* includes must be in the order shown */
2   #include <stdio.h>
3   BEGIN_SHARED_DECL  /* three different ways to share data are */
4   double tpi;        /* demonstrated in this program */
5   END_SHARED_DECL;
6   int nrecs, nprocs, time1, time2;
7   short *lock, *nodecount;
```

Lines 3–5 use a macro to define globally shared variables whose values may be changed by the processors. This macro can be used only once in a Uniform System program. Variables that need to be shared, but will not be redefined, can be shared by a macro named `Share` (see Line 23 in the following code) which merely makes the appropriate address available to each processor.

```
 8   UserInput()
 9   {
10      printf("\nNumber of rectangles is ...");
11      scanf("\n%d", &nrecs);
12      printf("\nNumber of processors is ...");
13      scanf("\n%d", &nprocs);
14   }
```

At Lines 8–14 the `nrecs` (number of rectangles) and `nprocs` (number of processes) are input by the user for each run. The program does not attempt to redefine these last two variables.

```
15   ShareData()
16   {
17      MakeSharedVariables;
18      nodecount = (short *) Allocate(sizeof(short));
19      *nodecount = nprocs;
20      lock = (short *) Allocate(sizeof(short));
21      *lock = 0.
22      SHARED tpi = 0;
23      Share(&nrecs); Share(&nprocs); Share(&nodecount);Share(&lock);
24   }
```

After the Uniform System has been initialized (see Line 70) `MakeSharedVariables` (Line 17) is a macro that must be called (only if the `SHARED_DECL` macros are used) to allocate the space and make necessary addresses available to each processor. Each variable declared by the `SHARED_DECL` macros can be referenced in subsequent code if the variable name is preceded by the word `SHARED` (e.g., Line 22). Alternatively, in the case of the variables `nodecount` and `lock`, the allocation is explicit, using the functions shown in Lines 18 and 20. The `Allocate(size)` routine allocates a block of storage of `size` bytes and returns a `char` type that is then cast into the desired result type. At Line 23 the pointers to four variables are passed to all processors. The variable pointed to when the `Share()` function is utilized *must* be four bytes in length. Other macros for sharing data are described in Appendix B2.

```
25   PrintAnswer()
26   {
27      int elapsed_time;
28      double pi;
29      if (time2 > time1)
30         {
31         elapsed_time = time2 - time1;
32         printf("\nTime is %d0, elapsed_time);
33         }
34      pi = 3.1415926535897932384626433;
35      pi = pi - SHARED tpi;
36      printf("\nCalculated pi is ... %27.20e\n", SHARED tpi);
37      printf("\nPi minus calculated pi is ... %27.20e\n", pi);
38   }
```

The function described in Lines 25–38 is called after the main body of the program. It merely outputs the value calculated for pi and compares that value with the known value. The value for pi shown in Line 34 is carried well beyond the double precision achievable (with one variable) with this machine.

In the main body of the following program, the routine named `GetRtc` is used to obtain the value of the system clock. After the computation this value is obtained again, and if the system clock has not been reset, the value is printed in response to the code on Line 32. The clock times are in units of 62.5 microseconds.

```
39   Dummy2() {};
40   Partial_Pi(Dummy2, index)
41   int index;
42   {
43      int me, n1, n2, j, section;
44      double h, x, sum;
45      {
46         me      = index;
47         h       = (double) 1.0 / nrecs;
48         section = nrecs / nprocs;
49         n1      = (me * section) + 1;
50         n2      = n1 + section - 1;
51         if (me == (nprocs - 1)) n2 = nrecs;
52         sum = 0.0;
```

Lines 39–64 define the computation sent to each processor. The main body of the program consists of the function `Partial_Pi(dummy2, index)` (Line 40). `Dummy2` is an argument that can be passed to a routine that is called on each processor before the `Partial_Pi` is executed. Similarly, this same argument can be passed to a routine that is executed after the main routine (in this case it is `Partial_Pi`) is executed. In this version, this automatic routine-calling capability is not used, but is described in the following discussion of the main program (Lines 65–75) that generates the tasks for each processor.

The `index` value (Lines 40 and 46) ensures that there will be a unique number for each processor executing the `Partial_Pi` code. The `index` values will be a compact set of integers in the range 0 to the number of processors previously requested minus one The variable `h` (Lines 44 and 47) is the width of the rectangles. The variable `x` (Lines 44 and 55) is the midpoint of a subinterval (base of a rectangle). Each processor uses its `index` value and the variable `section` to determine its range of integration (Lines 49–51).

```
53      for (j = n1; j <= n2; ++j)
54        {
55            x   = (j - 0.5) * h;
56            sum = sum + (4.0/(1.0 + x * x));
57        }
58      LOCK(lock, 0);
59          SHARED tpi = SHARED tpi + (h * sum);
60      UNLOCK(lock);
61      Atomic_add(nodecount, -1);
62      while (*nodecount > 0) UsWait(0);
63    }
64  }
```

The actual integration for each interval is performed at Lines 53-57. The LOCK and UNLOCK macros (capitalization required) at Lines 58 and 60 implement a busy-wait lock. The second argument is the number of tens of microseconds delay between attempts to obtain the lock. A value of zero results in a default time (approximately 1 millisecond). After `tpi` is atomically updated, a counter initially equal to the number of processors is atomically decremented, and another busy-wait macro named `UsWait(n)` (Line 62) is called to ensure that no code is executed past Line 62 until all processors finish their tasks. As before, the `n` argument to `UsWait` is the number of tens of microseconds, and a value of zero defaults to approximately 1 millisecond.

```
65   Dummy1() {}; Dummy3() {};
66   main ()
67   {
68      UserInput();
69      time1 = GetRtc();                /* system clock read */
70      InitializeUs();
71      ShareData();
72      GenOnIFull(Dummy1, Partial_Pi, Dummy3, 0, nprocs, 0, 0);
73      time2 = GetRtc();
74      PrintAnswer();
75   }
```

Last, we come to the main function, which invokes the other functions discussed. Line 68 calls `UserInput`, which requests the number of rectangles and the number of processors to be employed. Line 67 starts the timing clock. Line 70 installs and initializes the Uniform System followed by the call to share the necessary variables.

Line 72 invokes a *generator* to create the tasks for each processor. This is just one of many generators available to users of the butterfly machine. `GenOnIFull` causes `Partial_Pi` to be executed in parallel on `nprocs` processors. The processor that invokes `GenOnIFull` also completes a task and has an index value of zero. The routine `Dummy1` is called on each processor before `Partial_Pi`, and `dummy3` is called on each processor after `Partial_Pi`. The fourth argument to `GenOnIFull` (zero in the present case) is the argument that can be passed to `Dummy1` and/or `Dummy2` if this capability is invoked. The sixth argument (also zero in the present case) can limit the number of processors. A value of zero or minus one limits the number of processors to `nprocs`, and a positive value limits the number to that value. The seventh argument (if set to one) allows any processor to abort the call to `GenOn-IFull` if some condition is met. In this case, all processors return control to the processor that initiated the call to `GenOnIFull`, and no more task calculations are started. However, tasks in progress will be completed. The abort routine `AbortGen` returns the value passed to it when it was aborted.

Line 73 is reached only when all the tasks are completed, and at this time another reading of the system clock is taken, and Line 74 calls a function to print the results.

4.4 PERFORMANCE

At the present time the Butterfly is a single-user system. It requires a full minute to download the compiled Pi Program over a serial port from the front-end computer to the Butterfly. (The Ethernet would go faster). The time to install the Uniform System (i.e., to execute Line 70) is slightly less than two seconds. For the program described here, each processor carries out `nrecs/nprocs` iterations. The last iteration may do slightly more or less computation depending on the number of processors used. In any case, the load is well balanced. A single update to the shared variable `tpi` is done after each process finishes with all its iterations. Wall-clock time for 10,000,000 intervals (60,000,000 floating point operations) using 29 nodes averaged 18.0 seconds (or 3.3 Mflops).

Speedup results of timing with 10 million rectangles on different numbers of processors are shown in Fig. 4.5.

For runs up to 29 processors, the difference between the calculated value of pi and that assigned in Line 34 is approximately 10^{-15} or less, which is near the limit of double precision. For this example program, the −O and −O2 compile options did not speed up execution.

4.5   PITFALLS AND PROBLEMS

The Chrysalis operating system is in an early stage of development. Users familiar with UNIX will find a small subset of the commands and utilities that they have come to depend on. Yet there are many routines provided to give considerable implementation flexibility to the user. The Uniform System affords the simplest use of the machine and the example in this chapter uses this method exclusively. More explicit instructions allow more tailored use, but require much greater understanding of the operating system.

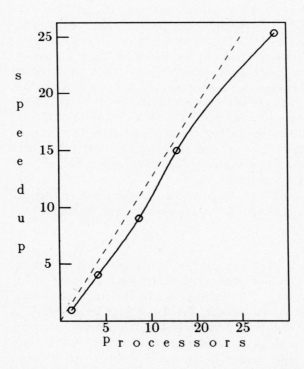

Figure 4.5   Speedup for 4 to 29 processors with 10,000,000 rectangles.

There are many low-level primitives available for managing global and local memory and communicating between processors. Calls to generators can be nested, but this can result in deadlock. As with most parallel processors, it is possible to write code that performs correctly with some data but incorrectly with other input. In other words, we were not prevented by the compiler from using some routines in an incorrect way. The documentation is usually, but not always, clear on such points.

The approach taken in implementing a program, especially the memory management scheme, can have a large effect on its performance. For example, frequent references to global variables by many processors can become a bottleneck since all global variables are allocated on the same physical memory.

4.6 CONCLUSIONS

The Butterfly architecture provides a convenient means to study parallel architecture. The combination of a local memory for each processor and each processor having fast access to shared memory supports an environment on which to map many parallel software strategies. Certain models may run into problems with memory contention. Admittedly, the tools available are limited, and the `ddt` debugger can be tedious for some users, but the versatility of process and memory management allows programming flexibility. It is not necessarily true, however, that existing code and algorithms will be easily ported to this machine and exhibit maximum performance with modest effort.

4.7 ACKNOWLEDGMENTS

Thanks are due to Mindy Garber of BBN Advanced Computers for her assistance in obtaining the documentation on the Uniform System Library Routines in Appendix B2 and for her help with a technical review of this chapter.

4.8 REFERENCES

[1]   BBN Laboratories Inc, "Butterfly™ Parallel Processor Overview", BBN Report No. 6148, Version 1, March 6, 1986.

[2]   BBN Laboratories Inc, "The Uniform System Approach to Programming the Butterfly™ Parallel Processor", BBN Report No. 6149, Version 2, June 16, 1986.

5
CRAY X-MP

Kurt B. Modahl

Machine/Model:	CRAY X-MP Model 22
Location:	National Magnetic Fusion Energy Computer Center, University of California, Lawrence Livermore National Laboratory
Processors:	2 CPUs sharing 2 M 64-bit words
Operating System:	CRAY Time Sharing System (CTSS)
Language:	Extended Fortran 77
Compiler:	CRAY Fortran Compiler (CFT version 1.14)

5.1 HARDWARE

The CRAY Research, Inc., CRAY X-MP 22[†] supercomputer is a multiprocessor extension of the CRAY-1. It contains two CRAY-1-like processors that share memory and I/O subsystems. The interleaved central memory bank can store 2 million 64-bit words. All banks can be accessed independently and in parallel during each machine clock period. The basic machine cycle time is 9.5 ns. Each CPU has 12 functional units, organized in four groups: address, scalar, vector, and floating point. Each functional unit is pipelined and can operate concurrently, yielding parallelism across units. Eight address (A), 64 address-save (B), eight scalar (S), 64 scalar-save (T), and eight 64-element vector (V) registers are used to stage data between main memory and the pipelined function units. A diagram of the architecture of a two-processor CRAY X-MP is shown in Fig. 5.1.

All arithmetic instructions are register-to-register: functional units take input operands from and store result operands to A, S, and V registers. Inter-processor

---

[†]The model number means "2 processors, 2 Mwords of memory". Another model, the X-MP 48, has four processors sharing 8 Mwords of memory. CRAYs with 8, 16, and 64 processors are currently under development.

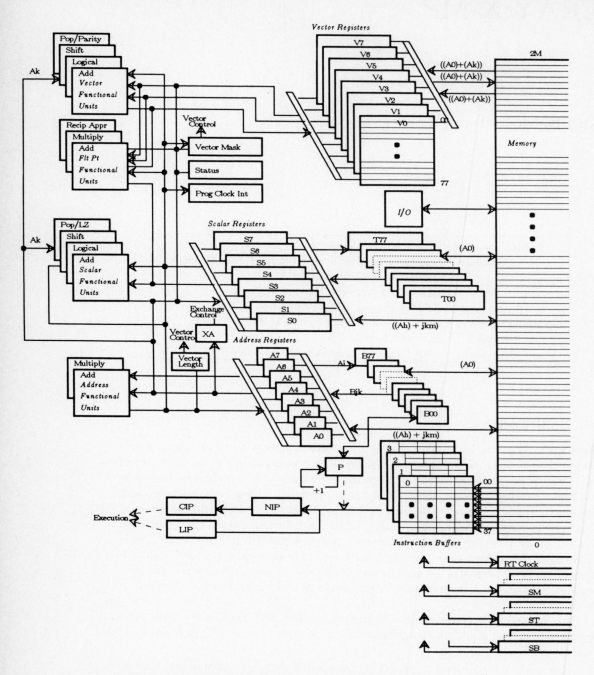

Figure 5.1(a)   Architecture of a two processor CRAY X-MP.

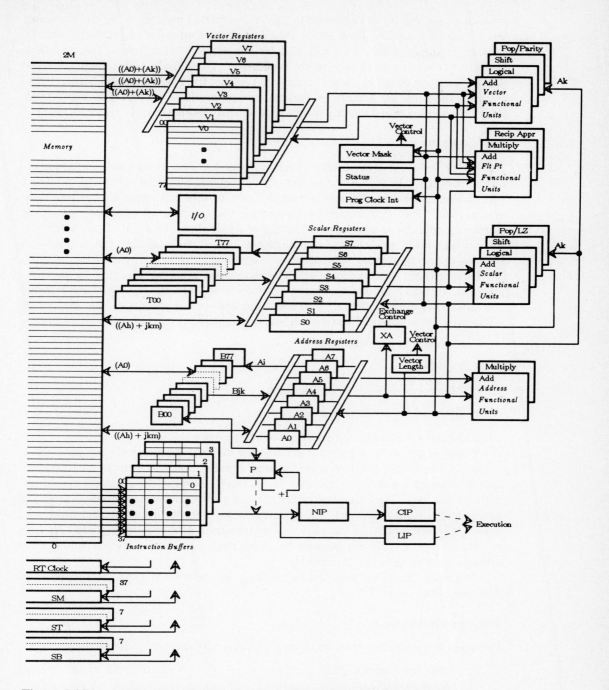

Figure 5.1(b) Architecture of a two processor CRAY X-MP (continued).

communication can be accomplished in CRAY Assembly Language (CAL) by accessing sets of shared registers. Each set of shared registers consists of eight shared address (SB), eight shared scalar (ST), and 32 1-bit semaphore (SM) registers. One real-time clock (RTC) register is shared by the processors. The CRAY Time Sharing System (CTSS) uses one of the hardware semaphore registers for synchronization between processors. The hardware semaphore registers are also available for access by users (from CAL), but were not used directly for the experiments reported in this chapter.

5.2 SOFTWARE

The CRAY X-MP, like the CRAY-1, achieves low-level parallelism through vectorization. The CRAY FORTRAN compiler (CFT) analyzes innermost DO loops to detect vectorizable sequences and then generates code to take advantage of the processor organization. The vectorization performed by the compiler is automatic, providing increased performance without restructuring or handcoding. In addition, the X-MP can achieve high-level parallelism via multitasking. All of the processors can cooperate to solve a problem by running separate tasks in parallel.

Under CTSS, any required task synchronization must by specified by the programmer via calls to the multitasking library (MULTILIB). Multitasking requires careful consideration of the algorithm at hand and data dependencies that may exist. CTSS provides a variety of facilities to support multitasking, including the necessary:

- Compiler linkage protocols;

- Utilities;

- Memory management facilities; and

- Multitasking synchronization routines

needed to support a multitasking environment (see Appendix C2).

A task is defined as a program unit capable of being independently assigned a processor. All tasks of a program share the same Fortran COMMON memory area, but each task is allocated a private environment for its local variables. All programs consist initially of one task. Any task can create a number of other tasks. All tasks created as descendants of the initial task run logically in parallel, but actual parallel processing across the two processors depends on instantaneous machine loading and available resources. Hence, it is not possible to easily determine for a particular run whether separate tasks actually ran in parallel.

For more details on parallel programming for the CRAY X-MP as supported by Cray Research, see [1] [2] [3].

Program Development

Preparing an application program under CTSS typically consists of the following steps:

1. Create the Fortran source code using trixgl, a line-oriented editor, or other editors available.

2. Compile the source code using the CFT compiler:

```
cft i=source,b=binary,l=listing,link=2
```

where `link` allocates local variables to the stack.

3. Link and load the binary version into an executable object:

```
ldr b=binary,lib=(multilib,fortlib),x=execute
```

where `multilib` is the library for the multitasking routines and `fortlib` contains the normal Fortran routines.

4. Run the executable object:

```
execute
```

5.3 PARALLEL PROGRAM EXAMPLE

The sequential and parallel versions of the Pi Program use the same source code. A main task generates n subtasks and waits for the tasks to finish calculation for their portion of the loop intervals. The portion of work done by the DO loop in each task is based on the total number of tasks and on its task number (1 to 4). The sums are returned to the main task through a single variable in COMMON. The main program waits for all subtasks to complete execution before printing the final result.

Annotated Source Code for the Main Program

```
1           REAL        SUM
2           INTEGER     TL(4), INTRVLS, NTASKS, TLOCK
3           COMMON SUM , TL ,INTRVLS , NTASKS , TLOCK
4           INTEGER     LSTAT
5           REAL        PI
6   C
7           INTEGER     ITC(3,4)
8           EXTERNAL TASK
9   C
```

Lines 1–2 declare variables in the COMMON block that will be accessed by each of the tasks (named TASK, declared EXTERNAL at Line 8):

- SUM is the final result that is used by each task to contribute its sum to accumulate the final total;

- TL is an array used to store each task's timing information;

- INTRVLS and NTASKS are the user input values for the number of intervals and tasks respectively;

- TLOCK is a multitasking lock variable used by each task to coordinate access to the shared SUM;

- LSTAT is used for the return status of the call that assigns and initializes TLOCK at Line 12;

- PI contains a reference value of pi to 23 decimal places; and

- ITC is the task control array used to initialize up to four subtasks.

The EXTERNAL TASK statement at Line 8 is required for the call to TSKSTART at Line 37.

```
10          CALL LINK('UNIT59=TTY//')
11          PI = 3.14159265358979323846433E0
12          CALL LOCKASGN (TLOCK,LSTAT)
13   C
14   C *** SET TASK CONTROL ARRAYS & START THE TASKS ***
15   C
16          DO 15 I = 1 , 4
17             ITC(1,I) = 3
18   C          *** SET TASK NUMBER IN CONTROL ARRAY ***
19             ITC(3,I) = I
20   15     CONTINUE
21   C
22   100    WRITE(59,*) 'ENTER INTERVALS & TASKS (UP TO 4) 0=>END'
23          READ (59,*,END = 10 , ERR = 10 ) INTRVLS,NTASKS
24          WRITE(59,*) ' INTERVALS = ', INTRVLS
25          WRITE(59,*) ' NUMBER OF TASKS = ', NTASKS
26          SUM = 0.0E0
27   C *** REPEAT UNTIL NO. OF INTERVALS = 0 ***
28          IF ( INTRVLS .EQ. 0 ) GO TO 999
29   C
30   C      *** GET STARTING WALL CLOCK TIME ***
31   C
32          ISTART = IRTC()
33   C
```

The CALL to LINK at Line 10 assigns a Fortran logical unit number for the user's terminal. Unit 59 is used subsequently for all terminal input and output. The program accepts the number of intervals and number of tasks (1, 2, or 4) as user input at Line 23. LOCKASGN at Line 12 initializes the lock variable TLOCK. LSTAT is set to one if TLOCK already contains a valid lock (which it should not at this point) or zero if TLOCK was initialized properly. The program could check the returned status at this point. The task control array used to initiate subtasks is initialized in the DO loop at Lines 16–20. The first element specifies the number of words in each task control array. The second element is assigned a unique task identifier as a result of the TSKSTART call, and the third element contains a *task value*, which in this program identifies each task's number (1–4).

The starting time in CRAY real-time clock (RTC) cycles for an execution is obtained by the call to the CFT intrinsic function IRTC at Line 32. The difference between the ending time and the starting time (in machine cycles) gave us an accurate measure of actual wall-clock time for various numbers of intervals and tasks. The call to IRTC is generated as in-line code, and it affects task timing very little.

```
34  C     *** START ALL TASKS ***
35  C
36        DO 50 I = 1 , NTASKS
37           CALL TSKSTART ( ITC(1,I) , TASK )
38  50    CONTINUE
39  C     *** NOW WAIT ON EACH TASK ***
40        DO 60 I = 1 , NTASKS
41           CALL TSKWAIT ( ITC(1,I) )
42  60    CONTINUE
43  C
```

Multitasking routines provide for the creation of new tasks by the initial main task. The calls to TSKSTART at Line 37 create, initialize, and start new tasks at a specified subroutine entry point, in this case TASK. The ITC array must be built by the calling program. Depending on the user input value for NTASKS, one, two, or four tasks are created by calls to TSKSTART in the DO loop at Lines 36–38. TSKWAIT is invoked for each of the tasks created in the DO loop at Lines 40–42, and it causes the main task to suspend execution until the task has completed. The calls to TSKWAIT execute sequentially. If a subtask never returns, the program calling TSKWAIT is blocked indefinitely.

```
44  C     *** GET ENDING WALL CLOCK TIME ***
45        IEND = IRTC()
46  10    WRITE(59,*) ' TASKS COMPLETED '
47        WRITE(59,*) ' PI COMPUTED = ' , SUM
48        WRITE(59,*) ' ERROR AMOUNT = ', PI - SUM
49        WRITE(59,*) ' CPU TIME =', TL
50        WRITE(59,*) 'ELAPSED WALL CLOCK TIME = ', IEND - ISTART
51  C
52  C     *** GO GET NEXT INTRVLS AND NTASKS ***
53  C
54        GO TO 100
55  C
56  999   CONTINUE
57        CALL EXIT
58        END
```

The finishing time for a given test execution is obtained at Line 45 with another call to IRTC. The final result SUM is output along with the individual timings from the tasks and the elapsed wall-clock time. The loop is repeated until the user enters a zero for INTRVLS.

Annotated Source Code for Subroutine TASK

```
59   C
60         SUBROUTINE TASK
61   C     *** TASKS 1-4 ***
62         REAL        SUM
63         INTEGER     TL(4), INTRVLS, NTASKS, TLOCK
64         COMMON SUM , TL ,INTRVLS , NTASKS , TLOCK
65   C
66         REAL        LSUM
67         INTEGER     ME1
68         INTEGER     TL1(3)
69   C
70         INTEGER     I
71         REAL        H , F , X
72         F(X) = 4.0E0 / ( 1.0E0 + X**2 )
```

TASK contains the code invoked by the CALL TSKSTART statement at Line 37 in the main program. The task name must be declared EXTERNAL in the main program. Lines 62–63 repeat the declarations for the variables used in COMMON. The local variable LSUM accumulates each task's contribution to the global sum. ME1 becomes the starting index for each task's share of the intervals. Timing information is inserted into the TL1 array. Line 72 defines an in-line statement function used to compute function values for values of X.

```
73   C
74   C *** TASK ENTRY ***
75   C
76         CALL TSKVALUE (ME1)
77         H = 1.0E0 / INTRVLS
78         LSUM = 0.0E0
79   C
80   C
81         DO 10 I = ME1 , INTRVLS , NTASKS
82            LSUM = LSUM + F ((I-0.50E0) * H )
83   10     CONTINUE
84   C
85         LSUM = LSUM * H
```

The TSKVALUE call at Line 76 retrieves the integer value inserted into the task control array by the main program at Line 19. As a result, ME1 is assigned a value (1–4) used to partition the intervals in the DO loop. For example, for four tasks, task 1 computes the sums for intervals 1, 5, 9, and so on.

Synchronization locks can be used for mutual exclusion between tasks when accessing shared memory or when separate tasks are doing parallel I/O operations. LOCKASGN must be called to initialize a new lock variable before it can be used by other lock routines. Lock variables must be stored in COMMON so that they can be accessed by those routines that will use them. LOCKON sets a lock and returns control to the calling task. If the lock is already set, the task is suspended until the lock is cleared. LOCKOFF clears a lock and returns control to the calling task. Clearing a lock may allow another task to resume execution. When a task sets a lock, it becomes the owner of that lock and is the only task that is allowed to perform a LOCKOFF operation. It is a fatal error for a task to attempt to:

- Clear a lock that another task has set; or

- Attempt to doublelock a lock that is already set.

```
86   C *** ADD RESULT TO SUM ***
87         CALL LOCKON (TLOCK)
88             SUM = SUM + LSUM
89         CALL LOCKOFF (TLOCK)
90   C
91         CALL TSKTIME ( TL1 , 3 )
92         TL(ME1) = TL1(1)
93         RETURN
94   C
95         END
```

After each task has computed its partial sum (LSUM), the task must add LSUM to the final answer SUM, which is global to all subtasks. Access to SUM must be controlled so that there is no contention between any two tasks for updating its value. The call LOCKON(TLOCK) at Line 87 attempts to lock the lock variable that is initialized by the main program. If TLOCK is already set, then the task is suspended until the lock is cleared (by a call to LOCKOFF) by the task that originally set it. Otherwise, TLOCK is set, and the calling task resumes control.

The call to TSKTIME at Line 91 returns the total task CPU time in clock cycles, I/O time, and system time. At Line 92, the total task CPU time is entered into the task's respective part of the global TL array. Note that all tasks can enter values into the TL array in parallel safely because they are each given different values for ME1.

5.4 PERFORMANCE

To achieve a reasonable level of accuracy for the integral, it had been suggested that 10,000,000 intervals were needed. (As it turned out, 50,000 to 100,000 intervals gave the most accurate answers). Unfortunately, using 10,000,000 intervals also gave the surprising result for the integral of 0.0 (although the code ran very fast!). This problem is caused by the limitation in CFT that DO loop index variables cannot exceed $2^{23}-1$) (8,388,607). This limitation arises because the loop index variable is stored in a 24-bit

A register. Since ordinary Fortran integers on the CRAY have 64-bit precision, this limitation was quite unexpected. To bypass the size restriction on the loop index, the upper limit of the loop can be divided in half. The original DO loop code at Lines 79 to 83 code is modified to:

```
79              INTEND = INTRVLS / 2
80              DO 10 I = ME1, INTEND, NTASKS
81                  LSUM = LSUM + F ((I-0.50E0) * H )
82                  LSUM = LSUM + F ((I+INTEND-0.50E0) * H )
83      10      CONTINUE
```

INTEND is the ending index for the DO loop. This version (V1 in the results) worked fine for 10,000,000 intervals, but of course will fail again if the loop variable I becomes larger than 2^{23}-1 (i.e., at 16,777,214 intervals). This version was subsequently modified to combine the two assignments in the DO loop body to become:

```
79              INTEND = INTRVLS / 2
80      C
81              DO 10 I = ME1, INTEND, NTASKS
82                  LSUM = LSUM + F((I-0.50E0)*H) + F((I+INTEND-0.50E0)*H )
83      10      CONTINUE
```

This version (V2) ran much faster than V1.

Execution results for 10,000,000 intervals are shown in Fig. 5.2 for version V1, for 1, 2, and 4 tasks. The slight differences between the computed and reference values of pi are due to round off in the different orders of summation for various numbers of

NTASKS	1	2	4
Total Cycles	705,539,734.8	715,635,474.2	715,919,421.6
Total Seconds	6.70263	6.79854	6.80123
Error	4.016E-08	+2.008E-08	+1.004E-08
Cycles/Task	705,539,734.8	357,817,737.1	178,979,855.4
Seconds/Task	6.70263	3.39927	1.70031
Parallel Mflops	9.698	19.1218	19.114
Serial Mflops	9.698	9.561	9.557

Figure 5.2. Execution results for V1 (two-statement DO loop).

tasks. Also listed are each task's total CPU time (in CRAY X-MP machine cycles) and seconds for the four runs. The times were determined by calls to TSKTIME, which returns the approximate number of CPU cycles (9.5 nanoseconds per cycle) charged to the job. The number of seconds was computed from the total number of cycles used, averaged across the number of tasks. Parallel Mflops was determined by multiplying the number of floating point operations per loop iteration (13) by the number of iterations (5,000,000), assuming that this program was the only job running on the CPUs. The parallel Mflop number thus represents the hypothetical maximum parallel speed, assuming that both CPUs were devoted to only this problem. The serial Mflop number represents the hypothetical serial speed, assuming there was no actual parallel execution.

Shown in Fig. 5.3 are execution results for the version (V2) with a one-statement DO loop body. The speedup differences of V2 over V1 are more interesting than those between 1, 2, and 4 tasks. V2 is approximately six times faster than V1 regardless of the number of tasks. A possible explanation for this speedup is that the second version is faster because it makes two fewer references to LSUM. A more likely explanation is that the CFT compiled source listing shows that only the second version is vectorized by the compiler. The speedup computed from the CPU time within each version is very close to linear with the number of tasks: 2 tasks are twice as fast as one, and so on.

The error differences between the two versions is rather interesting. V1 is over 50 times less accurate than V2. Again, the only differences between them are in memory accesses and vectorization.

A more realistic measure of performance on time-shared parallel processors is elapsed wall-clock time for serial versus parallel versions. If a user program does not run significantly faster in such an environment as a parallel program (or, worse yet, runs significantly slower), it is likely that few people will ever want to run parallel programs

NTASKS	1	2	4
Total Cycles	118,170,665.5	115,774,946.8	117,087,091.2
Total Seconds	1.12262	1.09986	1.11233
Error	6.279E-10	+3.139E-10	+1.570E-10
Cycles/Task	118,170,665.5	57,887,473.4	29,271,772.8
Seconds/Task	1.12262	0.54993	0.27808
parallel Mflops	57.900	118.197	116.872
serial Mflops	57.900	59.098	58.436
SPEEDUP (V2/V1)	5.97	6.18	6.11

Figure 5.3. Execution results for V2 (one-statement DO loop).

on such a system. Shown in Fig. 5.4 are wall-clock timing results (obtained by calls to IRTC) for the version V2 with a single statement DO loop body. The number of clock cycles, average time in seconds, and standard deviation in seconds are presented for 20 consecutive runs for 10,000,000 intervals and 1, 2, and 4 tasks. The tests were made on a normal weekday afternoon on the National Magnetic Fusion Energy (MFE) Computer Center CRAY X-MP, which is always quite heavily loaded, typically serving more than one hundred timesharing users.

A single task ran the slowest (for the same overall computation), with two tasks running a little faster, and four tasks running slightly slower than two. Since this is a two-processor machine, four tasks are slightly slower than two due to the overhead of creating and terminating the third and fourth tasks.

The standard deviations are quite large in all cases, but particularly large with one task. The 2.5-second difference in average wall-clock time between 1 and 2 tasks are certainly not worth the programming effort to parallelize even our small Pi Program, but for programs that might consume hours or even days of CRAY time, a possible advantage for parallel programming can be seen. According to discussions with staff members at the MFE Computer Center, there should be a definite wall-clock advantage for parallel processing (provided artificially by CTSS for programs with a high priority and large memory requirements). The lack of any overwhelming trend in these experiments may be due to the smallness of this job, both in memory requirements and execution time.

5.5   PITFALLS AND PROBLEMS

CTSS and trixgl are probably the biggest obstacles inexperienced users must overcome to get parallel programs running. Perhaps programmers unaccustomed to screen editors would have less difficulty in adapting to CTSS. Although most, if not all, of the documentation is available online, it appears cumbersome and laborious to use and may not be always be current. It can be difficult to tell where to search for document information when problems arise.

NTASKS	1	2	4
Cycles/Run (*10**6)	1031.879	768.335	837.8
Seconds/Run	9.803	7.299	7.959
Standard Deviation (cycles*10**6)	620.6	165.6	191.3
Wall-clock Mflops	6.631	8.905	8.167

Figure 5.4. Wall-clock timing results for V2 (one-statement DO loop).

The line-oriented editor suggested for use by novices on the system, `trixgl`, has some quite sophisticated commands that might be appreciated by hardcore CRAY users, but perhaps not so much by users of screen-oriented editors. Many of the compiler errors experienced while getting sample parallel programs debugged were directly or indirectly related to unfamiliarity with using `trixgl` to edit source code.

Files created or changed by the editor must be moved to more permanent storage using the `filem` utility. If a user forgets to use `filem` on an important file, then the user "loses-em" after 32 hours. The need to run a utility manually to permanently store files after creation or modification seems unnecessarily burdensome. Apparently a time-shared Cray does not have enough disk space for every user to keep all files on disk.

MPDOC, the program reference manual that describes the multitasking environment for the CRAY, gives details on the library calls available to the programmer. Excerpts from MPDOC are given in Appendix C2. The routines `TSKSTART`, `TSKTIME`, `TSKVALUE`, and `TSKWAIT` are used to implement the sample program. MPDOC's explanation of these routines is somewhat terse, and it can be difficult for novice parallel programmers to use them without some trial and error. MPDOC could especially use examples showing where, when and why a programmer would use the various parallel calls[†]. For example, a `WARNING` message from CFT complained of an argument error in the statement:

```
CALL TSKSTART ( ITC1, TASK, 1 )
```

in an earlier version of the sample program in which `ITC1` was the first task's control array. This was caused by illegal use of literals as arguments in calls to `TSKSTART`.

After a clean compile and loading, the first run with 1,000,000 intervals and 4 tasks executed, but gave a result for pi of `5.234....`, which was off by more than expected. The problem was not due to parallelism, but was caused by the omission of the statement:

```
H = 1.0E0 / INTRVLS
```

at Line 101. This illustrates a frustrating feature of parallel processing in which sequential errors can be confused with actual parallel bugs.

Another problem also occurred as the result of porting the program verbatim from a 32-bit machine to run on the CRAY. Although correct results were produced, the code ran about 25 times slower than expected (about 270 Kflops—approximately the speed of a VAX). The explanation is that the original ported code specifies `DOUBLE PRECISION` for real variables. `DOUBLE PRECISION` (128-bit floating point arithmetic) is emulated in software on the CRAY, which results in considerable overhead and the resulting slowdown in execution time.

[†] A new online document named INTROMP is now available at MFE to provide users with an introduction to multiprocessing.

5.6 CONCLUSIONS

It is an interesting experience to have access to one of the fastest existing parallel super-computers. Some of the program development tools, however, do not seem to be up to par with the hardware. On the other hand, the parallel library available under CTSS at MFE is fairly well documented and is consistent across several (parallel and non-parallel) supercomputers (CRAY-1, CRAY X-MP, and CRAY-2). It is nice to have cross-referenced source listings with messages telling where CFT is able to vectorize code, which made it easier to explain speed differences between the two versions.

5.7 ACKNOWLEDGMENTS

We would like to thank Danny Sorensen of Argonne National Laboratory for sharing some of his CRAY time allotment at MFE with our class for these experiments. Eugene Somdahl and George Spix of Cray Research, Inc., helped with multitasking as supported by Cray Research. The User Consultants at MFE were very helpful in providing help with CTSS and with CTSS Multitasking Facilities as implemented at MFE. We would also like to thank Kirby Fong and Larry Berdahl, also at MFE, for their help in reviewing this chapter and the excerpts from MPDOC in Appendix C2.

5.8 REFERENCES

[1]   John L. Larson, "Multitasking on the CRAY X-MP-2 multiprocessor", *Computer*, vol. 17, no. 7, July 1984, pp. 62–69.

[2]   Steve S. Chen, Chris C. Hsiung, John L. Larson, and Eugene R. Somdahl, "CRAY X-MP: A Multiprocessor Supercomputer" in *Vector and Parallel Processors: Architecture, Applications, and Performance Evaluation*, M. Ginsberg (ed.) Amsterdam: North Holland, (to appear in 1987).

[3]   Cray Research, Inc., "Multitasking User Guide", Cray Computer System Technical Note SN-0222, January 1985.

6

FPS T Series Parallel Processor

Phillip C. Miller, Charles E. St. John,
and Stuart W. Hawkinson

Machine/model:	T/20
Location:	Floating Point Systems, Beaverton, Oregon
Processors:	16 nodes, each with 1 Mbyte DRAM
Operating systems:	VMS on MicroVAX front end,
	TOPSYS B01 on T Series System Board,
	VB Main Process B01 on T Series Vector Board
Languages:	occam 1, VAX/VMS Fortran Version 4.2
Compiler:	Transputer Development System 2.2A

The T Series represents Floating Point Systems' entry in the field of massively parallel architectures. The system is configured as an n-dimensional hypercube, which means that there are communications paths between each node and its n closest neighbors. The architecture of the T Series makes use of three important developments:

1. The Inmos Transputer chip [1] [2];

2. The occam programming language; and

3. An innovative multiport memory scheme.

Even in the rapidly changing world of parallel architectures, these ideas represent challenging departures from the recent approaches taken by other parallel system design efforts.

In this chapter we discuss the T Series architecture and two programming examples, which were run on a small T Series system. The first of the examples demonstrates internode communications and the second illustrates use of the vector processing hardware and utilities.

6.1   HARDWARE

The T Series can be configured from the smallest system of eight (2^3) nodes, or vector boards, to a maximum of 16,384 (2^{14}) nodes. The peak performance at these two extremes ranges from 96 Mflops to 196 Gflops. The programming examples in this chapter were run on a 16-node system.

The overall system topology is a 14-dimensional hypercube in its largest configuration. Other user-defined topologies, such as mesh, torus, ring, and cylinder, are relatively easy to implement using the hypercube interconnection scheme. The basic T Series configuration consists of a module, made up of:

- A system control board;

- An 80-Mbyte system disk; and

- Eight vector boards.

Doubling the number of vector boards adds another dimension to the cube structure. Applications can be written to be independent of the size of the system, providing a simple means for running programs on T Series systems of various sizes.

System Control Board

The System Control Board (SCB) connects a T Series module to its eight attached vector boards, a disk subsystem, and optionally to a front-end computer. The SCB is not user programmable, but contains operating system software to handle user service requests, such as communication and data transfer to and from a front-end computer, vector boards, disk subsystem, and, for multimodule T Series configurations, other SCBs.

Vector Boards

Each vector board (or node) can be thought of as a single-board array processor with a host computer. As mentioned previously, there are eight vector boards attached to a single system board. Each vector board contains:

- A Transputer;

- A Link Adapter/MUX;

- 1 Mbyte of multiported RAM;

- An ALU section consisting of a floating point adder and multiplier (IEEE 32- or 64-bit floating point format); and

- 4K words of 64-bit static RAM, used for microcode control of vector routines.

The ALU and its microcode store are collectively referred to as a Vector Processing Unit (VPU). VPUs are programmed using a set of FPS-supplied occam procedures that run on the VB Transputer. The occam procedures provide a high-level interface to microcoded VPU operations.

There are six groups of occam procedures for programming the VPU:

1. *Multi-node Subroutines* perform operations on data distributed across multiple nodes. The operations are performed in parallel, and some internode data communications is performed in support of the operations.

2. *Single-node Subroutines* perform operations on data located on single nodes of a T Series. Operations here include many of the more common matrix and vector manipulation operations. The operations in this group do not perform internode communications.

3. *Math Library Utility Subroutines* provide the mechanism for data transfers, status handling, and establishing the operational modes of a VPU.

4. *Generic Subroutines* provide a lower level of interaction with the VPU. These subroutines support operations, such as Vector-Scalar-Multiply-Add operation, on a complete vector on the VPU.

5. *Parameter Block Subroutines* are still lower in the level of interaction with the VPU. These subroutines support operations such as the initiation, continuation, and termination of a vector operation.

6. *Vector Form Subroutines* are at the lowest level of interaction with the VPU. These subroutines initiate microcoded operations in the VPU. The operations establish the flow of data through the VPU, set operating modes, and modify VPU registers.

A VPU operates asynchronously from its controlling Transputer; that is, vector operations can be performed in parallel with user occam code. Typically the VB Transputer moves data to and from main memory, performing disk operations, adjusting array pointers, or doing other operations involving the input and result data. The VPU automatically moves data between main memory and the arithmetic units during the execution of the VP operations.

Vector Board Communications

There are four communication links to and from a Transputer chip. The serial links have a measured data transfer rate of half a megabyte per second.

Two procedures, `byte.slice.input` and `byte.slice.output`, perform input and output to the links. The Vector Board (VB) allows as many as 16 channels to be used as communication links to a Transputer. The 16 channels are multiplexed so that a user may select four of them at any given time. The four paths are selected by the system call `set.links`. This must be done prior to invoking the `byte.slice` procedures. The paths are deselected via the `release.links` call.

Two of the 16 channels are reserved for the system. The other 14 channels are available for use by the programmer as hypercube communication channels or for connecting to external I/O devices. One channel per dimension of the hypercube is used by each VB to communicate with its neighboring nodes; the remaining links are available for connection to external I/O devices. In the largest T series configuration (16,384 nodes), all 14 channels are used for communication with neighboring nodes, although the potential exists for dedicating one or more dimensions of the cube structure for additional disk storage.

Figure 6.1 illustrates how the vector boards can be configured into an 8-node hyper-cube structure. One of the two reserved system channels is connected to all eight vector boards and to one of the SCB links. One vector board at a time gets the SCB link and uses it for downloading application code and input data, or for sending result data back to the system board and out to the module system disk. The other system channel is reserved for future system development.

VB Memory System

To use the VPUs, it is essential to understand the structure of the VB main memory system. The VB Transputer and the VPU have exclusive access to the memory of a node; a VB does not directly read or write the memory of any other node; it passes data using communication primitives and procedures. The VB main memory consists of 1 Mbyte of multiported RAM used to hold the source and destination data for the vector routines. The random access port of main memory is used by the VB Transputer for transfers of data to or from the system disk. The sequential access ports are used by the VPU to access rows of data for vector operations; an entire row of data can be read from or written to anywhere in main memory.

On every clock cycle, each of the two sequential access ports, A and B, can transfer a vector element from the VB main memory to the VPU; a result from a previous VPU operation can also be stored. The VPU runs most efficiently for vectors of lengths that are multiples of 256 32-bit words or 128 64-bit words. Figures 6.2 and 6.3 show the structure of the memory system.

Further information on the architecture of the T Series can be found in Appendix D2 and in [3].

6.2 SOFTWARE

The most prominent feature of the T Series programming environment is the occam language. Occam is the primary language of the Transputer and is closely related to its architecture. Occam has a simple and natural notation for expressing parallelism. The reserved word PAR is used to specify statements or processes that are to run in parallel. Its counterpart is SEQ, which directs the compiler to produce statements that execute sequentially. PRI PAR allows prioritization of parallel processes. ALT causes the execution of the first process that is ready from among a selection of processes.

Interprocess communication is performed in occam by using the ? (input) and ! (output) operators. For transferring data between processors, FPS provides two pro-cedures, byte.slice.input and byte.slice.output, mentioned previously in Section 6.1.

Timing information is provided through use of the occam constructs TIME, WAIT, NOW, and AFTER. These constructs provide the capabilities for measuring time, delaying a process, comparing time values, and placing a time limit on a process.

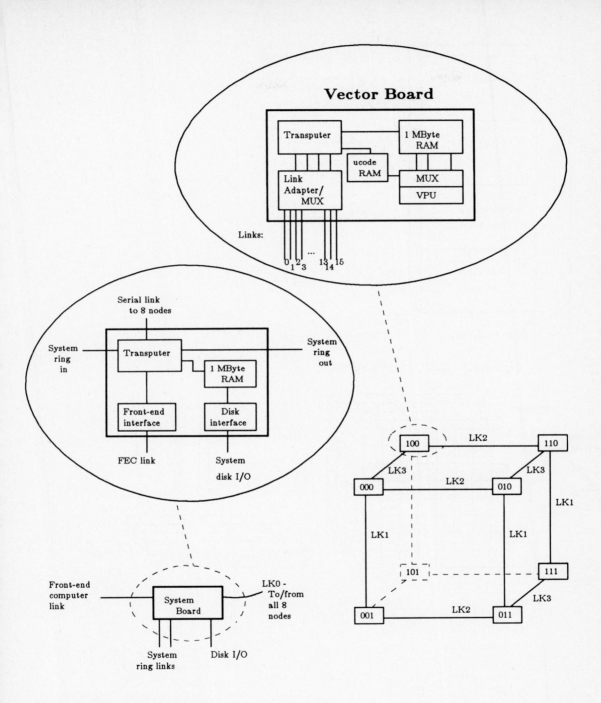

Figure 6.1   A T Series Module.

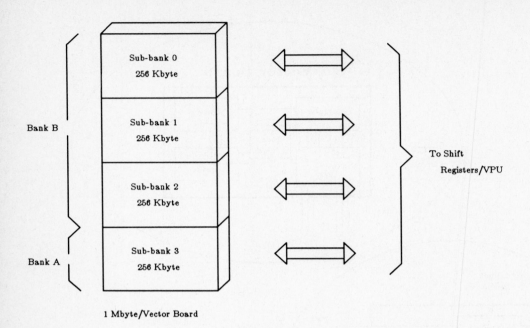

Figure 6.2 Main Memory Sub-bank.

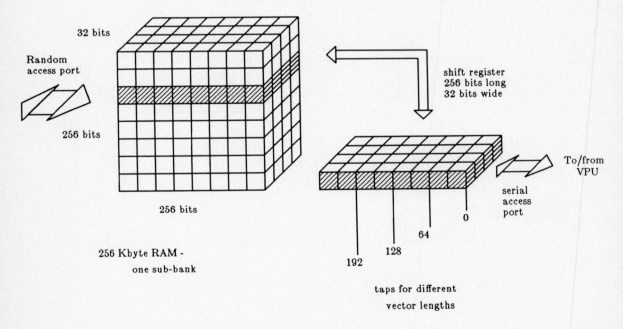

Figure 6.3 Vector Board Main Memory.

Further insight into the use of several of these language constructs and primitives is given in the examples and accompanying commentary.

Reference [4] is an excellent armchair guide to occam. The author gives many examples to show the features of occam. He also illustrates some of the thought processes involved in dividing a problem into parallel components and mapping a problem onto a Transputer-based system. For a more rigorous exposure to the occam language, see [5].

Program Development

T Series programs can be controlled from the front-end computer through the use of a host-resident program written in either C or Fortran. With the front-end program, a user can:

- Assign and release a T Series machine;

- Load an application program;

- Copy data files to and from T Series application disks;

- Delete files from those disks; and

- Report on the status of any of these operations.

There is also a utility provided for the user to convert data from the T Series IEEE floating point formats to the floating point formats of the front-end computer, and vice-versa.

User Disk Software

Each vector board can access the file system of its module system disk. The usual disk file operations are supported on the system: create file, open file, close file, delete file, and so forth. Since all files default to being temporary files, an additional command converts files to permanent files.

Occam Programming System

The Occam Programming System (OPS), provided by the Inmos Corporation, allows the user to develop the occam portions of a program and simulate its execution on the front-end computer, which is a Digital Equipment Corporation MicroVAX. Reference [6] describes the OPS in detail.

At the heart of this integrated programming environment is an editor specifically oriented toward the occam language. From within the editor, the user can invoke several utilities:

1. The *syntax checker* performs a syntax analysis on a portion of an occam program. In this way the user can save the overhead of a complete compilation.

2. The *occam compiler* produces an object module that can be linked and run on the front-end computer.

3. The *estimate* utility produces several interesting statistics about the user program. The most useful are the programs size and an estimate of the execution time (in machine cycles) for the program.

4. After successfully compiling a program, the user can exit the OPS session and link and run the program on the host. If the program aborts, the OPS system can be re-entered and the *locate error* utility can be invoked; the editor then displays the offending line of occam source code.

Transputer Development System

The Transputer Development System (TDS) is used to produce programs that are executable on Transputer-based systems [7]. The editor and its utilities are basically the same as those of the Occam Programming System. TDS is used to produce the executable programs for the T Series. FPS provides a sample template file as an aid to the user in developing T Series applications. This template file contains the software libraries used by a user program. For more information on programming the T Series, see [8].

6.3 PARALLEL PROGRAM EXAMPLES

This section contains two examples:

1. A simple occam program that runs on several processors and performs some simple interprocess communication.

2. An implementation of the Pi Program, which demonstrates use of the vector processing hardware.

Example 1: T Series Internode Communications

The following code represents the user process area of an occam program; not included are system variable definitions, configuration information, and run-time library procedures. These items are included in a template file supplied by FPS. This occam program causes each process running on a node to transmit messages to its nearest neighbors in the hypercube. The processes then conclude by printing a message indicating their position in the hypercube and the processes from which they received a message. For an 8-node system, the output is:

```
Vector Board # 0 received messages from VB's 1 2 4
Vector Board # 1 received messages from VB's 0 3 5
Vector Board # 2 received messages from VB's 0 3 6
Vector Board # 3 received messages from VB's 1 2 7
Vector Board # 4 received messages from VB's 0 5 6
Vector Board # 5 received messages from VB's 1 4 7
Vector Board # 6 received messages from VB's 2 4 7
Vector Board # 7 received messages from VB's 3 5 6
```

Note that the nearest neighbors to a node are those whose node number differs by one
bit when represented as a binary number. For example, processor number 7 (binary
111) has nearest neighbors 3 (binary 011), 5 (binary 101), and 6 (binary 110). The
number of the link that connects two adjacent nodes is equivalent to the sum of the bit
position of the differing bit plus one. It can therefore be seen that processor number 7
communicates with processor 3 over link number 3, processor 5 communicates with
processor 4 over link 1, and so on.

```
1    DEF dimension = 3
2    VAR neighbor[dimension]
3    DEF recvaddr = #80000:
4    PUTBYTE(processor,#40000)
```

Line 1 of the code for the first example declares a constant that represents the
number of dimensions in the cube. The value three means that the program uses eight
(2^3) processors. Line 2 declares an array (of integers) that holds the node numbers of
all nodes sending messages to this node. Line 3 declares a constant that represents the
address in VB memory where processor values received from neighboring nodes are
stored. Line 4 stores this node's processor number at byte address 40000 (hex) in VB
memory.

```
5    SEQ
6      -- internode communications example
7      set.links(4,1,2,3)
8      SEQ i = [1 FOR dimension]
9        PAR
10         byte.slice.output(i, #40000, 1)
11         byte.slice.input(i, recvaddr + (i - 1), 1)
12      release.links
13
```

Line 5 is an occam control structure that indicates that the following statements are executed sequentially. This control structure encloses all statements that are indented two
or more spaces to the right, or Lines 6–23. This is the occam method of representing
control structure hierarchy. Line 6 is an occam comment. Line 7 wires the link multiplexors for a particular pattern of communications between nodes: Links 1–4 will be
activated. Line 8 is an occam-style DO loop, to be executed sequentially. This
encloses Lines 9–11. The SEQ could be replaced with a PAR, causing the messages to
be sent and received over the three links in parallel.

Line 9 is an occam control structure that indicates that the following statements are
executed in parallel. This encloses Lines 10 and 11. A process may receive input data
or transmit output data in parallel. In the case of Lines 10–11, one byte of data (the
processor number) is output to link i from an address in VB main memory, and one
byte of data (a neighbor node's processor number) is input on link i to a different

address in VB main memory. Line 12 unwires the link multiplexors from this communications configuration.

```
14      hkeep(status)
15      -- Send the terminating messages to the monitor screens
16      hwrite.string("Vector Board #", 0, processor, status)
17      hwrite.int( processor, 0, processor, status)
18      hwrite.string(" received messages from VB's ",
19                      0, processor, status)
20      SEQ i = [0 FOR dimension]
21        SEQ
22          GETBYTE(neighbor[i], recvaddr + i)
23          hwrite.int( neighbor[i], 0, processor, status)
24          hwrite.string(" ", 0, processor, status)
25      hwriteln(0, processor, status)
26      hrelease(status)
```

Lines 14–26 print the termination message indicating node number (or address in the hypercube) and neighbor's node numbers.

Example 2: The Pi Program

Using the Rectangle Rule, the integral can be approximated by taking the sum of the areas of rectangular slices at intervals under the function curve. The greater the number of evaluation points, or rectangles, the greater is the accuracy of the result. This problem lends itself well to parallel processing since the integral's calculations can be spread over a large number of processing elements. In the following program, run on a T/20 system, each processor works on one panel of the interval [a,b]. Each panel consists of 16,384 evaluation points, for a total of 262,144 evaluation points for the integral.

```
1       -- source code
2       DEF one  =  TABLE[#00000000,#3FF00000]:
3       DEF half = TABLE[#00000000,#3FE00000]:
4       DEF four = TABLE[#00000000,#40100000]:
5       DEF pi   =  TABLE[#54442D18,#400921FB]:
```

We use the occam TABLE structure in Lines 2–5 to define floating point constants in IEEE format. There are two 32-bit table entries for each constant; the first comprises the least-significant half of the word, and the second is equal to the most-significant half. The constants are later referenced by their TABLE index values; for example, pi[0] is equivalent to the least-significant half of the 64-bit value for pi. Line 1 is a comment line.

```
6        VAR ftemp[2],temp,ntemp,xwrd,xn[2]:
7        VAR h[2],a[2],b[2],sum[2],new[2]:
8        VAR nt,np,npp,ns,lnsp,vlen,xoffs[2]:
9        VAR xa,x2a,xb,x2b:
10       VAR begin,mid1,mid2,mid3,end:
11       VAR elap1,elap2,elap3,elap4:
12       VAR h.adrs,xoffs.adrs,xn.adrs:
13       VAR sum.adrs,new.adrs,one.adrs:
```

The VAR statements in Lines 6–13 declare occam variables used as program
parameters, intermediate vector results, temporary integer values, and the integral's final
sum. Also declared are variables to be used in timing the four sections of the program
and variables used to hold vector memory addresses.

```
14       SEQ
15         -- define addresses
16         addr.v(h,h.adrs)
17         addr.v(xoffs,xoffs.adrs)
18         addr.v(xn,xn.adrs)
19         addr.v(sum,sum.adrs)
20         addr.v(new,new.adrs)
21         addr.v(one,one.adrs)
```

Lines 14–21 define VB memory addresses and the variables associated with each
address. The vector routines work with the addresses of variables, and the Transputer
operations reference the contents of the variables. At Line 14, the SEQ states that the
following 7 indented lines will be executed in sequential order.

```
22         -- report value of pi
23         IF
24           (processor=0)
25             SEQ
26               rel.control
27               hkeep(status)
28               hwrite.string(" True value for PI is  ",0,
29                       processor,status)
30               ct.hwrite.real64(pi,2,20,0,processor,status)
31               hwriteln(0,processor,status)
32               hwriteln(0,processor,status)
33               hrelease(status)
34               get.control
35           TRUE
36             SKIP
```

Lines 22–36 direct processor `0` to print the known value of pi to the terminal screen. Lines 26 and 34 release and obtain control of the system node interrupts. An `ELSE` must be provided for the other branch of the `IF` statement, and in this case we use the occam global constant `TRUE`. This, plus the `SKIP` at Line 36, indicates a no-op for processors other than number `0`. This value for pi, along with the value calculated using the Rectangle Rule, is printed at the end of program execution.

```
37        -- define x at BankA,B1 boundaries
38        xa := VP.BankA
39        xb := VP.BankB1
40        -- sync all processors for timing run
41        SEQ j=[0 FOR 5]
42          SEQ i = [1 FOR dimension]
43            set.links(i,-1,-1,-1)
44        release.links
45        TIME ? begin
```

In Lines 37–39, we define the location of the `x` vector (x from the integral of `1/(1+x**2)`), taken over the interval `[a,b]`) to start at the beginning of `Bank A` of VB memory. A second copy of the `x` vector is also stored, beginning at the start of `Bank B1` of VB memory. Each processor, as is seen later, has different parts of the total `x` vector in its VB memories, and works only on its own part.

Lines 41–44 force the synchronization of all processing elements by setting and releasing the internode communication links. This is necessary to ensure accurate timing measurements. At Line 45, the beginning time is obtained via the occam `TIME` statement.

```
46        -- partition domain
47        np := 1<<dimension   -- number of processors = 2^dim
48        vlen := 128          -- original vector length = slice
49        lnsp := 7            -- lnsp = log2(ns)
50        ns := 1<<lnsp        -- number of slices ns = 2^lnsp
51        nt := np*ns*128      -- total quad points (2^14 per node)
52        npp := nt/np         -- quad points per processor
```

Lines 46–52, as the comments indicate, assign parameter values used in determining each processor's share of the load, as well as in the calculations themselves. The number of processors is obtained by a left shift (<<) of the dimension value integer. The integral is partitioned into `262,144` evaluation points, with each of the 16 processors working on an equal share of the load, or `16,384` points each. These points can be thought of as the midpoints of `262,144` rectangles, each of width `h=1/262,144`.

```
53        -- specify interval [a,b]
54        a[0] := 0
55        a[1] := 0
56        b[0] := one[0]
57        b[1] := one[1]
58
59        -- compute h := (b-a)/nt
60        --              ftemp := float(nt)
61        IntegerToDReal(ftemp,nt)
62
63        --               h := b-a
64        DRealOp(h,b,Sub,a)
65
66        --               h := (b-a)/nt
67        DRealOp(h,h,Div,ftemp)
```

At Lines 53–57 we specify the beginning and ending points of the interval, 0 and
1. At Lines 61–67, the value of h (our rectangle width) is determined by dividing the
interval width by the number of evaluation points, in floating point format.

```
68        -- x[i] := xoffs + h*i
69
70        --              xoffs = a + (p*npp+0.5)*h
71
72        ntemp := processor*npp
73        IntegerToDReal(ftemp,ntemp)
74        DRealOp(ftemp,ftemp,Add,half)
75        DRealOp(xoffs,ftemp,Mul,h)
```

At Lines 72–75, each processor's offset into the evaluation space is determined and
set equal to the variable xoffs. Processor 0's offset is equal to the midpoint of the
first rectangle, processor 1's offset equal to the midpoint of the 16,364th rectangle,
and processor n's offset equal to the midpoint of the (16,384*n)th rectangle.

```
76        xwrd := (xa>>2)
77        SEQ i = [0 FOR vlen]
78          SEQ
79            PUTWORD(i,xwrd)
80            PUTWORD(0,xwrd+1)
81            xwrd := xwrd+2
```

At Lines 76–81, we create a seed vector of length 128 that is used to grow each
processor's portion of the total x vector. Line 76 converts VB memory byte address
xa into a word address, as required by the PUTWORD operations at Lines 79 and 80.

The loop of Lines 77–81 places the integers 1 to 128 in consecutive memory locations, beginning at address xa.

```
82      --              float sequence of integers & add offsets
83      GN.VO(xa,AF.Xfloat,xa,VP.null,vlen)          -- float i
84      GN.SVO(h.adrs,xa,MF.XYmul,xa,VP.null,vlen)   -- h*i
85      GN.SVO(xoffs.adrs,xa,AF.XYadd,xa,xb,vlen)    -- h*i+xoff
86
87      --              xn=float(vlen)*h
88      IntegerToDReal(ftemp,vlen)
89      DRealOp(xn,ftemp,Mul,h)
90      TIME ? mid1
```

Line 83 executes a single-node generic vector operation which converts the length 128 seed vector to floating point format and places it back into VB memory location xa. The parameters for the vector operation are:

- The input vector address;
- The arithmetic operation index;
- The first output vector destination address;
- The second output vector destination address (null in this case); and
- The number of elements to be operated on.

Line 84 executes a scalar-vector operation, multiplying our seed vector by h and replacing it in memory. Line 85 completes the generation of each processor's master slice by adding in each processor's offset value. This master slice is then stored in VB memory starting at locations xa (Bank A) and xb (Bank B).

At this point we have a vector whose elements are the midpoints of the first 128 evaluation rectangles of each processor. A doubling operation is used to expand this to a vector of length 16,384 on each node. Lines 88–89 set the variable xn equal to the first doubling width. Line 90 acquires the elapsed program time, in microseconds.

```
 91      --              vlen,xn and xi doubled lnsp times
 92
 93      SEQ j=[1 FOR lnsp]
 94        SEQ
 95          x2a := xa+(vlen*8)
 96          x2b := xb+(vlen*8)
 97          GN.VSO(xa,xn.adrs,AF.XYadd,x2a,x2b,vlen)
 98          DRealOp(xn,xn,Add,xn)
 99          vlen :=vlen+vlen
100      --              store x in both A and B banks
101      TIME? mid2
```

Lines 93–99 comprise the doubling loop, where the complete x vector is generated. During the first pass, the vector-scalar operation of Line 97 does an add of our 128-element seed vector with the scalar xn, with the result vector concatenated in memory with our original master slice. Our total x vector is now of length 256. The values for vlen and xn are doubled, and in the next pass, the next 256 evaluation midpoints are determined and again concatenated. After seven passes of the loop, our x vector is of length 16,384 (on each processor); one copy of x resides in VB memory Bank A, and one copy resides in VB memory Bank B. Line 101 gathers the current elapsed time.

```
102        -- compute sum over ns slices
103        --              1+x(i)*x(i)
104        GN.VVOSO(xa,xb,MF.XYmul,one.adrs,AF.XYadd,xb,VP.null,vlen)
105        SN.VRECIP(xb,1,xb,1,vlen)
106        GN.VRO(xb,AF.XYadd,sum.adrs,vlen)
107        TIME ? mid3
```

Lines 104–106 complete the integral calculations. Our x vector is squared and added to 1 with the vector-vector-scalar operation at Line 104. The vector multiply (in this case a squaring operation) is most efficiently done with each vector operand coming from a different VB memory bank. That is the reason for having two copies of the x vector. At this point, we have completed the $1+X**2$ portion of the calculation. Line 105 does a vector reciprocal operation on our intermediate result, and the following line does a vector reduction. Again, we obtain an elapsed time value at Line 107.

```
108        -- communicate and collapse sums over processors
109
110        rel.control
111        set.links(1,2,3,4)
112
113        SEQ i= [1 FOR dimension]
114          SEQ
115        --                              exchange sums
116            PAR
117              byte.slice.output(i,sum.adrs,8)
118              byte.slice.input(i,new.adrs,8)
119
120        --                              accumulate sums
121            DRealOp(sum,sum,Add,new)
122
123        release.links
```

At Lines 110–123, each processor's sum (corresponding to its portion of the integral calculation) is sent via hypercube communications to its nearest cube neighbors. The byte.slice procedures at Lines 117–118 have as their parameters the communication link number, the source/destination byte addresses in VB memory of the data to be sent/received across the link, and the number of bytes to be transferred. As a result of this exchange-and-accumulate operation, each processor should possess an identical sum result for the entire approximation interval.

```
124    -- compute sum := sum*4*h
125    DRealOp(sum,sum,Mul,four)
126    DRealOp(sum,sum,Mul,h)
127    TIME? end
128
129    -- output results
130    elap1 := mid1-begin
131    elap2 := mid2-begin
132    elap3 := mid3-begin
133    elap4 := end-begin
```

At Lines 125–133, each processor completes the pi approximation calculations and determines the number of microseconds spent in each of the four sections of the program.

```
134    hkeep(status)
135    hwrite.string(" Est. value for PI is  ",0,processor,status)
136    ct.hwrite.real64(sum,2,20,0,processor,status)
137    hwrite.string("   on processor ",0,processor,status)
138    hwrite.int(processor,0,processor,status)
139    hwriteln(0,processor,status)
140    hwrite.string("Elapsed times:float;gen.pts;sum pts;comm ",0,
141            processor, status)
142    hwriteln(0,processor,status)
143    hwrite.int(elap1,0,processor,status)
144    hwrite.string("   ",0,processor,status)
145    hwrite.int(elap2,0,processor,status)
146    hwrite.string("   ",0,processor,status)
147    hwrite.int(elap3,0,processor,status)
148    hwrite.string("   ",0,processor,status)
149    hwrite.int(elap4,0,processor,status)
150    hwrite.string("   ",0,processor,status)
151    hwriteln(0,processor,status)
152    hwrite.string(" total # pts, nt= ",0,processor,status)
153    hwrite.int(nt,0,processor,status)
154    hrelease(status)
155    get.control
```

Lines 134–155 direct each processor to write to the terminal screen:

- The approximated values of pi;
- The timing information; and
- The total number of evaluation points.

6.4   PERFORMANCE

For timing purposes, the Pi Program was partitioned into four sections, with elapsed times measured at the end of each section. The sections are as follows:

1. Section MID1: construct seed x vector;

2. Section MID2: generate complete x vector;

3. Section MID3: compute `1/(1+X**2)` for all elements of x;

4. Section END: sum over the cube.

Our program uses `262,144` evaluation points. A run was also completed using `32,768` evaluation points. The results for these two program runs are as follows:

```
32,768 evaluation points:

    Section MID1 elapsed time =  2.3 msec
    Section MID2 elapsed time =  1.3 msec
    Section MID3 elapsed time =  6.9 msec
    Section  END elapsed time =  2.1 msec

262,144 evaluation points:

    Section MID1 elapsed time =  2.3 msec
    Section MID2 elapsed time =  5.2 msec
    Section MID3 elapsed time = 53.2 msec
    Section  END elapsed time =  2.1 msec
```

If we count the program as having 8 floating point operations per vector element (2 vector multiplies, 3 vector adds, and 3 operations for reciprocal divide), an approximation of the performance we obtained can be calculated. For the 262K points case, we measured 37 Mflops for the entire system; with 32K points, this rating was about 21 Mflops. We assume that the difference in these two numbers is due to the constant overhead involved in setting up the processors, calculating offsets, doing format conversions, and so forth. As the amount of data being worked on increases, the ratio of overhead time to vector processing time is diminished.

For further information on performance characterization of the T Series, see reference [9].

6.5   PITFALLS AND PROBLEMS

Our experiences with writing and running occam programs were varied. Surprisingly, the overhead involved in learning the occam language was minimal. Previous exposure to a structured language such as Pascal can help considerably in learning occam. It is helpful to picture occam as being a "shell" that surrounds our vector routines and communication operations.

We actually wrote the Pi Program twice: the first time, using vector form subroutines, and the second using the generic subroutines (the latter version included in this chapter). Although the vector forms permit explicit control of the VPU, the generic subroutines call for less set-up and chaining overhead, which shortens the code.

The most challenging aspect of generating the parallel code was in determining exactly how the problem was to be partitioned across the n-cube and in determining what to define as a variable, a variable address, or simply a value to be passed to a vector or Transputer operation.

Most of our coding errors were due to incorrect implementation of either the communication or vector routines. It was easy to forget that whereas the `byte.slice` and vector operations take byte addresses, the former takes a byte count, whereas the latter take word counts. Also, care must be taken when setting up the `byte.slice` input and output. A sending node must have a receiving node, otherwise a deadlock can result.

In our early attempts to program the T Series, we found it helpful to debug our code by executing a small portion of the program at a time, after which an examination of memory contents could be made. As more software tools are developed, the partitioning and debugging of T Series programs will undoubtedly become much easier.

6.6   CONCLUSIONS

Occam is an interesting language, and it is probably indicative of the style of languages that will evolve to support massively parallel architectures, particularly architectures without global storage. The built-in control of parallelism and communications is probably the most distinctive feature of the language. The Transputer Development System is also a notable feature, although it sometimes leaves one wishing for some of the features of the conventional minicomputer development tools, such as libraries and a linker with the ability to locate entities at specific addresses. The Transputer will develop a larger following when more familiar languages, particularly Fortran and C, are available for the Transputer.

Our experiences clearly show the importance of carefully analyzing the nature of any candidate problem one wants to run on the parallel machine. The degree to which the problem's natural parallelism is recognized and exploited would seem to have a close relationship to the level of performance attained.

6.7   ACKNOWLEDGMENTS

The authors gratefully acknowledge the assistance of the many people who reviewed this manuscript, including Dr. John Gustafson, Jud Groshong, and Steve Oslon, the diligent work of Dr. Herman J. Migliore, who made the Pi Program work on the T Series, and most of all, the support of our wives.

6.8   REFERENCES

[1]   Paul Walker, "The Transputer, a building block for parallel processing", *Byte Magazine*, May, 1985.

[2]   Colin Whitby-Strevens, "The Transputer", in *Proceedings of the 12th Annual International Symposium on Computer Architecture*, IEEE Computer Society Press, 1985, p. 292.

[3]   John L. Gustafson, Stuart W. Hawkinson, and Ken Scott, "The architecture of a homogeneous vector supercomputer", *Journal of Parallel and Distributed Computing*, vol. 3, no. 3, Sept. 1986, pp. 297-304.

[4]   Geraint Jones, "Programming in occam, A tourist guide to parallel programming", Programming Research Group, Technical Monograph PRG-13, Oxford University Computing Laboratory, 1985.

[5]   Inmos Corporation, "Occam Programming Manual", 1985.

[6]   Inmos Corporation, "Occam Programming System", 1985.

[7]   Inmos Corporation, "Transputer Development System", 1985.

[8]   Donna Bergmark, "Programming the FPS T Series", to appear in *Proceedings of the 1987 ARRAY Conference*, Montreal, Canada, 1987.

[9]   Brenda K. Helminen and David A. Poplawski, "A performance characterization of the FPS T Series hypercube", to appear in *Proceedings of the 1987 ARRAY Conference*, Montreal, Canada, 1987.

7
IBM 3090

Michael S. Beckerman

Machine/Model:	IBM 3090-200VF
Location:	IBM Scientific Center, Palo Alto, California
Processors:	2, with 1 vector unit each,
	sharing 64 Mbytes central memory
	and 128 Mbytes expanded memory
Operating System:	VM/SP release 4 with CMS
Language:	Fortran 77
Parallel Environment:	VM/EPEX
Compiler:	VS FORTRAN Level 2.1.0 (Jan 1986)

The IBM 3090 described in this chapter was used during a normal work day at the IBM Scientific Center, with an average load of 200 users during our tests. Interactive response was excellent throughout the day. Editing of our programs was accomplished using `Xedit` [1], a block-mode editor that allows local screen editing and block transmission of the screen of text back to the host. Dr. Alan Karp was our host, providing technical expertise, typing services, and plenty of IBM background information and folklore.

7.1 HARDWARE

Each of the two central processors in the IBM 3090 uses a 64 Kbyte high-speed cache to provide access to instructions and data (see Fig. 7.1). This buffer is dynamically managed by hardware and is transparent to programs. Storage on the 3090 comes in two forms: central and expanded (optional). Processor storage is accessible with delays in the microsecond range and is dynamically managed by the real storage and system resource managers.

Our test machine had 64 Mbytes of central storage and 128 Mbytes of expanded storage. Error checking and correction code bits are stored with the data in central storage. Single-bit errors detected during transfer are corrected. Multiple-bit errors are flagged for follow-on action.

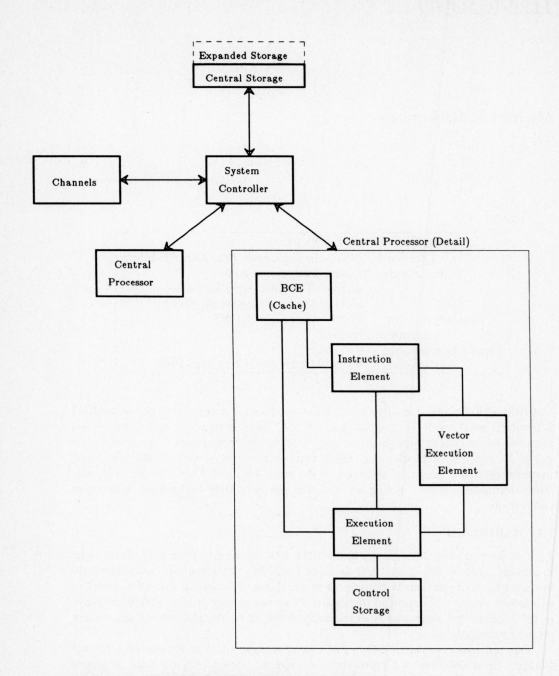

Figure 7.1   IBM 3090 Model 200VF functional elements.

Expanded storage is a high-speed, high-volume electronic repository for 4 Kbyte pages, providing synchronous movement of a 4 Kbyte page to or from central storage in approximately 75 microseconds (half hardware/half software). Expanded storage is transparent to subsystems and user programs. Error checking and correction code bits within expanded storage are used for both single-bit and double-bit error detection and correction. They also detect all triple-bit errors and some other multiple-bit errors. Errors are corrected when possible without the need for instruction retry. Unrecoverable errors are flagged.

Using the IBM XA channel design, the 3090 runs a single system image even though there are two processors. Intelligence is distributed from the central processors to the channel subsystem, the 3880 controller, and the 3380 head of string, all under the control of the MVS/XA or VM/XA Systems Facility. Channel-attached devices transfer information with delays in the millisecond range.

7.2   SOFTWARE

The software primarily involved with our test case is:

- REXX, a CMS command language;

- EPEX, an experimental parallel system available at the time of our runs only within IBM; and

- The VS FORTRAN compiler [2].

VM/EPEX was developed as part of the Research Parallel Processing Project (RP3), a highly parallel shared memory system consisting in its full configuration of 512 processors and currently under development at IBM Research in Yorktown [3]. The purpose of the EPEX system is to enable parallel application development prior to the availability of the RP3 hardware, although it can be used for parallel execution on current IBM multiprocessors, such as the 308X and 309X, that support up to four processors. VM/EPEX maps parallel processors (termed processes or tasks) onto separate VM virtual machines; process communication and synchronization is accomplished through shared memory, simulated by existing support under the VM operating system [4] [5]. Process synchronization is accomplished via directives that are embedded in the program. The operating system is not invoked for synchronization.

A number of computational models have been developed with the existing VM/OS support:

1. An EPEX-FORTRAN model, which supports a Single Program Multiple Data (SPMD) computation model in which all processes execute the same program but may execute different instructions at any particular instant, acting on different data according to synchronization directives and data values [6];

2. An EPEX-C computation model, characterized by forks and joins; and

3. A message-passing simulation environment that uses shared memory for message passing.

We had experience with the EPEX-FORTRAN environment, and in this chapter we concentrate on describing our experience with it.

In the EPEX environment, parallelism can be specified via EPEX-FORTRAN preprocessor constructs that are translated into both subroutines calls and in-line Fortran code. EPEX provides the user with:

- High-level support for shared data;

- Multiple forms of parallel loops;

- Serial code sections;

- Barriers; and

- EPEX reserved parameters known as *distinguished variables*.

Although our tests relied upon use of this preprocessor, (which at the time was not available for use outside IBM, except under special cooperative research agreements), the output of the preprocessor step uses only released hardware and software facilities. More details on the EPEX-FORTRAN environment can be found in the IBM Research Report reproduced in Appendix E4.

Developing Parallel Programs

Development and debugging of parallel programs is fairly simple with the help of the EPEX-FORTRAN preprocessor, Xedit, and REXX. Dr. Karp had previously written several REXX command files to aid in compiling EPEX-FORTRAN source files, and we used those in our tests. Had these not been available, we would have had to initiate the preprocessing, compilation, and load module generation phases manually, which would have added more work to our test runs.

Output from the VS FORTRAN compiler is quite verbose, detailing all options specified for the compilation and the resulting memory organization of the object. When the source is compiled with the vectorization option on, those program loops that the compiler vectorized are easily detectable in the listing. Each such loop is augmented by a graphical representation of loop nesting in the left margin. This representation shows the exact extent of the loop in the source statements. The listing also reports the results of compiler analysis with respect to inefficient use of vectorization. If the loop is vectorized, VECT appears to the left of the graphic loop. However, if a loop is eligible for vectorization but the compiler deems it inefficient in a particular case, ELIG appears instead. Thus it is easy to determine how the compiler treats the program under a given set of options. This determination can be made in the context of the source listing itself, rather than by examining an auxiliary compilation report.

An introduction to the facilities and concepts of the VM/EPEX Fortran preprocessor is given in [7].

7.3   PARALLEL PROGRAM EXAMPLE

The only input to the Pi Program is the number of intervals by which to subdivide the interval [0,1]. The program is designed so that when it is run as more than one process, each process calculates a portion of the total integral and then adds its sum to the total integration. Two different versions of the example program were run using combinations of scalar-mode, vectorizing-mode, and 1, 2, or 4 virtual processors.

The parallel version of the program is as follows:

```
1        IMPLICIT DOUBLE PRECISION (A-H,O-Z)
2        REAL*16 PI
3        DIMENSION T1(3), TIME(3)
4        @SHARED/COMM/ SUMALL
```

Lines 1–3 are standard Fortran declarations and are unaffected by the EPEX-FORTRAN preprocessor. The variable PI, declared as quadruple precision, is used later to store a reference value of pi for comparison with the value calculated by our parallel program. Arrays T1 and TIME are used to store the start and finish times of the program and provide run-time statistics. The EPEX-FORTRAN preprocessor @SHARED declaration on Line 4 declares SUMALL as a shared variable in the named COMMON storage area COMM.

```
5        F(X) = 4.D0/(1.D0+X*X)
6        PI   = 4.Q0*QATAN(1.Q0)
7        READ(5,*) INTRVL
```

Line 5 specifies F(X) as a statement function defining the function to be numerically integrated. On Line 6, PI is assigned a quadruple-precision reference value of pi for later use. On Line 7, INTRVL is read in from the user, thus establishing the number of subdivisions or intervals making up the integration for a particular test case.

```
8        CALL FCLOC(T1)
9        @SERIAL BEGIN
10          SUMALL = 0.D0
11       @SERIAL END
```

Line 8 is a call to a locally available procedure FCLOC, which stores current system time information into the three elements of T1. Times provided are: elapsed, user, and user+system. Lines 9–11 define the beginning, body, and end of a serial section of code. A serial code section is a section of code that is performed by only one process, rather than by all of the processes in the job. In addition, all other processes in the job wait until the process performing the serial section has finished executing the serial section. All processes (except one) that reach Line 9 wait at Line 11 until the work at Line 10 is completed. Note that this is not a synchronization point for all processes running the program. Processes that "arrive late" (after the serial section has been executed by *some* process) can skip the serial section and proceed without delay. The variable SUMALL is shared among the processes in our test case (the only shared data in the example program), and thus access to it must be carefully controlled. Here, by declaring the initialization in a serial section, we have ensured that it is initialized safely. If we did not perform the initialization in a serial section, one or more processes might initialize and subsequently modify SUMALL, only to have another process re-initialize it to zero.

```
12          WIDTH = 1.D0/INTRVL
13          SUM = 0.D0
14          DO 100 IC = @MYNUM, INTRVL, @NUMPROCS
15              SUM = SUM + WIDTH * F( (IC - 0.5D0) * WIDTH )
16      100 CONTINUE
17  C
18          CALL FCLOC(TIME)
```

At Lines 12–13 the width of the intervals being integrated and the process-local sum are initialized. The DO 100 loop is an example of a prescheduled DO loop. If the program is run with only one process, it is identical to a sequential program. If @NUMPROCS is greater than one, each process does every @NUMPROCS'th interval. For our initial tests we wanted to get an idea of how the program is affected by vectorization, so we compiled it with the vectorizing option on and then ran it as a single process (thus serially.) The result of the integration is accumulated in SUM at Line 15. This loop and calculation were indicated as vectorized by the VS FORTRAN compiler on the compiler source code listing.

After we gathered statistics for the serial run, we gathered statistics for parallel runs of the same program by running it several more times, specifying either 2 or 4 processes, and either ten-thousand, one-million, or ten-million intervals.

After the prescheduled runs of the Pi Program, we wanted to do the same for similar self-scheduled runs. The self-scheduled version of the program is identical to the prescheduled version with the exception of the DO 100 loop, which was altered to:

```
14          @DO 100 IC = 1, INTRVL, CHUNK = nnnn
15              SUM = SUM + WIDTH * F( (IC - 0.5D0) * WIDTH )
16      100 @ENDDO NOWAIT
17          T = DFNA(SUMALL, SUM)
```

The @DO ... @ENDDO loop is a parallel form of the usual serial DO loop defined as follows: when a process arrives at the beginning of the loop, it *asks for work*, represented by a value of the loop index. If it gets an index value, it performs the loop iteration for that index value and then asks for more work. For this to be correct in general, successive iterations of the loop must be independent. For more details on the @DO and other parallel constructs supported by EPEX, see Appendix E4.

There is no conflict in variable access since each process accumulates a local version of SUMALL. For greater efficiency, the optional CHUNK = nnnn construct can be specified in a @DO statement to assign a series (chunk) of index values to process, rather than a single value, each time it asks for work. Since our test case does very little work for each iteration of the loop, we experimented with several chunk sizes on the assumption that larger chunking would reduce the overhead and accounting penalties incurred while synchronizing and assigning iterations of the loop between processes. The NOWAIT option on the @ENDDO statement at Line 16 specifies that when a process finishes its share of work from the loop it need not wait for any other processes before continuing execution, even if those processes are working on statements that are either before or part of the same loop. In many applications the subsequent code after the loop depends on the results of the loop task, and thus each process must wait for the other processes to finish the work in the loop, but in our example this is not the case.

The call to the parallel library routine DFNA at Line 17 synchronously sums up the partial integration results from each process-local SUM variable into the final result SUMALL. DFNA is a library routine providing summation with a hardware process interlock. Thus it is guaranteed that only one process at a time performs that addition. This is of course important and necessary, since the result of two processes writing to the same memory location at the same time is unpredictable at best. The call to FCLOC records the finish times for the program.

```
19          DO 200 I = 1, 3
20            TIME(I) = 1.D-6*(TIME(I)-T1(I))
21     200 CONTINUE
22          ERR = SUMALL - PI
23          WRITE(6,'(A,F25.15,1.PD15.3)') 'SUMALL, ERR =', SUMALL, ERR
24          WRITE(6,'(A,3F10.4)') 'TIME =', TIME
25          END
```

Lines 19-21 compute the differences between the start and finish times provided by FCLOC. At Line 22 the difference or error between our calculated value of pi and the reference value is computed. Finally, Lines 24 and 25 write out the value found by the integration, the error, and the times. Note that all processes write the value of SUMALL even though only one prints the correct result. A @BARRIER statement between Lines 21 and 22 would avoid this inconvenience. In addition, an @SERBEG before Line 22 paired with an @SEREND after Line 24 would allow only one process to print out the results.

7.4   PITFALLS AND PROBLEMS

It was sunny and warm when we arrived early one Tuesday morning at the IBM Scientific Center in Palo Alto, California. That must have been a sign that things would go smoothly. We were met by Dr. Alan Karp, who was to be our guide and mentor for the day. We settled into his office and explained what we would like to do, including a description of the sample problem. Twenty minutes later we were recording the results of our first successful test run. Dr. Karp had been working with the 3090 and EPEX for quite some time, and, since he was doing all of the typing, our tests progressed quite rapidly. Also, he had available several REXX command-language files that he had previously created for his use of the EPEX-FORTRAN preprocessor and the VS FORTRAN compiler. These files greatly increased our productivity, invoking the tools in the proper sequence with no further manual intervention. This saved us considerable typing, since the EPEX-FORTRAN preprocessor consists of three phases that must be invoked explicitly.

Initially we ran a sequential version of the program to get a feel for the speed of the machine, the response time, and the user interface. Since we never actually touched the keyboard (because of certain legal issues), we did not get the benefit of being novices at work. However, we still gained an appreciation for the typical user's environment.

We brought along a listing of a serial version of the example program and gave it to Dr. Karp to enter. His knowledge of the EPEX environment allowed us to circumvent a bug he had previously encountered: the preprocessor failed to handle statement function declarations properly in certain circumstances and would place them improperly in the resultant Fortran source code, following an EPEX-FORTRAN preprocessor-generated subroutine call. When the VS FORTRAN compiler was invoked, an error message was generated. Had we been working on this alone for the first time (with no idea how to view the EPEX-FORTRAN preprocessor-generated Fortran source code), this bug might have been difficult to track down and thus brought an early end to our day.

Once we had results from our first serial prescheduled test run, our confidence was sufficiently bolstered to try some parallel prescheduled runs. Once again the results of our tests were quickly available. Dr. Karp then informed us that he had available a newer version of the VS FORTRAN compiler, and he wondered if we might want to try using that. Of course we were eager to use the very latest software, so Dr. Karp proceeded to make the necessary modifications to the command files. Again he submitted the job, but this time instead of results we got the message:

```
OPERAND EXCEPTION AT LINE 0006 OF BABB.
```

After investigating for a couple of minutes Dr. Karp discovered that one of his REXX command files needed to be updated to reference a different library. A quick edit, and we were back in business. We then ran some tests using self-scheduled @DO loops. Our tests went quite smoothly, and no more software bugs or obstacles were encountered for the rest of the day. We had now successfully run the example program as a serial prescheduled program, as a parallel prescheduled program, and as a parallel self-scheduled program, all with and without vectorization, using the latest software. We recorded our results for various tests conditions using combinations of different interval counts, 1, 2, or 4 processes, and varying chunk sizes where appropriate.

7.5   PERFORMANCE

All of our test runs were made during two different normal work days at the IBM Scientific Center, with no special consideration given for the runs. There were an average of 200 users on the system during the runs. On the first day, one user was running a very long production job that occupied 95% of one CPU, and 93% of the other. Figs. 7.2-7.4 shows a summary of our timing runs.

The average and range (for more than one process) of elapsed (wall-clock) times for each test run are plotted. Circles represent scalar runs, and squares represent vector runs. (Some times have been slightly offset horizontally for legibility).

It is interesting to note that the VM scheduler does not know that a given program is being run in parallel, and thus in some cases it gives one process sufficient CPU cycles to complete all of the work. This can be seen in the figure for 10^4 intervals self-scheduled, `chunk = 1000`, for the cases of 2 and 4 processes. Also, the relative speed of vector and scalar modes changes depending on chunk size for self-scheduled loops.

Appendix E3 contains complete tables of our experimental results and gives user (or virtual) CPU time and total time. Virtual CPU time is the CPU time charged to the job. Total time is an estimate of the wall clock time a program would take if it were running alone on the system (including system overhead for paging in the virtual memory system as well as some of the I/O charges).

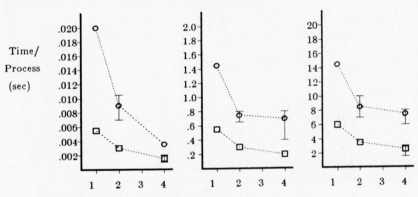

Figure 7.2   Prescheduled timing results.

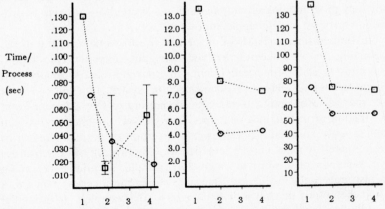

Figure 7.3   Self-scheduled timing results for chunk size 1.

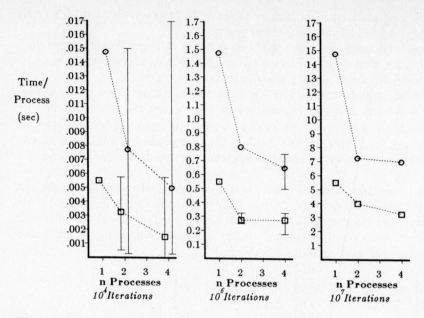

Figure 7.4   Self-scheduled timing results for chunk size 1000.

7.6   CONCLUSIONS

The performance and response of the IBM 3090-200VF we used for our tests were very impressive. Its response time under load was more than adequate for interactive use, and its run times were respectable. Although our exposure was limited, we found the combination of the REXX command language, the EPEX-FORTRAN preprocessor, and VS FORTRAN to be a highly flexible yet easy-to-work-with configuration of software tools that provides a fairly robust set of software constructs in support of parallel programming. Our impression is that once a new user overcomes the initial learning curve necessary to use any new programming environment, it is a straightforward task to produce or modify a wide variety of parallel applications.

Unfortunately our limited time at IBM did not allow use to work with any of the debugging tools available, so we have no personal debugging experience to report. There are no special tools available for parallel debugging beyond those normally used for sequential program debugging. However, one operating system function, PER, is especially useful for parallel debugging. It supports monitoring of five different event types. PER allows tracing of instructions of a specific type, such as branches. It can also trace, for example, only successful branches into a certain range of addresses or stores into an address range. A mask can be specified to allow tracing of only instructions that modify certain bits of a word to catch, for example, a variable becoming negative. One can also trace only instructions that alter storage in a certain range to a specific value (to find the culprit that set a divisor to zero, for example). In a parallel application, each virtual process specifies its own PER monitoring. A post-mortem comparison of the separate event histories can show the order in which specific instructions of a set of parallel processes modify various shared memory locations.

7.7 ACKNOWLEDGMENTS

We would like to express our thanks to the staff of the IBM Scientific Center, and in particular Dr. Alan Karp, without whose help this chapter would most surely have suffered. We would also like to express our appreciation to Frederica Darema-Rogers, a member of the RP3 group at the IBM T. J. Watson Research Center, for her assistance in arranging for access to the machine and helping us obtain permission to reprint the IBM Research Report in Appendix E4.

7.8 REFERENCES

[1]   "VM/SP Editor (Xedit)", IBM Program Product SC24-5220.

[2]   IBM, "VS/FORTRAN", IBM Program Product 5748-F03.

[3]   G. Pfister et al., "The IBM Research Parallel Processor Prototype (RP3): Introduction and Architecture", in *Proceedings of the 1985 International Conference on Parallel Processing,* Aug. 1985, pp. 764-771.

[4]   IBM, "VM/SP Introduction", IBM Program Product GC19-6200.

[5]   F. Darema-Rogers, D. A. George, V. A. Norton, and G. F. Pfister, "Environment and System Interface for VM/EPEX", IBM Research Report RC 11381 (#51260), Sept. 19, 1985.

[6]   F. Darema-Rogers, V. A. Norton, and G. F. Pfister, "Using a Single-Program-Multiple-Data computational model for parallel execution of scientific applications", IBM Research Report RC 11552 (#51726), Nov. 19, 1985.

[7]   J. M. Stone, F. Darema-Rogers, V. A. Norton, and G .F Pfister, "Introduction to the VM/EPEX Fortran preprocessor", IBM Research Report RC 11407 (#51329), Sept. 30, 1985.

8
Intel iPSC Concurrent Computer

Douglas M. Pase and Allan R. Larrabee

Machine/Model:	Intel iPSC Concurrent Computer d5
Location:	Oregon Graduate Center
	Beaverton, Oregon
Processors:	32 nodes (0.5 Mbytes local memory each)
Operating System:	XENIX (Version R3.0) on cube manager
	NX (Release 2.0 and 3.0) on nodes
Languages:	Fortran-286 and Ryan-McFarland Fortran
Compilers:	ftn286 V2.1 and rmfort V2.10

The Intel Personal SuperComputer (iPSC) is one of the first commercially available parallel (or concurrent) computers. The iPSC is a true Multiple Instruction Multiple Data (MIMD) machine. All processor nodes are identical and are connected by bidirectional links in a hypercube topology. In a 16-node hypercube (Fig. 8.1), each node is directly connected to four nearest neighbors. For any hypercube, if d is the dimension of the cube, it has d nearest neighbors, and 2^d nodes. The average distance between any two nodes is $d/2$, and the maximum distance is d. Although the basic machine ($d=5$) consists of a single 32-node unit, the architecture allows expansion to two or four units (64 or 128 nodes). The communication arrangement allows other topologies, such as meshes, rings, and trees, to be constructed in software by the user.

8.1 HARDWARE

An iPSC system consists of one, two, or four basic computational units plus an Intel 286/310 computer, referred to as the *cube manager* or *host*. Each unit consists of 32 identical single-board microcomputers or *nodes*. There is a total of 16 Mbytes of unshared memory evenly divided among the 32 nodes. Each node has a copy of a small operating system (NX), an Intel 80286 CPU, and an Intel 80287 floating point

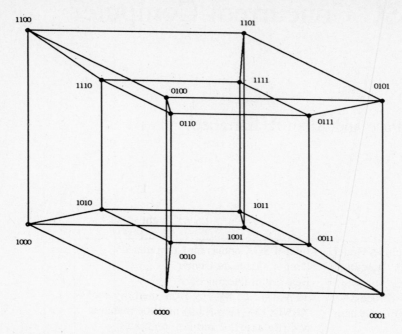

Figure 8.1   16-node hypercube.

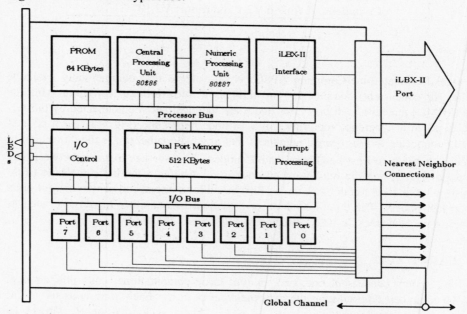

Figure 8.2   Node architecture.

coprocessor (see Fig. 8.2). The 80286/80287 combination has a throughput rate of about 30 Kflops, or just under one Mflop per 32-node unit[†].

Hardware options allow the addition of 4 Mbytes of memory per node, or a vector processor with each node. Such additions come at the expense of half of the nodes in each unit. Thus each basic computational unit can contain 16 nodes, each with 4.5 Mbytes of memory, or with a vector processor (but not both), or it may contain 32 nodes, each with 0.5 Mbytes of memory.

There are eight communication channels per node. The internode channels are implemented via seven Intel 82586 communication coprocessors per node. In addition, an eighth 82586 implements a *global Ethernet channel* for communication with the cube manager. Under NX (Release 3.0), message transmission to a nearest neighbor for messages of 0 to 1024 bytes take from 1 to 2.2 milliseconds. Longer hops and larger messages require more time. No message can be longer than 16 Kbytes in length. Host-to-node messages of the same size take approximately eight times as long (18 milliseconds for a 1-Kbyte message), and transmission rate is affected by size, just as node-to-node messages are.

Hypercube interconnections for a 32-node machine are implemented via backplane connections. Machines consisting of two or four 32-node computational units (32 nodes) are interconnected via external cables. The collection of nodes is controlled by a system cube manager, which is an Intel 286/310 computer. This computer uses the same processors as the nodes, but has 2 to 4 Mbytes of memory, a 140-Mbyte Winchester disk, a floppy disk drive, and it uses the XENIX operating system.

8.2   SOFTWARE

Processes communicate with other processes on the same or neighboring nodes by sending and receiving messages. Message passing is the only means available for internode communication and synchronization, since the iPSC has no shared memory. A message send can be either *blocked* or *unblocked*. A *blocked send* delays execution until the message is sent. (Note that this does not mean that the message has been received). Although use of unblocked sends can decrease execution time, a check must be made to determine whether or not the previous message has been sent before another message is sent (either blocked or unblocked) over the same communication channel, or the contents of the message buffer are modified. A separate problem is that it is possible for a program to generate messages faster than destination nodes can receive them.

All messages carry a type code, which is a non-negative integer. Message types allow receiving nodes to accept only messages of a desired type. In contrast, the cube manager receives messages regardless of type, but can decide alternate courses of action based on the message type. The time required for message passing depends on the number of 1-Kbyte packets (the basic unit that is sent) that must be formed and on the number of internode connections that must be traversed. In blocked message passing, no subsequent instructions are executed until the message has been sent (or received, in

---

[†]This calculation was performed using an equal proportion of additions, multiplications and divisions. Better or worse performance can be obtained by changing these proportions.

the case of a blocked receive). With unblocked message passing, the program continues executing after the send (or receive), and the message is handled by the operating system according to its own priorities. In the latter case, a call to `status` can determine whether a particular message buffer is available for reuse. These message-passing protocols allow users to construct correctly synchronized parallel applications and avoid message flow problems.

Timing programs between any two points in the cube manager program involves calling the subroutine `gettim` available with the Ryan-McFarland Fortran compiler. This subroutine accesses the current system time to the nearest hundredth of a second. Each node maintains its own independent clock, accessed by the integer function `clock()`. Clock times on the nodes can be used to obtain accurate timings across sections of code. However, because the clocks are independent, it is difficult to use them directly for synchronization (see [1]).

8.3 PROGRAM DEVELOPMENT

Design Considerations

On an iPSC with 32 nodes, the best speedup attainable for solving a single problem is 32 times the speed of a single node. Whether or not such increases in speed are actually attainable is heavily dependent upon the application to be run. Some applications are easily divided into independently executing tasks, whereas others can be divided, but require a great deal of communication to support their processing. Still other applications cannot be divided at all, but are inherently serial in nature. If a certain algorithm cannot be easily parallelized, it is possible that another algorithm can be found that can.

All distributed processing requires message passing in one form or another, at least for communicating results. Because communication can take CPU cycles that could otherwise be used for computing, or leave a processor idle while it waits for a message, it is very important that the execution time not be dominated by time spent passing messages. For example, if half of the total execution time is devoted to waiting for messages from other processors, then the machine speed has been effectively cut in half.

One possible solution is to reduce the amount of synchronization (processes waiting on messages from other processes) that must take place. If a large amount of time must be spent in synchronization, it may be useful to move away from the Single Program Multiple Data (SPMD) model and load more than one process on a node. Which process(es) should be loaded and where, however, is an exercise in load balancing. Optimal static load balancing, in general, is a very difficult problem (see [2] and Section III of [3]). However, the hypercube architecture is particularly well suited to a large number of common problems for which load balancing is a reasonable task (see [3] and [4]).

For a program to take maximum advantage of the iPSC, it must require enough CPU time to justify the overhead involved in initializing and loading the nodes. It is much easier to fully utilize the power of the iPSC if the problem in question can be decomposed into long-running processes that are computation-intensive, rather than communication-intensive.

A key program design consideration for making effective use of the iPSC, is to identify computational tasks that can run in parallel and represent a significant fraction of the total program effort. To justify the extra overhead involved in message passing, the ratio of executed instructions to messages sent (or received) must be large. Just how large is a function of the number of messages, the length of each message, the number of node-to-node connections the message must pass through, and whether the messages are between nodes or the cube manager and a node.

Results can be sent directly to the cube manager and then written into a XENIX file or displayed on a terminal. Another strategy is to dedicate one node to collecting and processing data from the other nodes. This master node can then manage the transmission of the final data to the cube manager. The nodes also can call the `syslog` function to write data (via the cube manager) to a logfile. The `syslog` facility can also be used by the nodes to output error or diagnostic messages.

Initializing and Loading the Cube

The following terminal session of commands could be used to execute two previously compiled programs (in this case, called `host` and `node_program`).

```
%getcube
 assigning cube
%load -c 5
```

(In this example, `%` is the XENIX prompt). The `getcube` command ensures that only one user has access to the hypercube at one time. The `load` command installs the Node Executive (NX) and the communication software onto a hypercube whose dimension is 5. The `-c` option runs a program that tests the correctness of the NX and communication software.

```
%load node_program
 Load successful
%host
%loadkill
 loadkill complete
%vi node_program.f
%make node_program
 .
 .
 .
%load node_program
 Load successful
%host
%relcube
 relinquishing cube
```

In this sample terminal session, the cube manager program is named `host`. After a successful loading of `node_program`, the cube manager program is started by entering its name. The command `loadkill` terminates all existing processes on the nodes and leaves only the operating system and communication software. This command interrupts active programs or removes terminated ones. During sessions with the cube, the `load` command is normally invoked only at the beginning. The `relcube` command releases exclusive access to the hypercube.

Message Primitives

Messages can be sent from any process to any other process existing on a node or the host. Each message is tagged with a type and a two-element address, consisting of a node ID and a process ID. Node IDs are in the range of 0 to 31 on a 32-node hypercube, with a special value, -32768, as the host ID. The process ID is a number associated with each channel and is specified at the time the channel is opened. Thus several channels can be opened with the same process ID. If those channels are opened by different tasks on the same node, each process is able to steal messages that might be intended for another. The message type allows a program to select its messages, but at the time the message is received rather than when the channel is opened.

Channels are opened and closed using the `copen` and `cclose` routines. `cid = copen(pid)` opens the channel, and `cclose(cid)` closes it. The value of `pid` is the process ID for the new channel. Process IDs unique to a task can be created on the nodes by making a call to `mypid()`.

Message passing is the same for all nodes, but it is different between the host and the nodes. The host is able only to send and receive blocked messages. It is also unable to select messages based on type. The host command:

- `sendmsg(cid,type,buf,len,node,pid)`

  Sends a message in `buf` to the node, channel, and type specified by `node`, `pid`, and `type`; and

- `recvmsg(cid,type,buf,len,cnt,node,pid`

  Receives messages sent to the host. All fields in this call except channel ID (`cid`) and buffer length (`len`) are filled in by the call. When `recvmsg` returns, the buffer, the byte count of the message (`cnt`), and the type of the message all contain values corresponding to the message received. The `node` and `pid` fields contain the node and process ID of the task and channel that sent the message.

The calls to `send`, `recv`, `sendw`, and `recvw` have exactly the same parameters as `sendmsg` and `recvmsg`, and they work just the same with the following exception. For `recvmsg`, the `type` parameter is modified by the call and cannot be used to select between incoming messages of different types. For `recv` and `recvw`, the `type` parameter is *not* modified and *does* select between incoming messages of different types. Other than that difference, `sendw` and `recvw` work exactly the same on the nodes as `sendmsg` and `recvmsg` do on the host.

The difference between `send` and `sendw`, and `recv` and `recvw`, is that `send` and `recv` do not block execution until the message has been sent. Judicious use of these routines can speed up program execution by keeping the program executing when it might otherwise be in an unnecessary sleep state. However, `status(cid)` must be called to find out if buffers may be re-used after a call to `send`. In addition, `status` can be used to check whether any messages waiting to be received on a particular channel.

A program can use `syslog` to transmit special logging messages that cannot be intercepted by any process and do not otherwise interfere with the normal execution of the program. A typical use for `syslog` is for debugging. Another use could be to indicate how far a computation has progressed by logging messages at different stages of the computation.

Host-to-Node Communication

Under NX Release 2.0, contention mode or polling mode were selectable by an option to the `load` system command. Contention mode allows the communication channels to be used only when there is actually a message to be received. The host (node) interrupts the node (host) when it sends a message, but otherwise leaves it free to perform its own tasks. In polling mode the host must cycle from node to node, asking if the node has any messages for the host. This mode tends to steal compute cycles from each node because of the time required by each node to service the host's requests. Originally, polling mode was recommended for reliability reasons, even though it was slower. Under Release 3.0, only contention mode is available, but we include timing information from Release 2.0 in both modes to illustrate the effects of different communication speeds on our simple program.

The difference in performance between polling and contention mode can be quite dramatic (see Fig. 8.3). For small messages, polling mode can take up to 20 times longer to send a message from the host to a node than contention mode. (We measured 0.028 seconds average time for a message of size 0 with the host operating in contention mode. In contrast, we measured 0.26 seconds for communication with some nodes and 0.52 seconds for others with the host operating in polling mode.)

Node-to-Node Communication

Communication between two nodes is much faster than communication between the host and any node (see Figs. 8.4 and 8.5). This difference can be used to advantage when a message must be broadcast to each node in the network. A naive approach would be to let the host cycle through each node, sending each the message over the host-to-node connection. A more sophisticated approach with much better performance is to send the message to a root node, which sends it to several neighbors, which in turn send it to their neighbors, following a *minimal spanning-tree* (see [5]). The results in Section 8.5 illustrate the effect such strategies can have on program performance.

All timings were obtained on an unloaded iPSC, and therefore represent message transmission times with no contention. If a message is sent when there are many messages in the system, transmission times can be significantly worse.

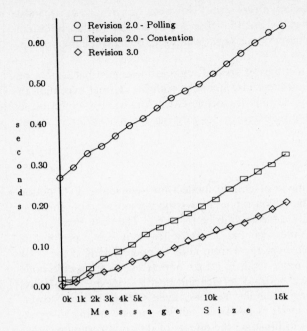

Figure 8.3   Host-to-node communication timing.

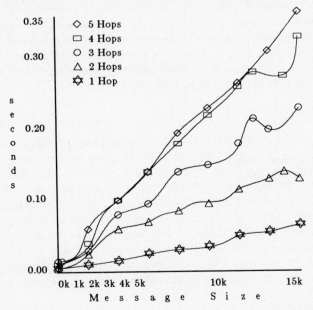

Figure 8.4   Node-to-node communication timing (NX Release 2.0).

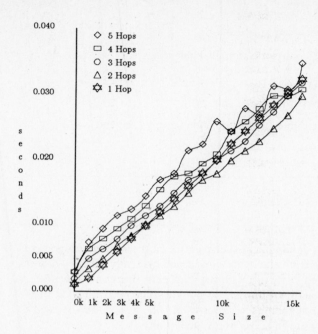

Figure 8.5   Node-to-node communication timing (NX Release 3.0).

8.4   PARALLEL PROGRAM EXAMPLE

In this section two versions of a simple numeric program are presented. The program computes the mathematical constant π. The first version takes a naive approach to communication, whereas the second version attempts to optimize the communication. The complete listings for both versions appear in Appendix F.

The basic strategy of the solution for the Pi Program example is to use each of the (32) nodes on the hypercube to compute an equal portion of the approximate integral. When the partial sum is complete, all nodes send their result to node 0. Node 0 then adds its contribution and sends the result back to the host.

Host Program—Unoptimized Version

```
1        program host
2        parameter (lenint=4, lendbl=8, npid=0)
3        integer cid, cnt, copen, nid, pid, processors, cubedim
4        integer type1, intervals, type
5        double precision sum
```

As shown on Lines 3 and 4, the following variables must be declared as integers:

- the communication channel ID `cid`;

- the length of the message received in bytes `cnt`;

- the function that creates the communication channel `copen`;

- the node ID `nid`;

- the type of the message `type1`;

- the function that returns the dimension of the cube `cubedim`; and

- the process ID `pid`.

```
6          data pid /0/, type1 /1/
7          cid = copen(pid)
8          processors = 2**cubedim()
```

A communication channel used to communicate between the host and node programs is opened at Line 7. Communications channels are closed automatically when a process exits, or the channels can be closed explicitly with the `cclose` function. The process ID (Line 6) is used to address the correct process on a node. The determination of the number of nodes is accomplished at runtime, as shown on Line 8, and can be used to allow programs to adapt themselves to run on a hypercube of any size.

```
9    10    write(*, *)
10          write(*, '(''Enter number of intervals'')')
11          read(*, *, err=10, end=20) intervals
12          if (intervals .le. 0) go to 20
13          do 15 i = 0, (processors - 1)
14             call sendmsg(cid, type1, intervals, lenint, i, npid)
15   15       continue
```

The range of integration [0, 1] divided by the value of `intervals` read in at Line 11 gives the size of the differential (dx) in the integration by the rectangle rule. The number of intervals is sent to every node by the call to `sendmsg` on Line 14. This is a blocked send since this program runs on the cube manager. Unlike the nodes, the cube manager supports only blocked message passing. The arguments to `sendmsg` are as follows:

- `cid` is the communication channel ID that is opened by the previous `copen` call (Line 7);

- `type1` specifies the message type which that is received by each node (used to discriminate between different messages sent to a specific channel);

- `intervals` gives the starting location for the integration (to send the contents of an entire COMMON block, this would be the identifier of the first variable of that block);

- lenint is the number of bytes to be sent; and

- i is the number of the node that receives the message.

Every open channel has an associated identifier, called the *process ID*. Process IDs need not be unique to a process, nor even to a channel. However, if more than one channel on a node is opened with the same process ID, reading a message from that channel can cause one task to steal a message intended for another task. In the example program, the variable npid is the process ID of the intended receiving process. There is only one process per node, and all node process IDs are set to zero. Each node determines its portion of the integration based on its node ID and the number of intervals.

```
16              call recvmsg(cid, type, sum, lendbl, cnt, nid, pid)
17              write(*, 100) sum/intervals
18              go to 10
19    100    format('Pi is ',f20.16)
20     20    end
```

Each node sends its result to node 0, which adds its contribution to the sum and sends the final result to the cube manager. The value is sent via the call to recvmsg (Line 16). This arrangement is faster than having each node send its result directly to the cube manager because node-to-node communication is much faster than is node-to-host communication. The arguments for the call to recvmsg are as follows:

- cid is the same channel ID as mentioned previously (notice that a channel may be used for both sending and receiving messages);

- type is set by the call to the message type of the next message;

- sum is the actual message received;

- lendbl specifies the (maximum) size of the message buffer;

- cnt is returned as the actual size of the message received (if cnt is less than or equal to lendbl then the entire message was received—if the message is larger than the available buffer, the message is truncated); and

- nid is set to ID of the node, and pid is set as the ID of the process that sent the message.

Node Program—Unoptimized Version

The following program is loaded onto each node. In this case each node runs a single program, but it is possible to load several processes onto one node.

```
21              program node
22              parameter (lenint=4, lendbl=8)
23              integer pid, cid, copen, nid, mynode, dim, cubedim
24              integer type, cnt, hid, node, processors, root
25              integer type1, type2, type3
26              integer intervals, i
27              double precision f, x, h, sum, work
28              data type1 /1/, type2 /2/, type3 /3/
29              data pid /0/, hid /-32768/, root /0/
30              f(x) = 4.0d0/(1.0d0 + x*x)
31              cid = copen(pid)
32              nid = mynode()
33              dim = cubedim()
34              processors = 2**dim
```

The system uses the value -32768 (minus 2^{15}) as the ID (hid, initialized at Line 29) for the cube manager. The call to the function mynode at Line 32 returns the node ID, which must be declared as an integer. The call to cubedim at Line 33 allows nodes to determine what fraction of the overall work each should accomplish. The pid value used to open the sending channel must have the same value as the pid used to open the receiving channel. For any message to be received, the type must also agree with the type of the message sent. The pid value used by all channels in this program is the value zero. The host uses a type of 1 to broadcast the intervals. The nodes use a type of 2 to communicate the partial results with node 0, and node 0 uses a type of 3 to transmit the completed result with the host.

```
35      10      continue
36              call recvw(cid,type1,intervals,lenint,cnt,node,pid)
37              if (intervals .le. 0) go to 30
38              h = 1.0d0/intervals
39              sum = 0.0d0
40              do 20 i = nid, intervals-1, processors
41                  x = (i + 0.5d0) * h
42                  sum = sum + f(x)
43      20      continue
```

At Line 36, the recvw call actually receives the message containing the number of intervals to be calculated. The variable lenint represents the value 4. When the message is received by the node, cnt is the length of the message actually received. If cnt is less than lenint, the message is truncated. Each node performs its portion of the integration (computes its partial sum) in the DO loop at Lines 40–43.

```
44                  if (nid .eq. root) then
45                      do 25 i = 1, (processors - 1)
46                          call recvw(cid,type2,work,lendbl,cnt,node,pid)
47                          sum = sum + work
48      25              continue
49                      call sendw(cid,type3,sum,lendbl,hid,pid)
50                  else
51                      call sendw(cid, type2, sum, lendbl, root, pid)
52                  end if
53                  go to 10
54      30      end
```

The partial sums are then sent to the collection point, node 0, by the call to `sendw` at Line 49. At Line 44, a check is made that this is not the root node, since node 0 need not send a message to itself. If a node determines that it is the root node (i.e., node 0) in the check at Line 44, it must receive and sum all partial results from the other nodes and send the total to the cube manager. The node program then loops back to start another integration.

Changes for Optimization

The differences between the optimized and unoptimized versions lie in the way they use the internode hypercube communication channels. In the unoptimized version, the host program sends the number of intervals to each node. In the optimized version, the host sends the interval count to one node, node 0, which sends it to its nearest neighbors, who in turn send it to theirs, and so on, until all nodes have the value. The scheme is optimally parallel. Lines 13–15 in the unoptimized program are replaced by:

```
13      c--
14              call sendmsg(cid, type1, intervals, lenint, root, npid)
15      c--
```

The root node (0) begins distribution when it receives the value from the host. This is done by replacing Line 36 in the unoptimized program with:

```
36              call grecvw(cid, type1, intervals, lenint, cnt, dim)
```

The collection of the distributed partial results is also optimized. In the unoptimized version (Lines 44–52) each node sends its partial result directly to the root node (node 0). This leaves the responsibility of summing the results and transmitting the total to the host with the root. This is sped up by having nodes that are far from the root send their results to a neighbor that is closer, which adds its result and in turn sends the accumulated partial result to a neighbor that is closer still. This is accomplished by the following code (see Appendix F4):

```
41          call gop(cid, type2, sum, 1, '+', root, dim, work)
42          if (nid .eq. root) then
43             call sendw(cid, type3, sum, lendbl, his, pid)
44          end if
```

The routines `grecvw` (global receive-wait) and `gop` (global op) are part of a library of communication utilities supplied by Intel [6].

The unoptimized version can also be significantly improved under NX Release 3.0 by replacing Lines 13–15 in the host program with:

```
13   c--
14          call sendmsg(cid, type1, intervals, lenint, -1, npid)
15   c--
```

The node program remains exactly as in the unoptimized version. This modification makes use of the Ethernet broadcast capability provided by Release 3.0, which is discussed further in the next section.

8.5 PERFORMANCE

Preliminary measurements of performance of the Intel iPSC with a scientific program involving a great many floating point calculations indicated that the cube manager is roughly three times slower than an unloaded VAX 11/780 with a floating point accelerator running Berkeley UNIX 4.2BSD. A single node is only 1.9 times slower than is an unloaded VAX 11/780.

We ran both the unoptimized and the optimized versions of the Pi Program discussed in the previous section under NX Release 2.0 with the host communications first in polling mode, then in contention mode. Each version ran with 8, 16, and 32 nodes. The results are shown in Figs. 8.6, 8.7, and 8.8. Fig. 8.9 compares the effects of communication optimization and polling/contention mode for 32 processors. We also ran both versions, plus an additional version that uses a system Ethernet broadcast capability, under NX Release 3.0 using 32 nodes (Fig. 8.10). The system broadcast feature is new with NX Release 3.0.

From these experiments we can see some of the effects that communication time can have on overall execution time. One can easily see that when a significant portion of the execution time is spent passing messages, reducing that time reduces the overall execution time. We were able to reduce the time spent communicating three ways:

1. Giving no thought to the program itself, we were able speed up its execution by simply *reducing* the number of nodes involved in the computation. There is a certain amount of overhead required for each node involved in the computation. Each node must do enough work to justify spending the time to get it started. If the problem is small enough, using less than the full cube can give better results. Of course, as the workload increases, the extra overhead is justifiable and additional nodes should be used.

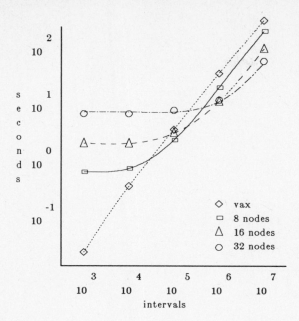

Figure 8.6 Unoptimized Pi Program—host in polling mode (NX Release 2.0).

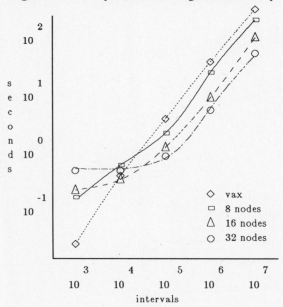

Figure 8.7 Unoptimized Pi Program—host in contention mode (NX Release 2.0).

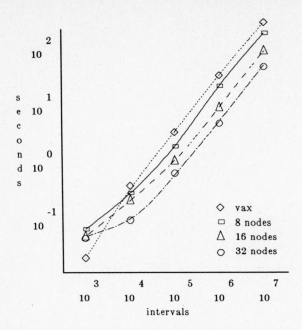

Figure 8.8 Optimized Pi Program—host in contention mode (NX Release 2.0).

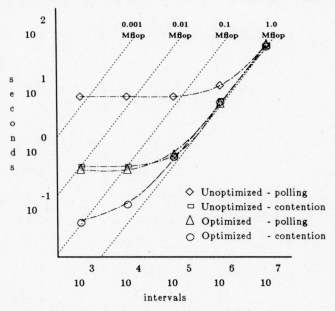

Figure 8.9 Comparison of communication strategies for 32 nodes (NX Release 2.0).

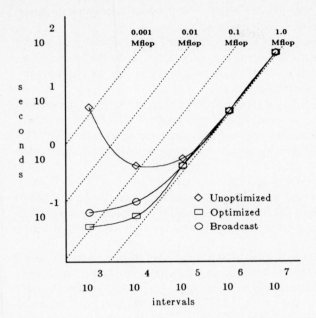

Figure 8.10   Optimized and unoptimized execution (NX Release 3.0).

2. One can also reduce the startup overhead by using contention mode rather than polling mode. Although the latest version (3.0) supports only contention mode, a programmer might be tempted to build in some form of polling behavior into an application, perhaps to synchronize program execution. Our results and some common sense suggest that this should be avoided when possible.

3. We can the overhead of involving additional processors by broadcasting messages over a minimal spanning-tree, rather than use the host-to-node connections. This approach is fairly simple, and it significantly improves broadcast times regardless of the environment or number of nodes involved. Its success comes because the broadcast is performed in parallel, with its longest path no longer than the diameter of the cube, and the communication is over fast links. This is opposed to the unoptimized form, which is a serial broadcast over slow links.

Another approach is to perform system-wide reduce operations (e.g., summing the results from every node) in parallel, which is the reverse of the spanning-tree broadcast. When results computed at each node are to be collected and combined, rather than all sent to some node (perhaps zero), each node can combine its result with those of a neighbor before passing it on, thus reducing the number of messages and the distance each must travel. Leaf nodes of a minimal spanning-tree would send their results immediately to the nearest inner node. Branch nodes would wait for the results of neighbor nodes farther from the root. When the results are received, they are combined with those generated at that node, and the new value is shipped to a node that is closer to the root. The final result is computed by the root node.

Our last approach is to use the system broadcast feature. It permits a rapid broadcast from a node to any sub-cube connected to that node, even up to the whole cube. The host is able to broadcast messages only to the whole cube, not to smaller sub-cubes. This is a relatively simple yet fast approach.

As the communication-to-computation time ratio decreases, effort spent optimizing the communication has less effect. When our program calculates 10,000,000 intervals, even the least efficient 32-node execution (unoptimized communication under NX 2.0 in polling mode) is no worse than the best (minimal spanning-tree communication under NX 3.0).

Another observation emerges from these experiments. If the number of messages is constant, the fraction of time devoted to message passing decreases as the computational load increases. As one might expect, message passing optimization is valuable only if the number of messages required is large or the time spent in message passing is dominant (or both).

Thus, for programs to be suitable for the iPSC, they must require relatively large amounts of processor time, must be intrinsically parallelizable, and, most important, must have a high ratio of computational operations to messages. A key program design consideration for making effective use of the iPSC is to separate out computational tasks that require much time, are parallelizable. and also represent a significant fraction of the total effort of the program. The size of this fraction is a function of the length of the message, the number of node-to-node connections the message must pass through, and whether the messages are node to node or between the cube manager and a node.

8.6 PITFALLS AND PROBLEMS

At the time our first experiments were run on the cube, there were not a lot of debugging capabilities available. Debug print statements (`syslog` calls) were embedded into node source code. Alternatively, messages sent by the nodes to the cube manager might be used to carry information—however, to be useful, such messages would need a corresponding receive on the cube manager. Recently a Concurrent Debugger [7] has become available. A brief description is given in Appendix F6. Because Fortran does no type checking on calls to subroutines, one must pay careful attention to the number and types of arguments to the message-passing utilities.

Because it is relatively expensive to send messages, when a task needs to send a large number of variables, it is generally not a good idea to send them individually. If the data is stored in an array, it is fairly obvious how to proceed. One merely uses the array as the buffer and the array length multiplied by the number of bytes in each array element as the buffer length. However, if the data is not arranged quite so conveniently, the programmer can still send the data without sending each variable individually.

The way this is done is by declaring each variable to be sent as part of a COMMON, using the first variable in the COMMON as the message buffer. The message length is simply the length, in bytes, of the COMMON. The receiving program must, again, have the same arrangement. Now, because no checking is made to guarantee that variables in a COMMON match either names or data types, it is very important that the programmer make sure that they do. As in sequential Fortran programs, if the order of two variables is reversed, or the wrong type is declared for a single variable, *every variable that occurs after the error* can be garbled beyond recognition.

Because many tasks are being performed in parallel, each requiring a different amount of time to complete, there is a much greater potential for time-related errors, such as deadlocks, data corruption and incoherence, or process-ordering violations.

8.7   CONCLUSIONS

The iPSC is a practical, usable parallel processor that also has the advantages of being expandable and flexible. Although no parallel machine is best for all applications, the iPSCs hypercube topology makes it fairly easy to exploit whatever large-grained parallelism is available in an application. The program development tools are both improving and expanding.

Because of the general familiarity of serial computers and the corresponding lack of familiarity with parallel computers and algorithms, additional care is needed when mapping sequential algorithms onto parallel architectures. In particular, message-passing machines seem to be most reliably programmed if work is partitioned by distributing a large data space over the memories of the node processors in such a way that communication and computation are balanced, and where each node runs the same program (or small set of programs).

As with any distributed machine, one must be careful to avoid creating too many processes, each of which contributes only a small amount to the overall computation. One must also use care to avoid delays because of unnecessary communication between nodes. In earlier releases, it was important to emphasize communication between nearest neighbors when possible. At least in Release 3.0, it appears that the distance between nodes has little effect on message transmission times and therefore might easily be ignored.

8.8   ACKNOWLEDGMENTS

We would like to thank Cleve Moler, Intel Scientific Computers, for his assistance as a reviewer of this chapter.

8.9   REFERENCES

[1]   Leslie Lamport, "Time, clocks, and the ordering of events in a distributed system", *Communications of the ACM,* vol. 21, no. 7, July 1978, pp. 558-568.

[2]   S. H. Bokhari, "On the Mapping Problem", *IEEE Transactions on Computers,* vol. C-30, no. 3, March 1981, pp. 207-214.

[3]   Michael T. Heath (ed.), *Hypercube Multiprocessors 1986, Proceedings of the First Conference on Hypercube Multiprocessors,* Knoxville, TN, Aug. 26-27, 1985. Philadelphia: SIAM, 1986. See especially Sections IV and V.

[4]   Geoffrey C. Fox, "Concurrent processing for scientific calculations", in *Proceedings of the IEEE COMPCON Spring 84,* San Francisco, CA, Feb. 27-Mar. 1, 1984, pp. 70-73.

[5]   Cleve Moler, "Matrix computation on a hypercube multiprocessor", in *Hypercube Multiprocessors 1986, Proceedings of the First Conference on Hypercube Multiprocessors,* Knoxville, TN, Aug. 26-27, 1985. Philadelphia: SIAM, 1986. pp. 181-195.

[6]   Cleve Moler and David S. Scott, "Communication Utilities for the iPSC", iPSC Technical Report No. 2, Intel Scientific Computers, Aug. 1986.

[7]   Intel Corporation, "iPSC Concurrent Debugger Manual", (2d ed.), March 1987.

9
Loral Dataflo LDF 100

David C. DiNucci

Machine/Model:	Loral Dataflo LDF 100
Location:	Loral Instrumentation, San Diego, California
Processors:	4 node processors (128 Kbytes local memory each)
	1 host processor (1 Mbyte local memory)
Operating Systems:	GENIX on host
	Dataflo Kernel (Version 1.0) on nodes
Languages:	Fortran 77 + Loral Data Graph Language (DGL)
Compiler:	Green Hills Fortran 77 (Version of June 19, 1986)
Other S/W Tools:	tass (Version 1.0) - (Tag Assigner)
	linker (Version 1.0)

The Loral Dataflo LDF 100 was originally developed by Loral Instrumentation to extend the capabilities of real-time data collection, analysis, and output devices manufactured by Loral. It is also sufficiently flexible to perform many general-purpose computation-intensive tasks. The *Dataflo* name describes the data flow (or data driven) nature of the computer, in which a process is scheduled for execution only after all of its run-time input values are available (because they have been produced as output by other processes).

Conventional dataflow has referred to computation models where machine instruction-level operations are triggered by the availability of operands that flow (conceptually) along arcs in a *dataflow graph*. This operation-level dataflow can be contrasted with Large-Grain Data Flow[1], in which the unit of computation scheduling is larger (perhaps very much larger) than a single machine instruction. The Loral Dataflo LDF 100 was designed to exploit this larger grain parallelism.

9.1   HARDWARE

The LDF 100 consists of a host processor, in which an application is prepared for execution, and from 1 to 256 node processors, where the application actually runs.

Each node processor consists of two sections, as shown in Fig. 9.1. The *Token Processing Section* (TPS), is involved only with receiving and assembling messages for the processes running on the node. The *Node Processing Section* (NPS), executes the process code supplied by the user. Each section of the node processor has its own NS32016 microprocessor, ROM (16 Kbytes), and static RAM (32 Kbytes for the TPS, 128 Kbytes for the NPS). The NPS also contains an NS32081 floating point processor, as well as memory management and interrupt control units. The two sections communicate with each other via 16 Kbytes of communication RAM.

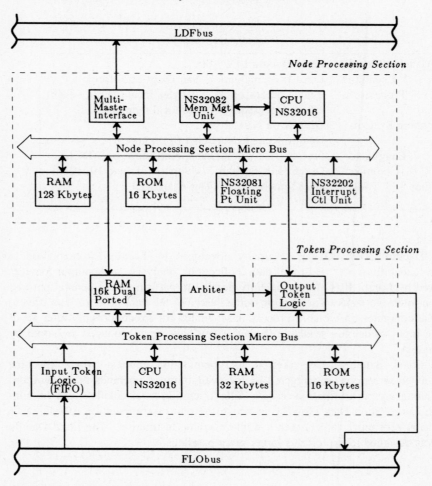

Figure 9.1   An LDF 100 Node Processor.

All messages sent between node processors in a single chassis pass over a common bus called a FLObus. To send a message, the application running on the NPS of the sending node processor copies data flow packets onto the bus. Each packet is 32 bits long and consists of 16 bits of data along with a 16-bit *tag* to identify the virtual data path, or *arc*, associated with the data. These 32-bit packets, or *tokens*, are copied off the FLObus by the TPS on all node processors that have processes requiring input from that arc. The receiving TPS strips the tags off and re-assembles the message. Messages are passed between the TPS and NPS via the communication RAM.

The host processor, where the program development environment resides, has essentially the same hardware that the node processors have, but has more memory (1 Mbyte dynamic RAM vs. 128 Kbytes static RAM). Both node and host boards run at 10 MHz without wait states.

Tokens needed by another chassis are copied off the FLObus by a *FLObus Network Interface (FNI)* board, which transfers them to a corresponding FNI board in another chassis to be deposited onto *its* FLObus. An FNI board resembles a standard node processor on the FLObus. Fig. 9.2 shows the configuration of the node processors and FNI boards within the system chassis. More details on the architecture of the LDF 100 can be found in [2] [3].

9.2 SOFTWARE

Each processing node is assigned zero or more processes to run. Each process receives data (from other processes or input devices) through one or more data arcs and can send data (to other processes or output devices) through zero or more (different) data arcs. Since these data arcs are implemented as tagged messages on a common bus, the number of arcs per process can be quite large. Although shared memory among node processors is supported by the architecture, it is provided mostly as a fallback to reduce overhead when very large data structures must be processed by several processes.[†]

Data arcs are implemented as queues and, like pipes in UNIX, buffer one or more messages until the consumer accepts them, being limited only by available memory (both the private RAM in the TPS and the communication RAM between the TPS and NPS). Multiple processes can receive data from a single data arc, in which case all consumer processes receive a copy of the data on that arc. Multiple processes cannot send on the same data arc, however, unless the messages are only 16 bits long and/or the content of the messages is immaterial. This is because messages are sent as tokens on the bus, with long messages corresponding to multiple tokens. The bus protocol is designed to guarantee a maximum latency for access to the bus and will therefore interleave long messages.

The TPS determines when a complete message has arrived on a data arc by counting the tokens that have arrived with the associated tag. In the default case, when a process has received one complete message on each of its input arcs, those messages are made available in communication RAM, and the process is scheduled to execute on

---

[†]Since shared memory was not available during our experimentation, it is not discussed further.

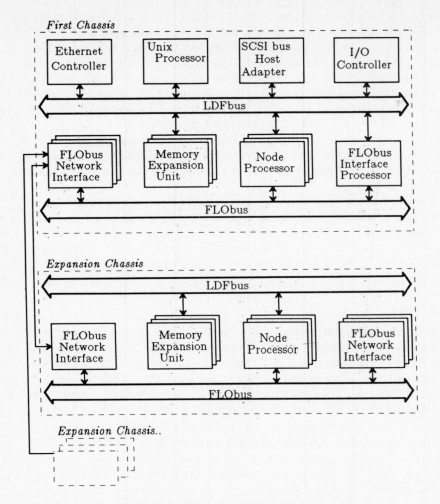

Figure 9.2 LDF 100 system chassis configurations.

the NPS. When it actually *fires* (wakes up), it can read all of its input data arcs and write any or all of its output data arcs. Of course, the data a process writes to an output arc is usually some transformation of the data read from its input arcs. If the process does not read an input arc during a particular execution, the corresponding message is irretrievably lost.

The programmer can specify other conditions for a node to be scheduled to run (or fire) based on which input arcs have received complete messages or on the content of the messages. This capability was not available when we performed our tests, and therefore it is not illustrated in this chapter. However, the default rule (firing after all inputs have been received) is sufficient to accomplish a wide variety of tasks.

Although parallelism is not explicitly stated in this model (as it is in most others), it is typical for many processes (on separate node processors) to run concurrently. If more than one process is assigned to a single node processor, only one runs at a time (even though several may have their firing rules satisfied).

Program Development

All editing, preprocessing, compiling, linking, and so forth, is performed on the host processor, which runs the GENIX operating system, a variant of UNIX. Preparing an application consists of the following steps:

1. Design a program data flow graph;

2. Encode the flow graph into Data Graph Language;

3. Process the Data Graph Language;

4. Write application code for the node processes;

5. Compile the node processes;

6. Link the compiled code with the data graph; and

7. Download and execute the node processes.

Steps 4 and 5 can be performed before, during, or after Steps 2 and 3, since all four steps simply implement the design from Step 1. In practice, bug fixes or revisions in the process code often lead to a revision of the Data Graph Language and vice versa, so Steps 2 and 4 are strongly interrelated.

Of these seven steps, only Steps 1, 2, and 4 need to be performed by the programmer. Steps 3, 5, and 6 can be handled by the UNIX `make` facility, and Step 7 can be performed by a UNIX shell script.

These steps are covered in some detail in [4] and [5].

9.3   PARALLEL PROGRAM EXAMPLE

There are a variety of ways to attack the example problem. The solution outlined in the following section illustrates each of the program development mentioned in the previous section.

Designing a Program Data Flow Graph

A program *data flow graph* (or *data graph*) defines connections between processes (represented in the graph by circles) and data arcs (represented in the graph by arrows). A data graph specifies the overall design of the application. It can require much thought and some skill to determine how the program should be broken down into data-activated processes in order to achieve maximum speedup.

At one extreme, the entire program can be made into one process, but this defeats concurrency. It is also possible to make a great many very small processes, each of which does only a very small amount of work, such as one statement or even one arithmetic operation, but the overhead required for each process to start is significant compared to the amount of work getting done. Although finding the optimum division of work among processes can involve some trial and error, the structure of the problem being solved often suggests some good first approximations.

After the data graph is drawn, every process and arc is labeled with an alphanumeric name, which is used in the Data Graph Language. It is also helpful to label each arc with the kind of data that is expected to pass over the arc.

Our design of the example program uses a variable number of `worker` processes that compute their portions of the integral and feed their separate results to a `summer` that adds up their contributions. The workers were told what portions of the integral they were to compute based on information provided to them by a `work distributor` process, as shown in Fig. 9.3.

In the program data flow graph, the arc labeled `d00` is used to obtain program parameters from the terminal for the work distributor. Arcs `d01` and `d02` carry work assignments from the `work distributor` to the `workers`, and `d04` and `d05` carry the `partial sums` to the `summer`.

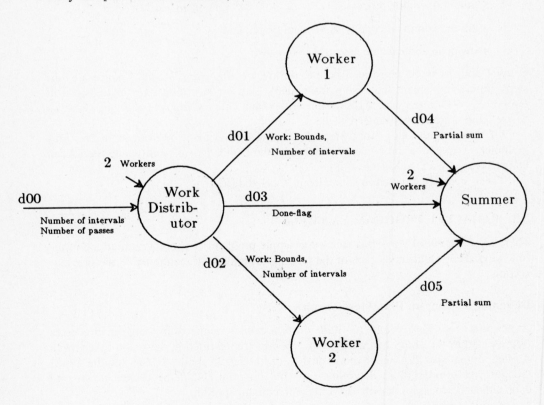

Figure 9.3 Data graph for the example program.

The diagram also shows the use of constant arcs. Constant arcs are input data arcs that are hard-wired to a particular constant value, which is specified within the Data Graph Language. These arcs do not have names or tags like other arcs. They are especially useful in describing the current configuration of a program with a flexible configuration. In our case, these constant arcs are used to notify the `work distributor` and `summer` processes of how many worker processes to use. The number of workers can easily be modified by changing the DGL, without requiring recompiling programs.

The use of data arc `d03` illustrates the kind of subtleties that sometimes arise in this style of data flow programming. This arc is not required to make a properly functioning program, but is present to allow us to experiment with changing the program from compute bound to what might be called *firing bound*. We accomplished this by requiring the workers to fire multiple times on a single run, each time performing a subset of their entire work load. This means that the `summer` routine also needes to fire multiple times and needs to know when it has its final answer in order to print it to the terminal.

It would seem that a simple counter would be sufficient to allow the `summer` to tell when it should print its answer. Unfortunately, there is a problem since the `summer` process starts from the beginning every time it fires, thereby precluding an initialization section. Unlike most looping programs, which consist of initialization statements followed by the loop body, the `summer` could be considered as completely within the loop body. This suggests a solution: initialize the counter above the loop body, in a process, such as the `work distributor`, that only executes once and send the value to the `summer`.

If the counter is an input arc to the `summer`, it must have a new message on it every time the `summer` fires. By making that message *be* the counter (or at least a flag telling whether the counter has reached its limit), the problem is solved. After summing the data from arcs `d04` and `d05` into the total sum on each firing, the `summer` also reads `d03` for a flag to determine whether or not it has the final answer.

Encoding the flow graph into Data Graph Language

Translating the data flow graph to Data Graph Language, or DGL, is straightforward. DGL corresponding to the data flow graph in Fig. 9.3 is shown in Fig. 9.4. In the DGL, each process is represented by a header and a list of import (input) and export (output) arcs. Details of the format of DGL are given in Appendix G2. Our biggest difficulty in performing this translation from flow graph to DGL was in deciding exactly how many words would be sent over each arc, since this depends on the data type and number of each of the variables on the arc (i.e., in a message sent over the arc).

The `<T 2000>` entry on `d00_int_npass` at Line 3 in Fig. 9.4 is an example of a *tag*. These tags are added to every data arc (and process) in the DGL by the tag assigner in a later step, but it is possible to pre-assign a tag to an arc by hand as we have done here. This is useful for data items that will be deposited onto an arc from the terminal since the tag for the arc must be known at runtime. If we did not use this method, it would be necessary to peek at the output from the tag assigner each time it runs to determine which tag it has assigned to the arc.

```
 1   work_distributor = "work_dist" <C0> <P11>
 2
 3   import {2;
 4           word[2] d00_int_npass <T 2000> }
 5   export {word[6] d01_lo_hi_int;
 6           word[6] d02_lo_hi_int;
 7           word    d03_done_signal}
 8
 9   work1 = "worker" <C0> <P10>
10
11   import {word[6] d01_lo_hi_int}
12   export {word[4] d04_sum}
13
14   work2 = "worker" <C0> <P9>
15
16   import {word[6] d02_lo_hi_int}
17   export {word[4] d05_sum}
18
19   summer = "summer" <C0> <P7>
20
21   import {2;
22           word[2] d03_done_signal
23           word[4] d04_sum;
24           word[4] d05_sum; 100}
```

Figure 9.4 DGL for the Pi Program.

Processing the Data Graph Language

Before the Graph Language can be used by the linker utility program (its ultimate target), each process must be assigned to a node processor, and each data arc and process must be assigned a 16-bit integer to be used as a tag (as described in Section 9.1). These assignments are performed by annotating the appropriate points in the Graph Language with special symbols. This work is typically performed automatically by the Graph Balancer gb and the Tag Assigner tass.

During our experiments, the gb utility was not available, so we performed its work by hand. This work consisted of adding two entries after each process heading line. An entry of the form <C#> gives the chassis number, and one of the form <P#> gives the processor board number within a chassis on which the process is to run.

The machine we were working with had one chassis (chassis 0) and node processors in slots 0, 2, 4, 6, 7, 9, 10, and 11. To avoid some shortcomings of the tag assigner (since repaired), it was suggested that we assign the node processor boards to processes in descending order (i.e., highest node processor to first process, etc.). The tag assigner was run with the command line

```
tass wirelist -o wirelist.tagged
```

where the file `wirelist` contains the DGL (as shown in Fig. 9.4) and `wirelist.tagged` is the output file.

Writing Application Code for the Node Processes

Overview

Each process is written as a main program in either Fortran (which we used) or C. To read from an arc, the process executes a `floread` call, and to write to an arc, a `flowrite` call. The arguments specify the arc to be read or written and the corresponding buffer.

If we ignore shared memory, these message-passing calls are the only support required for correct parallel execution, since explicit process synchronization is not needed in data flow models. Processes can begin execution as soon as all input data tokens have arrived[†].

Terminal I/O requires support beyond the `floread` and `flowrite` calls. The `fip` utility program, detailed in the next section, provides a means to deposit data values onto any arc (from the terminal), so terminal input is handled in this way. Terminal output is currently provided automatically by the `printf` function in C (with a little help from `fip`). Fortran programmers can also call a special version of the `printf` function for this purpose.

Experience

Writing the code brought few problems. Since we thought the problem through fairly thoroughly in order to create the data flow graph, we already had a good idea of the role of each module. If we had come upon any problems during the coding phase, it is likely that we would also have had to modify the data flow graph.

We had to remember that these processes are not subroutines, but programs that start afresh on every invocation. This means that data held in variables (e.g., sums) are, in general, not present on subsequent iterations. In the sample program this caused a problem, since the `summer` was required to add the `partial sums` from the `workers` to some total sum, which it needed to keep over all iterations of a particular run. We found, with some experimentation, that putting the variable into named COMMON would not only keep the value intact between runs, but would also ensure that the value of the (integer) variable stored there would be zero the first time it was used.

A purer data flow approach would have been to write the previous sum to an arc that circled back to feed it to the `summer` on its next execution cycle. Although this pure technique would result in more overhead for the process to fire, the resulting code would not be so dependent on the behavior of the particular loader and compiler we were using.

[†]Other data flow models add the restriction that a process cannot fire until after all previous output has been consumed. This *strict* activation rule leads to what is termed *demand driven* data flow, discussed in Section 9.5, which can limit concurrency to some extent.

Although we used the named COMMON facility to initialize a summing variable to zero, it could also be used to initialize a flag variable. This would then allow a program to have an initialization sequence by checking the flag variable at the beginning of each run and, if zero, performing the initialization sequence and setting the variable to a non-zero value. (Had we known this at the outset, we could have avoided using that special data arc d03, though with some loss of run-time control.)

Annotated Program Listings

```
1   C
2   C - Work Distribution
3   C - Sends work intervals to workers and flag to summer
4   C
5           REAL*4      LO, HI, SIZINTRVL
6           INTEGER     NSEGMENTS, INTRVLS, PASS, WORKER
7           INTEGER*2   FLAG, NWORKERS, TOTINTRVLS, NPASSES, SIZE
```

All variables that will be read from the terminal (via fip) or from a constant arc must be defined as INTEGER*2, as on Line 7.

```
8           COMMON /TERMIN/ NPASSES, TOTINTRVLS
9           COMMON /WORKARC/ LO, HI, INTRVLS
```

Variables are placed in COMMON at Lines 8 and 9 to force them into sequential memory storage. This is necessary when more than one value will be read from or written to an arc. In this case, we can think of two records being defined, one for each COMMON statement, although they could all be combined into a single COMMON statement with the same effect.

```
10          CALL FLOREAD(1, NWORKERS, 1, SIZE)
11          CALL FLOREAD(2, NPASSES, 2, SIZE)
```

The FLOREAD at Line 10 reads from the first import arc mentioned in the DGL for this process, as dictated by its first argument (1). In this case, this is a constant arc, so the value read is always 2. Note that for a constant arc, the variable being read (NWORKERS) must be defined as INTEGER*2 and the number of words being read (specified in the third argument) should be 1. The FLOREAD at Line 11 reads from the second import arc mentioned in the DGL for this process (d00_int_pass), as dictated by its first argument. This arc is not connected to any other processes (according to the DGL), so the only way this arc will ever obtain data is from a hardware device, or in this case a terminal executing the fip program. Since fip sends only 16-bit (1 word) values, and since this read is accepting two words (as shown in the third argument), it will obtain two INTEGER*2 values. The first is stored into NPASSES, whereas the second is stored into whatever variable follows NPASSES in memory. In this case, since the variable TOTINTRVLS follows NPASSES in

COMMON, it is guaranteed to follow it in memory and is therefore set to the second value entered via `fip` on this arc.

```
12              CALL PRINTF(" INTRVLS = %d npasses = %d nworkers = %d\n",
13      1                       TOTINTRVLS, NPASSES, NWORKERS)
```

The call to PRINTF at Lines 12–13 prints onto the terminal, but only if `fip` is running on the terminal and has been invoked with the −r option. For those who are not familiar with the C `printf` function, it works by printing the first (string) argument as is, except for the following substitutions:

- Replacement sequences (which begin with %) are replaced by the value from the next argument in the argument list. The letter following the % tells the type of the variable. In this case, %d represents decimal formatting of INTEGER∗2 variables.

- Escape sequences (represented by a backslash followed by a character) are replaced by a special (usually invisible control) character. In this case, \n is replaced by the newline character (which is displayed as a carriage return and linefeed).

```
14              NSEGMENTS = NPASSES * NWORKERS
15              INTRVLS = TOTINTRVLS
16              SIZINTRVL = 1.0 / NSEGMENTS
17              HI = 0
18              DO 100 PASS = 1, NPASSES
19                 DO 90 WORKER = 1, NWORKERS
20                    LO = HI
21                    HI = HI + SIZINTRVL
22                    CALL FLOWRITE(WORKER, LO, 6)
23      90         CONTINUE
```

The FLOWRITE call at Line 22 writes 6 words (12 bytes) starting with the variable LO to the export arc specified by WORKER. LO is only 4 bytes, and HI (4 bytes) and SIZINTRVL (4 bytes) immediately follow it in memory, as dictated by the COMMON statement. This sends a *work order* to the workers. Note that WORKER must be an INTEGER∗4 variable if used as the first argument to FLOREAD or FLOWRITE.

```
24              FLAG = NPASSES - PASS
25              CALL FLOWRITE(NWORKERS + 1, FLAG, 1)
26      100  CONTINUE
27           END
```

The FLOWRITE at Line 25 writes a non-zero value to the d03 arc on every iteration but the last, when a zero is written. SUMMER reads these values from this arc to tell when it has its final answer (when it reads a zero).

```
28    C
29    C - Worker (Code identical for each worker node)
30    C - Reads work assignment from work distributor, writes partial
31    C -    sum to summer
32    C
33          REAL        LO, HI
34          REAL*8      SUM, WIDTH, FARG, SIZE
35          INTEGER     INTRVLS, SLICE
36          COMMON   /INPATH/ LO, HI, INTRVLS
37          CALL FLOREAD(1, LO, 6, SIZE)
38          WIDTH = (HI - LO) / INTRVLS
39          SUM = 0.0
40          DO 100 SLICE = 1, INTRVLS
41             FARG = LO + (SLICE - .5) * WIDTH
42             SUM = SUM + WIDTH * (4.0 / (1.0 + FARG * FARG))
43    100   CONTINUE
44          CALL FLOWRITE(1, SUM, 4)
45          END
```

The WORKER routine (Lines 33–45) does the work. The FLOREAD at Line 37 reads a work order (which is written at Line 22). The process then computes the integral and sends the result to the SUMMER (at Line 44). Note that although both the FLOREAD and FLOWRITE refer to arc 1 (in their first argument), the FLOREAD is referring to the first import arc (either d01 or d02, depending on which worker this is), whereas the FLOWRITE is referring to the first export arc (either d04 or d05).

```
46    C
47    C - Summer (as in, one that sums)
48    C - Reads partial sum from each worker, adds them into a total sum
49    C
50          INTEGER SIZE
51          INTEGER*2    FLAG, ITER, NPASSES
52          REAL*4       TEMPSUM, TOTALSUM
53          COMMON /STATIC/ TOTALSUM
```

TOTALSUM is declared in COMMON (Line 53) so that it:

- Retains its value after each iteration; and

- Begins on the first iteration with a zero value. The name of the COMMON block is immaterial.

```
54              CALL FLOREAD(1, TEMPSUM, 4, SIZE)
55              TOTALSUM = TOTALSUM + TEMPSUM
56              CALL FLOREAD(3, TEMPSUM, 4, SIZE)
57              TOTALSUM = TOTALSUM + TEMPSUM
```

Lines 54–57 retrieve and add the partial sums from the workers to the variable TOTALSUM. Note that if the DGL is changed at some point to include more workers, this subroutine would have to be modified.

```
58              CALL FLOREAD(2, FLAG, 1, SIZE)
59              IF (FLAG .EQ. 0) THEN
60                  CALL PRINTF("pi is %F\n", TOTALSUM)
61                  CALL PRINTF("diff is %F\n",
62         &            TOTALSUM - 3.141592653589793238D0)
63                  TOTALSUM = 0
64              END IF
65              END
```

The FLOREAD at Line 58 reads FLAG to see whether this is the last iteration and, if so, writes the integral and the difference to the terminal. Note that the formatting specifications are now %F to write double precision floating point values.

Compiling the Node Processes

The processes are compiled with the standard UNIX f77 Fortran compile command. We had a few of the standard Fortran problems: a line longer than 72 characters and some improper indentation. Our most severe problem was with a one-line function that the compiler complained about, so we moved the associated calculations inline. The error probably was a result of including the function or its dummy argument in a type statement.

Each program is linked using the standard loader, using commands of the form

```
ld file.o -T 800 /u/software/lib/flolib.a -o file
```

(The -T 800 option forces a base address of 800 and is no longer required).

Linking the Compiled Code with the Data Graph

The whole program is tied together into one package with the linker utility[†]. It takes the tagged Data Graph Language and all of the object files as input and produces one combined file, containing all pertinent code and information, ready to download to the node processors. Only the name of the file containing the tagged Data Graph Language (produced by the tass program) is supplied to it on the command line,

---

[†]This name is confusing—we had already linked the program, in the traditional sense of resolving external references, with the ld utility, which is confusing enough all by itself!

since the names of the object files are present within this file. The `linker` is executed with the commands of the form:

```
linker wirelist.tagged -o wirelist.code
```

The file `wirelist.code` at this point contains all the information (program code and network description) needed to download and execute the program.

Downloading and Executing the Node Processes

The actual execution of the program is facilitated by the FLObus Interface Processor, or `fip`, which downloads the program to the processor nodes and supervises all node input and output. In a sense, the FLObus is a peripheral of the host processor, and `fip` is a program that communicates with this peripheral. There is a UNIX device driver which interacts with the FLObus. The three forms of the `fip` command used were:

1. `fip -g wirelist.code`

   This downloads `wirelist.code` (our output file from the `linker`) to the node processors.

2. `fip -r -s 2000 10000 -s 2000 10`

   The `-r` option causes `fip` to *listen* to the FLObus for `printf` output. The `-s` option causes the next two arguments to be taken as a tag number of an arc (`2000`, in our case) and a data item (`10000` and `10`). `Fip` then deposits the data item onto the arc (or more precisely, tags the data item with the specified tag and deposits it onto the FLObus). More than one set of arcs and/or data items can be given by respecifying the `-s` option, but all must fit on one line or be continued with a shell continuation character. The data item must be in the form of a decimal number that is passed to the application as an unsigned 16-bit integer.

3. `fip -i`

   This interrupts and initializes the node processors after an abnormal termination. The program must be downloaded again to be rerun after this command.

9.4   PERFORMANCE

At the time we performed this testing, there were no timing routines available for the node processes, so the program was timed with a stopwatch on a large number of iterations, with these results:

Intervals	Passes	Time
10000	100	98 sec
10000	10	10 sec
10000	50	50 sec
10000	70	69 sec
10000	90	88 sec

The principal loop in the program contains 8 floating point operations: three adds, one subtract, three multiplies, and one divide. For the last timing, this produces a speed of

$$\frac{90 \; Passes \times 10000 \; \dfrac{Loops/Worker}{Pass} \times 2 \; Workers \times 8 \; \dfrac{Floating \; ops}{Loop}}{88 \; Seconds}$$

$$= 0.164 \; Mflops$$

or an average of .082 MFlops/board.

9.5   PITFALLS AND PROBLEMS

Program Design

Even though the author had previous experience with data flow programming, subtle differences between this data flow model and others made the drawing of the data flow graph trickier and more time-consuming than originally expected. Although the basic rules of data flow are simple to understand, techniques for using these rules effectively will be developed only over time. It is necessary (and sometimes puzzling) to experiment with a specific data flow system to determine the most effective kinds of program structures that can be built with it.

We originally intended to have the `work distributor` create or maintain a *work to do list*, and have `workers` acess this common list for more work when they had finished with their last parcel. Work would not be divided in half at the beginning; one worker might end up doing a larger portion of the integral if it finished first. Although this technique (sometimes called the "hungry puppies" technique) would probably not be used to its full effectiveness in the integration since both `workers` would likely take the same amount of time to finish, there are plenty of applications (such as adaptive quadrature, which could be used to solve the same problem) where it could be.

Our first idea was to put the work to do list on a common arc, where the `worker` processes could contend for work. This approach has worked well in other data flow models, but the LDF 100 model of dataflow did not (at the time we ran these experiments) support contention for the data values on an arc. Rather, every process gets its own copy of the data on the arc.

We considered having each `worker` receive its orders from a different path from the `work distributor`, and having each process ask for more work by sending a message over a separate *demand arc* to the `work distributor` when done with its previous parcel. The absence (again, at the time) of an "or" firing rule ruled out having two separate demand arcs, since the `work distributor` must fire on a demand from either `worker`.

One possible solution would be to have the demand arcs merge into one to feed into the `work distributor`. Recall that this is possible only if the messages are one word long, which is sufficient in this case, since the messages need to consist only of a number identifying who is making the demand. It is important that when the program starts, a demand token for each of the `workers` is present on the arc to get them all going the first time. The `work distributor` would need to read the arc on each firing and use the data on the arc to determine on which output arc to send the next work order.

This idea of *demand* is important. Without demand arcs, the system implements no explicit flow control, leaving open the possibility that a process may receive data faster than it can be processed. The flow control mentioned previously might be called *any* flow control, in that the producing process fires when any of the consuming processes wants more input. *Every* flow control, where the producing process would fire only when every one of the consumers wants more input, could be modeled either by separate demand arcs for each consumer or by a merged data arc (like the *any* model), where the message length of the consumer is *n* times as long as the demand messages being sent by the *n* consumers. This latter technique has the advantage of using up only one tag for all consuming processes. With either of these *every* methods, no logic needs to be added to the producer, unlike the *any* method. Demand arcs on the LDF 100 are discussed further in [6].

Writing Processes

Message lengths were confusing. In the DGL, message lengths must be expressed in units of 16-bit words, which are somewhat arbitrary units to begin with. They must also be expressed as such in `FLOREAD` and `FLOWRITE` calls. However, lengths of variables within the program are typically specified in bytes (e.g., `INTEGER*4`).

In addition, all messages originating from the terminal or from constant arcs are 16-bit word (2 byte) integers. This is not the default length for an integer in either Fortran or C.

9.6   CONCLUSIONS

The Loral LDF 100 offers a fertile environment to explore the relatively new technique of data flow programming. As our example shows, this technique coerces the programmer to adopt a stepwise approach to programming, which, in the end, can actually increase the quality of the code. At the same time, it allows the programmer to avoid the complexities of synchronization inherent in most other parallel programming models and concentrate on the computations and algorithms that are central to the solution.

Although the speed of this particular machine is not quite on a par with some of the other computers we are reviewing here, the features of this architecture seem to offer promise for much faster parallel processors.

9.7   ACKNOWLEDGMENTS

We would like to express our appreciation to John Van Zandt, Loral Instrumentation, for providing us with the opportunity to run on the LDF-100, and to Ian Kaplan, also of Loral, for his assistance in running our experiments and reviewing this chapter.

9.8 REFERENCES

[1]   Robert. G. Babb II, "Parallel Processing with Large-Grain Data Flow Techniques," *Computer*, vol. 17, no. 7, July 1984, pp. 55–61.

[2]   John Van Zandt, "C^{3}I: Beyond the von Neumann Bottleneck", *Defense Electronics,* January 1986.

[3]   Ian L. Kaplan, "The LDF 100: A large grain dataflow parallel processor", to appear in *SIGARCH Computer Architecture News,* 1987.

[4]   Loral Instrumentation, "LDF 100 Getting Started Manual", Document no. 49055665(A), 1986.

[5]   Ian L. Kaplan, "Programming the Loral LDF 100 dataflow machine", to appear in *SIGPLAN Notices,* 1987.

[6]   Ian L. Kaplan, "Demand-Driven Data Flow", Loral Instrumentation Report, March 3, 1986.

10
Sequent Balance Series

Lise Storc

Machine/Model:	Sequent Balance 21000
Location:	Sequent Computer Systems, Inc.
	Beaverton, Oregon
Processors:	30
	16 Mbytes physical memory,
	8 Kbytes cache memory per processor,
	16 Mbyte virtual address space per process
Operating System:	DYNIX Version 2.1
Language:	Fortran 77
Compiler:	NS32000 Fortran 77 V2.6 Parallel Compiler

The Sequent Balance Series computers are shared memory multiprocessors running the DYNIX operating system, a version of UNIX 4.2BSD. Multitasking and sequential applications coexist in a multi-user environment. The Balance 21000 incorporates from 4 to 30 general-purpose, symmetric, 32-bit microprocessors[†]. DYNIX achieves dynamic load balancing via a system-wide run queue used to schedule executable processes. Even if no effort is made to parallelize a user application, all DYNIX processes can potentially run in parallel. This is termed *transparent multiprogramming*. For details on the parallel strategies used at the UNIX process level, see [1].

Sequent has modified certain UNIX utilities, such as `make`, to allow them to run multitasked automatically. DYNIX manual pages for various parallel compilers, utilities, and system calls can be found in Appendix H3.

In addition, users can specify explicit parallelism in which DYNIX processes can share memory. Multitasking libraries are available to assist in writing parallel applications.

[†]Another model, the Balance 8000, supports from 2 to 12 processors.

10.1 HARDWARE

The Balance Series computers contain from 2 to 30 32-bit general-purpose microprocessors, two to a board (see Fig. 10.1). A Balance system can contain up to 28 Mbytes of shared system memory. Blocks of memory are dynamically allocated to processes or process groups. This memory can be either local to a process or shared by a process group. All processors, together with memory modules and I/O controllers, are plugged into a single high-speed bus, the SB8000. This bus supports pipelined I/O and memory operations and can sustain a data transfer rate of 26.7 Mbytes per second.

The CPU used is the National Semiconductor 32032. All CPUs operate independently and can execute both user code and system code. All processors share a single

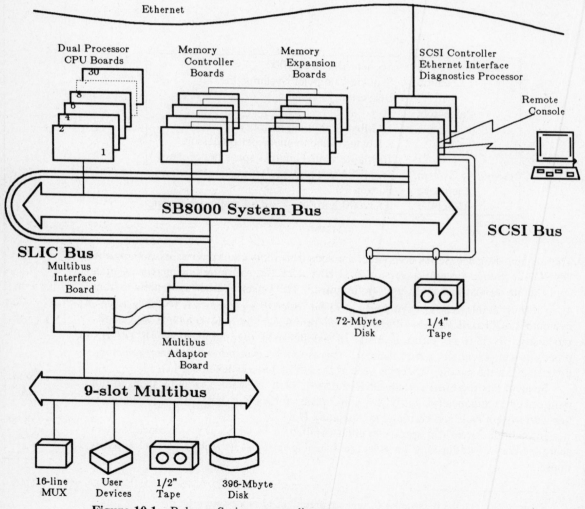

Figure 10.1 Balance Series system diagram.

copy of the DYNIX kernel. Communication with other processors and subsystems is managed by System Link and Interrupt Controller (SLIC) chips via a special SLIC bus. A processor has 8 Kbytes of cache RAM, which contains copies of the most recently read blocks of main memory. Each processor also has an NS32081 Floating Point Unit and an NS32082 Memory Management Unit that supports a 16-Mbyte virtual address space per process.

Atomic Lock Memory (ALM)

User-accessible hardware locks are available to allow mutual exclusion of shared data structures. There are 16K such *hard locks* in a set. One or more sets can be installed in a machine, one per MULTIBUS adapter board. Each lock supports an atomic test-and-set operation. Each 32-bit doubleword in the ALM represents one lock. The least-significant bit determines the state of a lock: locked (1) or unlocked (0). Reading a lock returns the value of this bit and sets it to 1, thus locking the lock. Writing 0 to a lock unlocks it. The locks can support a variety of synchronization techniques, including busy waits, counting/queuing semaphores, and barriers. For example, a process can execute a busy wait on a lock by simply reading the lock until it is unlocked by the process holding it (i.e., until the read returns 0). The process executing the busy wait can immediately continue, since the read automatically relocks the lock.

   More information on the parallel architecture of the Sequent Balance Series can be found in [2].

10.2   SOFTWARE

The DYNIX Operating System

DYNIX schedules processes from a system-wide run queue. A process runs without interruption on a processor until it blocks (e.g., to wait for an I/O operation to complete), terminates, or is pre-empted by another process with greater or equal priority. At any point, the user process with lowest priority is required to service the interrupts. Therefore, a parallel application runs best when it has a higher priority than other user processes and a number of processes that is one less than the number of processors available. It may also be advantageous to suspend processes that busy wait for a lock longer than some specified amount of time.

Shared Memory

DYNIX allows two or more processes to share a common region of system memory. From application languages, shared memory is read and written in the same way as ordinary program memory. In Fortran programs, shared variables are statically allocated in common blocks or in a shared stack. In C programs, each shared variable can be either statically or dynamically allocated. This memory can be used for interprocess communication (between both related and unrelated processes) and is more efficient than using UNIX system calls to share data between processes. Shared memory is implemented as a portion of a process's virtual address space (using the DYNIX `mmap()` system call).

New processes are created via the `fork()` system call, which has an overhead of about 55 milliseconds. The new (child) process is a duplicate copy of the current (parent) process, and it inherits data, register contents, program counter, and any shared memory and file access possessed by the parent. In a typical application, a parent process acquires a region of shared memory and one or more locks, then forks some number of child processes to share the work. Usually, no child process is terminated until the program is complete. It is possible, however, to relinquish a processor and reacquire it later, with an overhead of a few milliseconds.

DYNIX Parallel Programming Library routines are available to create, synchronize, and terminate parallel processes and allow for interprocess communication and mutual exclusion from C, Fortran, and Pascal programs. A preprocessor can be used to interpret compiler directives for loops in Fortran codes. The preprocessor automatically inserts code to create and synchronize processes executing the body of the loop in parallel [3].

Synchronization

Locks can be used to ensure exclusive access to a data structure in shared memory. The overhead incurred is only a few microseconds, since they are directly supported in hardware. Atomic Lock Memory (ALM) is mapped via `mmap()` into a process's virtual address space. Since direct access by user processes to the hardware locks can overload the bus, it is preferable for processes to spin on a *shadow lock* in cache. The processor spinning on the lock in its cache puts no load at all on the bus. When the state of the lock is changed, all processors spinning on that lock have their caches invalidated, and race to acquire the lock. Any number of *soft locks* can be built upon a single hard lock. These are referred to as multiplexed locks.

A processor can be relinquished during potentially long busy waits by using a system call such as `sigpause()`, if the overhead thereby incurred is tolerable to the application.

Program Development

The Sequent parallel programming documentation [4] describes two basic types of applications, along with techniques for analyzing and dealing with order dependencies within them. In general, an order dependency is a point where a task depends on the result of a previous task and cannot proceed until the previous task is finished.

Function partitioning is appropriate when multiple processes perform different operations on the same data set. One model for this is the *fork-join*, where processes are forked, do separate tasks, then meet at a barrier. This is the correct model when tasks are relatively independent. Another model is the *pipeline*, which handles dependencies by allowing a process to perform calculations on a subset of the data, write the results to shared memory, then notify the downstream process that the results are available for further work. This is then repeated on the next subset of data. A process can suspend or terminate when there is no more work to do.

Data partitioning is appropriate when multiple identical processes can perform the same operation on different data (e.g., loops that perform calculations on arrays). This is also referred to as *homogeneous multitasking*. Data partitioning tends to lead to automatic load balancing.

A simple example of an application for which data partitioning is appropriate is the following:

```
      DO 10 I=1,N
         A(I) = B(I)*C(I)
   10 CONTINUE
```

Iterations of the loop could execute in any order without affecting the final result and thus can be executed in parallel. This is an example of a fully independent loop, and it is a perfect candidate for data partitioning and parallel execution. No data is passed from one iteration to the next. Unfortunately, not all loops are of this type. Some loops have inherent dependencies that require some form of synchronization to preserve proper ordering. Others may have dependencies that result from the particular implementation. In this case, techniques such as rearranging statements and renaming can resolve the dependency.

All programs undergoing parallelization must undergo some degree of dependency analysis to uncover potential problems. The Balance Guide to Parallel Programming contains guidelines to aid this process. In addition, the `gprof` utility can be used to analyze a program to determine which loops are good candidates for dependency analysis and attempts at parallelization. Running `gprof` on a program results in a call graph and a profile indicating where the program spends its time. If no loop that is reasonably independent and compute-bound can be found, then function partitioning can be tried.

An example of dependency analysis and data partitioning is shown for the Pi Program in Section 10.3.

Compilation

A DYNIX command to compile the example parallel Fortran program (`pi.f`) is:

```
% fortran -e -u -g -mp pi.f
```

The −e flag specifies C language calling-sequence compatibility. The −mp option causes invocation of the parallel preprocessor. The −g option allows subsequent use of the `pdbx` parallel debugger described below under "Debugging". The −u flag can be used to retain a copy of the code produced by the preprocessor.

Performance

Program executions can be timed using the system routine `/bin/time`. However, this also times I/O.

The system calls `gettimeofday()` and `getrusage()` are available from within programs and are the basis of the C routines `start_timer`, `stop_timer`, and `fprt_timer`, which were written by Sequent. We used these three routines in the Pi Program. They provide user, system, and wall-clock times.

Debugging

Sequent offers an interactive parallel debugger, pdbx, based on the UNIX 4.2BSD debugger, dbx. Pdbx is almost identical to dbx when debugging sequential applications. However, pdbx can also be used to debug (possibly unrelated) multiple processes. In pdbx, processes can be started, stopped, traced, breakpointed, and examined independently. Pdbx assigns each process a number, which can be listed using the ps command and used to apply other pdbx commands to specific processes. Detectable events include forks, execs, and exits. Pdbx commands that put a process into execution accept an optional & to place the process into the background. Windowing is also available for viewing different processes on different screens. For more information, see [5].

10.3   PARALLEL PROGRAM EXAMPLE

```
 1   c - number of processes; status returned
 2         integer*4 nprocs, status
 3   c - number of rectangles; loop index
 4         integer*4 nrecs, i
 5   c - integration variables
 6         double precision h, x
 7   c - pi as found by the program
 8         double precision tpi
 9   c - pi to 16 decimal places, for comparison
10         double precision pi
11         pi = 3.1415926535897932d0
```

Lines 1–10 declare all variables used by the program. The user inputs nrecs (the number of rectangles) and nprocs (the number of processes) for each run. The status variable is used to store the return value of the library routine that actually sets the number of processes. The variable h is the width of the rectangles, and x is the midpoint of a subinterval (base of a rectangle). The program computes an approximation of pi in tpi and compares it against pi, which is initialized in Line 11 to the first 16 decimal places of the exact value of pi.

```
12      10 write(*,*) 'Number of rectangles: '
13         read(*,*) nrecs
14         if (nrecs.le.0) goto 30
15         write(*,*) 'Number of procs: '
16         read(*,*) nprocs
17         if (nprocs.le.0) goto 30
18         call start_timer
19         status = m_set_procs(nprocs)
20         if (status.ne.0) goto 20
```

Lines 12–22 set up the problem for one computation. The user input for the number of rectangles and number of processes is read in, and if either is zero, the program is terminated. The call to `start_timer` on Line 18 marks the beginning of the timed section of code, which includes everything except I/O. This routine, and the timing routines used later in the code, are furnished by Sequent. The library routine `m_set_procs` allows the program to set the number of processes that will execute in parallel at any subsequent call to `m_fork`.

The call to `m_fork` is generated automatically by the preprocessor when it encounters a `c$doacross` compiler directive (see Line 23 in the following code box). The return value (`status`) is zero if the `m_set_procs` call is successful. The program skips the computation section if the return value is non-zero. This occurs when `nprocs` is larger than either the preset system limit or the number of CPUs online minus one, or when previously created child processes are still in existence. If `m_set_procs` is not called, the number of processes defaults to half of the number of CPUs online.

```
21            h = 1.d0 / nrecs
22            tpi = 0.0d0
23  c$doacross share(h), local(x), reduction(tpi)
24            do 100 i = 1, nrecs
25               x = (i-0.5d0) * h
26               tpi = tpi + 4d0 / (1d0 + x * x)
27     100   continue
28            tpi = h * tpi
```

Lines 21–22 initialize the width of the rectangles and the approximation of pi for the bulk of computation to follow, in Lines 23–28. The `c$doacross` compiler directive is interpreted by the preprocessor, which automatically generates code to create and synchronize the processes executing the loop in parallel. The number of processes is determined by the previous call to `m_set_procs`. Synchronization information is extracted from the variable classifications in the `c$doacross` statement.

These variable classifications are the result of dependency analysis done by the programmer. The loop index itself (`i`) is not analyzed, nor are any variables present only in the loop control statement (`nrecs`). The variable classifications are:

- A *shared* variable (e.g., `h`) is a scalar that is read but never written, or an array in which each element is referenced by only one loop iteration. Thus, it can be placed in shared memory (by the preprocessor) to be used by processes that execute the loop, with no need for synchronization.

- A *local* variable (e.g., `x`) is a scalar that is initialized in each loop iteration before it is used. Each process can maintain its own local copy.

- A *reduction* variable (e.g., `tpi`) is used by the loop to accumulate a result across iterations. To qualify as a reduction variable, it must occur only in statements of the form:

$$var = var \; op \; expr$$

where *var* is the reduction variable, *op* is one of the operators:

$$+, \, -, \, *, \, /, \, and, \, or, \, exclusive \; or$$

and *expr* is an expression that does not include *var*. All such statements for a particular reduction variable must use the same operation. A variable of this type is handled by allowing each process to update first a local copy and then a shared copy under protection of a lock. This prevents excessive lock contention.

The preprocessor breaks the loop iterations into chunks, interprets the variable classifications and handles them appropriately, creates a subroutine containing the modified version of the loop, and creates the processes that execute the subroutine in parallel. The code generated by the preprocessor can be found in Appendix H2. In this code, *all* necessary synchronization is generated automatically from the `c$doacross` statement. Some applications contain loops that require additional compiler directives and/or library routine calls to be inserted by the user for correct synchronization (see Appendices H4 and H5).

```
29          call m_kill_procs
30      20  call stop_timer
31          if (status.ne.0) then
32             write(*,*) ' Error setting number of processes'
33          else
34             call fprt_timer(nprocs,nprocs,nprocs)
35             write(*,500) tpi
36     500     format(' Pi:      ',f18.16)
37             write(*,600) pi - tpi
38     600     format(' Error: ',f18.16)
39          endif
40          goto 10
41      30  stop
42          end
```

The call to `m_kill_procs` on Line 29 terminates the child processes created by the `c$doacross`. To save overhead, it is also possible to use `m_park_procs` to suspend the processes and `m_rele_procs` to resume them.

Lines 30–39 print the run results, and the program returns to the top to do another computation.

10.4 PERFORMANCE

Test runs were made with no other users on the system. The preprocessor divided loop iterations among the processes by allowing each process to carry out `nrecs/nprocs` iterations by executing the new loop with the control statement:

```
do 10 i = myid, nrecs, nprocs
```

where `myid` is the process id number (numbering starts at 0) returned by the library routine `m_get_myid`. This was appropriate for our loop, since each iteration involves the same amount of computation. Thus, the load was well balanced. A single update to the shared variable `tpi` was done after each process finished all its iterations. For 10^7 rectangles (corresponding to a total of 60 million floating point operations) we measured:

processors	1	29
seconds	794.79	27.30
Mflops	.081	2.20
Mflops/proc	.081	.070

(This is user time, but wall-clock is essentially the same).

Figs. 10.2 and 10.3 give the speedup results for the Pi Program for 10^7 rectangles and from 1 to 29 processors. The speedup $S(n)$ was computed by dividing a base

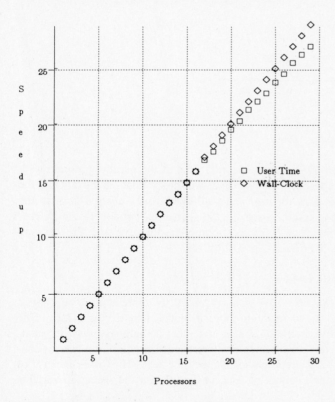

Figure 10.2   Speedup curves using $T(1)$.

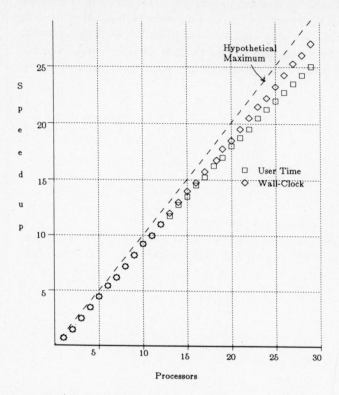

Figure 10.3   Speedup curves using *T(seq)*.

(sequential) time by *T(n)*, where *T(n)* is the execution time of the parallel program with *n* processors. Fig. 10.2 gives speedups for user and wall-clock times using *T(1)* as the base time. Fig. 10.3 gives speedups for user and wall-clock times using *T(seq)* as the base time, where *T(seq)* is the execution time for the sequential version of the Pi Program obtained by removing the c$doacross compiler directive and the calls to m_set_procs and m_kill_procs.

10.5   PITFALLS AND PROBLEMS

The Pi Program discussed in Section 10.3 was very easy to implement. The biggest obstacle was the tendency to try to make it more difficult than it really was. The c$doacross compiler directive is the only new statement actually *required* to parallelize the Pi Program. Only a few other statements are needed to allow the user to control the number of processes. The preprocessor handles the rest. However, because of the preprocessor, an inline function cannot be used in Line 26 for the reduction variable *expr*.

The dependency analysis for our example was uncomplicated, and the Sequent documentation is very good for this. A complete analysis of loop variables with the help of a variable classification scheme can be a great aid to parallelization and can reduce the chance of such errors as faulty synchronization. However, a user unfamiliar with the concepts involved might need some time to master them. Also, because the currently available tools do not do the analysis automatically, it could take an enormous amount of time to analyze a large and complex loop.

The familiarity of the UNIX environment made program development pleasant. The Sequent documentation is generally good, with some sample programs, but no documentation is *ever* perfect and more examples would be helpful.

Though we did not have to handle process creation, synchronization and termination, and shared memory allocation and use manually for the Pi Program, more complex parallel applications will require this. Some of the problems we encountered included:

- deadlock from forgetting to create a needed process;

- deadlock from forgetting to unlock a lock when done with it;

- deadlock from forgetting to put a variable in shared memory; and

- doubled output from forgetting to terminate a child process.

The `pdbx` parallel debugger was not needed for our Pi Program example, but for these earlier applications it proved valuable in debugging multiple processes and interprocess communication.

It is worth noting that multiple processes writing to the same file can cause problems. Also, processes tend to relinquish processors during disk accesses. Thus, it is best to put I/O in a sequential part of the code or to have an I/O server.

10.6 CONCLUSIONS

This is a very practical system in terms of offering a migration path into parallel processing. The system offers good solutions to most of the immediate problems of the transition into parallel execution, especially conversion cost and performance improvement. Much software that has been written for sequential computers can port directly and can exploit the increased system throughput and parallelized utilities transparently. The fact that DYNIX is an extension of a familiar and proven operating system (UNIX) is also a big plus.

The parallel processing support is varied enough to allow the programmer to ease into the parallel programming world slowly. The compiler directives, libraries, system calls, and the ability to implement custom parallel programming support routines can seem a bit confusing to the novice, but they can allow good fit between method and application. Some users may find dependency analysis too difficult, but it seems likely that this will be automated in the future.

10.7 ACKNOWLEDGEMENTS

We would like to thank Michael Squires, Gary Fielland, Joe DiMartino, and Anita Osterhaug, all at Sequent Computer Systems, for their tremendous help, and for allowing us virtually unlimited access to the Balance 8000 and the Balance 21000.

10.8 REFERENCES

[1]   B. Beck and D. Olien, "A parallel programming process model," in *Proceedings of the Winter 1987 USENIX Technical Conference*, Washington, D.C., Jan. 1987, pp. 84–101.

[2]   S. Thakkar, P. Gifford, and G. Fielland, "Balance: A shared memory multiprocessor," to appear in *Proceedings of the Second International Conference on Supercomputing*, Santa Clara, CA, May 1987.

[3]   G. Graunke, "Translating sequential languages for concurrent execution," in *Proceedings of the IEEE Spring CompCon 1987*, pp. 338–342.

[4]   Sequent Computer Systems, "Balance Guide to Parallel Programming," September, 1986.

[5]   Sequent Computer Systems, "DYNIX Pdbx Debugger User's Manual," September, 1986.

Appendix A
Alliant FX/8

CONTENTS

A1.   Pi Program Listing—No Explicit Concurrency

```
 1   C
 2   C - - Pi - Program loops over slices in interval, summing
 3   C - -  area of each slice
 4   C
 5         real tt1(2), tt2(2)
 6         integer*4 intrvls, cut
 7         double precision sumall, width, f, x
 8   C
 9         f(x) = 4d0 / (1d0 + x * x)
10   C
11         read(*,*) intrvls
12         t2 = etime(tt1)
13   C
14   C - - Compute width of cuts
15   C
16         width = 1.d0 / intrvls
17         sumall = 0.0d0
18   C
19   C - - Loop over interval, summing areas.
20   C
21         do 100 cut = 1, intrvls
22             sumall = sumall + width * f((cut - .5D0) * width)
23     100  continue
24   C
25   C - - Finish overall timing and write results
26   C
27         t1 = etime(tt2)
28         write(6, *) 'Time in main =', t1 - t2,', sum =', sumall
29         write(6, *) 'Error = ', sumall - 3.14159265358979323846d0
30         stop
31         end
```

A2.   Pi Program Listing—With Explicit Concurrency

```
1   C
2   C - - Main - This program starts the workers and writes out the
3   C        final answer as well as the times for all workers
4   C
5         double precision sumall, time(50)
6         real tt1(2), tt2(2)
7         integer*4 prcnum, nprocs, intrvls
8         common /comm/ sumall, time
9   C
10        read(*,*) nprocs, intrvls
11        t2 = etime(tt1)
12  C
13  C - - Call subroutine concurrently to do work
14  C
15  CVD$L CNCALL
16        do 100 prcnum = 1, nprocs
17           call work(prcnum, intrvls, nprocs)
18    100  continue
19        t1 = etime(tt2)
20        write(6, *) 'Time in main =', t1 - t2,', sum =', sumall
21        write(6, *) 'Error = ', sumall - 3.14159265358979323846d0
22        do 200 i = 1, nprocs
23           write(6, *) 'Process ', i, ' Time = ', time(i)
24    200  continue
25        stop
26        end
```

```
27              subroutine work(idproc, intrvls, nprocs)
28    CVD$R NOCONCUR
29    c
30    c - Computes integral for every nprocs-th slice, using a
31    c - rectangular approximation.  Number of slices is passed
32    c - to routine as integer * 4 message.
33    c
34            Integer * 4 cut, intrvls, idproc, nprocs
35            Real dummy(2)
36            Double precision sum, sumall, width, f, x, time(50)
37            common /comm/ sumall, time
38            common /synch/ lock
39            f(x) = 4d0 / (1d0 + x * x)
40    c
41            t1 = etime(dummy)
42    c
43    c - - Get number of cuts and compute width of cuts
44    c
45            width = 1.d0 / intrvls
46    c
47    c - - Calculate area in every "nprcss" cuts and sum
48    c - - (This is the WORK part)
49    c
50            sum = 0.0d0
51            do 100 cut = idproc, intrvls, nprocs
52                sum = sum + width * f((cut - .5D0) * width)
53      100   continue
54            time(idproc) = etime(dummy) - t1
55    c
56    c - - - Return answer to the base node
57    c
58            call lockon(lock)
59            sumall = sumall + sum
60            call lockoff(lock)
61            return
62            stop
63            end
```

A3.   Excerpts from the *FX/FORTRAN Programmer's Handbook*[†]

A3.1   CONCEPTS

FX/Fortran optimizes the following operations for concurrency and vectorization:

- *Array operations*—array operations run in vector-concurrent mode (or COVI mode; see below).

- *Iterative loops*—Iterative `DO` loops of the form `DO I = 1, N` that contain no restricted statements and no data dependencies that prevent optimization execute in vector-concurrent mode.   `DO` loops may run in vector, scalar-concurrent, or scalar mode due to restrictions.   `DO` loops may be split into several loops, some of which run in scalar mode and some of which run with some form of optimization, due to restrictions.

- `DO WHILE` *loops*—DO WHILE loops that contain no restricted statements and no data dependencies that prevent optimization run in scalar-concurrent mode.

- *All other*—All other code runs in scalar mode. Note that a series of scalar operations on an array is not optimized; for example, the following code is not optimized for concurrency or vectorization:

```
A(1) = A(1) + S
A(2) = A(2) + S
A(3) = A(3) + S
A(4) = A(4) + S
```

The modes of execution have the following meanings:

- *Scalar*—Operations are performed serially. The FX/Fortran processor schedules instructions as much as possible to take advantage of pipelining.

- *Vector*—Operations are performed in groups of 32 elements (or fewer if 32 elements are not available) by special vector instructions in the hardware.

- *Concurrent (scalar concurrent)*—Operations in different iterations of the same loop are performed by a number of computational elements (CEs) concurrently.

- *Vector concurrent*—Operations are performed in groups of up to 32 elements by a number of CEs concurrently.

Fig. A3.1 illustrates the various possible modes of execution.

Assuming a processor cycle time of 170 nanoseconds, the problem loop (8192 iterations of double precision arithmetic) executes in the following times: scalar mode —0.02 seconds, yielding 0.39 Mflops; vector mode—0.0041 seconds yielding 1.99

[†]This material is taken from Chapter 3, "Concurrency and Vectorization", of the *FX/FORTRAN Programmer's Handbook*, revised March 1986. Materials contained in Appendix A3 are reprinted with the permission of Alliant Computer Systems Corporation, which reserves all rights thereto.

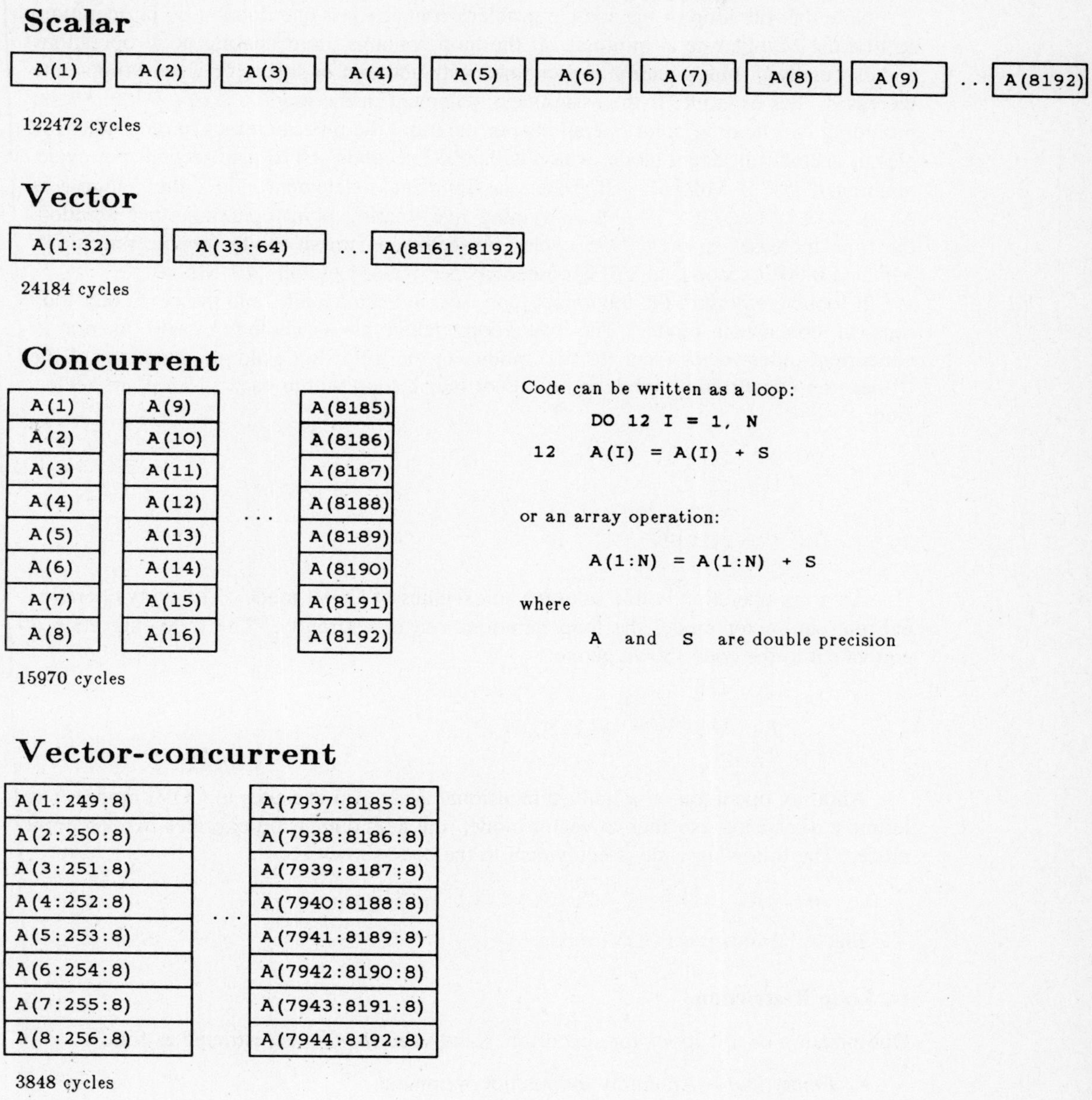

Scalar

| A(1) | A(2) | A(3) | A(4) | A(5) | A(6) | A(7) | A(8) | A(9) | ... | A(8192) |

122472 cycles

Vector

| A(1:32) | A(33:64) | ... | A(8161:8192) |

24184 cycles

Concurrent

A(1)	A(9)		A(8185)
A(2)	A(10)		A(8186)
A(3)	A(11)		A(8187)
A(4)	A(12)	...	A(8188)
A(5)	A(13)		A(8189)
A(6)	A(14)		A(8190)
A(7)	A(15)		A(8191)
A(8)	A(16)		A(8192)

15970 cycles

Code can be written as a loop:

```
      DO 12 I = 1, N
12    A(I) = A(I) + S
```

or an array operation:

```
      A(1:N) = A(1:N) + S
```

where

```
      A   and   S   are double precision
```

Vector-concurrent

A(1:249:8)		A(7937:8185:8)
A(2:250:8)		A(7938:8186:8)
A(3:251:8)		A(7939:8187:8)
A(4:252:8)	...	A(7940:8188:8)
A(5:253:8)		A(7941:8189:8)
A(6:254:8)		A(7942:8190:8)
A(7:255:8)		A(7943:8191:8)
A(8:256:8)		A(7944:8192:8)

3848 cycles

Figure A3.1   Modes of execution.

Mflops; scalar-concurrent mode (eight CEs)—0.0027 seconds, yielding 3.02 Mflops; vector-concurrent mode (eight CEs)—0.00065 seconds, yielding 12.5 Mflops.

Note that the loop in the sample problem contains just one floating point operation, so that the Mflops rate is minimal. If the loop contains more floating point operations and especially if multiplication is combined with addition or subtraction, the Mflops rate increases. For example, if the assignment statement in the loop is `A(I)=A(I)*T+S`, providing two floating point operations per iteration, the time increases to only 4883 cycles in vector-concurrent mode, which is 0.00083 seconds at 170 nanoseconds per cycle, yielding 19.7 Mflops. If the assignment statement in the loop is `A(I)=A(I)*T+S+A(I)*S+T`, providing five floating point operations per iteration, the time increases to only 9995 cycles in vector-concurrent mode (double precision), which is 0.0017 seconds at 170 nanoseconds per cycle, yielding 24.1 Mflops.

If loops are nested, the innermost loop runs in vector mode, and the next outer loop runs in concurrent mode. The two loops taken as a whole are said to run in concurrent-outer-vector-inner (COVI) mode. In the following example, iterations of the J loop run concurrently, while iterations of the I loop within each J loop are vectorized:

```
      DO 11 J = 1, L
         DO 12 I = 1, N
            A(I, J) = A(I, J) + S
12       CONTINUE
11    CONTINUE
```

An array operation within a loop also executes in COVI mode. The array operation executes in vector mode; the loop iterations run concurrently. The following code is equivalent to the code shown above:

```
      DO 11 J = 1, L
         A(1:N,J) = A(1:N,J) + S
11    CONTINUE
```

An array operation on a multi-dimensional array also executes in COVI mode. The leftmost dimension executes in vector mode; the next dimension executes in concurrent mode. The following code is equivalent to the code shown above:

```
      A(1:N, 1:L) = A(1:N, 1:L) + S
```

Fig. A3.2 illustrates COVI mode.

DO **Loop Restrictions**

Optimization of DO loops for concurrency and vectorization is restricted as follows:

- *Empty loop*—An empty loop is not optimized.

- *Statements*—A loop to be executed in vector, vector-concurrent, or COVI mode can contain only the following statements:

    data assignment
    comment

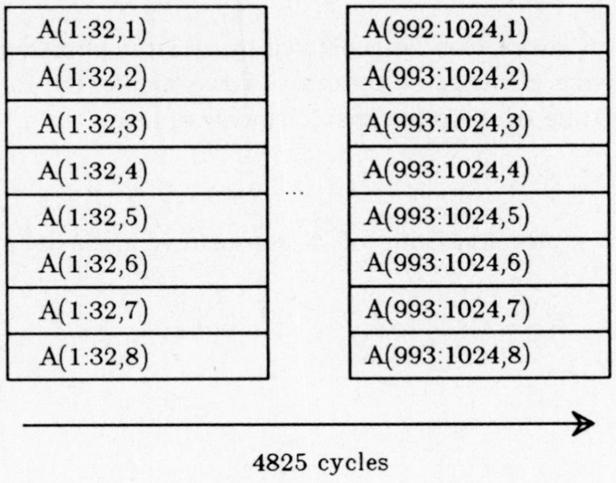

A(1:32,1)	A(992:1024,1)
A(1:32,2)	A(993:1024,2)
A(1:32,3)	A(993:1024,3)
A(1:32,4)	A(993:1024,4)
A(1:32,5)	A(993:1024,5)
A(1:32,6)	A(993:1024,6)
A(1:32,7)	A(993:1024,7)
A(1:32,8)	A(993:1024,8)

4825 cycles

Code can be written as a loop:

```
       DO 12 J = 1, L
       DO 12 I = 1, N
12     A(I,J) = A(I,J) + S
```

or an array operation:

$$A(1:N,1:L) = A(1:N),1:L) + S$$

where

$$N = 1024 \text{ and } L = 8$$

A and S are double precision

Figure A3.2   Concurrent-Outer-Vector-Inner (COVI) mode.

```
CONTINUE
GOTO forward label within loop
arithmetic IF to forward label
block IF, ELSE, END IF
logical IF
```

Note that no I/O statements are allowed.

Inclusion of the following statements in a DO loop inhibits vectorization but permits concurrency:

```
ELSE IF
block IF with nesting at a level greater than 3
GOTO forward label outside loop
RETURN
STOP
```

- *Character variables*—Inclusion of a character variable in a loop inhibits concurrency and vectorization.

- *Subprograms*—The inclusion of references to statement functions and intrinsic functions in loops does not prevent optimization. The inclusion of references to external procedures in loops does prevent optimization unless you explicitly allow the procedure.

- *Assigned* GOTO—A GOTO statement may not use a variable set by an ASSIGN statement.

Vector Constructs

Optimized code treats data as follows:

- *Vector*—A series of elements. A vector may be generated by an array operation or by iterative operations involving elements of an array. For example, the following code uses a vector consisting of N consecutive elements of array A:

```
A(1:N) = A(1:N) + S
```

The following code also uses a vector consisting of N consecutive elements of array A:

```
      DO 12 I = 1, N
         A(I) = A(I) + S
12    CONTINUE
```

Note that the scalar constructs A(1) through A(N) are vector elements.

- *Loop scalar*—A single element for purposes of the vector operation. A loop scalar is a reference to a scalar variable or a single array element. In a loop, an array reference is a loop scalar (rather than a vector) if the array subscript does not change between iterations. In the following example, the variable S and the array element B(J) are loop scalars with respect to the vector derived from array elements A(1) through A(N):

```
      DO 12 I = 1, N
         A(I) = A(I) + B(J) + S
12    CONTINUE
```

- *Index*—A single integer element whose value changes by a constant increment for every element of a vector. More specifically, an index must meet the requirements of a constant increment integer discussed in the next section. In the following example, I and J are indexes with respect to the vectors derived from array elements A(1) through A(N) and B(J) through B(J−N+1):

```
      DO 12 I = 1, N
         A(I) = B(J)
         J = J - 1
12    CONTINUE
```

Constant Increment Integers

A constant increment integer (CII) is an induction variable that is defined only as follows within the loop:

- *Recurrent CII*—The variable plus or minus an expression that is invariant within the loop.

- *In terms of a previous CII*—A previously occurring CII plus, minus, or times an expression that is invariant within the loop.

In the following example, I, J, and K are CIIs. I is incremented by a constant on each loop iteration. J is decremented by a constant on each loop iteration. K is assigned the value of a defined CII times a constant plus a constant.

```
      DO 12 I - 1, N
         J = J - 1
         K = I * 2 + 3
         A(J) = B(K)
12    CONTINUE
```

Violation of the rules means that the integer is not a CII. For example, if the first assignment statement read J = J * 2, J would not be a CII because the multiplication is not in terms of a previously defined CII. If the second statement read K = I / 2, I is a previously defined CII, but division is precluded, so K would not be a CII.

Indirect Addressing

Indexes must meet one of the following requirements for optimization to occur:

- *Direct addressing*—At least one of an array's subscripts must be transformable to the following form for the resulting vector to be addressed directly:

```
CII * invariant expression + or - invariant expression
```

- *Indirect addressing*—If a subscript is itself an element of an indexed array, the resulting vector is addressed indirectly. In addition, arrays whose subscripts do not meet the requirements for direct addressing result in vectors that are addressed indirectly.

Indirect addressing results in a performance loss. The performance loss could be significant if the possibility of storing twice into the same array element exists.

Scalar Promotion

A scalar variable stored into by an array on an optimized loop is temporarily (for the duration of the loop) promoted to a vector (vector-concurrent mode). In the following example, the compiler automatically replaces S with a temporary vector:

```
      DO 12 I = 1, N
         S = A(I) + B(I)
         C(I) = S(I) + 1.0 / S
12    CONTINUE
```

The need for the temporary array is apparent if you perform the same task using array constructs:

```
      S(1:N) = A(1:N) + B(1:N)
      C(1:N) = S(1:N) + 1.0 / S(1:N)
```

A3.2   MECHANICS

The O option to the fortran command turns on optimization and may be used in combination with the g, c, and v suboptions. The following combinations are useful:

- O—Global optimizations, concurrency, and vectorization.

- Og—Global optimizations only.

- Ogc—Global optimizations and concurrency (no vectorization).

- Ogv—Global optimizations and vectorization (no concurrency).

Omission of the O option results in no optimizations.

You might specify Ogc if all the loops in the program are short (three iterations or less). However, suppression of the vectorization is better controlled by the NOVECTOR directive.

The -AS (associative transformation) option, in conjunction with the -O option, causes certain loop constructs to be treated as reduction functions, permitting optimization where no optimization would otherwise occur. However, the order of evaluation of an associative transformation is undefined. Associative transformations can also be controlled by the ASSOC directive.

Optimization Directives

You can place directives in your source code to change the default optimization actions. Directives are effective only in programs compiled with the -O option and no suboptions or the -O option and suboptions that include c or v. The form of an optimization directive is shown in Fig. A3.3. The optimization directives and their defaults are shown in Fig. A3.4.

A3.3   SUPPRESSING OPTIMIZATION

In certain run-time situations, optimization of DO loops for vectorization or concurrency may degrade performance. Directives permit you to suppress optimization in these cases.

Suppressing Vectorization

The NOVECTOR directive inhibits vectorization. Suppressing vectorization might improve performance in the following situations. In all cases, you should time the code with and without vectorization to make sure you are really enhancing performance.

- *Few iterations*—If the number of loop iterations at run time results in vectors that are less than three elements in length, suppressing vectorization usually enhances performance. On a machine with eight CEs, for example, you should consider suppressing vectorization if the number of iterations of a non-nested loop is less than 24. Vectorization is automatically suppressed if a loop contains

CVD$[*s*] *directive*

where

s	Default	Description
G		Directive applies globally (to end of file)
R		Directive applies to end of routine
L	*	Directive applies to end of loop

Figure A3.3. Form of optimization directives.

directive	Default	Description
ASSOC		Optimize associative transformations
NOASSOC	*	
CNCALL		Allow subroutine and function references in loops
NOCNCALL	*	
CONCUR	*	Optimize for concurrency
NOCONCUR		
DEPCHK	*	Check for data dependencies between loop iterations.
NODEPCHK		
LSTVAL	*	Save last values of original indexes and promoted scalars.
NOLSTVAL		
SYNC	*	Check for synchronization problems between loop iterations.
NOSYNC		
VECTOR	*	Optimize for vectorization.
NOVECTOR		

Figure A3.4. Optimization directives.

an explicit iteration count of less than five. The following example codes a loop
twice, suppressing vectorization for short loops:

```
        IF (N .LT. 25) THEN
CVD$    NOVECTOR
        DO 12 I = 1, N
            A(I) = A(I) + S
12          CONTINUE
        ELSE
        DO 14 I = 1, N
            A(I) = 1, N
14          CONTINUE
        END IF
```

However, suppressing concurrency may obtain better results.

- *Conditional processing of array in loop*—A loop in which the array processing is conditional may result in few calculations per vector instruction actually occurring at run time. For example, if A(I) in the following loop contains many values that are less than EPS, you may want to suppress vectorization.

```
CVD$   NOVECTOR
       DO 12 I = 1, N
          IF (ABS(A(I)) .GT. EPS)  A(I) = A(I) + S
12     CONTINUE
```

However, if the program performs calculations on the same set of sparse elements several times, gathering the sparse elements for efficient vector processing may be worthwhile. The following routine collects in array J the subscripts of the elements to be processed:

```
       DO 12  I = 1, N
          IF (ABS(A(I)) .GT. EPS) THEN
             II = II + 1
             J(II) = I
          END IF
12     CONTINUE
```

Routines that follow access only the elements that are greater than EPS by using the elements of array J as subscripts. The NODEPCHK directive is necessary to optimize this code because the value of the subscript cannot be determined at compile time.

```
CVD$   NODEPCHK
       DO 14 I = 1, II
          A(J(I)) = A(J(I)) + S
14     CONTINUE
```

- *Multi-way branching*—When the code selects one of many possible branches each time through the loop, efficient grouping of scalar operations for vectorization is not likely. In the case of block IF structures containing ELSE IF statements, the multi-way branching situation is recognized, and vectorization is suppressed automatically. In other cases, you should manually suppress vectorization with the NOVECTOR directive. For example, if you use the logical if statement as a case statement, you should consider suppressing vectorization:

```
CVD$   NOVECTOR
       DO 12 I = 1, N
          IF (A(I) .EQ. 1) A(I) = A(I) + S1
          IF (A(I) .EQ. 2) A(I) = A(I) + S2
          IF (A(I) .EQ. 3) A(I) = A(I) + S3
          IF (A(I) .EQ. 4) A(I) = A(I) + S4
12     CONTINUE
```

- *Sparsely distributed iterations*—Even if the code splits into only a few branches (as in a simple `IF..ELSE` block), the branch which operates on the array may be the one least chosen. In such situations, you should manually suppress vectorization with the `NOVECTOR` directive.

You should time the code with and without vectorization to make sure that you are enhancing performance.

Suppressing Concurrency

The `NOCONCUR` directive inhibits concurrency. If your system contains only one CE, and you have no plans for upgrading to multiple CEs, you might try suppressing concurrency. You might also try suppressing concurrency for a loop in which most of the code cannot be optimized due to data dependencies. In either case, test the program with timings to ensure that a savings has been made.

Suppressing concurrency rather than vectorization may provide better performance for loops with few iterations (but not less than five). The following example suppresses concurrency for short loops with more than five iterations:

```
      IF (N .LT. 6) THEN
CVD$  NOVECTOR
      DO 10 I = 1, N
         A(I) = A(I) + S
10       CONTINUE
      ELSE IF (N .LT. 25) THEN
CVD$  NOCONCUR
      DO 12 I = 1, N
         A(I) = A(I) + S
12       CONTINUE
      ELSE
      DO 14 I = 1, N
         A(I) = A(I) + S
14       CONTINUE
      END IF
```

Under certain circumstances, you may want to alter the standard method (COVI) for processing nested loops. If the number of outer iterations is less than the number of CEs available, COVI mode does not use all available CEs. Simply running the inner loop in vector-concurrent mode may be more efficient. You can force this mode of operation by applying the `NOCONCUR` directive to the outer loop:

```
CVD$  NOCONCUR
      DO 12 J = 1, 4
         DO 11 I = 1, 2048
            A(I, J) = A(I, J) + S
11       CONTINUE
12    CONTINUE
```

COVI mode may also be inefficient if the inner loops are short. Again, you can force vector-concurrent mode by applying the NOCONCUR directive to the outermost loop.

A3.4   DATA DEPENDENCY

Data dependencies can restrict the optimization of DO loops. Data dependency between loop iterations (also called data recursion and data feedback) means that calculations during one iteration of the loop depend on results achieved in a previous iteration, so that the order in which operations occur must be maintained. A data dependency may inhibit all vectorization and concurrency for a loop; such a loop is commented as DATA DEPENDENT in the DO loop summary of a listing. A data dependency may partially inhibit vectorization and concurrency for a loop; such a loop is commented as VECTOR-CONCURRENT, VECTOR, or CONCURRENT in the DO loop summary of a listing, but with a Y under the DP? column.

Whether data dependencies actually occur at run time is not always clear from the source code. The FX/Fortran processor suppresses (or partially suppresses) optimization whenever the possibility of a data dependency exists. You can force optimization by specifying the NODEPCHK directive; however, you should be positive that no dependencies will in fact occur at run time.

The following subsections describe the common data dependency problems and point out those situations where you might safely force optimization.

Carry-around Scalars

A scalar variable that is stored into after being referenced in a loop is called a carry-around scalar because the value set in one iteration of the loop is carried around and used in the next iteration of the loop. Common uses of carry-around scalars are in reduction functions and recursive calculations. The following example shows a listing of a program that reduces elements of arrays A and B to the scalar S. As you can see, the loop is not optimized.

```
7          DO 12 I = 1, N
8             S = S * A(I) + B(I)
9    12    CONTINUE
```

```
Line 8   Informational message # 1219
            Concurrent and vector loop optimization inhibited by
            carry-around scalar -- S
```

The evaluation of S in each iteration of the loop depends on the value of S derived in the previous iteration as illustrated in Fig. A3.5. Consequently, the loop cannot be optimized. If, for example, the five iterations shown above were executed independently, S would attain five separate values (1, 2, 3, 4, and 5), four of which would be incorrect.

Never force optimization in this situation.

```
S = S * (A(I) + B(I))
```

where

```
        A = (1, 2, 3, 4, 5)
        B = (1, 2, 3, 4, 5)
        S = 0
```

```
Iteration 1: 0*1+1 = 1
        Iteration 2: 1*2+2 = 4
                Iteration 3: 4*3+3 = 15
                        Iteration 4: 15*4+4 = 64
                                Iteration 5: 64*5+5 = 325
```

Figure A3.5. Carry-around scalar.

Eliminating Carry-around Scalars

In certain situations, code can be rewritten to eliminate carry-around scalars. In the following example, the scalar T is defined, then carried around and referenced in the next iteration of the loop. In this case, the carry-around scalar does not accumulate or recursively calculate data, but simply saves the result of a calculation in the previous iteration:

```
        T = 0.0
        DO 12 I = 1, N
            S = A(I) * B(I)
            C(I) = S + T
            T = S
12      CONTINUE
```

The example can be written to perform the calculation again rather than carry it around, adding a multiplication to each iteration but permitting the loop to be fully optimized. Despite the extra multiplication, the example runs many times faster with full optimization:

```
        C(1) = A(1) * B(1)
        DO 12 I = 2, N
            C(I) = A(I) * B(I) + A(I-1) * B(I-1)
12      CONTINUE
```

Recursive calculations can often be replaced by explicit calculations, which are inefficient in scalar mode but which permit full optimization in an optimized mode. Suppose that a symmetrical matrix is stored as a vector, as illustrated in Fig. A3.6.

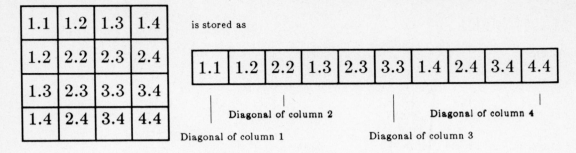

Figure A3.6   A symmetrical matrix stored as a vector.

The following code accesses the diagonal of the matrix using a recursive calculation to determine the subscript. The code cannot be optimized for concurrency or vectorization because of the feedback:

```
    J = 0
    DO 12 I = 1, N
       J = J + I
       A(J) = A(J) + B(I) * T
12     CONTINUE
```

However, the recursive calculation can be replaced by an explicit formula (the formula for calculating the sum of a series). The NODEPCHK directive is necessary because the subscript J does not meet the requirements of a CII:

```
CVD$   NODEPCHK
       DO 12 I = 1, N
          J = (I * I + I) * 0.5
          A(J) = A(J) + B(I) * T
12        CONTINUE
```

Associative Transformations

If the −AS option or the ASSOC directive is in effect, the FX/Fortran processor recognizes some recursions as reduction functions and optimizes these loops. The reduction functions recognized in loops are summation, product, dot product, maximum value, minimum value, and count. The following loop, for example, is recognized as a dot product and optimized:

```
       S = 0.0
CVD$   ASSOC
       DO 12 I = 1, 8192
          S = S + A(I) * B(I)
12        CONTINUE
```

The effect is the same as invoking the `dotproduct` intrinsic function for `A(1:N)` and `B(1:N)`. Note, however, that the optimized code does not treat as significant the order of computation. If the order of computation matters, for example, if the order in which the rounding occurs is significant, you should not allow optimization of associative transformations.

Feedback to Array Elements

Feedback occurs when an array element is defined during one iteration and referenced during a succeeding iteration. If the definition and reference occur in parallel, the results are not the same as if the reference follows the definition. This situation usually manifests itself as an incremented subscript on the left-hand side. The following example uses feedback to propagate a value through the elements of an array:

```
       A(1) = 1.0                          A(1) = 1.0
       DO 12 I = 1, N          or          DO 12 I = 2, N
          A(I+1) = A(I)                       A(I) = A(I-1)
12     CONTINUE                  12        CONTINUE
```

The value assigned to the array element in each loop iteration depends on the value assigned to the previous array element in the previous iteration, as illustrated below. If the operation were vectorized or performed concurrently, the lack of feedback would invalidate the results. Therefore, the code is not optimized. Fig. A3.7 compares the results for the above loop when `A = (1.0, 0.0, 0.0, 0.0)`.

Often, non-recursive techniques can be used to accomplish the same ends, permitting optimization. If the intent in the above example is to assign the value 1.0 to every element of the array section `A(1:N)`, the recursive code can be replaced by a simple array assignment:

```
       A(1:N) = 1.0
```

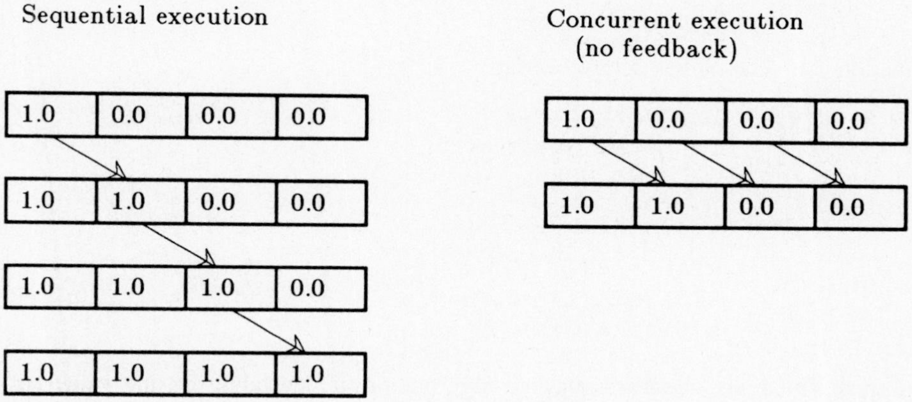

Figure A3.7 Sequential versus concurrent execution of array assignments.

Or a loop that assigns the value:

```
      DO 12 I = 1, N
         A(I) = 1.0
12       CONTINUE
```

These constructs *are* optimized. Accessing equivalenced data in the above manner also causes feedback.

Storing one array element from another does not necessarily result in feedback from one loop iteration to another. The following situations do not inhibit optimization:

Situation 1:   The store is into a previous element

```
            DO 11 I = 1, 3
               A(I) = A(I+1)
11          CONTINUE
```

where A = (1, 2, 3, 4)

```
      A(1) = A(2) = 2
      A(2) = A(3) = 3
      A(3) = A(4) = 4
```

Situation 2:   The stride means no overlap

```
            DO 11 I = 1, N, 2
               A(I+1) = A(I)
11          CONTINUE
```

where A = (1, 2, 3, 4, 5, 6)

```
      A(2) = A(1) = 1
      A(4) = A(3) = 3
      A(6) = A(5) = 5
```

Situation 3:   The ranges do not overlap

```
            DO 11 I = 1, 3
               A(I+3) = A(I)
11          CONTINUE
```

where A = (1, 2, 3, 4, 5, 6)

```
      A(4) = A(1) = 1
      A(5) = A(2) = 2
      A(6) = A(3) = 3
```

In some situations, feedback may or may not occur depending on the values of variables at run time. If you are *positive* that no feedback will occur, use the NODEPCHK to force optimization. Two examples used previously illustrate this point:

```
1.  CVD$   NODEPCHK
            DO 14 I = 1, II
               A(J(I)) = A(J(I)) + S
     14     CONTINUE


2.  CVD$   NODEPCHK
            DO 12 I = 1, N
               J = (I * I + I) * 0.5
               A(J) = A(J) + B(I) * T
     12     CONTINUE
```

In both cases, the subscripts of the arrays cannot be determined at compile time, and the possibility of feedback exists. However (in both cases), the programmer knows that the subscripts produced at execution time will not result in feedback, and forces optimization.

You should examine a loop that is not optimized or only partially optimized to see if the loop can be recoded in a manner that permits optimization. For example, the following loop is not optimized because elements of array A are defined in one iteration and referenced in the next iteration:

```
        DO 12 I = 2, N
           B(I) = A(I-1)
           A(I) = A(I) + C(I)
12      CONTINUE
```

However, the same work can be accomplished by two loops that do not involve any feedback:

```
        DO 12 I = 2, N
           A(I) = A(I) + C(I)
12      CONTINUE
        DO 14 I = 2, N
           B(I) = A(I-1)
14      CONTINUE
```

Some loops that are partially optimized for vector-concurrency run much faster in scalar-concurrency mode. For example, the FX/Fortran compiler partially optimizes the following loop by executing the first assignment in vector-concurrent mode and the second assignment in scalar-concurrent mode:

```
        DO 12 I = 2, N
           A(I) = A(I) + A(I) * B(I)
           B(I) = B(I-1) + A(I) + B(I)
12      CONTINUE
```

In practice, this loop may run faster if it is executed entirely in scalar-concurrent mode because the synchronization in scalar-concurrent mode makes for a better overlap of the running code on the CEs. Scalar-concurrent mode can be forced with a directive:

```
CVD$   NOVECTOR
       DO 12 I = 2, N
           A(I) = A(I) + A(I) * B(I)
           B(I) = B(I-1) + A(I) + B(I)
12     CONTINUE
```

Multiple Stores

Concurrency (but not vectorization) is suppressed if the possibility of storing multiple values into one array element exists, because the order of the stores must be preserved. This situation can occur when indirect addressing is used for the loop index. In the following example, the subscript for A cannot be determined at compile time:

```
       DO 12 I = 1, N
           A(J(I)) = B(I)
12     CONTINUE
```

For example, if array J contains the values 1, 2, 3, 1, and the following assignments take place:

```
       A(1) = B(1)
       A(2) = B(2)
       A(3) = B(3)
       A(1) = B(4)
```

If the potential for a multiple store is known not to manifest itself at run time, for example, if all the elements of J are known to have unique values, you can force optimization with the NODEPCHK directive:

```
CVD$L  NODEPCHK
       DO 12 I = 1, N
           A(J(I)) = B(I)
12     CONTINUE
```

Synchronization of Concurrent Operations

Operations in vector-concurrent and scalar-concurrent mode have the potential to corrupt data by storing into arrays out of sequence. Assume, for example, the following loop:

```
       DO 12 I = 1, N
           A(I) = A(I+1)
12     CONTINUE
```

If CE0 is processing A(32)=A(33) while CE1 is processing A(33)=A(34), CE0 must store the value of A(33) into A(32) before CE1 changes A(33). The FX/Fortran processor synchronizes operations in situations where the sequence of stores must be preserved; the synchronization does not result in a great loss of performance.

The NOSYNC directive forces a potential synchronization problem to be ignored and also turns off the NODEPCHK directive. You should only use the NOSYNC when you want to turn off synchronization (do not use NOSYNC as a substitute for NODEPCHK) and you are positive that the synchronization problem will not occur at runtime. In the following example, turning off synchronization is safe because no overlap is possible:

```
      K = N
CVD$L NOSYNC
      DO 12 I = 1, N
         A(I) = A(I+K)
12    CONTINUE
```

Note that the above code can be replaced by an array assignment statement:

```
      A(1:N) = A(1+K:N+K)
```

Last Value Saving

Optimized code does not need to maintain the original indexes in a loop. However, the values of indexes upon exit from the loop are calculated in case further processing in the program requires them, unless the processor can determine that the last value is not needed. Similarly, when a scalar variable is promoted to a temporary vector or to local scalars, the original scalar does not require maintenance in the loop. However, the scalar may be set to the last temporary value when the loop terminates.

If an index or scalar is not required after the loop terminates, you may enhance performance slightly by specifying the NOLSTVAL directive. The following example turns off last value saving for a program unit:

```
CVD$R NOLSTVAL
```

Conditional Stores into Scalars and Indexes

In a loop, a scalar variable that is set conditionally and then references outside the condition is a carry-around scalar and inhibits optimization. In the following example, incrementing S conditionally and using it unconditionally in the next statement prevents the loop from being optimized:

```
      DO 12 I = 1, N
         IF (A(I) .GT. X) S = B(I) + 2
         A(I) = S
12    CONTINUE
```

If the definition and any references are restricted to the same conditional use, the loop is optimized. The following example poses no problem:

```
        DO 12 I = 1, N
          IF (A(I) .GT. X) THEN
            S = B(I) + 2
            A(I) = S
          END IF
12      CONTINUE
```

If a scalar variable is used conditionally legally (that is, the store and reference are restricted to the same conditional use), and the last value of the scalar variable is preserved (the default case), the loop is optimized only for the scalar-concurrent use. If the last value is not preserved, the loop is fully optimized. In this instance, you should definitely use the NOLSTVAL directive if the scalar value (S in the above example) is not needed beyond the loop.

External Procedures

By default, a loop optimized for concurrency or vectorization cannot invoke an external procedure because the procedure cannot be checked for data dependencies. You can explicitly permit concurrent execution of loops containing references to external procedures with the CNCALL directive or through an appropriately specified Fortran interface block. The following example (although inefficient) demonstrates the concurrent execution of a subprogram:

```
      DOUBLE PRECISION A(8192)
      . . .
CVD$L CNCALL
      DO 12 I = 1, 8192
        CALL SUB(1.0D0, A(I))
12    CONTINUE
      . . .
      RECURSIVE SUBROUTINE SUB(S, A)
      DOUBLE PRECISION A, S
      A = A + S
      END
```

A Fortran subprogram invoked in an optimized loop must be reentrant. Reentrancy is implemented through inclusion of the RECURSIVE keyword in the FUNCTION or SUBROUTINE statement, as demonstrated above, or compilation of the subprogram with the -recursive option:

```
fortran -recursive -c sub.f
```

Each invocation of a reentrant subprogram allocates new storage for a unique copy of the subprogram's local variables. This practice differs from the default Fortran practice of storing local variables in one static area that is used by all invocations of the subprogram.

CNCALL *Directive*

The CNCALL directive explicitly permits the inclusion of an external routine in a loop optimized for concurrency. The following example demonstrates the CNCALL directive:

```
      DOUBLE PRECISION A(8192)
      ...
CVD$L CNCALL
      DO 12 I = 1, 8192
         CALL SUB(1.0D0, A(I))
12    CONTINUE
      ...
      RECURSIVE SUBROUTINE SUB(S, A)
      DOUBLE PRECISION A, S
      A = A + S
      END
```

No interface blocks or special command line options are needed when the CNCALL directive is used.

Fortran Interface Block

A Fortran interface block is a general mechanism for defining relationships between program units and is included in the proposed update to the Fortran standard. (The mechanism is not specified in the Fortran 77 standard.) FX/Fortran uses the interface block mechanism to permit the inclusion of subprograms in concurrent loops without the use of a directive in the source code and also to permit the building of libraries of concurrent programs.

To generate a Fortran interface block that defines a subprogram for inclusion in a concurrent loop, compile the subprogram with the -interface option. The -interface option creates a file containing the interface block; the name of the file is the same as the source program file with an extension of .interface instead of .f. The following example generates an object file named sub.o and an interface block named sub.interface:

```
fortran -O -c -recursive -interface sub.f
```

The invoking program unit, that is, the program unit containing the concurrent loop, must specify the -cncall option on the command line. The -cncall option identifies the interface file associated with the subprogram in the concurrent loop. The following example compiles a program that includes sub as a subprogram that can be invoked from a concurrent loop:

```
fortran -O -cncall sub.interface main.f sub.o
```

The name of the file containing the interface block must immediately follow -cncall. A command line can contain more than one -cncall option.

A `.interface` file can contain more than one interface block. For example, you can concatenate the output `.interface` files of many subprogram compilations to form a single library:

```
cat sub.interface >> lib.interface
```

If the interface file or files specified on the command line contain more than one interface block for the same subprogram, the first interface block is used, permitting the use of default libraries with an override mechanism.

An interface file is an ASCII file containing a series of interface blocks. Each interface block has the following format:

```
INTERFACE
FUNCTION or SUBROUTINE statement
[data-type statement for dummy argument ...]
[DIMENSION statement for dummy argument ...]
[INTENT statement for dummy argument ...]
END INTERFACE
```

The `INTENT` statement is included in the proposed update to the Fortran standard and is specified as follows[†]:

```
INTENT (in-out) dummy-name, ...
```

where *in-out* is one of the following:

- `in`—Names dummy arguments that are referenced but not defined in the subprogram.

- `out`—Names dummy arguments that are defined but not referenced in the subprogram.

- `inout`—Names dummy arguments that are both defined and referenced in the subprogram.

The following example demonstrates an interface block:

```
INTERFACE
RECURSIVE SUBROUTINE SUB(S,A)
DOUBLE PRECISION S
DOUBLE PRECISION A
INTENT (IN)    S
INTENT (INOUT) A
END INTERFACE
```

[†]The `INTENT` statement is not specified in the Fortran 77 standard.

Cautions

You must take great care in handling non-local data in subprograms invoked from a concurrent loop, since the code will be executed asynchronously on multiple processor. In particular, you must not access the same data element in COMMON or EQUIVALENCE storage by overlaying arguments (pass the same data element to two different dummy arguments), unless the data is never defined in the subprogram. For example, the following code, which sums array A when executed sequentially, does not work concurrently because many invocations of the subprogram reference and define the common variable S at the same time without synchronization. Do not optimize such code for concurrency.

```
C       ***EXAMPLE OF WHAT NOT TO DO***
        DOUBLE PRECISION A(8192), S
        COMMON S
        A(1:8192) = 1.0
CVD$ CNCALL
        DO 12 I = 1, 8192
           CALL SUB(A(I))
12      CONTINUE
        PRINT 1, S
1       FORMAT(G)
        END
        RECURSIVE SUBROUTINE SUB(A)
        DOUBLE PRECISION A, S
        COMMON S
        S = S + A
        END
```

You must be certain that the subprogram does not introduce undetected data dependencies into the program. For example, the following recursion goes undetected because the program units taken separately do not exhibit the recursion:

```
        DIMENSION A(8192)
        ...
        DO 12 I = 1, 8192
CVD$ CNCALL
           CALL SUB(A(I+1),A(I))
12      CONTINUE
        ...
        END
        RECURSIVE SUBROUTINE SUB(A1,A)
        A1 = A
        END
```

The use of pure functions is recommended to eliminate the danger of undetected data dependencies. (A pure function defines none of the arguments; only the return value is defined.) For example, if the above program were rewritten as follows, the recurrence would be trapped:

```
      DIMENSION A(8192)
      ...
      DO 12 I = 1, 8192
CVD$  CNCALL
          A(I+1) = FUNC(A(I))
12    CONTINUE
      ...
      END
      RECURSIVE FUNCTION FUNC(A)
      FUNC = A
      END
```

The use of Fortran interface blocks enables the detection of recurrences in situations such as the above. Recurrences introduced through the definition cannot be detected except through your own analysis of the combined program units. The following rules also apply to concurrent subprograms:

- A subprogram permitted by an interface block or CNCALL directive cannot execute an alternate return.

- A function reference cannot subscript an array in a loop even if an interface block or the CNCALL is in effect.

In addition, a reentrant (recursive) subprogram cannot save local data from invocation to invocation. All local data is initialized or undefined upon each invocation of the subprogram.

Concurrent Independent Subprograms

A DO loop can be used to execute separate subprograms or independent invocations of a subprogram concurrently by making each separate subprogram invocation conditional upon a certain iteration of the loop. If a single subprogram is invoked repeatedly, ensure that it is recursive. The following program executes three subroutines concurrently:

```
      DIMENSION X(512), Y(1024), Z(2048)
      ...
CVD$  CNCALL
      DO I = 1, 3
         IF (I .EQ. 1) THEN
            CALL XYZ(X, 512, XT)
         ELSE IF (I .EQ. 2) THEN
            CALL XYZ(Y, 1024, YT)
         ELSE IF (I .RQ 3) THEN
            CALL XYZ (Z, 2048, ZT)
         END IF
      END DO
```

```
T = (XT + YT + ZT) / 3
PRINT *, T
END

RECURSIVE SUBROUTINE XYZ(A, N, T)
DIMENSION A(N)
T = (SUM(A)-MAXVAL(A)-MINVAL(A)) / (N-2)
END
```

Appendix B
BBN Butterfly

CONTENTS

B1.   Pi Program Listing

```
1    #include <us.h>      /* includes must be in the order shown */
2    #include <stdio.h>
3    BEGIN_SHARED_DECL  /* three different ways to share data are */
4    double tpi;           /* demonstrated in this program */
5    END_SHARED_DECL;
6    int nrecs, nprocs, time1, time2;
7    short *lock, *nodecount;
8    UserInput()
9    {
10      printf("\nNumber of rectangles is ...");
11      scanf("%d", &nrecs);
12      printf("\nNumber of processors is ...");
13      scanf("%d", &nprocs);
14   }
15   ShareData()
16   {
17      MakeSharedVariables;
18      nodecount = (short *) Allocate(sizeof(short));
19      *nodecount = nprocs;
20      lock = (short *) Allocate(sizeof(short));
21      *lock = 0;
22      SHARED tpi = 0;
23      Share(&nrecs); Share(&nprocs); Share(&nodecount); Share(&lock);
24   }
25   PrintAnswer()
26   {
27      int elapsed_time;
28      double pi;
29      if (time2 > time1)
30          {
31              elapsed_time = time2 - time1;
32              printf("\nTime is %d\n", elapsed_time);
33          }
34      pi = 3.14159265358979323846264338;  /* pi to 24 decimal places */
35      pi = pi - SHARED tpi;
36      printf("\nCalculated pi is ... %27.20e\n", SHARED tpi);
37      printf("\nPi minus calculated pi is ... %27.20e\n", pi);
38   }
```

```
39   Dummy2() {};
40   Partial_Pi(Dummy2, index)
41   int index;
42   {
43      int me, n1, n2, j, section;
44      double h, x, sum;
45      {
46         me       = index;
47         h        = (double) 1.0 / nrecs;
48         section = nrecs / nprocs;
49         n1       = (me * section) + 1;
50         n2       = n1 + section - 1;
51         if (me == (nprocs - 1)) n2 = nrecs;
52         sum = 0.0;
53         for (j = n1; j <= n2; ++j)
54            {
55               x   = (j - 0.5) * h;
56               sum = sum + (4.0/(1.0 + x * x));
57            }
58         LOCK(lock, 0);
59            SHARED tpi = SHARED tpi + (h * sum);
60         UNLOCK(lock);
61         Atomic_add(nodecount, -1);
62         while (*nodecount > 0) UsWait(0);
63      }
64   }
65   Dummy1() {}; Dummy3() {};
66   main ()
67   {
68      UserInput();
69      time1 = GetRtc();              /* system clock read */
70      InitializeUs();
71      ShareData();
72      GenOnIFull(Dummy1, Partial_Pi, Dummy3, 0, nprocs, 0, 0);
73      time2 = GetRtc();
74      PrintAnswer();
75   }
```

B2.   Uniform System Library Routines[†]

This appendix documents each of the operations supported by the Uniform System Library. The operations are ordered alphabetically.

- `AbortGen`

  ```
  AbortGen(GenHandle, code)
  UsGenDesc * GenHandle;
  int code;
  ```

  Aborts the active task generator specified by `GenHandle` by preventing the generation of new tasks. Any tasks in progress run to completion. The value of `code` is returned as the result code for the generator. If `AbortGen` is called more than once for a given generator, the smallest `code` is returned as the generator result code.

  `GenHandle` must specify an abortable generator.

- `ActivateGen`

  ```
  UsGenDesc *
  ActivateGen(Init, Worker, Final, Arg, Range1, Range2,
      Type, Gen, Async, MaxProcsToUse Abortable, ResultP)
  int (* Init)(), (* Worker)(), (* Final)();
  int Arg, Range1, Range2, Type;
  int (* Gen)();
  int Async, MaxProcsToUse, Abortable, * ResultP;
  ```

  `ActivateGen` is the universal generator activator procedure. It is called by all of the `GenOn...` generator activator procedures. `ActivateGen` may be used directly by application programs to construct new generators.

  As with the generators described elsewhere in this appendix, `Init`, `Worker`, and `Final`, are respectively: the per-processor initialization routine; the task worker routine; and the per-processor post-processing routine.   `Arg` is a pointer to a data structure, which is passed to the `Init`, `Worker`, and `Final` routines.   `Type` must be `GENERATOR`, and `Range1` and `Range2` are integers. `Gen` is a task generation routine described in more detail below.   `Async` is a Boolean that specifies if the generator is synchronous (`true`) or asynchronous

---

[†]This appendix is taken from "The Uniform System Approach to Programming the Butterfly™ Parallel Processor", BBN Report No. 6149, Version 2, June 16, 1986. Reprinted by permission of BBN Advanced Computers Inc. For the most recent version of the Uniform System Documentation, please contact the marketing department at BBN Advanced Computers Inc., 10 Fawcett St., Cambridge, MA 02238, (617) 497-3700.

(false).   MaxProcsToUse specifies the processor limit for the generator;
0 or −1 indicates no processor limitation; a positive value indicates the maximum number of processors to be used on the generator.   Abortable is a
Boolean that indicates whether the generator is to be abortable. Finally,
ResultP is a pointer used when Abortable is true; it specifies a location
where the generator result code should be stored if the generator is aborted (so
that the generator activator routine can find it).

The task generation routine is of the form:

```
Gen(TD);
UsGenDesc * TD;
```

where TD is a pointer to a task descriptor data structure in globally shared
memory of the form (the type UsGenDesc is defined in usgen.h, an
#include file which must be used when ActivateGen is used):

```
struct
{   short started;
    short type;
    /* Defined types are: */
#define IDLETASK  1
#define GOAWAYTASK 2
#define GENERATOR 4
    short incarnation_number;
    short state;
    /* Defined states are: */
#define ACTIVE 1
#define INACTIVE 2
    short us_lock;
    short lock;
    int (*init)();
    int    (*call)();
    int    (*gen)();
    int    (*final)();
    int    arg;
    char *currentShare;
    int    range;
    int    range2;
    QH returnQ;
    int    post_pending;
    short MaxProcsToUse;
    int    end;
    int    abortable;
    short retcode;
```

```
      /* Defined retcodes are: */
#define genEXHAUSTED -1
    short endlock;
    union {
         long Long;
         short Short;
    } index;
    union {
         unsigned long Long;
         unsigned short Short;
    } index2;
    short locka[nlocks];
    short index1a[nlocks];
    short index2a[nlocks];
}
```

The Worker, Init, Final, Gen, Arg, Range1, Range2, Type, MaxProcsToUse, and Abortable parameters of ActivateGen are used to initialize the call, init, final, gen, arg, range, range2, type, MaxProcsToUse, and abortable fields of the task-descriptor data structure. The lock and the locka array fields are initialized to 0 and are available for use as locks by the Gen routine; the index and index2 fields, and the index1a and index2a array fields of the task-descriptor data structure are initialized to 0 and are available for use by the Gen routine for bookkeeping associated with generating the tasks. The remaining fields (e.g., started, state, shareCount, returnQ, etc.) are used by ActivateGen for internal bookkeeping.

After ActivateGen initializes the task-descriptor data structure, it makes the descriptor accessible to other processors. If Async is true, ActivateGen then returns control to its caller along with a pointer to the task descriptor data structure; otherwise, the processor on which ActivateGen is invoked calls the Gen task generation procedure. That processor, and others as they become free, use the task generator descriptor (TD) and the Gen task generation procedure to generate and execute calls on the Worker procedure.

• Allocate

```
char * Allocate(size)
int size;
```

Allocates a block of storage of size bytes in globally shared memory. The block is allocated from the memory with the most free space.

- AllocateC

```
char * AllocateC(size, class)
int size, class;
```

Allocates a block of storage of size bytes in globally shared memory. The block is allocated from the memory in the class specified with the most free space. See also UsSetClass.

- AllocateLocal

```
char * AllocateLocal(size)
int size;
```

Allocates from the memory of the local processor a block of globally shared storage of size bytes.

- AllocateOnPhysProc

```
char * AllocateOnPhysProc(physproc, size)
int physproc, size;
```

Allocates from the memory of the processor whose hardware processor number is physproc a block of globally shared storage of size bytes.

- AllocateOnUsProc

```
char * AllocateOnUsProc(proc, size)
int proc, size;
```

Allocates from the memory of the processor whose Uniform System processor number is proc a block of globally shared storage of size bytes.

- AllocateOnUsProcC

```
char * AllocateOnUsProcC(proc, size, class)
int proc, size, class;
```

Similar to AllocateOnUsProc, differing in that the block of memory will be allocated only if the processor is in the specified class; otherwise, it fails. See also UsSetClass.

- AllocScatterMatrix

```
char * * AllocScatterMatrix(nrows, ncolumns, element_size)
int nrows, ncolumns, element_size;
```

Allocates a matrix that is scattered by row over the memories of the machine. A vector of pointers nrows long is allocated, and nrows separate vectors, each containing ncols items of size element_size bytes. The vectors are allocated in separate memories. Returns a pointer to a vector of pointers to the scattered row vectors. Elements of an array A allocated in this way can be referenced using standard C array notation:

```
A[i][j]
```

- AllocScatterMatrixC

```
char * * AllocScatterMatrixC(nrows, ncolumns,
                             element_size, class)
int nrows, ncolumns, element_size;
```

Similar to AllocScatterMatrix, differing in that only memories of the machine that are in the specified class are used to hold the scattered rows of the matrix and the vector of row pointers. See also AllocScatterMatrix and UsSetClass.

- AsyncGenOnA

```
UsGenDesc *
AsyncGenOnA(Worker, Range1, Range2)
int (* Worker)();
int Range1, Range2;
```

Asynchronous version of GenOnA.   AsyncGenOnA is equivalent to:

```
AsyncGenOnAFull(0, Worker, 0, 0, Range1, Range2, 0, false)
```

- AsyncGenOnAAbortable

```
UsGenDesc *
AsyncGenOnAAbortable(Worker, Range1, Range2)
int (* Worker)();
int Range1, Range2;
```

Asynchronous version of GenOnAAbortable.
AsyncGenOnAAbortable is equivalent to:

```
AsyncGenOnAFull(0, Worker, 0, 0, Range1, Range2, 0, true)
```

- AsyncGenOnAFull

```
UsGenDesc *
AsyncGenOnAFull(Init, Worker, Final, Arg, Range1, Range2,
     Limited, Abortable)
int (*Init)(), (* Worker)(), (* Final)();
int Arg, Range1, Range2, Limited, Abortable;
```

Asynchronous version of GenOnAFull. AsyncGenOnAFull returns to the caller as soon as the task generator is activated, enabling the caller to work on other things while the tasks are executed. AsyncGenOnAFull returns a generator handle that can be used with WorkOn or WaitForTasksToFinish. See the description of GenOnAFull for an explanation of the parameters.

- AsyncGenOnALimited

```
UsGenDesc *
AsyncGenOnALimited(Worker, Range1, Range2, MaxProcsToUse)
int (* Worker)();
int Range1, Range2, MaxProcsToUse;
```

Asynchronous version of GenOnALimited. AsyncGenOnALimited is equivalent to:

```
AsyncGenOnAFull(0, Worker, 0, 0, Range1, Range2,
     MaxProcsToUse, false)
```

- AsyncGenOnHA

```
UsGenDesc *
AsyncGenOnHA(Worker, Range1, Range2)
int (* Worker)();
int Range1, Range2;
```

Asynchronous version of GenOnHA. AsyncGenOnHA is equivalent to:

```
AsyncGenOnHAFull(0, Worker, 0, 0, Range1, Range2, 0, false)
```

- AsyncGenOnHAAbortable

```
UsGenDesc *
AsyncGenOnHAAbortable(Worker, Range1, Range2)
int (* Worker)();
int Range1, Range2;
```

Asynchronous version of `GenOnHAAbortable`. `AsyncGenOnHAAbort-`
`able` is equivalent to:

`AsyncGenOnHAFull(0, Worker, 0, 0, Range1, Range2, 0, true)`

- `AsyncGenOnHAFull`

```
UsGenDesc *
AsyncGenOnHAFull(Init, Worker, Final, Arg, Range1, Range2,
                 Limited, Abortable)
int (* Init)(),   (* Worker)(), (* Final)();
int Arg, Range1, Range2, Limited, Abortable;
```

Asynchronous version of `GenOnHAFull`. `AsyncGenOnHAFull` returns to
the caller as soon as the task generator is activated, enabling the caller to work
on other things while the tasks are executed. It returns a generator handle that
can be used with `WorkOn` or `WaitForTasksToFinish`. See the description of `GenOnHAFull` for an explanation of the parameters.

- `AsyncGenOnHALimited`

```
UsGenDesc *
AsyncGenOnHALimited(Worker, Range1, Range2, MaxProcsToUse)
int (* Worker)();
int Range1, Range2, MaxProcsToUse;
```

Asynchronous version of `GenOnHALimited`. `AsyncGenOnHALimited` is
equivalent to:

`AsyncGenOnHAFull(0, Worker, 0, 0, Range1, Range2,`
`     MaxProcsToUse, false)`

- `AsyncGenOnI`

```
UsGenDesc *
AsyncGenOnI(Worker, Range)
int (* Worker)();
int Range;
```

Asynchronous version of `GenOnI`. `AsyncGenOnI` is equivalent to:

`AsyncGenOnIFull(0, Worker, 0, 0, Range, 0, false)`

- AsyncGenOnIAbortable

```
UsGenDesc *
AsyncGenOnIAbortable(Worker, Range)
int (* Worker)();
int Range;
```

Asynchronous version of GenOnIAbortable.
AsyncGenOnIAbortable is equivalent to:

```
AsyncGenOnIFull(0, Worker, 0, 0, Range, 0, true)
```

- AsyncGenOnIFull

```
UsGenDesc *
AsyncGenOnIFull(Init, Worker, Final, Arg, Range,
                Limited, Abortable)
int (* Init)(), (* Worker)(), (* Final)();
int Arg, Range, Limited, Abortable;
```

Asynchronous version of GenOnIFull. AsyncGenOnIFull returns to the caller as soon as the task generator is activated, enabling the caller to work on other things while the tasks are executed. It returns a generator handle that can be used with WorkOn or WaitForTasksToFinish. See the description of GenOnIFull for an explanation of the parameters.

- AsyncGenOnILimited

```
UsGenDesc *
AsyncGenOnILimited(Worker, Range, MaxProcsToUse)
int (* Worker)();
int Range, MaxProcsToUse;
```

Asynchronous version of GenOnILimited. AsyncGenOnILimited is equivalent to:

```
AsyncGenOnIFull(0, Worker, 0, 0, Range, MaxProcsToUse, false)
```

- Atomic_add_long

```
Atomic_add_long(loc, val)
int * loc, val;
```

Atomically adds val to the location pointed to by loc. The routine Atomic_add_long is similar to the Chrysalis 16-bit Atomic_add operation; it differs in that it operates on 32-bit quantities and does not support the "fetch" part of the "fetch-and-add" functionality provided by Atomic_add.

It is also important to note that in its current implementation, `Atomic_add_long` is atomic only with respect to other `Atomic_add_long` calls. In particular, it is possible for the execution of a read operation to be interleaved with an `Atomic_add_long` operation in a way that returns an inconsistent result to the read. This can occur if the high-order 16 bits returned by the read are obtained after the low-order 16 bits are incremented by the `Atomic_add_long`, but before the carry (if any) is propagated to the higher-order bits.

- `BEGIN_SHARED_DECL`

```
BEGIN_SHARED_DECL
    ...
    normal C declarations;
    ....
END_SHARED_DECL;
```

`BEGIN_SHARED_DECL` is a macro. It is used with `END_SHARED_DECL` to delimit the declaration of variables that are to be globally shared among all of the processors. Variables declared in this way are referenced using the `SHARED` prefix. Space for variables declared in this way must be allocated via `MakeSharedVariables` after `InitializeUs` is called and before they are referenced.

Only one `BEGIN_SHARED_DECL/END_SHARED_DECL` declaration can appear in a Uniform System program. All of the variables declared via `BEGIN_SHARED_DECL/END_SHARED_DECL` are allocated on the same physical memory. In some situations this may lead to memory contention.

- `ConfigureUs`

```
ConfigureUs(Spec, n)
int * Spec, n;
```

`ConfigureUs` can be used prior to calling `InitializeUs` to specify values for configuration parameters that differ from the values normally used by `InitializeUs`. `Spec` is an array (of `int`'s) that specifies the configuration; it contains `n` parameter specification blocks. Each parameter specification block contains an integer `configuration_code` that serves to identify the parameter being set, followed by one (or more) integer(s) that specify the value for the parameter.

The following `configuration_codes` are currently defined:

    Code   Parameter

    `configProcs`   `integer = number of processors to`
                        `include in Uniform System configuration`

    `configMaxSars`   `integer = number of segment attribute`
                        `registers (SARs) to use to define`
                        `process address spaces`

- `DistinctMemoriesAvailable`

  `DistinctMemoriesAvailable()`

  Returns an integer that is the number of memories available for use by the application program. This number is usually the same as `TotalProcsAvailable`, but there are cases where it will be a smaller number because memory cannot be obtained on a particular processor node.

- `END_SHARED_DECL`

  `END_SHARED_DECL` is a macro used with `BEGIN_SHARED_DECL` to delimit the declaration of variables that are to be globally shared.

- `FreeAll`

  `FreeAll()`

  Deallocates all globally allocated storage.

- `GenOnA`

  ```
  GenOnA(Worker, Range1, Range2)
  int (* Worker)();
  int Range1, Range2;
  ```

  Generates tasks that cause `Worker(0, index1, index2)` to be executed in parallel for all combinations of `index1` and `index2` for `0 <= index1 < Range1` and `0 <= index2 < Range2`. The processor that invokes `GenOnA`, and possibly other processors, is used to execute the tasks generated. When `GenOnA` returns, all of the tasks generated have been completed.

- GenOnAAbortable

```
GenOnAAbortable(Worker, Range1, Range2)
int (* Worker)();
int Range1, Range2;
```

Abortable version of `GenOnA`. The tasks generated are calls of the form `Worker(0, index1, index2, GenHandle)`, where `GenHandle` is an identifier for the task generator that can be used with `AbortGen` to abort it. `GenOnAAbortable` is equivalent to

```
GenOnAFull(0, Worker, 0, 0, Range1, Range2, 0, true)
```

Note that `GenOnAAbortable` returns a value that indicates whether `AbortGen` was used to abort the generator.

- GenOnAFull

```
GenOnAFull(Init, Worker, Final, Arg, Range1, Range2)
           Limited, Abortable)
int (* Init)(), (* Worker)(), (* Final)();
int Arg, Range1, Range2, Limited, Abortable;
```

Generates tasks that cause:

```
Worker(Arg, index1, index2)
```

 (if `Abortable` is `false`) or

```
Worker(Arg, index1, index2, GenHandle)
```

(if `Abortable` is `true`) to be executed in parallel for all combinations of `index1` and `index2` for `0 <= index1 < Range1` and `0 <= index2 < Range2`. The processor that invokes `GenOnAFull`, and possibly other processors, is used to execute the tasks generated.

The routine `Init(Arg)` is called on each processor used to execute the tasks generated before the `Worker` routine is called for the first time on the processor. The routine `Final(Arg)` is called on each processor used to execute the tasks generated after the `Worker` routine is called for the last time on the processor. The `Limited` parameter is used to control the number of processors used by the generator. If `Limited` is `0` or `-1`, there is no limitation on the number of processors; a positive value limits the processors used to that number or fewer.

When `GenOnAFull` returns, either all of the tasks generated have been completed, in which case `GenOnAFull` returns the value `genEXHAUSTED`, or if the `Abortable` parameter is `true`, the generator was aborted, and some

of the tasks may not have been performed, in which case `GenOnAFull` returns
the code passed to `AbortGen` when it was aborted.

- `GenOnALimited`

  ```
  GenOnALimited(Worker, Range1, Range2, MaxProcsToUse)
  int (* Worker)();
  int Range1, Range2, MaxProcsToUse;
  ```

  Limited version of `GenOnA`. `GenOnALimited` is equivalent to

  ```
  GenOnAFull(0, Worker, 0, 0, Range1, Range2, MaxProcsToUse,
        false)
  ```

- `GenOnArray`

  ```
  GenOnArray(Init, Worker, Arg, Range1, Range2)
  int (* Init)(), (* Worker)();
  int Arg, Range1, Range2;
  ```

  Generates tasks that cause `Worker(Arg, index1, index2)` to be executed in parallel for all combinations of `index1` and `index2` for $0\ <=$
  `index1` $<$ `Range1` and $0\ <=$ `index2` $<$ `Range2`. The processor that
  invokes `GenOnArray`, and possibly other processors, is used to execute the
  tasks generated. The routine `Init(Arg)` is called on each processor used to
  execute the tasks generated before the `Worker` routine is called for the first
  time on the processor. When `GenOnArray` returns, all of the tasks generated
  have been completed.

- `GenOnArrayA`

  ```
  GenOnArrayA(Init, Worker, Final, Arg, Range1, Range2)
  int (* Init)(), (* Worker)(), (* Final)();
  int Arg, Range1, Range2;
  ```

  Generates tasks that cause `Worker(Arg, index1, index2)` to be executed in parallel for all combinations of `index1` and `index2` for $0\ <=$
  `index1` $<$ `Range1` and $0\ <=$ `index2` $<$ `Range2`. The processor that
  invokes `GenOnArrayA`, and possibly other processors, is used to execute the
  tasks generated. The routine `Init(Arg)` is called on each processor used to
  execute the tasks generated before the `Worker` routine is called for the first
  time on the processor. The routine `Final(Arg)` is called on each processor
  used to execute the tasks generated after the `Worker` routine is called for the
  last time on the processor. When `GenOnArrayA` returns, all of the tasks generated have been completed.

- GenOnHA

```
GenOnHA(Worker, Range1, Range2)
int (* Worker)();
int Range1, Range2;
```

Generates tasks that cause `Worker(Arg, index1, index2)` to be executed in parallel for combinations of `index1` and `index2` that span the "half" array beneath the diagonal of a `Range1` by `Range2` array, as follows:

```
index2=0,    index1=1,...,(Range1-1)
index2=1,    index1=2,...,(Range1-1)
 ...
index2=R-2, index1=(R-1),...,(Range1-1)

where R = min(Range1, Range2)
```

The processor that invokes `GenOnHA`, and possibly other processors, is used to execute the tasks generated. When `GenOnHA` returns, all of the tasks generated have been completed.

- GenOnHAAbortable

```
GenOnHAAbortable(Worker, Range1, Range2)
int (* Worker)();
int Range1, Range2;
```

Abortable version of `GenOnHA`. The tasks generated are calls of the form `Worker(0, index1, index2, GenHandle)`, where `GenHandle` is an identifier for the task generator that can be used with `AbortGen` to abort it. `GenOnHAAbortable` is equivalent to

```
GenOnAFull(0, Worker, 0, 0, Range1, Range2, 0, true)
```

Note that `GenOnHAAbortable` returns a value that indicates whether `AbortGen` was used to abort the generator.

- GenOnHAFull

```
GenOnHAFull(Init, Worker, Final, Arg, Range1, Range2,
            Limited, Abortable)
int (* Init)(), (* Worker)(), (* Final)();
int Arg, Range1, Range2, Limited, Abortable;
```

Generates tasks that cause:

```
Worker(Arg, index1, index2)
```

(if `Abortable` is `false`) or

```
Worker(Arg, index1, index2, GenHandle)
```

(if `Abortable` is `true`) to be executed in parallel for combinations of `index1` and `index2` that span the "half" array beneath the diagonal of a `Range1` by `Range2` array as follows:

```
index2=0,   index1=1,...,(Range1-1)
index2=1,   index1=2,...,(Range1-1)
 ...
index2=R-2, index1=(R-1),...,(Range1-1)

where R = min(Range1, Range2)
```

The processor that invokes `GenOnHAFull`, and possibly other processors, is used to execute the tasks generated.

The routine `Init(Arg)` is called on each processor used to execute the tasks generated before the `Worker` routine is called for the first time on the processor. The routine `Final(Arg)` is called on each processor used to execute the tasks generated after the `Worker` routine is called for the last time on the processor. The `Limited` parameter is used to control the number of processors used by the generator. If `Limited` is `0` or `-1`, no limitation is placed on the number of processors; a positive value limits the processors used to that number or fewer.

When `GenOnHAFull` returns, either all of the tasks generated will have been completed in which case `GenOnHAFull` returns the value `genEXHAUSTED` or the `Abortable` parameter is `true`, the generator was aborted, and some of the tasks may not have been performed, in which case `GenOnHAFull` returns the code passed to `AbortGen` when it was aborted.

* GenOnHALimited

```
GenOnHALimited(Worker, Range1, Range2, MaxProcsToUse)
int (* Worker)();
int Range1, Range2, MaxProcsToUse;
```

Limited version of `GenOnHA`. `GenOnHALimited` is equivalent to

```
GenOnAFull(0, Worker, 0, 0, Range1, Range2, MaxProcsToUse,
    true)
```

- GenOnHalfArray

```
GenOnHalfArray(Init, Worker, Arg, Range1, Range2)
int (* Init)(), (* Worker)();
int Arg, Range1, Range2;
```

Generates tasks that cause `Worker(Arg, index1, index2)` to be executed in parallel for combinations of `index1` and `index2` that span the "half" array beneath the diagonal of a `Range1 x Range2` array, as follows:

```
index2=0,    index1=1,...,(Range1-1)
index2=1,    index1=2,...,(Range1-1)
 ...
index2=R-2, index1=(R-1),...,(Range1-1)

where R = min(Range1, Range2)
```

The processor that invokes `GenOnHalfArray`, and possibly other processors, is used to execute the tasks generated. The routine `Init(Arg)` is called on each processor used to execute the tasks generated before the `Worker` routine is called for the first time on the processor. When `GenOnHalfArray` returns, all of the tasks generated have been completed.

- GenOnI

```
GenOnI(Worker, Range)
int (* Worker)();
int Range;
```

Generates tasks that cause `Worker(0, index)` to be executed in parallel for all values of `index` in the range `0 <= index < Range`. The processor that invokes `GenOnI`, and possibly other processors, is used to execute the tasks generated. When `GenOnI` returns, all of the tasks generated have been completed.

- GenOnIAbortable

```
GenOnIAbortable(Worker, Range)
int (* Worker)();
int Range;
```

Abortable version of `GenOnI`. The tasks generated are calls of the form

```
Worker(0, index, GenHandle)
```

where `GenHandle` is an identifier for the task generator that can be used with `AbortGen` to abort it.   `GenOnIAbortable` is equivalent to

```
GenOnIFull(0, Worker, 0, 0, Range, 0, true)
```

Note that `GenOnIAbortable` returns a value that indicates whether `AbortGen` was used to abort the generator.

- `GenOnIFull`

```
GenOnIFull(Init, Worker, Final, Arg, Range,
          Limited, Abortable)
int (* Init)(), (* Worker)(), (* Final)();
int Arg, Range, Limited, Abortable;
```

Generates tasks that cause

```
Worker(Arg, index)
```

(if `Abortable` is `false`) or

```
Worker(Arg, index, GenHandle)
```

(if `Abortable` is `true`) to be executed in parallel for all values of `index` in the range `0 <= index < Range`. The processor that invokes `GenOnIFull`, and possibly other processors, is used to execute the tasks generated.

The routine `Init(Arg)` is called on each processor used to execute the tasks generated before the `Worker` routine is called for the first time on the processor. The routine `Final(Arg)` is called on each processor used to execute the tasks generated after the `Worker` routine is called for the last time on the processor. The `Limited` parameter is used to control the number of processors used by the generator. If `Limited` is `0` or `-1` there is no limitation on the number of processors; a positive value limits the processors used to that number or fewer.

When `GenOnIFull` returns, either all of the tasks generated have been completed, in which case `GenOnIFull` returns the value `genEXHAUSTED`, or if the `Abortable` parameter is `true`, the generator was aborted, and some of the tasks may not have been performed, in which case `GenOnIFull` returns the code passed to `AbortGen` when it was aborted.

- `GenOnILimited`

```
GenOnILimited(Worker, Range, MaxProcsToUse)
```

Limited version of `GenOnI`. `GenOnILimited` is equivalent to:

```
GenOnIFull(0, Worker, 0, 0, Range, MaxProcsToUse, false)
```

- GenOnIndex

```
GenOnIndex (Init, Worker, Arg, Range)
int (* Init)(), (* Worker)();
int Arg, Range;
```

Generates tasks that cause `Worker(Arg, index)` to be executed in parallel for all values of `index` in the range `0 <= index < Range`. The processor that invokes `GenOnIndex`, and possibly other processors, is used to execute the tasks generated. The routine `Init(Arg)` is called on each processor used to execute the tasks generated before the `Worker` routine is called for the first time on the processor. When `GenOnIndex` returns, all of the tasks generated have been completed.

- GenOnIndexA

```
GenOnIndexA(Init, Worker, Final, Arg, Range)
int (* Init)(), (* Worker)(), (* Final)();
int Arg, Range;
```

Generates tasks that cause `Worker(Arg, index)` to be executed in parallel for all values of `index` in the range `0 <= index < Range`. The processor that invokes `GenOnIndexA`, and possibly other processors, is used to execute the tasks generated. The routine `Init(Arg)` is called on each processor used to execute the tasks generated before the `Worker` routine is called for the first time on the processor. The routine `Final(Arg)` is called on each processor used to execute the tasks generated after the `Worker` routine is called for the last time on the processor. When `GenOnIndexA` returns, all of the tasks generated have been completed.

- GenTaskForEachProc

```
GenTaskForEachProc(Worker, Arg)
int (* Worker)();
int Arg;
```

Generates exactly one task of the form `Worker(Arg)` for every processor.

- GenTaskForEachProcLimited

```
GenTaskForEachProcLimited(Worker, Arg, NProcs)
int (* Worker)();
int Arg, NProcs;
```

Generates exactly one task of the form `Worker(Arg)` for each of `NProcs` processors.

Warning: If `ProcsInUse()` is less than `NProcs`, this call will hang.

- `GenTasksFromList`

```
GenTasksFromList(Routine_List, Arg_List, n)
int * (* RoutineList)();
int * Arg_List;
int n;
```

`Routine_List` is a list of n routines, `r1,...,rn`, and `Arg_List` is a list of n arguments, `arg1,...,argn`. `GenTasksFromList` generates n tasks, where the i'th task is of the form `ri(argi)`.

- `GetRtc`

```
GetRtc()
```

Returns the time since the system was booted in units of 62.5 microseconds.

- `InitializeUs`

```
InitializeUs()
```

Initializes the Uniform System. This includes creating and starting a Uniform System process on every available processor, setting up the memory that is globally shared among all Uniform System processes, and initializing the Uniform System storage allocator. `InitializeUs` must be called before any other Uniform System routine is used, and it should be called only once.

- `InitializeUsForBenchMark`

```
InitializeUsForBenchMark()
```

Initializes the Uniform System. Similar to `InitializeUs`, differing in that the King Node is used by the program if the program is started on a non-King node (via the `-on` switch of the `run` command or the `us` utility). This is useful when benchmarking a program, where it is desirable that the measurements not be affected by the processing requirements of the terminal handler and window manager that run on the King Node.

- LOCK

```
LOCK(lock, n)
short * lock;
int n;
```

Sets the lock specified by `lock`. The `short` pointed to by `lock` is assumed to have been initialized in the unset state to the value `0`. LOCK implements a "busy wait" type of lock. The `int` `n` specifies the time to wait in tens of microseconds between attempts to set the lock. Using zero for `n` forces use of a default that is about 1 millisecond. LOCK does not return until it has set the lock. (See UNLOCK.)

- MakeSharedVariables

```
MakeSharedVariables;
```

This is a macro. It allocates space in globally shared memory for variables declared as globally shared (via BEGIN_SHARED_DECL and END_SHARED_DECL) and makes the location of the variables known to other processors. MakeSharedVariables should be called after Initial-izeUs, and only if BEGIN_SHARED_DECL and END_SHARED_DECL are used.

- MemoriesAvailable

```
MemoriesAvailable()
```

Returns an integer that is the amount of memory available to the application program. The value returned is in units of 64 Kbytes.

- PhysProcToUsProc

```
PhysProcToUsProc(PhysProc)
int PhysProc;
```

Returns the Uniform System processor number corresponding to the physical processor number `PhysProc`.

- ProcsInUse

```
ProcsInUse()
```

Returns an integer that is the number of processors available to an application program. The value returned does not count any processors that have been removed by the `TimeTest` or `TimeTestFull` routines.

- SHARED

  SHARED is a macro.
  It is used as a prefix to access variables which have been declared as globally
  shared using `BEGIN_SHARED_DECL` and `END_SHARED_DECL`.
  For example, if N has been declared in this way, it may be referenced
  as `SHARED N`:

  ```
  SHARED N = SHARED N % 7;
  ```

  Warning: Before such a variable can be referenced, space for it must be allocated using `MakeSharedVariables`.

- Share

  ```
  Share(N)
  int * N;
  ```

  Passes the value pointed to by N to all processors used to execute tasks generated subsequently. N must point to a variable allocated in process private
  memory and declared to be a global or a static. In addition, the variable pointed
  to by N must be 4 bytes in size. Share causes the value pointed to by N (in
  the processor invoking Share at the time Share is invoked) to be copied into
  the location specified by N in each processor used to perform tasks generated by
  task generators activated subsequent to the call of Share.

- ShareBlk

  ```
  ShareBlk(X, size)
  int * X;
  int size;
  ```

  Passes the block of data of size bytes pointed to by X to all processors used
  to execute tasks generated subsequently. X must point to a variable allocated in
  process private memory and declared to be a global or a static. ShareBlk
  causes the block of data pointed to by X (in the processor invoking ShareBlk
  at the time ShareBlk is invoked) to be copied into the location beginning at
  X in each processor used to perform tasks generated by task generators activated
  subsequent to the call of ShareBlk.

- SharePtrAndBlk

```
SharePtrAndBlk(P, size)
int * * P;
int size;
```

Passes the pointer pointed to by P and the block of data of size bytes to which it points to all processors used to execute tasks generated subsequently. P must point to a pointer variable allocated in process private memory and declared to be a global or a static. SharePtrAndBlk causes a copy of the pointer pointed to by P and the block of data to which it points (in the processor invoking SharePtrAndBlk at the time SharePtrAndBlk is invoked) to be made for each processor used to perform tasks generated by task generators activated subsequent to the call of SharePtrAndBlk as follows: a block of storage is allocated in the memory of the processor, and the block of data pointed to by the pointer pointed to by P is copied into the newly allocated storage block; a pointer to the newly allocated storage block is stored in the location pointed to by P.

- ShareScatterMatrix

```
ShareScatterMatrix(P, nrows)
int * * * P;
int nrows;
```

P points to a global or static variable allocated by

```
AllocScatterMatrix(nrows, ncols, element_size)
```

ShareScatterMatrix makes a copy of the vector of row pointers allocated by AllocScatterMatrix in the memory of each processor used to execute tasks generated subsequently. It then sets the location pointed to by P to point to that copy. ShareScatterMatrix is functionally equivalent to SharePtrAndBlk, but operates much faster, since it is careful to make its copies from other copies as well as from the original.

- TimeTest

```
TimeTest(Init, Execute, PrintResults)
int (* Init)(), (* Execute)(), (* PrintResults)();
```

Times execution of the routine Execute on various processor configurations as specified by the user from the keyboard. TimeTest runs the routines Init, Execute, and PrintResults in sequence on each of the processor configurations specified. It times only the Execute routine and passes the execution time, the number of processors, and the effective number of processors to the specified `PrintResults` routine:

```
PrintResults(time, procs, effprocs)
int time, procs;
float effprocs;
```

The effective number of processors is a `float` equal to:

```
(time 1 proc) / (time n procs)
```

This is a good measure of the speedup the `Execute` routine achieves over one processor when n processors are used. If the first test run uses more than one (=k) processors, then the effective number of processors is

```
 k * (time k proc) / (time n procs)
```

The `PrintResults` routine is specified by the application program. The Uniform System Library contains a routine (see `TimeTestPrint` below) that can be used for this purpose, or users can supply their own routine.

`TimeTest` asks the user to specify the processor configurations to be used by specifying a `start` configuration, a step (`delta`), and an `end` configuration. The first run uses `start` processors, the next uses `start + delta` processors, and so forth, up to the final run, which uses `end` processors. If `start` (or `end`) is zero, the test is run from (to) the end of the range of available processors. In particular, it is run for the limiting processor case whether or not it is in the normal progression specified by `delta`. If `delta` is specified to be zero, the number of processors used increases by powers of two (1, 2, 4, 8, etc.). The rules for `start` and `end` still apply.

- `TimeTestFull`

```
TimeTestFull(Init, Execute, PrintResults, start, delta, end)
int (* Init)(), (* Execute)(), (* PrintResults)();
int start, delta, end;
```

`TimeTestFull` is similar to `TimeTest` (see above). It differs only in that it accepts the `start`, `delta`, and `end` parameters that specify the processor configurations to be timed, rather than asking for them from the keyboard. If the `delta` specified is negative, `TimeTestFull` asks the user to supply values for `start`, `delta`, and `end` at the start of the run.

- TimeTestPrint

  ```
  TimeTestPrint(runtime, procs, effprocs)
  int runtime, procs;
  float effprocs;
  ```

  Used with `TimeTest` or `TimeTestFull` to print the timing results for a particular processor configuration. It prints the execution time, the number of processors used, the effective number of processors used (= speedup achieved over 1 processor), and the efficiency with which processors were used for the given processor configuration. `TimeTestPrint` outputs this information in the format:

  ```
  [procs] time = runtime ticks = S sec; ep = effprocs;
  eff = E where E = effprocs / procs.
  ```

  (See `TimeTest` and `TimeTestFull`.)

- TotalProcsAvailable

  ```
  TotalProcsAvailable()
  ```

  Returns the total number of processors available to the application program. The value returned includes any processors that may have been removed by `TimeTest` or `TimeTestFull`.

- UNLOCK

  ```
  UNLOCK(lock)
  short * lock;
  ```

  Clears the lock specified by `lock`. (See LOCK.)

- UsProcToPhysProc

  ```
  UsProcToPhysProc(UsProc)
  int UsProc;
  ```

  Returns the physical processor number corresponding to the Uniform System processor number `UsProc`.

- UsSetClass

  ```
  UsSetClass(proc, class)
  int proc, class;
  ```

  Adds the memory of the specified Processor Node to the specified `class`. Initially all memories are in class `0`. See also `AllocateC`, `AllocScatterMatrixC`, `AllocateOnUsProcC`.

- UsWait

  ```
  UsWait(n)
  int n;
  ```

  Waits for `10*n` microseconds. Using zero for `n` forces use of a default value, which is about 1 millisecond. `UsWait` is a "busy wait".

- WaitForTasksToFinish

  ```
  WaitForTasksToFinish(GenHandle)
  UsGenDesc * GenHandle;
  ```

  Waits for the task generator specified by `GenHandle` to complete. `GenHandle` must specify an asynchronous generator activated by the calling process. `WaitForTasksToFinish` returns a value (the result code for the generator), which indicates whether the generator ran to completion or was aborted by `AbortGen`.

- WorkOn

  ```
  WorkOn(GenHandle)
  UsGenDesc * GenHandle;
  ```

  Works on tasks generated by the task generator specified by `GenHandle`. `GenHandle` must specify an asynchronous generator activated by the calling process. `WorkOn` returns a value (the result code for the generator), which indicates whether the generator ran to completion or was aborted by `AbortGen`.

Appendix C
CRAY X-MP

CONTENTS

C1. Pi Program Listing (V2)

```
1              REAL          SUM
2              INTEGER       TL(4), INTRVLS, NTASKS, TLOCK
3              COMMON SUM , TL ,INTRVLS , NTASKS , TLOCK
4              INTEGER       LSTAT
5              REAL          PI
6    C
7              INTEGER       ITC(3,4)
8              EXTERNAL TASK
9    C
10             CALL LINK('UNIT59=TTY//')
11             PI = 3.14159265358979323846433E0
12             CALL LOCKASGN (TLOCK,LSTAT)
13   C
14   C *** SET TASK CONTROL ARRAYS & START THE TASKS ***
15   C
16             DO 15 I = 1 , 4
17                 ITC(1,I) = 3
18   C            *** SET TASK NUMBER IN CONTROL ARRAY ***
19                 ITC(3,I) = I
20   15      CONTINUE
21   C
22   100     WRITE(59,*) 'ENTER INTERVALS & TASKS (UP TO 4) 0=>END'
23           READ (59,*,END = 10 , ERR = 10 ) INTRVLS,NTASKS
24           WRITE(59,*) ' INTERVALS = ', INTRVLS
25           WRITE(59,*) ' NUMBER OF TASKS = ', NTASKS
26           SUM = 0.0E0
27   C *** REPEAT UNTIL NO. OF INTERVALS = 0 ***
28           IF ( INTRVLS .EQ. 0 ) GO TO 999
29   C
30   C       *** GET STARTING WALL CLOCK TIME ***
31   C
32           ISTART = IRTC()
33   C
34   C       *** START ALL TASKS ***
35   C
36           DO 50 I = 1 , NTASKS
37               CALL TSKSTART ( ITC(1,I) , TASK )
38   50      CONTINUE
```

```
39   C        *** NOW WAIT ON EACH TASK ***
40            DO 60 I = 1 , NTASKS
41               CALL TSKWAIT ( ITC(1,I) )
42   60       CONTINUE
43   C
44   C        *** GET ENDING WALL CLOCK TIME ***
45            IEND = IRTC()
46   10       WRITE(59,*) ' TASKS COMPLETED '
47            WRITE(59,*) ' PI COMPUTED = ' , SUM
48            WRITE(59,*) ' ERROR AMOUNT = ', PI - SUM
49            WRITE(59,*) ' CPU TIME =', TL
50            WRITE(59,*) 'ELAPSED WALL CLOCK TIME = ', IEND - ISTART
51   C
52   C        *** GO GET NEXT INTRVLS AND NTASKS ***
53   C
54            GO TO 100
55   C
56   999      CONTINUE
57            CALL EXIT
58            END
59   C
60            SUBROUTINE TASK
61   C        *** TASKS 1-4 ***
62            REAL         SUM
63            INTEGER      TL(4), INTRVLS, NTASKS, TLOCK
64            COMMON SUM , TL ,INTRVLS , NTASKS , TLOCK
65   C
66            REAL         LSUM
67            INTEGER      ME1
68            INTEGER      TL1(3)
69   C
70            INTEGER      I
71            REAL         H , F , X
72            F(X) = 4.0E0 / ( 1.0E0 + X**2 )
73   C
74   C *** TASK ENTRY ***
75   C
76            CALL TSKVALUE (ME1)
77            H = 1.0E0 / INTRVLS
78            LSUM = 0.0E0
79            INTEND = INTRVLS / 2
80   C
```

```
81          DO 10 I = ME1, INTEND, NTASKS
82             LSUM = LSUM + F((I-0.50E0)*H) + F((I+INTEND-0.50E0)*H )
83   10     CONTINUE
84   C
85          LSUM = LSUM * H
86   C *** ADD RESULT TO SUM ***
87          CALL LOCKON (TLOCK)
88             SUM = SUM + LSUM
89          CALL LOCKOFF (TLOCK)
90   C
91          CALL TSKTIME ( TL1 , 3 )
92          TL(ME1) = TL1(1)
93          RETURN
94   C
95          END
```

C2.   Excerpts from "MPDOC—CTSS Multiprocessor Support"[†]

FUNCTION: MPDOC is a program reference manual that describes the multitasking environment a code is in when it executes. The multitasking environment includes compiler linkage protocols,
libraries, utilities, memory management, multitasking routines,
and operating system modifications needed to support multitasking.

AVAILABILITY: The CRAYs.

C2.1   INTRODUCTION

Multiprocessor architectures imply significant changes to software development procedures and concepts. Machines with small numbers of processors are available commercially; Machines with more processors are likely to be considered in the 1988-1990
time frame. Our problem was to develop software approaches that would efficiently
support increasing numbers of processors during this period. As a comparison, it took
over five years of active effort to develop software to efficiently support and utilize
vector technology. Multiprocessor support and utilization is significantly more difficult.

The target machine architectures that we are considering have multiple homogeneous processors sharing a single monolithic main memory. We are not considering
the support of a distributed processor environment at this time. It is expected that such
an architecture must also include machinery to guarantee exclusive access to shared data
and the ability for one processor to interrupt or halt any set of the remaining processors.
The software environment on such a machine will be the current uniprocessing software
environment with extensions to effectively utilize the machine.

Processors are most efficiently utilized when the cost of applying them to a user
code is small relative to the time spent there. Speedups obtained when this is true can
approach the number of processors. From a system point of view, assignment of the
available processors on a program-by-program basis to obtain higher overall throughput
represents the best guess in the absence of other information on how to most efficiently
utilize the processors. The modifications to the CTSS operating system necessary to
support a multiprocessor on this basis are few, and there are no other changes necessary
to the vast body of underlying software. The necessary work for this to be accomplished are now sketched briefly.

With a small number of processors, a job load consistently greater than or equal to
the number of processors, and a scheduling strategy biased towards throughput, the
opportunity to apply more than one processor to a program is small. This opportunity
occurs primarily with full or close to full memory jobs. However, we expect that the

---

[†]MPDOC describes Cray Time Sharing System (CTSS) support facilities for multitasking as implemented at the
National Magnetic Fusion Energy Computer Center (NMFECC). This version of MPDOC is dated February 13,
1986.

number of processors relative to the memory size will be increasing in the future so that the ability to apply multiple processors to a single program will become increasingly important. The changes necessary to the support software and to the application codes to do this are substantial. The design of this facility is the main thrust of this paper.

Providing for the support of multiprocessors necessitates cooperative planning among a number of heavily interdependent facilities. These include the system, compiler, libraries, memory managers, basic utilities, and application codes.

C2.2   TASK STRUCTURE

A task is a unit which is capable of being independently assigned a processor. All tasks of a program share the same memory area, but each task is allocated a private environment. The task structure consists of a stack and a task descriptor. These are allocated from the Heap when the task is created. The task descriptor includes a state save area, a standard pair of links to queue the task while it is waiting for any reason, a system call area, plus other information about the task. A task needs rapid access to its associated descriptor; hence, its method of access is necessarily dependent on the chosen linkage convention and stack design.

A standard queuing mechanism has been established and is used throughout so that this becomes a basic attribute of the task structure. The standard pair of queue links mentioned above are denoted `(TaskQp,TaskQn)` and are the absolute locations of the previous and next task's links (or queue head) respectively. Each queue of tasks has a head of queue constructed in the identical manner.

```
TaskQp(qhead)=TaskQn(qhead)=qhead
```

represents the empty state of all task queues. All task queues are doubly linked circular lists. Designers of multitasking support facilities are provided with standard queuing machinery that can be invoked any time a task wants to wait for any reason.

The Run Queue

The run queue (`RunQ`) is the queue of tasks that are ready to run but not currently assigned a processor. Tasks are added to this queue when they are first created or when the event they are waiting on occurs (e.g., system call completion, exclusive access granted, etc.). The head of the `RunQ` is located at an absolute location known to the system. This happens to be at absolute word 3 of the program. `RunQfp(3)=RunQbp(3)=3` when the `RunQ` is empty. It initially contains the root task that is set up by the loader.

Task Creation

The initial task is created by the loader (via the CTSS `LDR` command). Hence all programs consist initially of one and only one task. This and all subsequent tasks, however, may cause *any* number of other tasks to be created at any point during their lifetime. All coexisting tasks run logically in parallel and may in fact run in parallel at various intervals of the program's life. The amount of actual parallel calculation depends on the instantaneous machine loading, the physical number of processors, and whether the system finds multiple tasks to start when processors do become available.

The rapidity with which tasks can be created, terminated, and switched between are the primary factors that determine whether multiple tasks can be used effectively. Task creation and management require extra memory and CPU overhead. Hence use of fewer tasks can result in greater efficiency. Since no more tasks can actively compute than there are CPUs, two tasks are optimal on the CRAY X-MP/22 and four tasks on the CRAY-2. Creating many extra tasks serves no useful purpose.

The task creation algorithm is:

1. Allocate memory from the heap for a task descriptor.

2. Allocate memory from the heap for a stack.

3. Initialize the fields in the task descriptor.

4. Initialize the stack. This consists of inserting a dummy stack frame for TSKTERM to implicitly terminate the task if the task head executes a return.

5. Queue the new task descriptor on the RunQ for execution when a processor is available.

Task Switching

The ability to do a rapid task switch is one of the keys upon which a successful multiprocessing capability is built since the rapidity with which this can be done directly determines the extent to which a user is penalized for specifying parallelism. As discussed previously, we would like users to be able to specify a large amount of parallelism without worrying too much about the overhead of specifying more than can be realized by the actual number of processors. So while overhead still exists, it can be made cheap: it in fact costs only about as much as a normal subroutine call and return. The task-switching machinery described here is the heart of the multitasking capability.

A call to Q8WAIT[†] looks like any other call. Hence all context is in either memory or the B and T registers before the call to Q8WAIT. This includes all of the vector register context. Hence it is necessary only to save all of the Bs and all of the Ts upon entry in order to save the entire task state. The locks are well behaved due to the fact they protect only the linking convention, whose duration is very short. Hence all processors are eventually granted access within a finite (short) amount of time. Memory for the state save must be available on the stack regardless of linkage convention. With the current linkage convention, an overflow buffer is provided for the subroutine entry sequence. Hence the subroutine entry sequence and state save share this area and no extra memory is needed for the state save.

[†]The system interface routine Q8WAIT suspends the current task and starts another task (from the RunQ) if possible. If no user tasks are available on the RunQ, it executes an exchange to the operating system to give up the CPU. Q8WAIT is used internally by the multitasking library, MULTILIB, and is not called directly by user programs. (ed.)

If one attempts to disassociate the queuing logic from the context switch, race conditions and hazards can develop that can be overcome only by introducing more structure and complication into the queuing machinery. For example, if we had to adopted a convention that the caller would queue and then call `Q8WAIT` (with no arguments, that would simply save `B` and `T` registers to suspend), it would then be possible for the task to be dequeued before the switch was complete. To avoid this we would have had to include "can't take me" information that would be set while in the queuing critical region, unconditionally cleared by `Q8WAIT` after the state save, and checked on every attempt to dequeue. This would have unnecessarily complicated construction of all of the multitasking facilities. With the mechanism presented above, we have a tool with centralized complication upon which all other synchronization facilities can be cleanly built.

Most multiprocessor architectures have synchronization hardware based on memory (actual locks on memory cells, test-and-set on location, lock/unlock on location implemented as address cache or in the memory structure). The CRAY multiprocessor architectures have a few hardware semaphore bits that cannot be variably assigned. Hence it can be laborious to variably lock/unlock a hardware semaphore. However, our scheme must be targeted toward general multiprocessor architectures so that the implementation can be developed in a reasonably portable manner. Considering all multiprocessors, a single global semaphore approach is general enough.

Task Termination

The `TSKTERM` routine is responsible for task termination. Task termination results in the deallocation of all associated stack segments. Hence the disposal algorithm is designed so that it can deallocate all of its own memory.

Intertask Communication

All tasks of the same program share the same memory space. Hence, the most efficient method for one task to communicate with another is to use memory directly. The system neither supports nor prohibits message passing among tasks of the same program. If a task wants to communicate with another external to this program, it can do so by using the system's standard message facilities and include its own protocol within this message.

C2.3 MULTITASKING ROUTINES

The following multitasking routines were implemented by Cray Research Inc. (CRI). We have also implemented these with some changes and extensions. This facility is basically an experiment and hence needs wide support in order to benefit from the experience of others and to contribute our own.

1. Our naming convention is as follows:

   A. Names are eight characters in length or shorter.

   B. Names are of the form: `<prefix><mnemonic>`

C. The prefixes for the managers are as follows:

```
EV    :  Event Manager
LIB   :  Library Manager
LOCK  :  Lock Manager
MZ    :  Memory Manager
NZ    :  Interrupt Manager
$STK  :  Stack Manager
TSK   :  Task Manager
```

2. Where possible, we have followed CRI's naming conventions, calling sequences, and functionality. Extensions are implemented as separate routine calls.

3. Difficulties with CRI's CRAY X-MP multitasking conventions, and how NMFECC has fixed the problems:

   A. *ALTERNATE RETURN LABELS* may not be used because CIVIC[†] and CFT pass statement labels in different ways that are totally incompatible. Instead we return an integer variable indicating whether or not the routine was completed successfully.

   B. *LOGICAL FUNCTIONS and VALUES* are not used because CIVIC and CFT use different values for ".TRUE.". An integer function could have been implemented that returns 0 for .FALSE., and −1 for .TRUE., but instead we use a subroutine that returns an integer argument containing 0 or +1 to indicate the appropriate condition.

   C. A Fortran function must have a name that begins with a letter in the range I through N in order to make that function implicitly integer. Because of the naming conventions used, the EVENT and TASK manager functions would be implicitly real. This would have required that the user remember to explicitly declare each function in each subroutine that it is used in. Since that proved to be a major source of mistakes, it was decided to change all integer functions into subroutines that contain an additional integer argument used to return the value that was previously returned by the function.

C2.4   LOCK MANAGER

LOCKASGN - Create a New Lock Identifier

LOCKASGN creates a new lock to be used for synchronization. If the variable lockvar contains a valid lock identifier when LOCKASGN examines it, then the subroutine call acts as a no-op and returns with the value of lockvar unchanged. If it

---

[†]CIVIC is the compiler for LRLTRAN, an extended version of Fortran 77. CTSS and its utilities are written in LRLTRAN. (ed.)

does not, then a new lock is created and its ID is stored in `lockvar`. This subroutine must be called prior to the use of `lockvar` with any other lock routine.

Calling sequence[†]:

```
CALL LOCKASGN(lockvar,asgnstat)
```

lockvar   :=: An integer variable to contain the lock identifier.
asgnstat   :=   The status of the LOCKASGN subroutine call.

Notes:

1. asgnstat .EQ. 0   if a new lock was created and assigned by this call
             .EQ. 1   if `lockvar` already contained a valid lock identifier at the time of this call

2. The initial status of the lock is OFF (unlocked).

LOCKOFF - Clear a Lock

LOCKOFF clears a lock and returns control to the calling task. The act of clearing the lock may allow some other task to resume execution, but this is transparent to the task calling LOCKOFF.

Calling sequence:

```
CALL LOCKOFF (lockvar)
```

lockvar   :   an integer variable containing the lock identifier that is to be cleared

Notes:

1. It is a fatal error to try to clear a lock that this task did not set.

LOCKON - Set a Lock

LOCKON sets a lock and returns control to the calling task. If the lock is already set, the task is suspended until the lock is cleared by another task and can be set by this one. In either case, the lock is set by the task when it next resumes execution of user code.

When a lock is set, the task identifier of the task that set the lock is associated with the lock. This association is referred to as ownership of the lock, i.e., the owner of the lock is the task ID of the only task that may clear the lock (it set the lock, only it may clear the lock).

[†]In the argument descriptions, : means input only (read, not modified), := means output only (written, but not read), and :=: means both input and output.

Calling sequence:

```
CALL LOCKON (lockvar)
```

lockvar   :   an integer variable containing the lock identifier that is to be set

Notes:

1. It is a fatal error to attempt to doublelock a lock that this task has already set.

LOCKPARM - **Set the Lock Manager Parameters**

LOCKPARM changes the values of the parameters that control the execution of the lock manager.

Calling sequence:

```
CALL LOCKPARM(parmlist,numparm)
```

parmlist   :   an integer array containing the values of the parameters that are to be changed

numparm   :   the number of words/parameters being passed in the array parmlist—must be greater than zero

Notes:

1. If parmlist(i) = -2, then the parameter i is to be reset to its original default value.

2. If parmlist(i) = -1, then the value of parameter i is not to be changed from its current value.

3. The layout and meaning of the parameter list is as follows:

> parmlist(1) = The lock manager debug flag:
> = 0,   minimum argument checking is performed
> = 1,   maximum argument checking is performed
>
> parmlist(2) = initial number of lock descriptors to allocate when the first call to LOCKASGN is made
>
> parmlist(3) = the subsequent number of lock descriptors that are to be allocated when no more free lock descriptors remain and another one is needed to satisfy a call to LOCKASGN

4. The defaults for the lock manager parameters are as follows:

```
parmlist(1) = 1
parmlist(2) = 10
parmlist(3) = 10
```

LOCKREL - Release a Lock Identifier

LOCKREL releases the lock associated with the lock identifier. The lock variable containing the lock identifier is zeroed. If an attempt is then made to use the released lock variable, or a copy of the original lock identifier, an error results. The lock variable may be re-used following another call to LOCKASGN. Releasing a lock is equivalent to destroying it.

Calling sequence:

```
CALL LOCKREL (lockvar)
```

lockvar   :=: an integer variable containing the lock identifier—set to zero on return

Notes:

1. It is a fatal error to access a lock that has been released, i.e., to pass a lock identifier that has been released to another lock manager routine.

2. It is a fatal error to try to release a lock that is owned by another task.

3. It is a fatal error to try to release a lock upon which other tasks are currently waiting.

LOCKSET - Set a Lock

LOCKSET works in a similar way to LOCKON, except that it does not terminate with an error if the task attempts to set a lock that it already has set, and that it returns status information concerning the lock.

Calling sequence:

```
CALL LOCKSET (lockvar,lockstat,lockownr)
```

lockvar   :   an integer variable containing the lock identifier

lockstat   :=   the status of the lock at the instant that the CALL LOCKSET was made, either clear or set

```
.EQ.-1       the lock was owned by another task
.EQ. 0       the lock was previously clear
.EQ. 1       the lock was owned by this task
```

`lockownr`   := The task ID of the task that owns the lock at the instant that the CALL LOCKSET was made. If the lock is clear, then `lockownr = 0`.

Notes:

1. The values `lockstat` and `lockownr` are set after the lock has been set by this task, i.e., the lock `lockvar` also protects the arguments `lockstat` and `lockownr`.

LOCKSTAT - Get the Status of a Lock

LOCKSTAT returns the status of the specified lock. This includes whether the lock is set or clear, the task ID of the owner if the lock is set, and if tasks are waiting on the lock or not.

Calling sequence:

```
CALL LOCKSTAT(lockvar,statlock,lenstat,maxstat)
```

`lockvar`   :   an integer variable containing the lock identifier

`statlock` := an integer array to contain status information concerning the lock specified

`lenstat`   := the number of words contained in the `statlock` array

`maxstat`   :   the maximum number of words to return in `statlock`, which must be dimensioned at least `maxstat` words long

Notes:

1. The layout of `statlock` is as follows:

   ```
   statlock(1)  indicates whether the lock is set or clear
   statlock(2)  is the task ID of the owner, if any
   statlock(3)  indicates whether any other tasks are waiting for the
                lock to become available
   ```

2. The values returned in `statlock` are as follows:

   ```
   statlock(1)  = -1 if the lock is set by another task
                =  0 if the lock is clear
                =  1 if the lock is set by this task
   ```

```
statlock(2)  =  0  if the lock is clear
             =     task ID of the owner of the lock if the lock is
                   set
statlock(3)  =  0  if the lock is clear
             =  0  if the lock is set and no tasks are waiting on
                   the lock
             =  1  if the lock is set and one or more tasks are
                   waiting on the lock
```

LOCKTEST - Test and Set a Lock

LOCKTEST performs a test-and-set operation on the lock specified. The value of 0 is returned if the lock was set by this task, and a value of +1 is returned if the lock was set before the call to this routine. If the lock was previously clear, then it is set. No waiting is ever done by this routine.

Calling sequence:

```
CALL LOCKTEST(lockvar,lockstat)
```

lockvar   :   an integer variable containing the lock identifier. A lock identifier is made up of two parts: a unique lock identifier that is never re-used, and a lock descriptor index that points to the lock descriptor maintained by the lock manager.

lockstat   :=   The status of the lock identifier, either set/clear

         .EQ. 0   the lock was previously clear, it is now owned by this task

         .EQ. 1   the lock was owned by this or another task

Notes:

1. It is a fatal error to execute LOCKTEST on a lock which is owned by this task (see LOCKTSET).

LOCKTSET - Test and Set a Lock

LOCKTSET works in a similar way to LOCKTEST, except that it does terminate with an error if the task attempts to test a lock that it already has set, and that it returns additional status information concerning the lock.

Calling sequence:

```
CALL LOCKTSET(lockvar,lockstat,lockownr)
```

lockvar   :   an integer variable containing the lock identifier `lockstat` `:=`   the status of the lock identifier, either set/clear

> `.EQ.-1`   the lock was owned by another task
> `.EQ. 0`   the lock was previously clear
> `.EQ. 1`   the lock was owned by this task

`lockownr` `:=:`   the task ID of the task which owns the lock. If the lock is clear, then `lockownr = 0`.

Notes:

1. If the lock was owned by this task prior to the call, then `lockstat` is returned equal to 1 and `lockownr` is set equal to the task ID of this task (see `Q8TASKID`).

Lock Manager Errors

```
1  = Argument already contains a legal lock identifier
2  = Incorrect number of arguments passed to subroutine
3  = Address of argument is below 200 octal
4  = Address of argument is beyond field length (>FLL)
5  = Argument is not a valid lock identifier
6  = Argument which should contain a lock identifier instead contains
     either a legal event, library, or task identifier
7  = Argument does not contain a meaningful value
8  = An item in the parameter list does not contain a meaningful value
9  = Operation is invalid on lock that is currently owned
     by another task
10 = Operation is invalid when other tasks are waiting on the lock
11 = Free event/lock descriptor is not set up properly
12 = Attempt to double lock a lock which is already owned by this task
13 = Attempt to clear a lock which was not set by this task
14 = Attempt to clear a lock which is not set
15 = Address of task descriptor from RunQ is below 200 octal
16 = Address of task descriptor from RunQ is beyond field length (>FLL)
17 = Attempt to double lock the hardware semaphore
18 = Attempt to clear the hardware semaphore when it was not set
19 = MZEALLOC error, insufficient memory allocated for routine
20 = Illegal wait queue condition in lock descriptor
```

C2.5   EVENT MANAGER

EVASGN - Create a New Event Identifier

EVASGN creates a new event to be used for task signaling. If the variable `eventvar` contains a valid event identifier when EVASGN examines it, then the subroutine call acts as a no-op and returns with the value of `eventvar` left unchanged. If it does not, then a new event is created and its ID is stored in `eventvar`. This subroutine must be called prior to the use of `eventvar` with any other event manager subroutine.

Calling Sequence:

```
CALL EVASGN (eventvar,asgnstat)
```

`eventvar` :=: the integer variable that is to be assigned the new event's identifier

`asgnstat` :=   the integer status of the `EVASGN` subroutine call

Notes:

1. `asgnstat = 0` if a new event was created and assigned by this call
   `asgnstat = 1` if `eventvar` already contained a valid event identifier at the time of this call

2. The initial status of the event is CLEAR

EVCLEAR - **Clear an Event**

`EVCLEAR` clears an event and returns control to the calling task. In situations in which a single event is required (a simple signal), `EVCLEAR` should be called immediately after `EVWAIT` to note that the posting of the event has been detected. An event may be cleared any number of times by any task, regardless of when or by whom it was last posted.

Calling sequence:

```
CALL EVCLEAR (eventvar)
```

`eventvar` :   the integer event identifier to be cleared

EVPARM - **Set the Event Manager Parameters**

`EVPARM` sets a list of parameters used to control the execution of the event manager. The contents of the list have not yet been defined, but it may contain things like the initial number of event descriptors to allocate, the number to expand by when the event manager runs out, debug flags, etc.

Calling sequence:

```
CALL EVPARM (parmlist,numparm)
```

`parmlist` :   an integer array containing the values of the parameters which are to be changed

numparm   :   the number of words/parameters being passed in the array
                  parmlist—must be greater than zero

Notes:

1. If `parmlist(i) = -2`, then the parameter i is to be reset to its original
   default value.

2. If `parmlist(i) = -1`, then the value of parameter i is not to be changed
   from its current value.

3. The layout and meaning of the parameter list are as follows:

   parmlist(1) =   event manager debug flag
              = 0, disable the event manager debugger
              = 1, enable the event manager debugger

4. The defaults for the event manager parameters are as follows:

   parmlist(1) = 1,   enable the event manager debugger

EVPOSCLR - Post and Then Clear an Event

EVPOSCLR performs a POST/CLEAR operation, one immediately after the other. All
tasks waiting on the event resume execution.
   Calling sequence:

       CALL EVPOSCLR (eventvar)

   eventvar   :   the event identifier of the event to be posted and then cleared

EVPOST - Post an Event

EVPOST posts an event and returns control to the calling task. The act of posting the
event causes all tasks waiting on that event to resume execution. An event may be
posted any number of times by any task, regardless of when or by whom it was last
cleared.
   Calling sequence:

       CALL EVPOST (eventvar)

   eventvar   :   the integer event identifier of the event to be posted

EVREL - Release an Event Identifier

EVREL releases the event associated with the event identifier. The event variable containing the event identifier is zeroed. If an attempt is then made to use the released
event variable, or a copy of the original event identifier, an error results. The event

variable may be re-used following another call to `EVASGN`. Releasing the event is equivalent to destroying it. It is a fatal error to release an event for which other tasks are waiting, or to access an event which has been released.

Calling sequence:

```
CALL EVREL (eventvar)
```

`eventvar` `:=:` the event identifier that is to be released. After the call, `eventvar` contains a zero value.

Notes:

1. It is illegal to release an event while tasks are waiting on it.

`EVSTAT` - Get the Status of an Event

`EVSTAT` returns the status of the specified event. This includes whether the event is posted or cleared, the task ID of the task that last changed the status, and if tasks are waiting on the event or not.

Calling sequence:

```
CALL EVSTAT (eventvar,statevnt,lenstat,maxstat)
```

`eventvar` `:` the integer event identifier of the event whose status is desired

`statevnt` `:=` an integer array to contain status information concerning the event specified

`lenstat` `:=` the number of words returned in the `statevnt` array

`maxstat` `:` the maximum number of words to return in `statevnt`— `statevnt` should be dimensioned at least `maxstat` words in length

Notes:

1. The layout and values of `statevnt` are as follows:

    `statevnt(1)` indicates whether the event is posted or cleared
      `= 0` if posted
      `= 1` if cleared (have to wait when `EVWAIT` is called)
        `statevnt(2)` is the task ID of the task that last called `EVPOST` or `EVCLEAR` for this event

    `statevnt(3)` `= 0` if the event is posted (then no tasks are waiting)
      `= 0` if the event is cleared and no tasks are waiting on the event
      `= 1` if the event is cleared and tasks are waiting on the event

EVTEST - **Test an Event State**

EVTEST returns information concerning the state (posted/cleared) of the specified event.
   Calling sequence:

```
CALL EVTEST (eventvar,evntstat)
```

eventvar   :   the event identifier of the event to test

evntstat   :=:   the integer variable to contain the status of the specified event,
                 either posted or cleared

Notes:

   1. evntstat = 0 if the event is posted
      evntstat = 1 if the event is cleared

EVWAIT - **Wait for the Event to be Posted**

EVWAIT waits until the specified event is posted. If the event is already posted, the
task continues execution without waiting.
   Calling sequence:

```
CALL EVWAIT (eventvar)
```

eventvar   :   the event identifier of the event to wait for

Event Manager Errors

   1 = Argument already contains a legal event identifier
   2 = Incorrect number of arguments passed to subroutine
   3 = Address of argument is below 200 octal
   4 = Address of argument is beyond field length (>FLL)
   5 = Argument is not a valid event identifier
   6 = Argument which should contain a event identifier instead contains
       either a legal library, lock, or task identifier
   7 = Argument does not contain a meaningful value
   8 = An item in the parameter list does not contain a meaningful value
   9 = Event descriptor is in an impossible state,
       tasks are waiting on an event which is posted
  10 = Operation is invalid when other tasks are waiting on the event
  11 = Free event descriptor is not set up properly

C2.6   TASK MANAGER

TSKPARM - **Set the Task Manager Parameters**

TSKPARM sets a list of parameters used to control the execution of the task manager. The contents of the list have not yet been defined, but it may contain things like the initial number of task descriptors to allocate, the number to expand by when the task manager runs out, debug flags, initial stack segment size, subsequent stack segment size, maximum number of arguments, etc.

Calling sequence:

```
CALL TSKPARM (parmlist,numparm)
```

parmlist   :   an integer array containing the values of the parameters that are to be changed

numparm   :   the number of words/parameters being passed in the array parmlist—must be greater than zero

Notes:

1. If parmlist(i) = -2, then the parameter i is to be reset to its original default value.

2. If parmlist(i) = -1, then the value of parameter i is not to be changed from its current value.

3. The layout and meaning of the parameter list variables are as follows:

```
parmlist(1) = task manager debug flag (0=off, 1=on)
parmlist(2) = unused
parmlist(3) = unused
parmlist(4) = word/parcel address check mode = "PARCEL" or
              "WORD"
parmlist(5) = initial stack segment size
parmlist(6) = default subsequent stack segmentation size
parmlist(7) = task descriptor disposal method during task termina-
              tion
parmlist(8) = maximum number of arguments to TSKSTART
```

The values in parmlist 5 and 6 are overridden if the Task Common Table, $TASKCOM, is present, and these values are defined therein.

4. The defaults for the task manager parameters are as follows:

```
parmlist(1) = 1
parmlist(2) = N/A
parmlist(3) = N/A
parmlist(4) = "WORD     "
```

```
parmlist(5) = 2500B
parmlist(6) = 2500B
parmlist(7) = 0
parmlist(8) = 100
```

TSKSTART - Create and Start a New Task

To create, initialize, and start a new task at the specified subroutine entry point with the specified optional argument list. TSKSTART creates a new task. A call to TSKSTART is identical to CALL SUBENTPT(subargs) except that SUBENTPT is executed as a new task instead of as a subroutine, and when SUBENTPT returns, the new task terminates instead of the execution resuming after the call. Abnormal or alternate returns are not allowed across the task boundary.

Calling sequence:

```
CALL TSKSTART (tkcontrl,subentpt[,subargs])
```

tkcontrl :=: the integer Task Control Array. This array must be built by the calling program. At a minimum, the array must be two words in length. A third word can be optionally included. At a later date, additional words may be defined, but these are also be optional, thereby allowing existing codes to continue to run.

subentpt : the external entry point at which task execution is to begin. This name must be declared EXTERNAL in the routine calling TSKSTART. NOTE: CFT does not allow a subroutine to use its own name in this parameter.

subargs : optional list of arguments to be passed to the subroutine specified by subentpt when the new task begins execution. The arguments MUST not be literals (e.g., 1) or expressions (e.g., x*y)(see Note 2). Alternate returns are not allowed across task boundaries. If one of the arguments is to be an entry point address of a subroutine or function, then TSKPARMS must be called before TSKSTART, in order to insure that proper address checking is performed.

Notes:

1. The current task control array structure is as follows:

    tkcontrl(1) : the integer length, in words, of the task control array. This value must be either 2 or 3, depending on the optional use of task value. This value must be set by the calling task before the call to this subroutine is made.

tkcontrl(2) :=   the task descriptor identifier, assigned by the task manager when a task is created. This identifier uniquely identifies the task among all the tasks that may be created by this program.

tkcontrl(3) :   the task value (optional). This value is set to any value by the caller before creating the task. If task value is used, tkcontrl(1) must be set to a value of 3. The task value can be used for any purpose. A suggested use for this value includes a pointer to the task local storage area. During execution, a task may retrieve its own task value by calling TSKVALUE. A task may also retrieve another active task's task value by using TSKINFO.

2. Literals and expressions are represented by compiler temporaries and may disappear before the task actually runs.

TSKSTAT - Get the Status of a Task

TSKSTAT returns the desired amount of information about a specified task. The contents of this list have not yet been defined, however, it will probably contain information about the task state, task control words, task information block address, etc.

Calling sequence:

```
CALL TSKSTAT (tkcontrl,stattask,lentstat,maxstat)
```

tkcontrl :   the integer task control array from TSKSTART

stattask :=   an integer array to contain status information concerning the task specified

lenstat   :=   the number of words returned in the stattask array

maxstat   :   the maximum number of words to return in stattask— stattask should be dimensioned at least maxstat words long

TSKTERM - Terminate This Task, But Not the Code

TSKTERM may be either called implicitly or explicitly. If the subroutine specified in the argument list of TSKSTART executes a RETURN statement, it implicitly calls TSKTERM. A task may also explicitly call TSKTERM at any point within the tasks execution. TSKTERM terminates the task that calls it without terminating the code. Any tasks waiting for this task to terminate are allowed to resume execution (see TSKWAIT).

Calling sequence:

```
CALL TSKTERM
```

TSKTEST - **Test to See If a Task Has Terminated Yet**

TSKTEST tests to see whether the specified task has terminated yet.
   Calling sequence:

```
CALL TSKTEST (tkcontrl,taskstat)
```

tkcontrl   :   the integer task control array from TSKSTART

taskstat   :=   An integer variable whose value on return indicates whether the task was terminating/terminated at the instant that the CALL TSKTEST was made. If taskstat = 0, then the task no longer exists. If taskstat = 1, then the task has not terminated yet.

Notes:

1. It is an error to CALL TSKTEST with an illegal or never created task identifier in the task control array, i.e., tkcontrl(2), has to contain a value returned from some call to TSKSTART.

TSKTIME - **Return Task Timing Information**

TSKTIME returns the timing information of the calling task. This information includes total CPU, system, and I/O time.
   Calling sequence:

```
CALL TSKTIME (timelist,timelen)
```

timelist   :=   the integer array to hold the timing information

timelen   :   the number of words of timing information to return

Notes:

1. timelist is laid out as follows:

   timelist(1) =   total task CPU time in the same units as the real-time clock in machine cycles (12.5 nanoseconds for the CRAY-1 and 9.5 nanoseconds for the CRAY X-MP)
   timelist(2) =   total task I/O time
   timelist(3) =   total task system time

2. timelist should be dimensioned to be at least timelen words in length.

TSKVALUE - Get the Calling Task's Task Value Word

TSKVALUE retrieves the 64-bit word passed into the TSKSTART routine as the third word of the task control array for this task's creation. This word may be used for any single word value that the user desires. Common usages are things like a pointer to a task's work area or shared area.

Calling sequence:

```
CALL TSKVALUE (taskval)
```

taskval   :=   the 64-bit word that is to contain this task's task value word

TSKWAIT - Wait for a Task to Terminate

TSKWAIT causes this task to suspend execution and wait until the specified task has terminated. If the task has already terminated, then the execution of this task resumes immediately.

Calling sequence:

```
CALL TSKWAIT (tkcontrl)
```

tkcontrl   :   the integer task control array as set up by TSKSTART

Task Manager Errors

1 = User has over written task manager COMMON TASK_COM
2 = Wrong number of arguments to task manager routine
3 = Address of argument < 200B
4 = Address of argument > field length (FLL)
5 = Argument is not a valid task identifier
6 = Argument which should contain a task identifier, instead contains either a legal event, library, or lock identifier
7 = Argument does not contain a meaningful value
8 = An item in the parameter list does not contain a meaningful value
9 = Free task descriptor integrity error, check words invalid
10 = Free task descriptor stack size not large enough to handle number of subroutine arguments in call to TSKSTART
11 = Free task descriptor is not set up properly, TKDESCID <> "FREEDESC"
12 = Task control array length is invalid (< 2 or > 3)
13 = TSKWAIT called to wait on calling task's task identifier
14 = Error creating new (free) task descriptors in TSKSTART / TSK_XPN
15 = Parcel address of subroutine is not on a word boundary
16 = Cannot set task parameter MMSTKLEN after first call to TSKSTART
17 = Task parameter MMSTKLEN cannot exceed any stack segment's size
18 = Error return from system call

19 = Free task descriptor size is incorrect
20 = Summation of task common sizes referenced by this task does not match the sum specified in the `$TASKCOM` template (loader integrity error detected)
21 = Internal discrepancy detected, notify the consultants

Appendix D
FPS T Series

CONTENTS

D1.   Pi Program Listing

```
1     -- source code
2    DEF one  =  TABLE[#00000000,#3FF00000]:
3    DEF half = TABLE[#00000000,#3FE00000]:
4    DEF four = TABLE[#00000000,#40100000]:
5    DEF pi   =  TABLE[#54442D18,#400921FB]:
6    VAR ftemp[2],temp,ntemp,xwrd,xn[2]:
7    VAR h[2],a[2],b[2],sum[2],new[2]:
8    VAR nt,np,npp,ns,lnsp,vlen,xoffs[2]:
9    VAR xa,x2a,xb,x2b:
10   VAR begin,mid1,mid2,mid3,end:
11   VAR elap1,elap2,elap3,elap4:
12   VAR h.adrs,xoffs.adrs,xn.adrs:
13   VAR sum.adrs,new.adrs,one.adrs:
14   SEQ
15     -- define addresses
16     addr.v(h,h.adrs)
17     addr.v(xoffs,xoffs.adrs)
18     addr.v(xn,xn.adrs)
19     addr.v(sum,sum.adrs)
20     addr.v(new,new.adrs)
21     addr.v(one,one.adrs)
22     -- report value of pi
23     IF
24       (processor=0)
25         SEQ
26           rel.control
27           hkeep(status)
28           hwrite.string(" True value for PI is   ",0,
29                     processor,status)
30           ct.hwrite.real64(pi,2,20,0,processor,status)
31           hwriteln(0,processor,status)
32           hwriteln(0,processor,status)
33           hrelease(status)
34           get.control
35       TRUE
36         SKIP
37     -- define x at BankA,B1 boundaries
38     xa := VP.BankA
39     xb := VP.BankB1
```

```
40      -- sync all processors for timing run
41      SEQ j=[0 FOR 5]
42        SEQ i = [1 FOR dimension]
43          set.links(i,-1,-1,-1)
44      release.links
45      TIME? begin
46      -- partition domain
47      np := 1<<dimension   --     number of processors = 2^dim
48      vlen := 128          --     original vector length = slice
49      lnsp := 7            --     lnsp = log2(ns)
50      ns := 1<<lnsp        --     number of slices ns = 2^lnsp
51      nt := np*ns*128      --     total quad points (2^14 per processor)
52      npp := nt/np         --     quad points per processor
53      -- specify interval [a,b]
54      a[0] := 0
55      a[1] := 0
56      b[0] := one[0]
57      b[1] := one[1]
58
59      -- compute h := (b-a)/nt
60      --              ftemp := float(nt)
61      IntegerToDReal(ftemp,nt)
62
63      --              h := b-a
64      DRealOp(h,b,Sub,a)
65
66      --              h := (b-a)/nt
67      DRealOp(h,h,Div,ftemp)
68      -- x[i] := xoffs + h*i
69
70      --              xoffs = a + (p*npp+0.5)*h
71
72      ntemp := processor*npp
73      IntegerToDReal(ftemp,ntemp)
74      DRealOp(ftemp,ftemp,Add,half)
75      DRealOp(xoffs,ftemp,Mul,h)
76      xwrd := (xa>>2)
77      SEQ i = [0 FOR vlen]
78        SEQ
79          PUTWORD(i,xwrd)
80          PUTWORD(0,xwrd+1)
81          xwrd := xwrd+2
```

```
82    --            float sequence of integers & add offsets
83    GN.VO(xa,AF.Xfloat,xa,VP.null,vlen)              -- float i
84    GN.SVO(h.adrs,xa,MF.XYmul,xa,VP.null,vlen)    -- h*i
85    GN.SVO(xoffs.adrs,xa,AF.XYadd,xa,xb,vlen)      -- h*i+xoff
86
87    --            xn=float(vlen)*h
88    IntegerToDReal(ftemp,vlen)
89    DRealOp(xn,ftemp,Mul,h)
90    TIME? mid1
91    --            vlen,xn and xi doubled lnsp times
92
93    SEQ j=[1 FOR lnsp]
94      SEQ
95        x2a := xa+(vlen*8)
96        x2b := xb+(vlen*8)
97        GN.VSO(xa,xn.adrs,AF.XYadd,x2a,x2b,vlen)
98        DRealOp(xn,xn,Add,xn)
99        vlen :=vlen+vlen
100   --            store x in both A and B banks
101   TIME? mid2
102   -- compute sum over ns slices
103   --            1+x(i)*x(i)
104   GN.VVOSO(xa,xb,MF.XYmul,one.adrs,AF.XYadd,xb,VP.null,vlen)
105   SN.VRECIP(xb,1,xb,1,vlen)
106   GN.VRO(xb,AF.XYadd,sum.adrs,vlen)
107   TIME? mid3
108   -- communicate and collapse sums over processors
109
110   rel.control
111   set.links(1,2,3,4)
112
113   SEQ i= [1 FOR dimension]
114     SEQ
115   --                    exchange sums
116       PAR
117         byte.slice.output(i,sum.adrs,8)
118         byte.slice.input(i,new.adrs,8)
119
120   --                    accumulate sums
121       DRealOp(sum,sum,Add,new)
122
```

```
123    release.links
124    -- compute sum := sum*4*h
125    DRealOp(sum,sum,Mul,four)
126    DRealOp(sum,sum,Mul,h)
127    TIME? end
128
129    -- output results
130    elap1 := mid1-begin
131    elap2 := mid2-begin
132    elap3 := mid3-begin
133    elap4 := end-begin
134    hkeep(status)
135    hwrite.string(" Est. value for PI is  ",0,processor,status)
136    ct.hwrite.real64(sum,2,20,0,processor,status)
137    hwrite.string("   on processor ",0,processor,status)
138    hwrite.int(processor,0,processor,status)
139    hwriteln(0,processor,status)
140    hwrite.string("Elapsed times:float;gen.pts;sum pts;comm ",0,
141              processor,status)
142    hwriteln(0,processor,status)
143    hwrite.int(elap1,0,processor,status)
144    hwrite.string("   ",0,processor,status)
145    hwrite.int(elap2,0,processor,status)
146    hwrite.string("   ",0,processor,status)
147    hwrite.int(elap3,0,processor,status)
148    hwrite.string("   ",0,processor,status)
149    hwrite.int(elap4,0,processor,status)
150    hwrite.string("   ",0,processor,status)
151    hwriteln(0,processor,status)
152    hwrite.string(" total # pts, nt= ",0,processor,status)
153    hwrite.int(nt,0,processor,status)
154    hrelease(status)
155    get.control
```

D2.   "T Series Overview"[†]

Richard K. Helm and Phillip C. Miller

D2.1   INTRODUCTION

Overview

The FPS T Series is a massively parallel computer architecture organized in a hyper-cube configuration. The system is attached to a front-end computer which provides facilities for program development and system control. System control functions are characterized by application program loading and system initialization.

Hardware

Fig. D2.1 depicts the configuration for a T Series T-40 model computer. The basic unit of the T Series is a node, known more formally as a Vector Board. A Vector Board is essentially a single-board array processor. It includes an Inmos T414 Transputer, a Vector Processing Unit (VPU), and main memory.

The Inmos T414 Transputer is the control unit of the Vector Board. It controls the VPU and handles all communications between the VPU and external devices. The VPU is the vector arithmetic unit of a node containing a single adder and multiplier and four

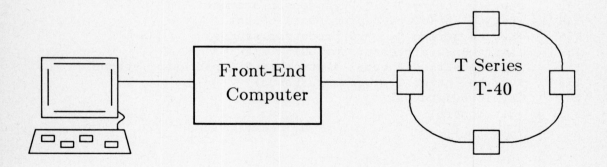

Figure D2.1   Release A00 configuration.

[†]This appendix is a condensed version of the following FPS manuals: "Programming the FPS T Series: Program Development Guide", (Release B), FPS Order No. 860-0001-003; "Programming the FPS T Series: System Services Reference Manual", (Release B), FPS Order No. 860-0001-004A; "Programming the FPS T Series: Math Library Manual", (Release B), FPS Order No. 860-0001-008B. Reprinted by permission of Floating Point Systems, Inc.

shift registers. Main memory for the Vector Board consists of four banks of 64K words each. The Transputer has direct access to each bank of main memory, whereas the VPU has access to memory via the shift registers.

A Module is the basic building block of the T Series. It consists of eight Vector Boards, a System Board containing an Inmos T414 Transputer, and a System Disk. Fig. D2.2 shows the components of a module.

Two networks are used to connect the T Series: the system network and the hyper-cube network. The system network is used by the operating system and connects

- An FEC to a System Board for external communications
- System Boards to other System Boards for ring communications
- A System Board to its 8 Vector Boards for ray communications

Fig. D2.3 depicts the system network connections in a T Series.

Software

FPS T Series software is categorized according to the main hardware components of the machine. Software components of the T Series include the following:

- Front-End Computer software;
- System Board software; and
- Vector Board software.

Front-End Computer software consists of program development tools supporting the Inmos occam programming language and FEC software libraries to support the interface to the T Series computer. Tools provided by Inmos are the Occam Programming System (OPS), and the Transputer Development System (TDS).

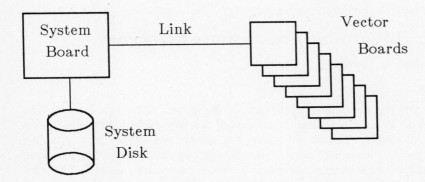

Figure D2.2   Components of a module.

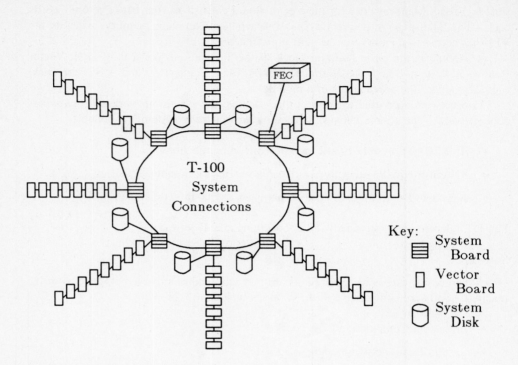

Figure D2.3   System network connections.

System Board software consists of an operating system capable of managing file resources, system communication, and communication between Vector Boards and the FEC.

Vector Board software provides vector arithmetic operations, data transfers to and from the System Disk, RS232 UART communication, and hypercube communication. Fig. D2.4 is a block diagram of the software for the T Series release.

D2.2   FRONT-END COMPUTER PROGRAMMING ENVIRONMENT

Occam Programming Tools

Occam language

Occam is the primary development language of the Inmos Transputer family. The development of occam centers around the concept of describing a system as a collection of concurrent processes. Occam programs are constructed using three primitive processes: assignment, input, and output. Occam processes can be combined to form sequential, parallel, or alternative constructs. Interprocess communication and synchronization are achieved through the use of occam channels.

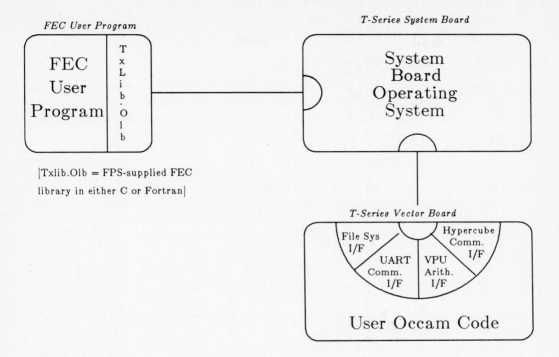

FEC User Program

T-Series System Board

[Txlib.Olb = FPS-supplied FEC
library in either C or Fortran]

T-Series Vector Board

Figure D2.4   T Series software.

Occam Programming System

The Occam Programming System (OPS) is an occam programming environment developed by the Inmos Corporation. The OPS enables the programmer to create and compile occam source code which will execute on the Front-End Computer. It should be noted that the OPS does not produce code which is executable on the T Series. That is the function of the Transputer Development System (TDS). The major functions of the OPS are:

- Editing occam source programs;

- Syntax checking of occam source code;

- Compilation of occam source code; and

- Simulation of occam programs on the Front-End Computer.

Transputer Development System

The Transputer Development System (TDS) is an occam programming environment developed by the Inmos Corporation for the purpose of creating occam programs which execute on Transputers. The TDS operations are almost identical to those of the Occam

Programming System (OPS), with the added support for the occam PLACED PAR, PROCESSOR, and PLACE AT specifiers; these allow occam processes to be "mapped" onto the T Series Vector Boards.

Front End Computer Programming Tools

A simple operating system, the T Series Session Executive (TSE), is provided for running programs and maintaining the runtime environment. This is a useful tool for running the most common class of programs. For more specialized applications, the user has Fortran and C access to the services of the T Series operating system.

T Series Session Executive

The TSE executes on the Front-End Computer system and allows the user to interactively control the execution of T Series programs. Commands in the T Series Command Language may be used to control the execution of T Series programs. The following commands are provided in TCL.

LOGIN	Allocates a T Series system
LOGOUT	Releases a T Series system
RUN	Runs a program on the assigned T Series system
SHOW	Shows the date and time
COPY	Copies files from (to) FEC to (from) T Series system node disk
DELETE	Deletes a file from a T Series system node disk
RENAME	Changes the name of a file on a T Series system node disk
DIRECTORY	Lists the directory of a T Series system node disk
QUIT	Ends a TSE session

TSM session subroutines

The T Series Service Module provides the services of the T Series operating system within the Fortran and C environments. Programmers may use the TSM software to develop customized FEC-resident control programs for T Series applications. Some of the services include:

- Acquiring (logging into) the T Series;
- Starting and stopping T Series programs;
- Communications with T Series vector nodes;

- File utilities for the System Disk;

- Conversion between FEC and T Series data types; and

- Conversion of error codes to error messages.

D2.3   T SERIES SOFTWARE

The user programs T Series vector nodes using the occam language and a library of math routines, communications routines, and system service routines. The user writes a program using the vector board programming template and these system and math libraries, all described below.

Vector Board Programming Template

Included with the release software for the T Series computer is a prefabricated template program which contains all software libraries needed to program the Vector Boards in a T Series computer. Within this example program is an area known as the "UserProcess" area in which the user may insert code for execution on the T Series.

Vector Programming Unit Software

The user can choose from several levels of math library routines. At the highest level, the user can call subroutines which distribute computation all over the system, automatically communicating partial results between nodes.

Toward the middle level, the user can perform operations on local data sets independently of other nodes. Interprocessor communications may be introduced by the user. Disk file operations may also be performed to system node disks.

At the lower levels, the user can program in what amounts to a vector assembler language. Here the user can program the vector hardware, with operations performed on "slices" of data in vector registers and banks of memory.

Although the user has fairly explicit control over the vector hardware and communications paths, it is worth pointing out that the user does not have to resort to microcoding the vector hardware.

D2.4   DEFINITION OF TERMS

Bank A

256 Kbyte main memory component consisting of one sub-bank labeled `sub-bank 3`.

Bank B

768 Kbyte main memory component consisting of three sub-banks labeled `sub-bank 0`, `sub-bank 1`, and `sub-bank 2`.

Byte Address

Integer value indicating a main memory location where main memory is considered a collection of 8-bit elements.

External Communication

Communications between the Front-End Computer and a System Board.

FEC

Front-End Computer. Used to perform program development, applications program downloading to the T Series, and applications program data transfers to the System Disks.

Hypercube

A point-to-point interconnection scheme used to describe the inter-Vector Board connections in a T Series computer. The Vector Board interconnects can be visualized as an n-dimensional cube in Cartesian n-Space, whose corners and edges respectively represent the Vector Boards, and the hypercube communications interconnect.

Hypercube Network

A Vector Board to Vector Board communications network used by application programs. Each Vector Board has N nearest-neighbor serial link connections in a T Series configuration of N-cube topology.

Link

Transputer serial link connection providing concurrent message passing capability between Vector Boards.

Main Memory

The 1 Megabyte dynamic storage component of a Vector Board; Main Memory is partitioned into 2 Banks, A and B, and is referenced as four sub-banks, 0 through 3.

Module

A term given eight Vector Boards connected to a T Series System Board and System Disk. As a minimum hardware configuration, a Module represents a T Series T-10 model computer.

n-Cube

A T Series hypercube containing 2 to the nth power Vector Boards.

Node

Vector Board.

Occam

The primary programming language of the T Series computer.

OPS

The Inmos Occam Programming System (OPS). The OPS is an occam program development tool which executes on the Front-End Computer (FEC). The OPS contains a simulator which can be used to develop and test programs in the Front-End Computer environment.

Ray Communications

Communications within a Module between a System Board and its eight Vector Boards.

Ring Communications

Communications between System Boards arranged in a ring topology.

Shift Register

The term given to the registers within the VPU component of a Vector Board. Each Shift Register is used for transferring and manipulating data between Vector Board main memory and the VPU arithmetic components.

Sub-bank

Term given a 256 Kilobyte segment of main memory. Four sub-banks comprise the total main memory.

System Board

The part of a T Series Module performing communications and data transfer between its 8 attached Vector Boards, an attached Front-End Computer, and to adjacent System Boards. Each System Board also acts as an interface to an attached disk controller. The disk interface capability is used for Vector Board mass storage via the T Series File System, and storage of the T Series System Board operating system software.

System Network

A T Series low-bandwidth communications network functionally composed of three communications sub-networks which are classified as External Communication, Ray Communication and Ring Communication. The System Network is used for system communication between Front-End Computers and System Boards, System Boards and their attached nodes, and from each System Board to any adjacent System Boards.

System Ring

The term given to the portion of the System Network consisting of System Boards configured in a ring topology.

TDS

The Inmos Transputer Development System (TDS). The TDS is an occam program development tool which executes on the Front-End Computer. The TDS is used to develop programs for execution within a T Series computer.

Transputer

The Inmos T414 Microprocessor that is used as the control processor within a Vector Board.

Vector Board

The basic processing element of a hypercube. A Vector Board consists of a Vector Processing Unit (VPU), an Inmos T414 Transputer, 1 Megabyte of Main Memory, and 16 multiplexed external Hypercube Network links. Also referred to as a node.

Vector Form

User interface to the microcoded functions of the Vector Board VPU.

VPU

Vector Processing Unit. The arithmetic component of a Vector Board which performs high-speed vector calculations.

Word

Four bytes.

Word Address

Integer value indicating a main memory location where main memory is considered a collection of 32-bit elements.

Appendix E
IBM 3090

CONTENTS

E1. Pi Program Listing—EPEX Preprocessor Input

```
1              IMPLICIT DOUBLE PRECISION (A-H,O-Z)
2              REAL*16 PI
3              DIMENSION T1(3), TIME(3)
4              @SHARED/COMM/ SUMALL
5              F(X) = 4.D0/(1.D0+X*X)
6              PI   = 4.Q0*QATAN(1.Q0)
7              READ(5,*) INTRVL
8              CALL FCLOC(T1)
9              @SERIAL BEGIN
10                 SUMALL = 0.D0
11             @SERIAL END
12             WIDTH = 1.D0/INTRVL
13             SUM = 0.D0
14             @DO 100 IC = 1, INTRVL, CHUNK = 1000
15                 SUM = SUM + WIDTH * F( (IC - 0.5D0) * WIDTH )
16      100    @ENDDO NOWAIT
17             T = DFNA(SUMALL, SUM)
18             CALL FCLOC(TIME)
19             DO 200 I = 1, 3
20                TIME(I) = 1.D-6*(TIME(I)-T1(I))
21      200    CONTINUE
22             ERR = SUMALL - PI
23             WRITE(6,'(A,F25.15,1.PD15.3)') 'SUMALL, ERR =', SUMALL, ERR
24             WRITE(6,'(A,3F10.4)') 'TIME =', TIME
25             END
```

E2.   Pi Program Listing—EPEX Preprocessor Output

```
 1   C            *** Processed by the VM/EPEX preprocessor ***
 2   C
 3            IMPLICIT DOUBLE PRECISION ( A-H, O-Z)
 4            REAL*16 PI
 5            DIMENSION T1(3), TIME(3)
 6   C
 7   C         ***** generated by the VM/EPEX preprocessor *****
 8            COMMON/$$PRIV/C28903(100)
 9            INTEGER*4 C28903
10   C         @SHARED_UNIQUE/C38478/I46759(26)
11            COMMON/C38478/I46759(26)
12            INTEGER*4 I46759
13   C
14   C         @SHARED/COMM/ SUMALL
15            COMMON/COMM/ SUMALL
16            INTEGER M85788/0/
17            INTEGER Y76575/0/
18            INTEGER R07643/0/
19            INTEGER X18274/0/,C27253/0/
20   C
21   C         ***** generated by the VM/EPEX preprocessor *****
22            F(X) = 4.D0/(1.D0+X*X)
23            PI   = 4.Q0*QATAN(1.Q0)
24            READ(5,*) INTRVL
25            CALL FCLOC(T1)
26   C         @SERIAL BEGIN
27   C         Synch array is at I46759(7)
28   C         Private clock variable is M85788
29            CALL SERSET(M85788,0,I46759(7),*1)
30                SUMALL = 0.D0
31   C         @SERIAL END
32            CALL SEREND(M85788,I46759(7))
33   1        CONTINUE
34            Y76575 =0
35   2        IF(M85788.LE.I46759(7))GOTO 3
36            CALL $$WAIT(2, Y76575)
37            GOTO 2
38   3        CONTINUE
```

```
39            WIDTH = 1.D0/INTRVL
40            SUM = 0.D0
41   C        @DO 100 IC = 1, INTRVL, CHUNK = 1000
42   C        Synch array is at I46759(18)
43   C        Private clock variable is R07643
44            CALL DOSET(R07643,I46759(18),*100)
45   4        CALL DOBEG(1,INTRVL,1,1000,X18274,C27253,R07643,I46759(18),*100)
46            DO 5 IC=X18274,C27253,1
47               SUM = SUM + WIDTH * F( (IC - 0.5D0) * WIDTH )
48   C 100    @ENDO NOWAIT
49   5        CONTINUE
50            GO TO 4
51     100    CONTINUE
52            T = DFNA(SUMALL, SUM)
53            CALL FCLOC(TIME)
54            DO 200 I = 1, 3
55               TIME(I) = 1.D-6*(TIME(I)-T1(I))
56     200    CONTINUE
57            ERR = SUMALL - PI
58            WRITE(6,'(A,F25.15,1.PD15.3)') 'SUMALL, ERR =', SUMALL, ERR
59            WRITE(6,'(A,3F10.4)') 'TIME =', TIME
60            END
```

E3.   Pi Program Timing Results

One Process					
Intervals	Error In Pi	Process	Time		
			Elapsed	Total	Virtual
10000	8.330D-08	1	0.0020	0.0015	0.0014
1000000	-8.428D-11	1	1.4288	1.3978	1.3876
10000000	-8.431D-10	1	14.6937	13.9871	13.8895

Two Processes					
Intervals	Error In Pi	Process	Time		
			Elapsed	Total	Virtual
10000	8.328D-10	1	0.0106	0.0072	0.0071
		2	0.0071	0.0071	0.0070
1000000	-5.389D-11	1	0.7099	0.7006	0.6930
		2	0.7520	0.7028	0.6924
10000000	-5.392D-10	1	9.8704	7.0020	6.9408
		2	7.6181	6.9838	6.9341

Four Processes					
Intervals	Error In Pi	Process	Time		
			Elapsed	Total	Virtual
10000	8.333D-10	1	0.0037	0.0036	0.0035
		2	0.0036	0.0036	0.0035
		3	0.0036	0.0036	0.0035
		4	0.0036	0.0036	0.0035
1000000	-6.448D-12	1	0.8185	0.3.506	0.3464
		2	0.3976	0.3498	0.3462
		3	0.7543	0.3516	0.3467
		4	0.7909	0.3508	0.3468
10000000	-6.532D-11	1	8.3449	3.5032	3.4692
		2	7.5709	3.4983	3.4661
		3	8.0620	3.5009	3.4678
		4	6.0459	3.4937	3.4650

Table E3.1 Prescheduled DO, scalar mode.

One Process			Time		
Intervals	Error In Pi	Process	Elapsed	Total	Virtual
10000	8.333D-10	1	0.0054	0.0054	0.0053
1000000	-5.766D-13	1	0.5525	0.5354	0.5288
10000000	-6.577D-12	1	5.8726	5.3389	5.8931

Two Processes			Time		
Intervals	Error In Pi	Process	Elapsed	Total	Virtual
10000	8.333D-10	1	0.0028	0.0028	0.0027
		2	0.0030	0.0029	0.0027
1000000	-3.401D-13	1	0.2707	0.2677	0.2642
		2	0.3033	0.2675	0.2643
10000000	-4.211D-12	1	3.8384	2.6780	2.6448
		2	3.0279	2.6655	2.6405

Four Processes			Time		
Intervals	Error In Pi	Process	Elapsed	Total	Virtual
10000	8.333D-10	1	0.0015	0.0015	0.0015
		2	0.0015	0.0015	0.0013
		3	0.0018	0.0015	0.0014
		4	0.0014	0.0014	0.0013
1000000	3.008D-14	1	0.2233	0.1336	0.1320
		2	0.2287	0.1341	0.1321
		3	0.1930	0.1343	0.1322
		4	0.1905	0.1342	0.1320
10000000	-5.097D-13	1	2.9375	1.3336	1.3209
		2	3.0489	1.3358	1.3213
		3	1.4391	1.3293	1.3199
		4	2.4349	1.3353	1.3202

Table E3.2 Prescheduled DO, vector mode.

One Process					
Intervals	Error In Pi	Process	Time		
			Elapsed	Total	Virtual
10000	8.325D-10	1	0.0694	0.0694	0.0674
1000000	-8.428D-11	1	7.0048	6.7714	6.7200
10000000	-8.431D-10	1	75.2523	67.8334	67.2660

Two Processes					
Intervals	Error In Pi	Process	Time		
			Elapsed	Total	Virtual
10000	8.328D-10	1	0.0694	0.0679	0.0674
		2	0.0003	0.0002	0.0000
1000000	-5.389D-11	1	3.9872	3.7903	3.7621
		2	3.9682	3.6304	3.5983
10000000	-5.392D-10	1	56.4691	33.4573	33.2051
		2	56.4216	37.4653	37.1796

Four Processes					
Intervals	Error In Pi	Process	Time		
			Elapsed	Total	Virtual
10000	8.333D-10	1	0.0691	0.0678	0.0673
		2	0.0020	0.0002	0.0000
		3	0.0009	0.0003	0.0000
		4	0.0007	0.0001	0.0000
1000000	-6.448D-12	1	4.2897	1.8742	1.8519
		2	4.2179	1.9124	1.8942
		3	4.2842	1.8427	1.8225
		4	4.1860	1.7670	1.7542
10000000	-6.532D-11	1	54.7136	16.6669	16.5160
		2	54.6479	18.2826	18.1065
		3	54.6089	18.8680	18.6773
		4	54.4742	18.5009	18.3273

Table E3.3 Self-scheduled DO, scalar mode, chunk = 1.

One Process					
Intervals	Error In Pi	Process	Time		
			Elapsed	Total	Virtual
10000	8.325D-10	1	0.1321	0.1305	0.1284
1000000	-8.428D-11	1	13.4511	12.9499	12.8273
10000000	-8.431D-10	1	137.123	129.6471	128.3561

Two Processes					
Intervals	Error In Pi	Process	Time		
			Elapsed	Total	Virtual
10000	8.326D-10	1	0.01156	0.1146	0.1125
		2	0.0245	0.0183	0.0176
1000000	-5.389D-11	1	8.0273	6.7808	6.7042
		2	7.9383	6.7869	6.7146
10000000	-5.392D-10	1	75.3012	70.3458	69.8364
		2	75.1876	65.3354	64.7479

Four Processes					
Intervals	Error In Pi	Process	Time		
			Elapsed	Total	Virtual
10000	8.333D-10	1	0.0785	0.0129	0.0121
		2	0.0674	0.0622	0.0613
		3	0.0714	0.0637	0.0611
		4	0.0002	0.0002	0.0000
1000000	-6.448D-12	1	7.2567	0.8142	0.79999
		2	7.3504	0.9684	0.9544
		3	7.2740	5.9992	5.9994
		4	7.3552	5.8263	5.7680
10000000	-6.532D-11	1	73.8832	12.5445	12.4309
		2	73.8736	48.3848	47.9689
		3	73.7840	36.8797	36.5658
		4	73.8058	37.9934	37.6852

Table E3.4 Self-scheduled DO, vector mode, chunk = 1

One Process					
Intervals	Error In Pi	Process	Time		
			Elapsed	Total	Virtual
10000	8.325D-10	1	0.0148	0.0141	0.0139
1000000	-8.428D-11	1	1.48000	10.3866	1.3740
10000000	-8.431D-10	1	14.6604	13.8518	13.7366

Two Processes					
Intervals	Error In Pi	Process	Time		
			Elapsed	Total	Virtual
10000	8.333D-10	1	0.0152	0.0142	0.0139
		2	0.0002	0.0002	0.0000
1000000	-5.333D-11	1	0.8177	0.6181	0.6106
		2	0.7926	0.7707	0.7631
10000000	-5.392D-10	1	7.4026	7.0571	6.9978
		2	7.3618	6.8075	6.7489

Four Processes					
Intervals	Error In Pi	Process	Time		
			Elapsed	Total	Virtual
10000	8.327D-10	1	0.0169	0.0117	0.0111
		2	0.0003	0.0002	0.0000
		3	0.0031	0.0031	0.0029
		4	0.0002	0.0002	0.0000
1000000	-9.320D-12	1	0.7573	0.4464	0.4409
		2	0.6892	0.3669	0.3623
		3	0.5144	0.2222	0.2190
		4	0.6603	0.3552	0.3509
10000000	-6.532D-11	1	7.3033	3.1434	3.1154
		2	7.2640	3.0425	3.0170
		3	7.2298	3.6701	3.6402
		4	7.1587	4.0045	3.9679

Table E3.5 Self-scheduled DO, scalar mode, chunk = 1000.

One Process					
Intervals	Error In Pi	Process	Time		
			Elapsed	Total	Virtual
10000	8.333D-10	1	0.0055	0.0055	0.0054
1000000	-5.914D-13	1	0.5479	0.5423	0.5371
10000000	-6.753D-12	1	5.4705	5.4081	5.3699

Two Processes					
Intervals	Error In Pi	Process	Time		
			Elapsed	Total	Virtual
10000	8.333D-10	1	0.0058	0.0057	0.0054
		2	0.0004	0.0001	0.0000
1000000	-3.392D-13	1	0.3131	0.3017	0.2979
		2	0.2493	0.2436	0.2398
10000000	-4.244D-12	1	4.1860	2.8657	2.8391
		2	4.1006	2.5610	2.5369

Four Processes					
Intervals	Error In Pi	Process	Time		
			Elapsed	Total	Virtual
10000	8.333D-10	1	0.0058	0.0057	0.0054
		2	0.0002	0.0002	0.0000
		3	0.0002	0.0002	0.0000
		4	0.0001	0.0001	0.0000
1000000	-3.898D-14	1	0.3445	0.0790	0.0765
		2	0.1738	0.0824	0.0802
		3	0.3303	0.1686	0.1657
		4	0.2392	0.2183	0.2157
10000000	-9.030D-13	1	3.2052	0.9967	0.9855
		2	3.1790	1.1946	1.1819
		3	3.1421	1.3291	1.3152
		4	3.0911	1.9163	1.8961

Table E3.6 Self-scheduled DO, vector mode, chunk = 1000.

E4.   "The VM/EPEX FORTRAN Preprocessor Reference"[†]

```
RC 11408 (#51330) 9/30/85
Computer Science
```

Janice M. Stone, Frederica Darema-Rogers, V.Alan Norton, and Gregory F. Pfister

IBM T.J. Watson Research Center

Yorktown Heights, NY

Abstract:

The VM/EPEX preprocessor extends a programming language by adding a set of high-level parallel constructs. In VM/EPEX, a program is executed concurrently by several different VM virtual machines, all of which have read/write access to the same shared segment of virtual memory. The preprocessor translates the parallel constructs into subroutine calls and in-line code in the target language. This document describes the Fortran version of the preprocessor.

[†]Reprinted by permission from IBM Corporation.

Preface

The VM/EPEX system evolved in the RP3 project, as part of a continuing research effort to understand the issues of large-scale parallel processing. This report is one of a collection describing the VM/EPEX system. In each report, the primary author appears first, followed by the other contributors, in alphabetical order. The reports are:

- F. Darema-Rogers, D. A. George, V. A. Norton, and G. F. Pfister, "VM/EPEX - A VM Environment for Parallel Execution", IBM Research Report RC11225 (#49161) 1/23/85.

- F. Darema-Rogers, D. A. George, V. A. Norton, and G. F. Pfister, "Environment and System Interface for VM/EPEX".

- E. A. Melton and G. F. Pfister, "A Writeable Shared Segment Operating System".

- J. M. Stone, F. Darema-Rogers, V. A. Norton, and G. F. Pfister, "Introduction to the VM/EPEX FORTRAN Preprocessor".

- J. M. Stone, F. Darema-Rogers, V. A. Norton, and G. F. Pfister, "The VM/EPEX FORTRAN Preprocessor Reference".

The contributors are listed below, and with each name is listed that aspect of VM/EPEX with which that individual is most concerned. Readers are invited to contact any of the authors for further details about the system. The contributors are:

Frederica Darema-Rogers	Applications and system design
David A. George	VM system interface
Evelyn A. Melton	Operating system design
Alan Norton	Applications and system design
Gregory F. Pfister	System design
Kimming So	Performance analysis
Janice M. Stone	High-level language preprocessor

E4.1   INTRODUCTION

The VM/EPEX preprocessor extends a programming language by adding a set of high-level parallel constructs. It operates in the VM parallel environment, in which a program is performed concurrently by several different VM virtual machines, all of which have read/write access to the same shared segments of virtual memory. The preprocessor translates the parallel constructs into a combination of subroutine calls and in-line code.

This document describes the Fortran version of the preprocessor. The VM/EPEX FORTRAN macros are:

- Shared data: `@SHARED`

- Distinguished variables: `@MYNUM`, etc.

- Parallel loop: `@DO ... @DOEND`, `@SCRAM`

- Serial section: `@SERIAL BEGIN ... @SERIAL END`

- Process gathering: `@BARRIER, @WAITFOR`

The use of the macros is introduced informally in the next section by a series of examples. The syntax and semantics of these macros are discussed in the sections that follow.

We wish to express our thanks for the advice, fruitful discussions, and suggestions we have received from Allan Gottlieb of NYU. We also wish to thank our initial users for their patience and willingness to put up with the errors that are inevitable in any new software system: Pat Teller of NYU, Paolo Carnevali of the IBM Rome Scientific Center, Andrei Heilper of the IBM Haifa Scientific Center, and Jim Kajiya of Cal Tech; and special thanks to Alan Karp of the IBM Palo Alto Scientific Center and Tim Kay of Cal Tech, early users who contributed execs (command files) that developed into EPEX features.

E4.2   THE VM/EPEX ENVIRONMENT

VM/EPEX, the environment for parallel execution under VM, was conceived as a means for gaining experience in parallel programming, with the additional performance advantage of enabling an application to utilize multiple concurrent processors. In this parallel environment, programs are written as if many different processors are acting on them simultaneously. Under VM, each such idealized processor is a VM virtual machine. In this document we shall refer to these virtual machines as processes. The various virtual machines execute the same program, but may at a given moment be performing different instructions on different portions of shared data. All the processes have read/write access to the same shared segments of virtual memory.

Applications run in this environment are usually derived from existing serial programs in a very straightforward way: the programmer specifies which loops can be executed in parallel and which data structures are to be shared among concurrent processes. The VM/EPEX preprocessor augments VS FORTRAN by adjoining several parallel constructs and shared-data declarations that have proved useful. The extended language is called EPEX-FORTRAN. The preprocessor acts as a source-to-source translator, converting the parallel constructs into appropriate in-line Fortran code and subroutine calls. The output files of the preprocessor are suitable input to the VS FORTRAN compiler. After compilation, the resulting TEXT files can be loaded and run under the WSSOS (Writeable Shared Segment Operating System) supervisor. This document describes the VM/EPEX preprocessor, with examples of how VM/EPEX programs are written and preprocessed.

E4.3   USING THE PREPROCESSOR

The VM/EPEX FORTRAN preprocessor operates in three phases: PPREPROC, PPBLOCK, and EPEXLOAD. PPREPROC translates EPEX declarations and commands into VS/FORTRAN. PPBLOCK generates a BLOCK DATA subprogram for shared-data declarations. EPEXLOAD produces an executable module. Their role in program preparation and compilation is shown in Fig. E4.1.

In the first phase, the preprocessor acts on an EPEX-FORTRAN source file, translating it into a VS FORTRAN source file. During the second phase, the preprocessor examines a collection of Fortran source files that were produced by the first phase to consolidate their shared references into a single BLOCK DATA subprogram specifying those data items that are to be allocated in shared memory. To determine the sizes of the COMMON blocks declared for the shared-data blocks, it reads the corresponding TEXT files.

When the user's source program is contained in one EPEX-FORTRAN file, the three phases of the preprocessor are performed consecutively. The first phase produces a VS FORTRAN source file, which must then be compiled. The second phase reads the FORTRAN and TEXT files, and produces a VS FORTRAN BLOCK DATA file. The third phase generates an executable module. For a program comprising several files, the first phase translates each component file separately, then each is compiled, and finally the second phase operates on the collection of translated and compiled files to produce the single BLOCK DATA file.

Invoking the Preprocessor

The first phase of the preprocessor is invoked by

PPREPROC *source-file* [*, destination-file*]

where any valid CMS file specifications are acceptable, and square brackets indicate an optional parameter. The default source file type is XFORT, and the default type of the destination file is FORTRAN.

Avoid using FORTRAN as the file type for the source file. It is inappropriate, anyway, as EPEX-FORTRAN is a proper extension of Fortran, and it is especially unwise when omitting the default destination file specification, because in that case the default destination file has the same name as the source file. The preprocessor asks for confirmation in this case, to warn the user of possibly inadvertent file specification conflict. However, it will, after confirmation, write its output to the input file.

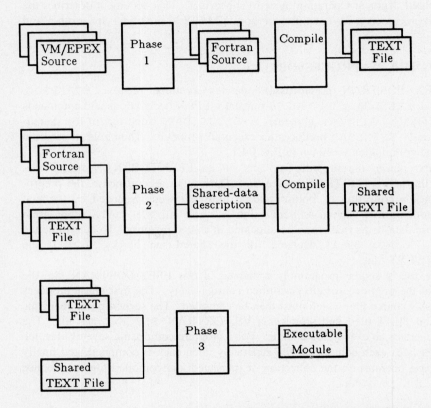

Figure E4.1   The three phases of the VM/EPEX FORTRAN preprocessor.

Invoking the Preprocessor from XEDIT

The preprocessor's first phase may also be invoked from within XEDIT, during editing of the source file, by issuing the subcommand:

PPREP [*destination-file*]

The preprocessor will return control to the terminal with the destination file as XEDIT's current file. Issuing FILE or QUIT will cause control to be returned to the terminal with the source file in XEDIT, as at the start.

The PPREP XEDIT macro is merely the second layer of the VM/EPEX preprocessor's first phase. In the outer layer, at the level of the CMS environment, the PPREPROC macro stacks a QUIT command, a FILE command, and a call to the PPREP macro. PPREPROC then invokes XEDIT to edit the source file, and the stacked `PPREP` command is the first one XEDIT performs. `PPREP` creates the destination file. When `PPREP` exits, the commands stacked by `PPREPROC` cause the writing of the destination file and the exit from XEDIT back to `PPREPROC`, which at that point returns to CMS.

Invoking the Second Phase

The second phase of the preprocessor creates a `BLOCK DATA` subprogram for the shared variables and data structures of a program. It is invoked by:

`PPBLOCK` *filename*   [, *filename* ...] : *destination-file*

where the default file type of the source and destination files is FORTRAN. In the normal case, the source files are those produced by the first phase of the preprocessor.

`PPBLOCK` scans a source file for shared-data declarations. This kind of declaration is a generalization of the usual definition of global variables, as data that is shared not only among subprograms of a program but also among concurrent processes. The form and use of the shared-data declaration are discussed in detail below. In the Fortran program produced by `PPREPROC`, the shared-data declarations have been translated into declarations of named `COMMON` blocks.

After identifying the shared-data declarations in the FORTRAN file, `PPBLOCK` reads the TEXT file for that program to ascertain the size of the `COMMON` block determined for it by the compiler, and produces in the `BLOCK DATA` subprogram a `COMMON` declaration for each distinct shared-data declaration.

A Fortran program may comprise several separate source files. A shared-data declaration will usually appear repeatedly and may occur in any of the component source files. The component XFORT files are translated independently by the first phase of the preprocessor, producing the corresponding FORTRAN files. The FORTRAN files are compiled independently. Then `PPBLOCK` scans each FORTRAN file in turn for shared-data declarations. The corresponding TEXT files are read, and for each shared-data declaration, the resulting named `COMMON` block is declared with the size of the largest `COMMON` block of that name.

If changes are made to one of several source files for a program, that one may be recompiled separately. Then `PPBLOCK` should normally be rerun on the collection to generate an updated `BLOCK DATA` subprogram for the entire program.

Invoking Phase Three

The third phase of the preprocessor is invoked by the command

`EPEXLOAD`

`EPEXLOAD` is an exec command file that creates an executable load module for EPEX programs. It creates either a load module for execution in the EPEX environment, or a load module for execution in the user's own virtual machine. In the interactive mode, `EPEXLOAD` asks the user to specify the main file, the block data file, and any other files to be loaded, the load address, load-module name, and entry point. In addition, the user specifies whether the load module will run under EPEX or on the user's virtual machine.

Alternatively, EPEXLOAD may be invoked with its parameters specified on the command line or in a separate file, to avoid the interactive screen package. This is the method to be used for calling EPEXLOAD from an exec. The EPEXLOAD parameters are given by name-value pairs, with any value that requires more than one word enclosed in single quotes. The parameters are shown in Fig. E4.2.

The main program and shared-data file must be specified. The other parameters are optional, with default values as indicated. The environment parameter indicates whether the module will run in the VM/EPEX environment or in the user's own virtual machine. To run under EPEX, the module includes subroutines that communicate with EPEX. To run in the user's virtual machine, the module operates in single-process mode, with alternate subroutines that substitute for communication with EPEX. In the alternate subroutines, a wait operation causes the program to terminate abnormally with a message. This is done because wait operations usually occur when a process is waiting for some condition to change. In a single-process situation, such change can never occur.

To specify the parameters on the command line, invoke the exec this way:

`EPEXLOAD MAIN:` *mainprog*`, SHARED-DATA:` *shared-data-file*   `,` *...*

where each parameter is given by a name-value pair as shown. If the value is not a single blank-delimited word, enclose it in quotes. The parameters may be specified in any order.

To instruct `EPEXLOAD` to take its parameters from a file, invoke the exec as follows:

`EPEXLOAD` @*file-spec*

where the parameter file is composed of lines of this form:

<parameter-name> `:` *<value>*

TXTLIB	Global Text Library Specification
MAIN	Main Program
SHARED-DATA	Shared-Data File
LOAD-ADDR	Load address for main program
SHARED-DATA-ADDR	Load address for shared data
OTHERS	Other files to load
OPTIONS	Genmod options
LOAD-MODULE	Load-module name
ENTRY-MODULE	Entry-module
LOAD-MODULE-MODE	Mode of load module
ENVIRONMENT	EPEX or Own

Figure E4.2. EPEXLOAD parameters.

and the parameter names and values are as defined above. An example of a parameter file for `EPEXLOAD` is shown in Fig. E4.3.

`EPEXLOAD` saves in a file named `EPEXLOAD RUN` the values of all its parameters, whether set explicitly or by default. It can be invoked with the same parameters again by issuing:

```
EPEXLOAD @EPEXLOAD RUN
```

or simply:

```
EPEXLOAD @
```

to invoke the module generator.

E4.4   TRANSLATION OF THE PARALLEL CONSTRUCTS

The VM/EPEX preprocessor's functions can be roughly divided into two categories: declaration of shared data and implementation of parallel constructs.

Declaration of Shared Data

Data to be shared among concurrent processes must be so identified. Any variable is private, available only to the process executing the program, unless it is explicitly declared as shared.

The VM/EPEX preprocessor handles declarations for three categories of memory:

1. Explicitly declared shared data for use by several participating processes.

2. A small block of private memory for distinguished variables that store the number of participating processes, the process number assigned to the process itself, and the values of some system parameters

3. Implicitly generated shared data for synchronization of access to shared memory.

The uses of these categories of memory are described in the sections that follow.

```
MAIN : FFTEST
SHARED-DATA : FFTSHARE
LOAD-ADDR : 20000
SHARED-DATA-ADDR : 200000
LOAD-MODULE : FFTEST
ENVIRONMENT : EPEX
```

Figure E4.3. An `EPEXLOAD` parameter file.

Explicitly Declared Shared Data

Storage for data structures to be shared among processes is declared explicitly, as shown in Fig. E4.4.

This construct is a generalization of the named COMMON block, as data that is shared not only among various subprograms in a program, but also among various concurrent processes. If one of the processes that share such data changes a shared value, then all of the sharing processes immediately have access to the new value.

The syntax of the @SHARED declaration corresponds to that of named COMMON statements; if the string @SHARED is replaced by COMMON, the resulting statement must conform to the Fortran specification of named COMMON blocks.

During the first phase of preprocessing, all @SHARED blocks are converted to COMMON blocks of the same name. The second phase copies all of these COMMON blocks into a BLOCK DATA subprogram and ensures that every such @SHARED block appearing in a collection of source files will appear exactly once in the output BLOCK DATA file.

The BLOCK DATA subprogram is generated by scanning the component FORTRAN files for shared-data declarations and then reading their corresponding TEXT files to determine the size of the COMMON block allocated for each such block. For a multifile program, the largest space allocated for the block is chosen. Then each block is declared as an array of variables of type REAL*8, which aligns the block on a doubleword boundary.

As with a COMMON statement, an @SHARED declaration must be included in every subprogram that refers to its shared variables. Instead of explicitly stating the declaration in every subprogram, a programmer may create a separate file containing a set of @SHARED declarations and incorporate it where needed, using @INCLUDE.

In contrast, the INCLUDE feature of VS FORTRAN incorporates into the source file statements from a library. It is anticipated that in the future the preprocessor will accomplish the function of the FORTRAN INCLUDE also. Fig. E4.5. illustrates the @INCLUDE.

When the preprocessor encounters an @INCLUDE, it performs an XEDIT Get to copy the specified file into its working file at the point of the @INCLUDE. The default file type is the same as the default file type for the preprocessor. For the VM/EPEX FORTRAN preprocessor, this is XFORT. Preprocessing is carried out with the destination file as XEDIT's current file. This means that a Get with unspecified file type would access a file with the same type as the destination file. Since this is not generally

@SHARED / *blockname* / *variable* [, *variable* ...]

Figure E4.4. The @SHARED declaration.

@INCLUDE *file-spec* [, *file-spec* ...]

Figure E4.5. The @INCLUDE directive.

what is wanted, the preprocessor does not leave the file type unspecified, but rather fills in its own default.

A restricted kind of @SHARED declaration is used internally by the preprocessor. Called @SHARED_UNIQUE, this declaration, which is discussed later under the heading *Implicitly Generated Shared Storage for Synchronization*, may also be used in application programs.

Declaration of Distinguished Variables

The preprocessor recognizes a few distinguished variables that store the number of participating processes, the process number assigned to the process itself, and the values of some system parameters. They are referred to in VM/EPEX programs by special variable names that are not valid Fortran variable names. The list of distinguished variables, still evolving, is currently as follows:

- @NUMPROCS, the number of participating processes. The value of this variable should not be changed by the program.

- @MYNUM, the identifying number of the executing process. This is a private variable, providing a unique ID to each process, such that

    0 < @MYNUM <= @NUMPROCS

    This variable should not be modified by the program.

- @DAGW, the time in microseconds used in subroutine DAGW, which causes the calling process to be immediately swapped out; the process becomes eligible for dispatching after an elapsed time of @DAGW microseconds. This variable is given a default value at execution time but may be altered by the user program. Each process must modify its own copy, if such a change is desired.

- @MAXWAIT, the maximum number of times a process will wait for a shared resource or lock before terminating execution. This is given a default value that the program may modify. When the number of attempts to obtain a lock exceeds @MAXWAIT, the program is considered to be deadlocked, and that process is terminated. It may be necessary to modify the value of @MAXWAIT according to the number of participating processes or the system load. If a process repeatedly terminates with a message that waiting time is exceeded, the relevant algorithm should be investigated. Experience has shown that this kind of termination is often caused by waiting for satisfaction of a condition that can never be met. If the algorithm seems correct, consider increasing @MAXWAIT experimentally.

While the values assigned to these variables are information shared between the operating system and the process, the variables themselves are private to a process. Each process is provided with its own private copy of these variables. That is, they are private to a process, and global within it. For Fortran, the preprocessor declares an integer array in a named COMMON block, $$PRIV, for the distinguished variables. Because this block is shared among subprograms, possibly compiled independently, the name $$PRIV is reserved for this purpose and may not appear as a block name in any user-generated COMMON declarations. The preprocessor generates a unique variable name for the array to contain the private copies of the variables @NUMPROCS, @MYNUM, @DAGW, and @MAXWAIT. References to these variables are replaced by references to the corresponding elements of the array. The values of the variables are set by an initialization subroutine that communicates with the operating system. The preprocessor inserts a call to the initialization subroutine as the first executable statement of any main program.

Implicitly Generated Shared Storage for Synchronization

Certain shared variables, invisible to the application programmer, are declared by the preprocessor and managed by VM/EPEX subroutines. These include, for example, synchronization locks, flags, and loop counters. Space for these variables is provided in a synchronization array in an @SHARED block, called the synchronization block, that is declared by the preprocessor for this purpose. Almost every VM/EPEX construct causes expansion of the synchronization array.

For each source file, the preprocessor declares one synchronization block and generates a unique name for it. This means that in a multi-file program there is one synchronization block for each file. It is essential that there be no duplication of synchronization-block names in the component files of a multi-file program. As shown in Fig. E4.1, component files receive first-phase preprocessing independently. While the likelihood of assigning duplicate names is minimized by giving the blocks randomly generated names that are unique within the source file, it is not possible to guarantee that synchronization-block names are unique over a collection of files. However, it is possible to detect a violation of this condition. In the unlikely event that the preprocessor's first phase generates the same name for the synchronization blocks of different files, the situation is recognized in the second phase. Such a duplication results in an error note and the inclusion in the BLOCK DATA subprogram of the corresponding COMMON declaration, which will, by duplicating the block label, cause compilation of the BLOCK DATA subprogram to fail. The duplication can be corrected manually or by repeating the first phase for one or more of the files.

The requirement for a unique block name is indicated by declaring the block not merely @SHARED, but @SHARED_UNIQUE. The preprocessor's second phase interprets @SHARED_UNIQUE as meaning that while declarations of the block may occur repeatedly within a file, as they must, for example, in component subprograms, nevertheless the block name may not be duplicated among files. The @SHARED_UNIQUE declaration may also be used by application programmers.

At the end of the first phase of the preprocessor, the declarations for the distinguished variables and the synchronization block are copied into each FUNCTION and SUBROUTINE subprogram in the file, they are available in every such subprogram.

Parallel Constructs

The preprocessor converts VM/EPEX macro calls into compilable source code. This frees the application programmer from certain repetitive activities during conversion to parallel code and allows exploitation of the basic operations of designating parallel loops and serial code sections. Each instance of a VM/EPEX macro is replaced by subroutine calls and in-line code. The VM/EPEX macros are:

- Parallel loop: @DO ... @DOEND

- Serial section: @SERIAL BEGIN ... @SERIAL END

- Process gathering: @BARRIER, @WAITFOR

The syntax and semantics of these macros are discussed in the sections that follow.

The Parallel Loop: @DO...@DOEND

This construct provides a parallel form of the usual serial DO loop. It allows concurrently participating processes to perform the task of the loop in parallel by assigning successive values of the loop index to various processes and letting each process do one iteration at a time.

The form of the usual serial DO loop is shown in Fig. E4.6. The loop has a scope, a loop index with an initial value and a final value, and a loop body, or task.

The scenario for performing a loop in parallel assumes that the iterations are mutually independent. When a process arrives at the beginning of the loop, its private loop-index "index" is assigned a value, and the process proceeds into the loop. At the end of the loop, the process returns to the beginning of the loop to be assigned another value of the loop index, until the loop's task is completed. In its simplest form, shown in Fig. E4.7, the parallel loop corresponds to the traditional serial loop.

```
    DO 100 index = n1,n2

        ... loop body ...


100   CONTINUE
```

Figure E4.6. The usual serial DO loop.

```
    @DO   [ stmt# ]  indx = n1,n2

        ... loop code ...

[stmt#]  @ENDO
```

Figure E4.7. Simple form of the parallel loop.

Like the serial loop, the parallel loop has a scope and a loop index with an initial value and a final value. As with serial loops, the parallel loop permits an optional increment value as well. In addition, there is a second analogue of the increment. It is sometimes more efficient to assign a series, or "chunk", of index values each time, rather than a single value. The @DO construct offers the optional CHUNK specification to accomplish this. For example, if the chunk size is specified as 10, the first process to enter the loop will execute the loop with the first 10 index values, the second will be assigned the next 10, etc. This option is attractive in situations in which there is only a small amount of work involved in any one loop iteration, and the overhead involved in accessing the shared index dominates the execution time.

Fig. E4.8 shows the full syntax of the parallel loop. This figure illustrates the conventions followed in stating the syntax of the VM/EPEX constructs:

- Reserved words are capitalized.

- Default values appear in boldfaced type.

- The required portion of a word is capitalized, and the rest appears in lower case.

- Optional items appear in square brackets.

- Alternatives are separated by a vertical bar.

For example:

        @ENDO [*label*]   [Wait | NOWait]

indicates that @ENDO is a reserved word, *label* is optional, the default option is WAIT, for which W suffices, and the alternative option is NOWAIT, for which NOW suffices. The preprocessor is not sensitive to case, so in actual practice reserved words, labels, and variables may appear in upper or lower case, according to the requirements of the target language. However, successive instances of a label must match with respect to case.

The interpretation of the parallel loop, shown in Fig. E4.8, differs from the usual Fortran DO loop in several significant respects:

- The loop index must be a private integer variable because various values of the index are assigned to the various participating processes.

- The initial value, *n1*, the final value, *n2*, and the optional increment, *n3*, must be integer expressions. The values of *n1*, *n2*, and *n3* should be the same for all

        @DO [*label* | *stmt#*] *index* = *n1*,*n2* [,*n3*]   [CHUNK=*chunksize*]

        ... *loop code* ...

[*stmt#*] @ENDO [*label*]   [Wait | NOWait]

Figure E4.8. The syntax of the parallel loop.

processes. Consideration of the description below of how these loops are controlled will make clear the fundamental applicability of this condition. While it is not enforced, one should realize that disregarding this advice may result in inconsistent or erroneous results.

- For the loop to be performed at least once, the initial value $n1$, must be less than or equal to the final value $n2$. Unlike the case for conventional Fortran DO loops, the @DO loop will not be executed at all if $n1$ is greater than $n2$. Similarly, the loop increment $n3$, if used, must be a positive integer. A performance advantage is achieved by limiting loop scheduling to positive iteration, and, since the loop iterations must be independent, the order in which they are performed must be of no significance.

- In order for a program to execute properly, the values of $n1$, $n2$ and $n3$ must not change while processes are still in the loop.

- To coordinate the passage of various processes through the loop, a program must not branch into or out of an @DO loop. The preprocessor flags as an error any GOTO statement whose target is not within the scope of the @DO loop. Non-standard exits from an @DO loop can be accomplished using the @SCRAM macro.

- Similarly, there must be no branches into an @DO loop.

- The end of the @DO loop is indicated by the @ENDO. The preprocessor accepts the following as mutually synonymous:

@ENDO
@ENDDO
@ENDOO[†]
@END_DO
@DOEND

- A process arriving at the end of the @DO loop will be assigned another loop-index value, or chunk of values, and will perform one or more additional iterations of the loop. When all values of the loop index have been assigned, there is no more work to be assigned. In general, there will be an interval in which all the work has been assigned but is not yet completed. For some programs, the subsequent code can be executed immediately, before the loop task is completed, as soon as there is a process available to do it. On the other hand, in some situations the subsequent code is dependent on the results of the loop task, and processes must wait until that task is done. The synchronization option at the end of the loop allows the programmer to control what a process does when there is no more work to be done in the loop. The default, WAIT, specifies that a process must wait for the completion of all the iterations of the loop before proceeding. The NOWAIT option permits the process to continue as soon as all

---

[†]This is not a typo. It was included because an early EPEX user wanted to use it. (ed.)

the work of the loop task has been assigned, even though other processes may still be completing some of the loop iterations. If WAIT is specified, explicitly or by default, the preprocessor inserts code that causes processes to wait until the loop iterations are completed before any of them proceed.

- The optional label may be an arbitrary alphanumeric string. If used, it must also appear in the statement that ends the loop.

Caveats

A parallel loop is appropriate in some but not all circumstances. For example, the interpretation of @DO makes nesting of @DO loops incoherent because not all combinations of loop indices will be assigned to processes. For this reason, nesting of @DO loops is flagged as an error by the preprocessor.

A typical application of parallel loops is shown in the example in Fig. E4.9, in which a series of parallel loops is embedded in a serial loop. Every process executing this code has the same general flow of control, in the sense that each one proceeds to the beginning of each loop, interacts with the loop, and continues to the next loop. The code generated by the preprocessor is satisfactory for this kind of situation. If, however, conditional branches direct the flow of control so that on different iterations of the

```
      DO 100 I=1,1000

         ...

      @DO 10 J1=1,10000

         ... loop body ...

10    @ENDO NOWAIT

         ...

      @DO 90 J9=1,200,20

         ... loop body ...

90    @ENDO WAIT

         ...

100   CONTINUE
```

Figure E4.9. Parallel loops embedded in a serial loop.

outer serial loop the process performs different parallel loops, the preprocessor's code is unsuitable. The reason for this is apparent in the discussion of implementation details, which is left to Section E4.6.

This restriction does not mean that every process must have the same flow of control. For example, processes may be diverted to various portions of a program on the basis of ID number. This means that a process chooses the same path every time it arrives at the choice point. When this holds, the preprocessor's code is satisfactory.

Even if this condition does not hold, it is possible that for some particular program this restriction does not apply. A careful study of the implementation details of the preprocessor will facilitate analysis of individual situations.

It is anticipated that a subsequent extension of the preprocessor will remove this restriction.

Nonstandard Loop Exit: @SCRAM

This construct is used to terminate execution of a loop in an abnormal way, presumably before all loop indices have been assigned. When a process encounters an @SCRAM statement, it proceeds to the @DOEND statement immediately, and other processes operating in the loop will proceed to the @DOEND as soon as they next request an index value or chunk of index values. It is important to note that iterations that have already been assigned to other processes will be completed.

The preprocessor replaces the @SCRAM with a call to a subroutine that causes the loop index to be incremented beyond its final value, effectively terminating further assignment of work in the loop.

The Serial Section: @SERIAL BEGIN...@SERIAL END

The serial section construct is used to specify a section of code that is to be executed by one process only. The programmer may choose whether the code is to be executed by the first process to arrive at the beginning of the section or by a particular process. The syntax of the serial section is shown in Fig. E4.10.

This construct has the same label and synchronization options as the parallel loop. The optional process number gives the identifying number of a particular process that is to execute the serial code. If no particular process is specified, the first process to arrive executes the serial code.

```
       @SERial BEGin  [label  |  stmt#]  [PROCESS=process-no]

           ... serial code ...

 [stmt#]  @SERial END   [label]   [ Wait | NOWait ]
```

Figure E4.10. The syntax of the serial section.

As with the @DO loop, the preprocessor expands the synchronization array to include space for the synchronization variables for a @SERIAL section. If WAIT is specified, explicitly or by default, the preprocessor inserts code that causes processes to wait until the loop iterations are completed before any of them proceed.

More Caveats

The discussion of parallel loops included restrictions on their use within program segments that are executed repeatedly. The same restriction applies to serial sections. In code that is performed repeatedly, the flow of control should be such that a process either always arrives at the serial section or never does. As with parallel loops, it is possible that analysis of a particular program, including a thorough understanding of the implementation details of the preprocessor, will lead to the conclusion that this restriction does not apply.

Rounding up Processes: @BARRIER and @WAITFOR

Two macros control how a process can wait for some or all of the participating processes to arrive at a particular point. A barrier is a widely used technique, in which all the participating processes assemble at a single point in the code. The @WAITFOR macro bars any processes that arrive at that point in the code from proceeding until a specified condition is met. Both of these macros are discussed in this section.

The @BARRIER macro forces all processes to wait until all the participating processes have arrived at this point in the program, before any are allowed to proceed. Its syntax is simply:

        @BARRIER

A process arriving at the barrier "checks in" by performing a fetch-and-add to the barrier's arrival counter. While the arrival counter remains less than the total number of processes in the job, @NUMPROCS, the process waits at the barrier. Notice that deadlock can result if there is a process that never arrives at the barrier. If this occurs, the waiting processes are terminated after attempting a delay as many times as allowed, according to the value of @MAXWAIT.

While the barrier macro creates a barrier that persists until all the participating processes have arrived, the wait macro sets up a barrier that persists until a specified condition is met. The form of the wait command is:

        @WAITFOR (*wait-condition*)

where a *wait-condition* is a logical combination of *wait-expressions*:

	wait-expression
or	(*wait-expression*)
or	.NOT. *wait-expression*
or	*wait-expression* [*logical-operator wait-expression* ...]

A *wait-expression* is:

> an EPEX label of a parallel construct
> or   a relational expression of Fortran and EPEX variables

A *logical operator* is

```
.AND. | .OR. | .EQV. | .NEQV.
```

An EPEX label can be referenced in a *wait-expression* only in the subprogram in which it appears. A reference to an EPEX label is interpreted as an implicit wait for completion of the specified parallel loop or serial section. This condition is satisfied when the shared clock for the loop or section is at least as great as the process's corresponding private clock. See Section E4.6 for details of implementation.

Examples:

1. *Wait-condition* is a simple logical expression:

```
@WAITFOR (N .GE. 256)
```

2. *Wait-condition* involves Fortran and EPEX variables:

```
@WAITFOR (ALPHA.NE.0.AND.@NUMPROCS.GE.4)
```

3. Wait for a labeled parallel loop or serial section to be done:

```
@WAITFOR (@100)
```

4. *Wait-condition* is an expression involving variables and labels:

```
@WAITFOR ((X.LS.10.AND.(@LOOP10.OR.(.NOT.XFUNC(Y)))))
```

Initialization

The preprocessor inserts in the user's main program, immediately prior to the first executable statement, a call to an initialization subroutine. The subroutine sets the values of the distinguished variables @NUMPROCS, @MYNUM, @DAGW, and @MAXWAIT. It delays the process until enough processes have been allocated to the job, according to the job's specification of minimum and maximum number of processes. When enough processes have been allocated, all are allowed to proceed. The actual number of processes allocated to the job is passed to the calling program as the value of the variable @NUMPROCS and should not be specified or modified in the source code.

The preprocessor inserts in the program the call to the initialization subroutine, of the form:

```
CALL GETNUM (distinguished-vars, synchr-vars)
```

where *distinguished-vars* refers to the array of distinguished variables in the $$PRIV COMMON block, and *synchr-vars* is the synchronization array declared by the preprocessor.

E4.5   PROGRAMMING EXAMPLES

Example of Parallel Loops that Wait

The example given in Fig. E4.11 shows two @DO loops with WAIT specified explicitly. Since the default synchronization option is WAIT, its explicit appearance is for purposes of emphasis and documentation. In this example, the WAIT causes execution of the first loop to be completed before the second loop is begun. A process that cannot be assigned further work in the first loop must wait until all the processes that were assigned work complete their iterations. Then all the processes can proceed into the second loop. Similarly, when a process can no longer be assigned work in the second loop, it must wait until all the iterations of *secondloop* are done.

Example of WAIT and NOWAIT Parallel Loops

The example given in Fig. E4.12 shows three @DO loops with various mutual dependencies. In this example, execution of the second loop is allowed to begin before the first loop has finished because of the NOWAIT option. Because the second loop is by default a WAIT loop, the third loop is allowed to begin only after all the work of the second is completed. Note, however, that some processes may still be executing the first loop when the third one is started.

```
@DO firstloop I = 20,50
    ... loop text ...
@DOEND firstloop WAIT

@DO secondloop J = 1,100
    ... loop text ...
@DOEND secondloop WAIT
```

Figure E4.11. Example of two parallel WAIT loops.

```
@DO firstloop I = 20,50
    ... loop text ...
@DOEND firstloop NOWAIT

@DO secondloop J = 1,100
    ... loop text ...
@DOEND secondloop

@DO thirdloop K = 2,30
    ... loop text ...
@DOEND thirdloop
```

Figure E4.12. Example of three parallel loops

Example of Pipelined Parallel Loops

The example shown in Fig. E4.13 illustrates a pipeline effect obtained by two `NOWAIT` loops embedded in code that is performed repeatedly. Processes arrive at *loop1* and are assigned work in it until all values of its loop index have been assigned. Suppose that process 7 runs out of work in *loop1*, or perhaps arrives too late to get any work in `loop1`. It proceeds immediately to *loop2*, even though other processes may still be completing their assigned iterations of *loop1*. When process 7 can no longer be assigned work in *loop2*, it proceeds to statement `200` and returns to the beginning of the sequence, to arrive a second time at *loop1*. At this time, other processes may still be completing work in *loop2*. Indeed, it is even possible that other processes are still completing the work in *loop1* that was in progress when process 7, finding that there was no more work to be assigned in *loop1*, left it for the first time.

In this case, process 7 is delayed at the beginning of *loop1* until the work of the previous instance of *loop1* is finished. When every process doing work in its first visit to *loop1* is done, then process 7 may begin its second visit.

This aspect of process synchronization is managed using a private *loop1-clock* for each process and a global *loop1-clock*. Details of the preprocessor's implementation are discussed in Section E4.6.

Skirting the Caveat, Diverting Processes

In Fig. E4.14, two processes are diverted from the others to perform one loop, while the others are allowed to start a different loop concurrently. While processes 1 and 2 are performing *loop1*, the other processes perform *loop2* and may finish it and proceed to *loop3*. It is not possible for *loop2* and *loop3* to be performed concurrently because *loop2* is by default a `WAIT` loop, so *loop3* cannot be started until all the iterations of *loop2* are completed. The `@BARRIER` ensures that no process will continue before all the processes executing the job arrive at that point. The caveat about potential synchronization problems inherent in divergent processes does not apply to this case because the path followed by any particular process is always the same. If this code were performed repeatedly, say inside a serial loop, and if the conditional branch in statement `1` were controlled on the basis of arrival order instead of ID number, a

```
100    @DO loop1 I = 20,50
       ...
       @DOEND loop1 NOWAIT

       @DO loop2 J = 1,100
       ...
       @DOEND loop2 NOWAIT

200    IF ( ... condition ... ) GOTO 100
```

Figure E4.13. Example of pipelined loops.

```
1     IF(@MYNUM.GT.2) GOTO 100
C  Here is a parallel loop to be done by two processes:

      @DO loop1   I = 1,1000
      ...compute some function of I...
      @DOEND loop1 NOWAIT

      GOTO 200

C  The other processes do the following two loops,
C  finishing the first one before starting the second.

100   @DO loop2 J=1,25
      ...do something with J...
      @DOEND  loop2

      @DO loop3 K=2,50,2
      ...do something for even values of K...
      @DOEND  loop3

C  Wait until all processes get here before proceeding
200   @BARRIER
      ...
```

Figure E4.14. Example of divergent processes.

process might sometimes be diverted to *loop1* and sometimes to *loop2*. It has been mentioned earlier that this can cause unsatisfactory results.

E4.6   IMPLEMENTATION OF VM/EPEX MACROS

The VM/EPEX macros are implemented in Fortran as subroutine calls to routines in the EPEXLIB text library. For each instance of a parallel construct, the preprocessor declares a set of shared variables for synchronization of processes and access to shared data. Control of critical sections is managed by subroutines that implement a variation of the Readers-Writers algorithm. This algorithm is a specialized form of the version of Readers-Writers code[†], which provided a starting point for the VM/EPEX algorithm.

[†]Allan Gottlieb, B. D. Lubachevsky, Larry Rudolph, "Basic Techniques for the Efficient Coordination of Very Large Numbers of Cooperating Sequential Processors", *ACM Transactions on Programming Languages and Systems*, vol. 5, no. 2, April 1983.

Implementation of the Parallel Loop

The semantics of the loop constructs are shown in the figures that follow. Fig. E4.15 shows a simple parallel loop. It does not specify a chunk size and is a NOWAIT loop. Its interpretation is shown below it.

The preprocessor declares a set of SHARED INTEGER variables for controlling the loop. To do this, it enlarges its single synchronization array, referred to here as ISYNCR, by the size of the required set of variables. References to the loop's set of variables are made by referring to the first of these array elements: ISYNCR(L), for some value of L. Also for each loop, the preprocessor declares a private integer, initialized to zero, with a unique name substituted for MYTIME.

If the loop is a WAIT loop, the preprocessor inserts after the loop the code to control delay of the process until the loop task is completed. Fig. E4.16 shows the form of the code generated by the preprocessor to control this delay. The delay is controlled by comparing the process's private loop-clock to the shared loop-clock for the loop. The preprocessor declares an integer variable for the private loop-clock. The shared loop-

The macro specification:

```
100    @DO 200 I=I1,I2,I3
         ... loop body ...
200    @ENDDO  NOWAIT
```

Its interpretation:

```
C100   @DO 200 I=I1,I2,I3
100    CALL DOSET(I1,I2,I3,MYTIME,ISYNCR,*200)
101    CALL DOBEG(I,MYTIME,ISYNCR,*200)
         ... loop body ...
       GOTO 101
C200   @ENDDO  NOWAIT
200    CONTINUE
```

Figure E4.15. Implementation of a parallel loop.

The interpretation of WAIT:

```
       switch = 0
300    IF(privateclock.LE.sharedclock)GOTO 301
       CALL $$WAIT(1, switch)
       GO TO 300
```

Figure E4.16. The code generated for WAIT.

clock is one of the shared variables in the loop's synchronization array, referred to here as ISYNCR. The private clock is incremented in the VM/EPEX loop-management subroutine before the process leaves the loop. The shared clock is incremented only by the last process to leave the loop, after the final iteration of the loop task is complete. After that occurs, the waiting process continues.

Fig. E4.17 shows a parallel loop that specifies a chunk size. Its interpretation, shown below it, shows the addition of an inner loop that implements the performance of a "chunk" of loop iterations. The preprocessor declares the variables J1 and J2, as well as MYTIME, and generates unique names for them.

The preprocessor provides the @SCRAM macro to permit a process to leave a loop prematurely and cause assignment of work in the loop to cease. Fig. E4.18 shows the implementation of @SCRAM.

Implementation of the Serial Section

The semantics of serial sections are shown in the figures that follow. Fig. E4.19 shows the code generated for a serial section that specifies which process is to perform it.

If the process's ID number is not 1, the process branches around the serial section and proceeds immediately to succeeding portions of the program. Otherwise, the process performs the serial section and then proceeds. If the process number is not specified, the preprocessor-generated call to SERSET gives zero instead of a process ID number, directing the SERSET subroutine to let the first process to arrive perform the serial section. If the program had not used a statement number on the @SERIAL END, the preprocessor would have generated a valid statement number for it.   WAIT and

The macro specification:

```
100     @DO 200  I=I1,I2,I3   CHUNK=10
          ... loop body ...
200     @ENDDO   NOWAIT
```

Its interpretation:

```
C100    @DO 200  I=I1,I2,I3   CHUNK=10
100     CALL DOSET(MYTIME,  ISYNCR,*200)
101     CALL DOBEG(I1,I2,I3,10,J1,J2,MYTIME,ISYNCR,*200)
          DO 102 I=J1,J2,I3
          ... loop body ...
102     CONTINUE
          GOTO 101
C200    @ENDDO   NOWAIT
200     CONTINUE
```

Figure E4.17. Implementation of a parallel loop with chunksize.

NOWAIT have the same effect as in parallel loops. If the WAIT option is in effect, the preprocessor inserts code that delays the process until the serial section has been performed.

The macro specification:

```
100    @DO 200 I=I1,I2,I3
          ...
       IF  (... condition ...) GOTO 150
       @SCRAM
          ...
200    @ENDDO  NOWAIT
```

Its interpretation:

```
C100    @DO 200 I=I1,I2,I3
100     CALL DOSET(I1,I2,I3,MYTIME,ISYNCR,*200)
101     CALL DOBEG(I,MYTIME,ISYNCR,*200)
          ...
        IF  (... condition ...) GOTO 150
        CALL SCRAM(ISYNCR, I2, *200)
          ...
        GOTO 101
C200    @ENDDO  NOWAIT
200     CONTINUE
```

Figure E4.18. Implementation of a parallel loop with @SCRAM.

The macro specification:

```
    100    @SERIAL BEGIN PROCESS=1
           ... serial code ...
    200    @SERIAL END
```

Its interpretation:

```
    C100    @SERIAL BEGIN PROCESS=1
    100     CALL SERSET(MYTIME,1,ISYNCR,*200)
                ... serial code ...
            CALL SEREND(MYTIME,ISYNCR)
    C200    @SERIAL END
    200     CONTINUE
```

Figure E4.19. Implementation of a serial section.

Implementation of the Barrier

The barrier forces a process to wait until all the processes in the job have arrived. The code generated by the preprocessor for a barrier is shown in Fig. E4.20.

Implementation of `@WAITFOR`

The `@WAITFOR` macro forces a process to wait until the specified condition is satisfied. The implementation of `@WAITFOR` is shown in Fig. E4.21.

E4.7   VM/EPEX SUBROUTINES

The VM/EPEX macros are implemented by means of calls to various synchronizing subroutines. We provide here a list of those subroutines, which may in fact be employed by the user as well as by the macro preprocessor. These subroutines are available in the text library EPEXLIB. The user must allocate the appropriate shared-memory locations, which can be done with the `@SHARED` declaration.

The macro specification:

```
@BARRIER
```

Its interpretation:

```
C       @BARRIER
C       Synch array is at syncharray
C       Private clock variable is privateclock
        CALL BARRIE(privateclock,syncharray)
```

Figure E4.20. Implementation of `@BARRIER`.

The macro specification:

```
@WAITFOR  ( ...condition... )
```

Its interpretation:

```
C         @WAITFOR ( ...condition... )
  537     SWITCH =0
  538     IF( ...condition...)GOTO 539
          CALL $$WAIT(4, SWITCH)
          GO TO 538
  539     CONTINUE
```

Figure E4.21. Implementation of `@WAITFOR`.

High-level Subroutines

- Initialize distinguished variables:

  GETNUM(IPRIVS,ISYNCR)

- Initialize parallel loop:

  DOSET(MYTIME,ISYNCR,*snum)

- Assign loop task:

  DOBEG(I1,I2,I3,ICHUNK,II1,II2,MYTIME,ISYNCR,*snum)

- Nonstandard exit from parallel loop:

  SCRAM(ISYNCR,I2,*snum)

- Initialize serial section:

  SERSET(MYTIME,IPROCNO,ISYNCR,*snum)

- Terminate serial section:

  SEREND(MYTIME,ISYNCR)

- Obtain (nonexclusive) access to resource:

  BEGRDR(S)

- Release (nonexclusive) access to resource:

  ENDRDR(S)

- Obtain (exclusive access to) resource:

  BEGWTR(S)

- Release (exclusive access to) resource:

  ENDWTR(S)

Low-level Subroutines

The assembly-language subroutines that support the high-level EPEX subroutines are also available to the application programmer.

- CS(I,JSHARE,K)

  This subroutine performs a 370 compare-and-swap operation: If JSHARE is equal to I then JSHARE is set equal to K. Otherwise I is set equal to JSHARE. This is used primarily to set locks: JSHARE will be a shared lock, for which JSHARE is equal to 0 when unlocked, and JSHARE is not equal to 0 when locked. One calls this routine with K nonzero and I a variable with value 0. If the resulting value in I is zero, the lock was obtained, and JSHARE was set to the value in K. Otherwise the lock was not obtained, and I contains the previous value of JSHARE.

- DAGW(N)

  This subroutine causes a SLEEP of N microseconds. The value of N should be chosen large enough to ensure that the scheduler will terminate the program's time slice. (This depends on the parameters in the VM scheduler, but usually 20000 is enough). This subroutine should be called whenever this process must wait for other processes to proceed, for example, when waiting for a lock to be released.

- LOCKUP(L)

  This subroutine causes the process to obtain the lock L, using the compare-and-swap subroutine CS, described above. If L is not available, it waits (using DAGW) until it becomes available.

- UNLOCK(L)

  This unlocks L by setting it to zero.

- LOKTRY(L)

  This logical function tries to lock L, and returns .TRUE. if successful, .FALSE. if not. It is useful in situations where a process has other useful work to perform while waiting for the lock to become available.

Fetch-and-Op Subroutines

The fetch-and-op subroutines perform atomic read-modify-write operations, as described below.

The target variable of such an operation is normally a shared variable. Declare it as an array to ensure that it is passed to the fetch-and-op routine by reference rather than by value. This requirement is emphasized in the subsequent descriptions by using array notation to refer to the target variable.

- IFNA(ISHARE,MYVAL)

  This is an integer function that uses the compare-and-swap subroutine CS to perform an integer fetch-and-add, adding MYVAL to the shared location ISHARE(1). The returned value is the previous value of ISHARE(1); after the call, ISHARE(1) will be increased by MYVAL.

- IFAND(ISHARE,MYVAL)

  This is an integer function that performs a fetch-and-AND, ANDing MYVAL to the shared location ISHARE(1). The returned value is the previous value of ISHARE(1).

- IFOR(ISHARE,MYVAL)

  This is an integer function that performs a fetch-and-OR, ORing MYVAL to the shared location ISHARE(1). The returned value is the previous value of ISHARE(1).

- `IFMIN(ISHARE,MYVAL)`

  This integer function performs a fetch-and-min. The previous value of the shared variable `ISHARE(1)` is returned. It is replaced by the value of `MYVAL` if `MYVAL` is smaller than `ISHARE(1)`.

- `IFMAX(ISHARE,MYVAL)`

  This integer function performs fetch-and-max, similar to the above, replacing minimum by maximum.

- `ISWAP(I,J)`

  This integer function causes the shared integer variable `I(1)` to be replaced by `J` and returns the previous value of `I(1)`. This may be thought of as a swap, or as a fetch-and-store.

- `FADD(SUM,ADD)`

  This subroutine call is similar to the fetch-and-add above, but does a floating point addition of `ADD` to the shared floating point variable `SUM(1)`. No value is returned. This is useful for obtaining a global floating point sum. Because the hardware of RP3 will not implement a floating point fetch-and-add, frequently accessed shared floating point sums should instead be maintained with integer fetch-and-adds, with suitably large integer fields. It will be possible to add to such a sum with two or three integer fetch-and-adds; however, it is more difficult to obtain the previous floating point value without explicit locks.

Appendix F
INTEL iPSC

CONTENTS

F1.   Unoptimized Pi Program—Host Program Listing

```
 1          program host
 2          parameter (lenint=4, lendbl=8, npid=0)
 3          integer cid, cnt, copen, nid, pid, processors, cubedim
 4          integer type1, intervals, type
 5          double precision sum
 6          data pid /0/, type1 /1/
 7          cid = copen(pid)
 8          processors = 2**cubedim()
 9    10       write(*, *)
10             write(*, '(''Enter number of intervals'')')
11             read(*, *, err=10, end=20) intervals
12             if (intervals .le. 0) go to 20
13             do 15 i = 0, (processors - 1)
14                call sendmsg (cid, type1, intervals, lenint, i, npid)
15    15       continue
16             call recvmsg(cid, type, sum, lendbl, cnt, nid, pid)
17             write(*, 100) sum/intervals
18             go to 10
19   100    format('Pi is ',f20.16)
20    20    end
```

F2. Unoptimized Pi Program—Node Program Listing

```
21              program node
22              parameter (lenint=4, lendbl=8)
23              integer pid, cid, copen, nid, mynode, dim, cubedim
24              integer type, cnt, hid, node, processors, root
25              integer type1, type2, type3
26              integer intervals, i
27              double precision f, x, h, sum, work
28              data type1 /1/, type2 /2/, type3 /3/
29              data pid /0/, hid /-32768/, root /0/
30              f(x) = 4.0d0/(1.0d0 + x*x)
31              cid = copen(pid)
32              nid = mynode()
33              dim = cubedim()
34              processors = 2**dim
35      10      continue
36              call recvw(cid,type1,intervals,lenint,cnt,node,pid)
37              if (intervals .le. 0) go to 30
38              h = 1.0d0/intervals
39              sum = 0.0d0
40              do 20 i = nid, intervals-1, processors
41                 x = (i + 0.5d0) * h
42                 sum = sum + f(x)
43      20      continue
44              if (nid .eq. root) then
45                 do 25 i = 1, (processors - 1)
46                     call recvw(cid,type2,work,lendbl,cnt,node,pid)
47                     sum = sum + work
48      25          continue
49                 call sendw(cid,type3,sum,lendbl,hid,pid)
50              else
51                 call sendw(cid, type2, sum, lendbl, root, pid)
52              end if
53              go to 10
54      30  end
```

F3.   Optimized Pi Program Listing—Host Program Listing

```
 1            program host
 2            parameter (lenint=4, lendbl=8, npid=0)
 3            integer cid, cnt, copen, nid, pid, root
 4            integer type1, type
 5            integer intervals
 6            double precision sum
 7            data pid /0/, root /0/, type1 /1/
 8            cid = copen(pid)
 9     10        write(*, *)
10            write(*, '(''Enter number of intervals'')')
11            read(*, *, err=10, end=20) intervals
12            if (intervals .le. 0) go to 20
13            call sendmsg(cid, type1, intervals, lenint, root, npid)
14            call recvmsg(cid, type, sum, lendbl, cnt, nid, pid)
15            write(*, 100) sum/intervals
16            go to 10
17    100   format('Pi is ',f20.16)
18     20   end
```

F4.   Optimized Pi Program—Node Program Listing

```
19          program node
20          parameter (lenint=4, lendbl=8)
21          integer pid, cid, copen, nid, mynode, dim, cubedim
22          integer type, cnt, hid, node, processors, root
23          integer type1, type2, type3
24          integer intervals, i
25          double precision f, x, h, sum, work
26          data type1 /1/, type2 /2/, type3 /3/
27          data pid /0/, hid /-32768/, root /0/
28          f(x) = 4.0d0/(1.0d0 + x*x)
29          cid = copen(pid)
30          nid = mynode()
31          dim = cubedim()
32          processors = 2**dim
33    10      continue
34            call grecvw(cid,type1,intervals,lenint,cnt,dim)
35            if (intervals .le. 0) go to 30
36            h = 1.0d0/intervals
37            sum = 0.0d0
38            do 20 i = nid, intervals-1, processors
39               x = (i + 0.5d0) * h
40               sum = sum + f(x)
41    20      continue
42            call gop(cid,type2,sum,1,'+',root,dim,work)
43            if (nid .eq. root) then
44               call sendw(cid,type3,sum,lendbl,hid,pid)
45            end if
46            go to 10
47    30    end
```

F5. "C Language and the Cube Manager"

Conceptually, algorithms written in C for the iPSC are the same as those written in Fortran. However, the C language offers a flexible data structure definition facility and a direct interface to the XENIX operating system, neither of which are available to Fortran language users. Unlike Fortran, C uses a "call-by-value" mechanism for passing parameters to subroutines. Thus each routine, when called, has access only to the contents of each variable in the parameter list, not the memory location where the value is stored. For example, the code fragment:

```
x = 3;
y = f(x);
```

passes the value 3 to the function f, not the memory location of the variable x. If a programmer intended to allow f to modify the *value* of x, the *address* of x must be passed:

```
y = f(&x);
```

and the function f must dereference x when its value is desired, e.g.:

```
z = 5 + *x; /* reference the value of x */
*x = z/2;   /* assign a new value to x */
```

One may use this feature to pass single values (integer, float, etc.), arrays, or structures as messages. The key to remember is that all send (send, sendw, sendmsg) and receive (recv, recvw, recvmsg) routines expect the address of the message, not its value. The only twist is that array identifiers represent the address of the first element of the array, so no "&" should precede an array reference. Since C distinguishes between addresses of different storage types, a type coercion or *type cast* (char *) generally must precede the buffer name.

Consider the following example:

```
int ci, type, node, pid, cnt;
struct s_ship {
   char name[20];
   float px,py,pz;
   float vx,vy,vz;
   float mass;
} ss, sr;

ci = copen(mypid());
...
sendw(ci, type, (char *) &ss, sizeof(ss), node, pid);
...
recvw(ci, &type, (char *) &sr, sizeof(sr), &cnt, &node, &pid);
...
cclose(ci);
```

The calls to `sendw` and `recvw` would work equally well if `ss` and `sr` were declared as type `float`, `int`, or `double`, for example. If `ss` and `sr` instead were arrays of any type, or even structures, one need only drop the `&` which precedes the `ss` and `sr`. For example:

```
int ci, type, node, pid, cnt;
struct s_ship {
    char name[20];
    float px,py,pz;
    float vx,vy,vz;
    float mass;
} as[5], ar[5];

ci = copen(mypid());
...
sendw(ci, type, (char *) as, sizeof(as), node, pid);
...
recvw(ci, &type, (char *) ar, sizeof(ar), &cnt, &node, &pid);
...
cclose(ci);
```

would be appropriate.

Message buffer space on the iPSC host computer is limited. When all buffers fill, no additional messages can be sent or received until one or more buffers are emptied. If a host process expects to produce all data for the nodes, then consume the results only after the last data has been shipped out, a dead-lock may occur if the results from the nodes occupy more buffer space than is available. One obvious way to avoid this is to have two asynchronous processes executing on the host. The parent process spawns a child process (via `fork()`), which produces data for the nodes, then exits when it is finished. The parent then waits for the results to come in and processes them as quickly as they arrive. The input and output channels may be opened before or after the fork with no conflicts. Both processes may even use the same channel. As long as they do not both try to read from the same channel, there will be no conflicts. If they do both try to read from the same channel, one process may steal messages from the other. For example:

```
ci = copen(...);
proc = fork();
if (proc != 0) {  /* parent process */
    while(...) {
        recvmsg(ci, ...);
    }
    exit(0);
}
```

```
else {             /* child process */
    while(...) {
        sendmsg(ci, ...);
    }
    exit(0);
}
```

would allow the child to be the producer and the parent to be the consumer process. The forking of processes is currently supported only on the host.

F6.   Excerpts from the "iPSC Concurrent Debugger Manual"[†]

F6.1   INTRODUCTION

Purpose

This manual describes the iPSC Concurrent Debugger, a tool designed to help developers debug their concurrent applications on iPSC systems.

Overview

The Concurrent Debugger offers developers a source-level debugging tool for their C and Fortran applications on iPSC systems. It provides source-level debug support for user processes running on both the cube manager and the nodes, with minimum interference.

The Concurrent Debugger provides two levels of debug capabilities:

- The first level concentrates on the sequential nature of the processes and provides debug capabilities on the user-defined objects usually seen in a sequential applications debugger. These include such functions as data access, conditional breakpointing/tracing, and execution monitoring. This level of debugging support can be used to debug one process at a time or processes that have little or no intercommunications.

- The second level provides a set of features at the process level designed specifically to assist you in debugging applications in the concurrent environment. This level can be used to debug process-level synchronization and communications activities in the user program. Among these additional features are process monitoring, process communications control, and node/message status monitoring.

F6.2   DESCRIPTION

The Concurrent Debugger runs on both the cube manager and the cube. The component that resides on the cube manager is called the *cube manager debug process*, while the other resides on each node and is called the *cube debug process*. They communicate using the Ethernet global channel.

Cube Manager Debug Process

The cube manager debug process controls the user processes running on the cube manager and performs such tasks as handling user debug commands from the terminal, executing debug commands such as loading user processes, creating/maintaining a small debug data base for symbol information and debugger local objects, evaluating

---

[†]Reprinted by permission of Intel Scientific Computers.

expressions, handling breakpoints, supporting cube manager-to-cube communications, handling keyboard signals, and managing virtual memory.

Cube Debug Process

The cube debug process (one per node) controls the execution of user processes running on the nodes and serves as the execution vehicle. It performs such major tasks as accessing memory, handling breakpoints, monitoring/controlling the invocation and intercommunications among the processes, controlling process execution, and monitoring the system queues. Cube debug processes interface with the node operating system and interact with the cube manager debug process.

F6.3   FUNCTIONS

The Concurrent Debugger offers the following debug capabilities:

- Program Execution Control
- Data and Status Access
- Process Loading
- Debugger Control

Program Execution Control

The *Program Execution Control Commands* provide mechanisms for initiating, suspending, and resuming execution of processes. They also allow you to set, remove, suspend, and restore various breakpoints/tracepoints (both data and code) and their associated actions.

In addition to allowing you to set breakpoints/tracepoints at the user-defined objects, including variables, statements, labels, and subprograms, the Concurrent Debugger allows these watchpoints to be set at the process level. This capability, coupled with the process event specification, helps you to gain insight into the inter-process communications and synchronization activities within the user program.

Data and Status Access

The *Data and Status Access Commands* help you to examine the state of a process after execution has been suspended. In addition to examining the source program, you can also examine and modify data values. The Concurrent Debugger has knowledge of formatting rules when displaying the value of any data type under the current language environment. It also does the checking of assignment compatibility when new values are assigned to variables.

In addition, the Concurrent Debugger allows you to inspect the status of the nodes and the status of the messages. This capability should help you to determine if a deadlock or race condition has occurred.

Process Loading

The *Process Loading Commands* allow you to load user processes into either the cube manager or the nodes. The loaded processes can then be executed under Concurrent Debugger control. Normally, these are the first commands used after the Concurrent Debugger is invoked.

Debugger Control

The *Debugger Control Commands* provide mechanisms to control operations of the Concurrent Debugger. These operations include executing debug command scripts, escaping to the XENIX system for services, defining aliases, and debug help facilities.

Appendix G
Loral Dataflo LDF 100

CONTENTS

307

G1.   Pi Program Listings

A listing of the three node programs follows; the `work distributor`, the `workers`, and the `summer`. Each source program was stored in a separate file.

```
 1    C
 2    C - Work Distribution
 3    C - Sends work intervals to workers and flag to summer
 4    C
 5          REAL*4      LO, HI, SIZINTRVL
 6          INTEGER     NSEGMENTS, INTRVLS, PASS, WORKER
 7          INTEGER*2   FLAG, NWORKERS, TOTINTRVLS, NPASSES, SIZE
 8          COMMON /TERMIN/ NPASSES, TOTINTRVLS
 9          COMMON /WORKARC/ LO, HI, INTRVLS
10          CALL FLOREAD(1, NWORKERS, 1, SIZE)
11          CALL FLOREAD(2, NPASSES, 2, SIZE)
12          CALL PRINTF(" INTRVLS = %d npasses = %d nworkers = %d\n",
13         1                        TOTINTRVLS, NPASSES, NWORKERS)
14          NSEGMENTS = NPASSES * NWORKERS
15          INTRVLS = TOTINTRVLS
16          SIZINTRVL = 1.0 / NSEGMENTS
17          HI = 0
18          DO 100 PASS = 1, NPASSES
19             DO 90 WORKER = 1, NWORKERS
20                LO = HI
21                HI = HI + SIZINTRVL
22                CALL FLOWRITE(WORKER, LO, 6)
23     90       CONTINUE
24             FLAG = NPASSES - PASS
25             CALL FLOWRITE(NWORKERS + 1, FLAG, 1)
26    100   CONTINUE
27          END
28    C
29    C - Worker (Code identical for each worker node)
30    C - Reads work assignment from work distributor, writes partial sum
31    C -    to summer
32    C
33          REAL        LO, HI
34          REAL*8      SUM, WIDTH, FARG, SIZE
35          INTEGER     INTRVLS, SLICE
36          COMMON   /INPATH/ LO, HI, INTRVLS
```

```
37          CALL FLOREAD(1, LO, 6, SIZE)
38          WIDTH = (HI - LO) / INTRVLS
39          SUM = 0.0
40          DO 100 SLICE = 1, INTRVLS
41              FARG = LO + (SLICE - .5) * WIDTH
42              SUM = SUM + WIDTH * (4.0 / (1.0 + FARG * FARG))
43   100    CONTINUE
44          CALL FLOWRITE(1, SUM, 4)
45          END
46   C
47   C - Summer (as in, one that sums)
48   C - Reads partial sum from each worker, adds them into a total sum
49   C
50          INTEGER SIZE
51          INTEGER*2   FLAG, ITER, NPASSES
52          REAL*4        TEMPSUM, TOTALSUM
53          COMMON /STATIC/ TOTALSUM
54          CALL FLOREAD(1, TEMPSUM, 4, SIZE)
55          TOTALSUM = TOTALSUM + TEMPSUM
56          CALL FLOREAD(3, TEMPSUM, 4, SIZE)
57          TOTALSUM = TOTALSUM + TEMPSUM
58          CALL FLOREAD(2, FLAG, 1, SIZE)
59          IF (FLAG .EQ. 0) THEN
60              CALL PRINTF("pi is %F\n", TOTALSUM)
61              CALL PRINTF("diff is %F\n",
62       &         TOTALSUM-3.141592653589793238D0)
63              TOTALSUM = 0
64          END IF
65          END
```

G2.   DGL Format

When encoding a data flow graph into Data Graph Language, each process is given a heading, a list of import (input) arcs, and a list of export (output) arcs in the form:

nodename = "nodecode"

```
import { arc_type arc_list ;
         arc_type arc_list ;
            . . .               }


export { arc_type arc_list ;
         arc_type arc_list ;
            . . .               }
```

where:

- *nodename* is a name used to uniquely identify the node;

- *nodecode* is the name of the file containing the linked code for the process from the loader ld (via the compiler);

- *arc_type* is either open (meaning variable length) or word[*n*] where *n* is an integer representing the number of 16 bit words comprising a complete message—if *n* is 1 then [*n*] can be omitted; and

- *arc_list* is a comma-separated list of user-created arc names (usually from the flow graph), used later by the tag assigner to determine arc connections.
  A constant arc is represented by entering the desired integer constant in place of the *arc_type arc_list* combination.

G3.   DGL—As Output from Tag Assigner

The tag assigner adds tags of the form `<T#>` to each arc and each process in the Data Graph Language that does not already have such a tag pre-assigned by the user. The tags on the arcs are used to identify the data packets for the arc, while the tags on the processes are used to identify code being downloaded to the processor. Shown below is a listing of our DGL after being processed by the tag assigner.

```
1    work_distributor = "work_dist" <C0> <P11> <T64335>
2
3    import {2;
4            word[2]  d00_int_npass <T2000> }
5    export {word[6]  d01_lo_hi_int <T64319>;
6            word[6]  d02_lo_hi_int <T64318>;
7            word     d03_done_signal <T64317>}
8
9    work1 = "worker" <C0> <P10> <T64351>
10
11   import {word[6]  d01_lo_hi_int <T64351>}
12   export {word[4]  d04_sum <T64316>}
13
14   work2 = "worker" <C0> <P9> <T64367>
15
16   import {word[6]  d02_lo_hi_int <T64318>}
17   export {word[4]  d05_sum <T64315>}
18
19   summer = "summer" <C0> <P7> <T64399>
20
21   import {2;
22            word[2]  d03_done_signal <T64317>
23            word[4]  d04_sum <T64316>;
24            word[4]  d05_sum <T64315>; 100}
```

G4. FLOREAD and FLOWRITE (Fortran)

In Fortran, the FLOREAD and FLOWRITE calls have the form

> CALL FLOREAD (*iarcno, record, ireclen, ngot*)

> CALL FLOWRITE (*iarcno, record, ireclen*)

where

- *iarcno* is the number of the arc to be read or written—the first import and export arc listed in the Data Graph Language for a process is arc 1;

- *record* is the name of the record (or variable or constant) to read or write;

- *ireclen* is the length of the record area in 16-bit words; and

- *ngot* is an integer variable that is set by FLOREAD to the number of words actually read from the arc—this value is typically the same as *ireclen* unless the type in the Data Graph Language is open.

If only one value (variable, or constant) is to be read or written, then *record* is simply that value, but if more than one value is to be processed, they must be lined up in a (named) common block, and the name of the first variable in the block must be supplied as *record*. In either case, it is up to the user to figure out how many 16-bit words are being supplied in the call (remembering that integers and single precision reals are 32 bits).

G5. Floread **and** Flowrite **(C)**

In C, the `floread` and `flowrite` functions have the form:

```
ngot = floread(arcno, &read_buf_ptr);
flowrite(arcno, &write_buf, sizeof(struct wr_fields));
```

where the arguments are defined as:

```
int arcno;              /* See Fortran description, above */

struct rd_fields *read_buf_ptr;
                        /* Where the type "struct rd_fields"
                           is defined by the user to contain
                           the fields to be read          */

int ngot;               /* See Fortran description, above */

struct wr_fields write_buf;
                        /* Where the type "struct wr_fields"
                           is defined by the user to contain
                           the fields to be written        */
```

Note that the `floread` call modifies the pointer `read_buf_ptr` to point to the internal buffering area ("communication" RAM) on the processor, so an incorrect reference through this pointer (i.e., past the end of the record) could have very undesirable effects.

G6.   PRINTF **(Fortran)**

To print from a node (in Fortran), use:

CALL PRINTF (*formatstring*, *value*, *value*, . . .)

where

(bu *Formatstring* is a character string containing the formatting codes used in C. Differences are that the conversion characters d and f are used only for INTEGER*2 and REAL*4 (default) values, respectively. INTEGER*4 values must use the D conversion character, and REAL*8 values must use the F conversion character.

(bu *value* is a variable or constant to be printed.

Since the printf function is not defined as part of the C language, Fortran programmers may need the help of a C resource (person or manual) to use this call effectively.

G7. Makefile Listing for the Pi Program

As mentioned in Section 9.2, many of the steps of program development can be aided
by the Unix `make` facility. Shown below is a listing of the makefile we used to process the DGL and node programs:

```
1   OBJS   = summer.o work_dist.o worker.o
2   LIBROOT= /u/software/lib
3   LINKED = summer worker work_dist
4   FLAGS  = -I/u/software/include
5   TAGGED = wirelist.tagged
6   CODE   = wirelist.code
7   GRAPH  = wirelist
8
9   ACTIVENODE = 800
10
11  CC = cc $(FLAGS)
12
13  doit: $(CODE)
14
15  $(CODE): $(OBJS) $(LINKED) $(TAGGED) $(LIBROOT)/flolib.a
16      /u/software/src/graph.lang/linker/linker $(TAGGED) -o $(CODE)
17
18  $(TAGGED): $(GRAPH)
19      cc -E $(GRAPH) |
20      /u/software/src/graph.lang/tag.ass/tass -o $(TAGGED)
21
22  summer: summer.o
23      ld -msummer.map    summer.o    -T $(ACTIVENODE)
24          $(LIBROOT)/flolib.a -o summer
25
26  worker: worker.o
27      ld -mworker.map    worker.o    -T $(ACTIVENODE)
28          $(LIBROOT)/flolib.a -o worker
29
30  work_dist: work_dist.o
31      ld -mwork_dist.map work_dist.o -T $(ACTIVENODE)
32          $(LIBROOT)/flolib.a -o work_dist
```

Appendix H
Sequent Balance Series

CONTENTS

H1.   Pi Program Listing—Before Preprocessing

```
 1   c - number of processes; status returned
 2           integer*4 nprocs, status
 3   c - number of rectangles; loop index
 4           integer*4 nrecs, i
 5   c - integration variables
 6           double precision h, x
 7   c - pi as found by the program
 8           double precision tpi
 9   c - pi to 16 decimal places, for comparison
10           double precision pi
11           pi = 3.1415926535897932d0
12      10  write(*,*) 'Number of rectangles: '
13           read(*,*) nrecs
14           if (nrecs.le.0) goto 30
15           write(*,*) 'Number of procs: '
16           read(*,*) nprocs
17           if (nprocs.le.0) goto 30
18           call start_timer
19           status = m_set_procs(nprocs)
20           if (status.ne.0) goto 20
21           h = 1.d0 / nrecs
22           tpi = 0.0d0
23   c$doacross share(h), local(x), reduction(tpi)
24           do 100 i = 1, nrecs
25               x = (i-0.5d0) * h
26               tpi = tpi + 4d0 / (1d0 + x * x)
27     100   continue
28           tpi = h * tpi
29           call m_kill_procs
30      20  call stop_timer
31           if (status.ne.0) then
32               write(*,*) ' Error setting number of processes'
33           else
34               call fprt_timer(nprocs,nprocs,nprocs)
35               write(*,500) tpi
36     500     format(' Pi:     ',f18.16)
37               write(*,600) pi - tpi
38     600     format(' Error: ',f18.16)
39           endif
40           goto 10
41      30  stop
42           end
```

H2.   Pi Program Listing—After Preprocessing

```
1    $system
2    $line 3 pi.fpp
3          external do100%
4          INTEGER m_fork
5    $line 2 pi.f
6          integer*4 nprocs, status
7          integer*4 nrecs, i
8          double precision h, x
9          double precision tpi
10          double precision pi
11          pi = 3.1415926535897932d0
12      10 write(*,*) 'Number of rectangles: '
13          read(*,*) nrecs
14          if (nrecs.le.0) goto 30
15          write(*,*) 'Number of procs: '
16          read(*,*) nprocs
17          if (nprocs.le.0) goto 30
18          call start_timer
19          status = m_set_procs(nprocs)
20          if (status.ne.0) goto 20
21          h = 1.d0 / nrecs
22          tpi = 0.0d0
23   c$doacross share(h), local(x), reduction(tpi)
24          if (m_fork(do100%,1,nrecs,1,h,tpi).ne.0) stop 'do 100  '
25          tpi = h * tpi
26          call m_kill_procs
27      20 call stop_timer
28          if (status.ne.0) then
29             write(*,*) ' Error setting number of processes'
30          else
31             call fprt_timer(nprocs,nprocs,nprocs)
32             write(*,500) tpi
33     500    format(' Pi:      ',f18.16)
34             write(*,600) pi - tpi
35     600    format(' Error: ',f18.16)
36          endif
37          goto 10
38      30 stop
39          end
40   $line 50 pi.fpp
41          subroutine do100%(i%1,i%2,i%3,h,tpi%)
```

```
42          integer i%1,i%2,i%3,i%chunk,m_get_myid,m_get_numprocs,i%end
43          integer is%1,is%2,is%3,is%4,is%5,is%6,is%7
44          INTEGER i
45          DOUBLE PRECISION x,h,tpi,tpi%
46          i%end = i%2
47          i = m_get_numprocs()
48          if (i .gt. 1) then
49             i%chunk = i%3 * i
50             i = i%1 + i%3 * m_get_myid()
51          else
52             i%chunk = i%3
53             i = i%1
54          endif
55 99998 tpi = 0
56          do 99996, i = i, i%end, i%chunk
57 $line 26 pi.f
58          x = (i-0.5d0) * h
59          tpi = tpi + 4d0 / (1d0 + x * x)
60   100  continue
61 $line 71 pi.fpp
62 99996 continue
63 99997 call m_lock
64          tpi% = tpi% + tpi
65          call m_unlock
66          end
```

H3.   Parallel Compilers, Utilities, and System Calls

Parallel programming on the Balance Series can be done in three languages: C, Fortran, and Pascal. DYNIX Manual pages[†] for the corresponding compilers are included in this Appendix. For more information on parallel programming in a particular language, see the appropriate *Compiler User's Manual*.

The `make` utility maintains program groups by updating files only when necessary. A *Makefile* consists of command sequences specifying dependencies. A *target file* is updated if it is dependent on files that have been modified, or if the target does not exist. The `make` utility has been extended by Sequent to allow prerequisite files to be made simultaneously. See the Parallel Support section of the `make` manual page for more details.

`Pdbx` was discussed briefly in Chapter 10. For more information, see the *DYNIX Pdbx Debugger User's Manual*.

`Mmap` is used by Sequent in the implementation of shared memory and in accessing the hardware-based locks.

[†]DYNIX manual pages in Appendices H3 and H5 are reprinted courtesy of Sequent Computer Systems Inc. Some manual pages have been excerpted to emphasize parallel aspects that differ from the corresponding standard (sequential) UNIX utilities.

NAME

cc – C compiler

SYNOPSIS

cc [option] ... file ...

DESCRIPTION

Cc is the DYNIX C compiler. The DYNIX compiler supports parallel programming (refer to the *Balance Guide to Parallel Programming*).

Cc accepts several types of arguments. Arguments whose names end with ".c" are taken to be C source programs; they are compiled, and each object program is left on the file whose name is that of the source with ".o" substituted for ".c". The ".o" file is normally deleted if a single C program is compiled and loaded all at once. In the same way, arguments whose names end with ".s" are taken to be assembly source programs; they are assembled, producing ".o" files.

The following options are interpreted by cc. See ld(1) for load-time options.

-c   Suppress the loading phase of the compilation; force an object file to be produced even if only one program is compiled.

-g   Have the compiler produce additional symbol table information for pdbx(1). Also pass the -lg flag to ld(1).

-go   Have the compiler produce additional symbol table information for the obsolete debugger sdb(1). Also pass the -lg flag to ld(1).

-w   Suppress warning diagnostics.

-p   Produce code that counts the number of times each routine is called. If loading takes place, replace the standard startup routine with one that automatically calls monitor(3) at the start and arranges to write out a mon.out file at normal termination of execution of the object program. An execution profile can then be generated by using prof(1).

-pg   Produce counting code in the manner of -p, but invoke a run-time recording mechanism that keeps more extensive statistics and produces a gmon.out file at normal termination. Also, a profiling library is searched, in lieu of the standard C library. An execution profile can then be generated by using gprof(1).

-O   Invoke an object-code improver. Do not use on programs that contain asm statements, as the result may not be correct.

-Y   Causes all external or static variables not explicitly declared as shared or private to be shared. (Refer to the *Balance 8000/21000 C Compiler User's Manual* for information on the shared and private keywords.)

323

-i   Suppress optimizations that are incorrect when memory locations might spontaneously change value. Memory-mapped registers have this property. This option has no effect if -O is not selected.

-R   Passed on to as, making initialized variables shared and read-only.

-S   Compile the named C programs and leave the assembler-language output on corresponding files with a ".s" suffix.

-SO   Compile the named C programs and send the assembler-language output to standard output.

-E   Run only the macro preprocessor on the named C programs and send the result to the standard output.

-C   prevent the macro preprocessor from removing comments.

-o output
        Name the final output file output. If this option is used, the file a.out will be left undisturbed.

-v   List (on standard output) the utilities called by cc and their arguments. Information produced by the -v flag is useful for debugging.

-vn   Like -v, but cc does not actually call the utilities.

-D name=def

-D name
        Define the name to the preprocessor, as if by "#define". If no definition is given, the name is defined as "1".

-U name
        Remove any initial definition of name. (The C preprocessor initially defines sequent, ns32000, and unix as "1".)

-I dir "#include" files whose names do not begin with "/" are always sought first in the directory of the file argument, then in directories named in -I options, then in directories on a standard list.

-B string
        Find substitute compiler passes in the files named string with the suffixes cpp, ccom, and c2. If "string" is empty, use a standard backup version.

-t [p02]
        Find only the designated compiler passes in the files whose names are constructed by a -B option. In the absence of a -B option, the string is taken to be "/usr/c/o".

-M   Run only the macro preprocessor on the named C programs, requesting it to generate Makefile dependencies and send the result to standard output.

Other arguments are taken to be loader option arguments, C-compatible object programs produced by an earlier `cc` run, or libraries of C-compatible routines. These programs, together with the results of any compilations specified, are loaded (in the order given) to produce an executable program with the name `a.out`.

FILES

`file.c`	input file
`file.o`	object file
`file.s`	assembly file
`a.out`	loaded output
`/tmp/ctm?`	temporary
`/lib/cpp`	preprocessor
`/lib/ccom`	compiler
`/lib/c2`	optional optimizer
`/lib/crt0.o`	runtime startoff
`/lib/mcrt0.o`	startoff for profiling
`/usr/lib/gcrt0.o`	startoff for gprof-profiling
`/lib/libc.a`	standard library, see intro(3)
`/usr/lib/libc_p.a`	profiling library, see intro(3)
`/usr/lib/libpps.a`	Parallel Programming Library, see intro(3)
`/usr/include`	standard directory for "#include" files
`/usr/local/include`	local directory for "#include" files
`mon.out`	file produced for analysis by prof(1)
`gmon.out`	file produced for analysis by gprof(1)

SEE ALSO

B. W. Kernighan and D. M. Ritchie, *The C Programming Language*, Prentice-Hall, 1978
B. W. Kernighan, *Programming in C—A Tutorial*
D. M. Ritchie, *C Reference Manual*
Balance 8000/21000 C Compiler User's Manual
Balance Guide to Parallel Programming
monitor(3), prof(1), gprof(1), ddt(1), ld(1), pdbx(1), as(1)

DIAGNOSTICS

The diagnostics produced by C are intended to be self-explanatory. Occasional messages may be produced by the assembler or loader.

BUGS

The compiler ignores advice to put `char`, `unsigned char`, `short`, or `unsigned short` variables in registers.

NAME

fortran – Fortran compiler

SYNOPSIS

```
fortran [ option ] ... file ...
```

DESCRIPTION

Fortran is the DYNIX Fortran compiler. DYNIX Fortran is compatible with ANSI standard Fortran 77, but has extensions and a preprocessor to support parallel programming. (For more information on parallel programming, refer to the *Balance Guide to Parallel Programming*).

Fortran accepts several types of arguments. Arguments whose names end with ".f" or ".for" are taken to be Fortran source files; a suffix of ".p" or ".pas" implies a Pascal source file; and a suffix of ".c" implies a C source file. The named source files are compiled, and each object module is written to the file x.o, where x is the basename of the original source file. In the same way, arguments whose names end with ".s" are taken to be assembly source files and are assembled, producing a ".o" file.

Unless the −c option is specified, the ".o" files are linked with the Fortran, Pascal, and C run-time libraries and loaded all at one go. The ".o" files are deleted unless the −c option is specified.

The following options are interpreted by fortran. See ld(1) for load-time options.

−O[0−4]

> Compile at specified level of optimization. The optimization levels are defined as follows: Level 0 performs no optimization. Level 1 enables constant folding, a technique whereby the compiler calculates the values of constant expressions and places the values in the object code. Level 2 enables constant folding and allocates registers on a per-subroutine basis. Level 3 enables constant folding and allocates registers over ranges smaller than one subroutine. Level 4 performs the same optimizations as Level 3, plus it optimizes array index computation within DO loops. The default optimization level is 4.
>
> The −O option and the −g option are not compatible. If both options appear in a fortran command, the option that appears first supercedes the other, and the compiler generates a warning message. If the −g option supercedes, the optimization level is set to 1.

−mp

> Invoke parallel preprocessor. This preprocessor generates Fortran code for parallel DO loop execution.
>
> If program units containing parallel DO loops are compiled separately, the −mp option must be used for each separate compilation in order to ensure that all variables are in shared memory. If a subprogram called from a parallel DO loop is compiled separately, the subprogram must also be compiled with the −mp option.

-v   Verbose mode. Display the steps of a compile.

-vn   Like -v, but does not actually compile the program.

-c   Suppress the loading phase of the compilation and force an object file to be produced even if only one module is compiled.

-e   Compile for C language compatibility. Arguments will be popped at the calling site rather than at the return site. This enables C modules to be linked with Fortran and Pascal. External names (used by ld (1)) are converted to lowercase. (By default, external names are converted to uppercase). Refer to the *Balance 8000/21000 Fortran Compiler User's Manual* for further details.

-L listname
            Generates a listing on the file "listname". If no name is specified, the default name is list.

-x   Generate a cross-reference in the listing file.

-prompt
            Prompt to standard input whenever a compile time error is detected. This prevents error messages from scrolling off the screen before you can read them.

-p   Compiles the code for profiling. The load sequence picks up the libraries for the prof utility. Fortran, Pascal, and C run-time libraries are also profiled.

-pg   Compiles the code for profiling. The load sequence picks up the libraries for the gprof utility. Fortran, Pascal, and C run-time libraries are also profiled.

-P   Compiles the code for profiling. The load sequence picks up the libraries for the prof utility. Run-time libraries are NOT profiled.

-PG   Compiles the code for profiling. The load sequence picks up the libraries for the gprof utility. Run-time libraries are NOT profiled. The flag -Pg is interpreted exactly the same as -PG.

-u   Do not delete ".obj" files. For each source file, the compiler produces an intermediate file with an ".obj" suffix. Under normal circumstances (-u omitted), these files are deleted when compilation is complete, since they serve no other function in the current implementation.

-o output
            Name the final output file output. If this option is used, the file a.out will be left undisturbed.

-g   Build a file of debug information for the pdbx debugger in the current working directory. The file will have .dbg as a suffix. For Fortran modules, information for COMMON variables is dumped only for variables that are referenced in that program unit (subroutine, function, or main). This speeds the loading of very large programs, but prevents you from examining COMMON variables that are never referenced.

The −O and −g options are not compatible. If both options appear in a fortran command, the option that appears first supercedes the other and the compiler generates a warning message. If the −g option supercedes, the optimization level is set to 1.

−gv   Build a file of debug information for the pdbx debugger in the current working directory. The file will have ".dbg" as a suffix. For Fortran modules, information for all COMMON variables is dumped, even if the variables are never referenced. This flag increases debugger-initialization time for very large programs. The −O option and the −gv option are not compatible. If both options appear in a fortran command, the option that appears first supercedes the other, and the compiler generates a warning message. If the −g option supercedes, the optimization level is set to 1.

−ansi   Flag as errors any deviations from the ANSI Fortran 77 standard. By default, the compiler ignores certain deviations from the standard and issues warning messages for others.

−charequ

       Allow numeric and CHARACTER variables to be EQUIVALENCEd or to share the same COMMON area and allow numeric variables to be initialized with CHARACTER data constants. Specifying this option is equivalent to including the $CHAREQU compiler option at the beginning of each source file.

−c72   Ignore all characters beyond column 72 in each source line. Specifying this option is equivalent to including the $COL72 compiler option at the beginning of each source file.

−dc   Compile debug code. By default, any source line that contains a lowercase or uppercase "D" in column 1 is treated as a comment. When this option is specified, the compiler processes the line as if the "D" were a space.

Other arguments are taken to be either loader options, or object modules, or perhaps libraries of compatible routines. These modules, together with the results of any compilations specified, are loaded (in the order given) to produce an executable program with the name a.out.

FILES

file.f or file.for	input file
file.dbg	file of information for pdbx(1)
file.o	object file
a.out	loaded output
/usr/lib/fppdoall	parallel preprocessor
/usr/lib/fortran	compiler front-end
/usr/lib/fncode	compiler code generator
/usr/lib/fjlinker	object code reformatter

`/usr/lib/libc.a`	C run-time support library
`/usr/lib/libf.a`	Fortran run-time support library
`/usr/lib/libpps.a`	Parallel Programming Library
`/usr/lib/libf_p.a`	Pascal run-time support library

SEE ALSO

ld(1), ddt(1), pdbx(1)

Balance 8000/21000 Fortran Compiler User's Manual

DIAGNOSTICS

The diagnostics produced by `fortran` itself are intended to be self-explanatory. Occasional messages may be produced by the loader.

NAME
pascal – Pascal compiler

SYNOPSIS
pascal [option] ... file ...

DESCRIPTION
Pascal is the DYNIX Pascal compiler.   Pascal accepts several types of arguments:

Arguments whose names end with ".p" or ".pas" are taken to be Pascal source files; a suffix of ".f" or ".for" implies a Fortran source program; and a suffix of ".c" implies a C source program. The named source files are compiled, and each object module is written to the file x.o, where x is the basename of the original source file. In the same way, arguments whose names end with ".s" are taken to be assembly source files and are assembled, producing a ".o" file.

Unless the −c option is specified, the ".o" files are linked with the Pascal and C run-time libraries and loaded all at one go. The ".o" files are deleted unless the −c option is specified.

The following options are interpreted by pascal. See ld(1) for load-time options.

−c   Suppress the loading phase of the compilation and force an object file to be produced even if only one program is compiled.

−e   Compile for C language compatibility. Arguments will be popped at the calling site rather than at the return site. This enables C modules to be linked with Fortran and Pascal. External names (used by ld (1)) are converted to lowercase. (By default, external names are converted to uppercase. Names declared cexternal are passed unchanged to ld regardless of whether −e is specified.) Refer to the *Balance 8000 Pascal Compiler User's Manual* for further details.

−L listname
          Generates a listing on the file listname. If no name is specified, the default name is list.

−prompt
          Prompts to standard input whenever a compile-time error is detected. This prevents error messages from flying off the screen.

−p   Compiles the code for profiling. The load sequence picks up the libraries for the prof utility. Pascal and C run-time libraries are also profiled.

−pg   Compiles the code for profiling. The load sequence picks up the libraries for the gprof utility. Pascal and C run-time libraries are also profiled.

−P   Compiles the code for profiling. The load sequence picks up the libraries for the prof utility. Run-time libraries are NOT profiled.

-PG　　　Compiles the code for profiling. The load sequence picks up the libraries for the `gprof` utility. Run-time libraries are NOT profiled. The flag `-Pg` is interpreted exactly the same as `-PG`.

-u　　　Do not remove ".obj" files. For each source file, the compiler produces an intermediate file with an ".obj" suffix. These files are required for the secure separate compilation feature. For details, refer to the *Balance 8000 Pascal Compiler User's Manual*.

-o output

Name the final output file `output`. If this option is used, the file `a.out` will be left undisturbed.

-g　　　Causes the compiler to build a file of debug information for dbg(1) or dbx(1) in the current working directory. The file will have ".dbg" as a suffix.

-gv　　　Build a file of debug information for dbg(1) or dbx(1) in the current working directory. The file will have ".dbg" as a suffix. For Pascal modules, `-g` and `-gv` have the same effect. (For Fortran modules, information for all COMMON variables is dumped, even if the variables are never referenced. This flag increases debugger-initialization time for very large programs.)

Other arguments are taken to be either loader options, or object modules, or perhaps libraries of compatible routines. These modules, together with the results of any compilations specified, are loaded (in the order given) to produce an executable program with the name `a.out`.

FILES

`file.f` or `file.for`	input file
`file.dbg`	file of information for dbg(1) or dbx(1)
`file.o`	object file
`a.out`	loaded output
`/usr/lib/r`	messages

SEE ALSO

Balance 8000 Pascal Compiler User's Manual
ld(1), ddt(1), dbg(1), dbx(1)

DIAGNOSTICS

The diagnostics produced by `pascal` itself are intended to be self-explanatory. Occasional messages may be produced by the loader.

NAME

    make – maintain program groups

SYNOPSIS

    make [-f makefile] [option] ... file ...

DESCRIPTION

Make executes commands in makefile to update one or more target names.   Name is typically a program. If no -f option is present, "makefile" and "Makefile" are tried in order. If makefile is "-", the standard input is taken. More than one -f option may appear.

Make updates a target if it depends on prerequisite files that have been modified since the target was last modified, or if the target does not exist.

Makefile contains a sequence of entries that specify dependencies. The first line of an entry is a blank-separated list of targets, then a colon, then a list of prerequisite files. Text following a semicolon, and all following lines that begin with a tab, are shell commands to be executed to update the target. If a name appears on the left of more than one "colon" line, then it depends on all of the names on the right of the colon on those lines, but only one command sequence may be specified for it. If a name appears on a line with a double colon "::" then the command sequence following that line is performed only if the name is out of date with respect to the names to the right of the double colon, and is not affected by other double colon lines on which that name may appear.

Two special forms of a name are recognized. A name like a(b) means the file named b stored in the archive named a. A name like a((b)) means the file stored in archive a containing the entry point b.

Sharp and newline surround comments.

The following makefile says that "pgm" depends on two files "a.o" and "b.o", and that they in turn depend on ".c" files and a common file "incl".

```
pgm:  a.o b.o
     cc a.o b.o -lm -o pgm
a.o:  incl a.c
     cc -c a.c
b.o:  incl b.c
     cc -c b.c
```

Makefile entries of the form

    string1 = string2

are macro definitions. Subsequent appearances of $(string1) or ${string1} are replaced by string2. If string1 is a single character, the parentheses or braces are optional.

Make infers prerequisites for files for which makefile gives no construction commands. For example, a ".c" file may be inferred as prerequisite for a ".o" file and be compiled to produce the ".o" file. Thus the preceding example can be done more briefly:

```
pgm:   a.o b.o
       cc a.o b.o -lm -o pgm
a.o b.o: incl
```

Prerequisites are inferred according to selected suffixes listed as the "prerequisites" for the special name ".SUFFIXES"; multiple lists accumulate; an empty list clears what came before. Order is significant; the first possible name for which both a file and a rule as described in the next paragraph exist is inferred. The default list is

```
.SUFFIXES: .out .o .c .e .r .f .y .l .s .p
```

The rule to create a file with suffix s2 that depends on a similarly named file with suffix s1 is specified as an entry for the "target" s1s2. In such an entry, the special macro $* stands for the target name with suffix deleted, $@ for the full target name, $< for the complete list of prerequisites, and $? for the list of prerequisites that are out of date. For example, a rule for making optimized ".o" files from ".c" files is:

```
.c.o: ; cc -c -O -o $@ $*.c
```

Certain macros are used by the default inference rules to communicate optional arguments to any resulting compilations. In particular, "CFLAGS" is used for cc(1) options, "FFLAGS" for fortran(1) options, "PFLAGS" for pascal(1) options, and "LFLAGS" and "YFLAGS" for lex and yacc(1) options. In addition, the macro "MFLAGS" is filled in with the initial command line options supplied to make. This simplifies maintaining a hierarchy of makefiles as one may then invoke make on makefiles in subdirectories and pass along useful options such as -k.

Another special macro is "VPATH". The "VPATH" macro should be set to a list of directories separated by colons. When make searches for a file as a result of a dependency relation, it will first search the current directory and then each of the directories on the "VPATH" list. If the file is found, the actual path to the file will be used, rather than just the filename. If "VPATH" is not defined, then only the current directory is searched.

One use for "VPATH" is when one has several programs that compile from the same source. The source can be kept in one directory, and each set of object files (along with a separate makefile) would be in a separate subdirectory. The "VPATH" macro would point to the source directory in this case.

Command lines are executed one at a time, each by its own shell. A line is printed when it is executed unless the special target ".SILENT" is in makefile, or the first character of the command is "@".

Commands returning nonzero status (see intro(1)) cause `make` to terminate unless the special target ".IGNORE" is in `makefile` or the command begins with <tab><hyphen>.

Interrupt and quit cause the target to be deleted unless the target is a directory or depends on the special name ".PRECIOUS".

Other options:

-P n   Permit n command sequences to be done in parallel with "&". See "PARALLEL SUPPORT" section below. If this option is present multiple times on the command line, the least value for n supercedes the others. If this option is missing, `make` looks for the environment variable PARALLEL and uses its numeric value for n. If this fails, n defaults to 3.

-i   Equivalent to the special entry ".IGNORE:".

-k   When a command returns nonzero status, abandon work on the current entry, but continue on branches that do not depend on the current entry.

-n   Trace and print, but do not execute the commands needed to update the targets.

-t   Touch, i.e., update the modified date of targets, without executing any commands.

-r   Equivalent to an initial special entry ".SUFFIXES:" with no list.

-s   Equivalent to the special entry ".SILENT:".

PARALLEL SUPPORT

`Make` includes a parallel processing ability. If the string separating a target from its prerequisites is ":&" or "::&", `make` can run the command sequences to make the prerequisites simultaneously. If two names are separated by an ampersand on the right side of a colon, those two may be created in parallel.

For example, in this Makefile, the objects "a.o", "b.o", and "c.o" may be built in parallel:

```
pgm:&    a.o b.o c.o
         cc -o pgm a.o b.o c.o
a.o:     a.c defs.h
b.o:     b.c defs.h
c.o:     c.c defs.h
```

In this example, only "a.o" and "b.o" are built in parallel, with "c.o" being started after the other two complete:

```
pgm:     a.o & b.o c.o
         cc -o pgm a.o b.o c.o
a.o:     a.c defs.h
b.o:     b.c defs.h
c.o:     c.c defs.h
```

The -P option controls the number of simultaneous command streams. Make invoked with an argument of -P1 selects no parallelism, and is useful when error messages from parallel command sequences are intermingled, obscuring the actual source of error. (A useful technique for searching the output for error messages is to look for lines that do not begin with a tab character.)

To execute command sequences in parallel, make forks off processes without waiting for them, and indicates they've been forked by appending an ampersand and the process ID while printing the command (similar to using the ampersand to indicate asynchronous jobs in the shell). If the forked-off command sequence returns a non-zero exit status, make precedes the error (or warning) message with the process ID, to help determine the source of the error.

Not all command sequences can be parallelized. Some command sequences generate filenames in the current directory that do not depend on the file being built. For example, operations involving two or more usages of yacc, lex, or xstr in the same directory cannot be parallelized.

While building the prerequisites in parallel, only the last (or only) command in a multiple command sequence is eligible to be forked for asynchronous execution. Other commands will be executed sequentially. For example, in this Makefile, only "lastcommand" is run in parallel; "firstcommand" and "secondcommand" are processed before any of the commands to build "b" are invoked:

```
pgm:& a b
a:
        firstcommand
        secondcommand
        lastcommand
b:
        b-firstcommand
        b-secondcommand
        b-lastcommand
```

To circumvent this, make all the commands be considered as one long shell command, as in:

```
pgm:& a b
a:
        firstcommand; \
        secondcommand; \
        lastcommand
b:
        b-firstcommand; \
        b-secondcommand; \
        b-lastcommand
```

The backslash at the end of the command line causes the following line to be regarded as a continuation. A Makefile set up in this way will have all the commands to build "a" be run in parallel with all the commands to build "b". Note that all three commands to build "a" are now executed by the same shell (rather than three separate invocations of the shell). Commands interpreted by the shell directly (to change directory, for example) are thus no longer isolated to one particular command line. This should be taken into consideration when altering the Makefiles in this way.

FILES

    makefile, Makefile

SEE ALSO

    sh(1), touch(1), fortran(1), pascal(1)
    S. I. Feldman, "Make – A Program for Maintaining Computer Programs".

BUGS

    Some commands return nonzero status inappropriately. Use -i to overcome the difficulty. Commands that are directly executed by the shell, notably cd(1), are ineffective across newlines in make.

    "VPATH" is intended to act like the System V "VPATH" support, but there is no guarantee that it functions identically.

    The ":&" and "::&" syntax is incompatible with previous versions of make. Where portability is desired, use ":$(P)" or "::$(P)" and type P="&" on the command line.

NAME
>
> pdbx, dbx – parallel debugger [excerpts]

SYNOPSIS
>
> pdbx [-r][-i][-u][-a][-c file] [-I dir]...[objfile [coredump]]
>
> pdbx [-r][-i][-u][-a][-c file] [-I dir]...\
>   [-O objfile]...[-C coredump]...

DESCRIPTION

Pdbx is a tool for source level debugging and execution of both conventional and parallel programs under DYNIX.   Pdbx is an enhanced version of the UNIX 4.2BSD dbx debugger and can be invoked as either pdbx or dbx; both names are links to the same program. When used to debug conventional one-process, one-program applications, pdbx performs almost identically to UNIX 4.2BSD dbx (refer to Appendix A of the *DYNIX Pdbx Debugger User's Manual* for a list of differences).

The objfile is an executable object file produced by a compiler with the -g flag specified to produce symbol information. Currently, cc(1), pascal(1), and fortran(1) produce the appropriate source information. The machine level facilities of pdbx can be used on any program.

The object file contains a symbol table that includes the names of all the source files translated by the compiler to create it. These files are available for perusal while using the debugger.

If a file named core exists in the current directory or one or more coredump files are specified, pdbx can be used to examine the state of the program when it faulted.

The first form of the pdbx command shown above is used when debugging an application that consists of one or more processes running the same program. The second form is used when debugging applications that consist of multiple programs (e.g., client/server applications or processes that exec); each -O option specifies a program to be debugged.

If the file .dbxinit exists in the current directory, then the debugger commands in .dbxinit are executed. Pdbx also checks for a .dbxinit in the user's home directory if there isn't one in the current directory.

The command line options and their meanings are:

-r   Execute objfile immediately. If it terminates successfully, pdbx exits. Otherwise the reason for termination will be reported and the user offered the option of entering the debugger or letting the program fault. Pdbx will read from /dev/tty when -r is specified and standard input is not a terminal.

-i   Force pdbx to act as though standard input is a terminal (e.g., prompt for commands).

-u   Preserve the case of identifiers for Fortran and Pascal programs. The Fortran and Pascal compilers are case insensitive and translate identifiers to uppercase only. Normally, `Pdbx` translates Fortran and Pascal identifiers to lowercase only. If this option is specified, Fortran and Pascal identifiers will remain all uppercase.

`-a`   Run all processes asynchronously (i.e., in the background). As soon as `pdbx` starts a process running, it prompts immediately for another command. No process may read from the terminal.

`-c file`
     Execute the `pdbx` commands in the `file` before reading from standard input.

`-I dir` Add `dir` to the list of directories that are searched when looking for a source file. Normally `pdbx` looks for source files in the current directory and in the directory where `objfile` is located. The directory search path can also be set with the `use` command. When more than one object file is specified, each `-I` option applies to the program specified by the next `-O` option.

`-O objfile`
     Identifies `objfile` as a program to be debugged. If there is only one program, it can be specified without the `-O` using the first form of the `pdbx` command shown in the SYNOPSIS.

`-C coredump`
     Identifies `coredump` as a core file to be analyzed. The `-C` option is useful if there is more than one program or more than one core file. The position of `-C` options relative to `-O` options is not important; `pdbx` matches each core file with the appropriate object file.

Unless `-r` is specified, `pdbx` just prompts and waits for a command.

Compiling Programs for Use with `Pdbx`

The `-g` flag given as a command line argument to cc(1), pascal(1), or fortran(1) causes the compiler to produce symbolic information for `pdbx`. If you invoke ld (1) directly to link your program, you must include the `-lg` flag in the `ld` command line. For C programs, the symbolic information is encoded in the symbol table of the object file. For Fortran and Pascal programs, the symbolic information is placed in a separate file with the extension `.dbg`. When `pdbx` is invoked on an object file `objfile`, it will read the symbolic information in the file `objfile.dbg` (if such a file exists) as well as the symbolic information in `objfile`.

If separate compilation is used, several `.dbg` files will be produced: one for each source file. These should be concatenated (with cat(1)) into `objfile.dbg`.

Code compiled with the `-g` flag cannot be optimized using the compiler's `-O` flag. Otherwise, the `-g` flag does not change the code that the compiler generates.

Debugging Multiprocess Applications

Pdbx can control multiple processes and their descendants. When a process is created (e.g., via the run command), it is assigned a process number. The first process created is number 1, and the process created most recently by pdbx is referred to as the "current process". Certain pdbx commands operate on the current process by default, but can operate on a specified process (e.g., "%2") or on all processes. Process numbers can be listed using the pdbx ps command, and the "current process" designation can be changed using the "%" command.

To run a process in the background, append an ampersand (&) to the command that starts the process running (e.g., run, cont, step). Pdbx will prompt for another command without waiting for the process to stop.

Execution and Tracing Commands

run [objfile] [args] [< filename] [> filename] [&]

rerun [objfile] [args] [< filename] [> filename] [&]
> Start executing objfile, passing args as command line arguments; < or > can be used to redirect input or output in the usual manner. When rerun is used without any arguments, the previous argument list is passed to the program; otherwise it is identical to run. Run and rerun terminate any existing processes before creating the process to be run.

> NOTE: The objfile parameter must be included if more than one objfile was specified when pdbx was invoked; otherwise it must be omitted.

create [objfile] [args] [< filename] [> filename]
> Create a process as with run, but do not run the process and do not terminate any existing processes. The created process can be run using the cont command.

terminate [%n]
terminate all
> Terminate the specified process (defaults to the current process). The ps command does not list terminated processes.

ps [%n]
> Report the status, DYNIX process ID, and parent process of process n. If no process is specified, print a numbered list of all processes, indicating the status of each. For core dumps, ps reports which type of signal caused the program to abort.

%n   Make process n the current process.

trace [procid] [in procedure/function] [if condition]
trace [procid] source-line-number [if condition]
trace [procid] procedure/function [in procedure/function] [if condition]

```
trace [procid] expression at source-line-number [if condition]
trace [procid] variable [in procedure/function] [if condition]
```
Have tracing information printed when the program is executed. A number is associated with the command that is used to turn the tracing off (see the `delete` command).

For multiprocess applications, the optional `procid` parameter specifies which process is to be traced (defaults to all processes associated with the current source file). A `procid` of the form `%n` specifies that process `n` is to be traced. A `procid` of the form `%objfile` specifies that all processes created from `objfile` are to be traced.

The next argument describes what is to be traced. If it is a `source-line-number`, then the line is printed immediately prior to being executed. Source line numbers in a file other than the current one must be preceded by the name of the file in quotes and a colon, e.g. `"mumble.p":17`.

If the argument is a procedure or function name, then every time it is called, information is printed telling what routine called it, from what source line it was called, and what parameters were passed to it. In addition, its return is noted, and if it's a function then the value it is returning is also printed.

If the argument is an `expression` with an `at` clause, then the value of the expression is printed whenever the identified source line is reached, just before it is executed.

If the argument is a variable, then the name and value of the variable is printed whenever it changes. Execution is substantially slower during this form of tracing.

If no argument is specified, then all source lines are printed before they are executed. Execution is substantially slower during this form of tracing.

The clause `"in procedure/function"` restricts tracing information to be printed only while executing inside the given procedure or function.

`Condition` is a boolean expression and is evaluated prior to printing the tracing information; if it is false, then the information is not printed.

```
stop [procid] if condition
stop [procid] at source-line-number [if condition]
stop [procid] in procedure/function [if condition]
stop [procid] variable [if condition]
stop all
```
Stop execution when the given line is reached, procedure or function called, variable changed, or condition true. "stop all" immediately stops all running processes; all other forms of the `stop` command set some form of breakpoint.

For multiprocess applications, the optional `procid` parameter specifies which process the breakpoint applies to. By default, the breakpoint is set in all processes created from the current program, and only the process that encounters the breakpoint is stopped. A `procid` of the form `%n` specifies that the breakpoint applies only to process n. If the `procid` is `all`, all processes are stopped if any process encounters the breakpoint. A `procid` of the form `%objfile` specifies that the breakpoint applies to each process created from `objfile`.

If a process is running, the `stop` command does not take effect in that process until it is stopped.

```
status [> filename]
```
Print out the currently active `trace` and `stop` commands.

```
delete command-number ...
```
Cancel the traces or stops corresponding to the given numbers. The numbers associated with traces and stops are printed by the `status` command.

```
catch[signal]
ignore [signal]
```
Start or stop trapping a signal before it is sent to the program. This is useful when a program being debugged handles signals such as interrupts. A signal may be specified by number or by a name (e.g., `SIGINT`). Signal names are case insensitive, and the "SIG" prefix is optional. By default all signals are trapped except `SIGCONT`, `SIGCHILD`, `SIGALRM`, and `SIGKILL`. When entered without parameters, `catch` lists the signals and events that will be caught, and `ignore` lists the signals and events that will be ignored.

```
catch event
ignore event
```
Catch or ignore the specified event, which may be `fork`, `exec`, or `exit`. By default, execs and exits are caught, and forks are ignored. If you direct Pdbx to catch forks, the child process is stopped immediately after a fork, but the parent is not stopped. If you direct Pdbx to catch execs, the process is stopped just before the new

program begins execution. If you direct Pdbx to catch exits, the process is stopped just before it is removed by the system; no matter how you resume execution of the process, it will exit.

signal [procid] signal
> Send the specified signal to the specified process (defaults to the current process). Procid may be all or %n.

cont [procid] [signal] [to linenumber] [&]
> Continue execution from where it stopped. For multiprocess applications, the optional procid parameter specifies which process is to be continued (defaults to the current process). procid may be all or %n.
>
> If a signal is specified, the process continues as though it received the signal (any signal previously caught is canceled). A signal of zero indicates that execution should continue as if the process had never been stopped. Otherwise, the process is continued with whatever signal was just received. If the process has multiple signals pending, the signal parameter overrides only the signal that was caught.
>
> If the optional linenumber parameter is specified, execution continues until the specified source line is executed, then stops.

step [procid] [&]
> Execute one source line. Any signal previously caught is canceled. For multiprocess applications, the optional procid parameter specifies which process to execute. Procid may be all or %n.

next [procid] [&]
> Execute up to the next source line. Any signal previously caught is canceled. Procid may be all or %n. The difference between next and step is that if the line contains a call to a procedure (or function), the step command will stop at the beginning of that procedure, while the next command will stop after completion of the procedure.

return [procedure]
> Continue until a return to procedure is executed, or until the current procedure returns if none is specified.

call procedure()
call procedure(parameters)
> Execute the object code associated with the named procedure or function.

window [%n] on ttyname
> Make ttyname the debugging window for process n. This command can be used to simplify the debugging of multiprocess applications by providing a different control

terminal for each process. The specified process (defaults to the current process) will be used as the current process when interpreting commands from `ttyname`. If a process is explicitly specified, `ttyname` will be used for the specified process's standard input, standard output, standard error, and debugger messages. `Ttyname` may specify a BSS/PC-Shells window (see shells(1)) or an ordinary terminal with login disabled. `Ttyname` may be a complete device name (e.g., "`/dev/ttyp9`") or its two-character suffix (e.g., "`p9`").

Printing Variables and Expressions

Names are resolved first using the static scope of the current function, then using the dynamic scope if the name is not defined in the static scope. If static and dynamic searches do not yield a result, an arbitrary symbol is chosen, and the message "`[using qualified name]`" is printed. The name resolution procedure may be overridden by qualifying an identifier with a block name, e.g., "`module variable`". A `module` is considered to be the subroutines and data inside a source file and is named by the file name without "`.c`", "`.f`", or "`.p`". The Fortran and Pascal compilers are case insensitive, so identifiers for these languages must be specified as lowercase only (or uppercase only if the `-u` option is specified when `Pdbx` is invoked).

Expressions are specified with an approximately common subset of C and Pascal syntax. Indirection can be denoted using either a prefix "`*`" or a postfix "`^`", and array expressions are subscripted by brackets ("`[ ]`"). The field reference operator ("`.`") can be used with pointers as well as records, so "`.`" can be used in place of the C operator "`->`" (but "`->`" is also supported).

For multiprocess applications, an expression of the form `n:expr` yields the value of `expr` when interpreted in the context of process `n`. Process `n` must be stopped when the expression is evaluated. If the `n:` prefix is omitted, the current process is used.

            *   *   *   (4 pages omitted)   *   *   *

FILES

`a.out`	object file
`name.dbg`	symbolic information from Fortran and Pascal

SEE ALSO

cc(1), pascal(1), fortran(1), ddt(1)

DYNIX Pdbx Debugger User's Manual

COMMENTS

`Pdbx` suffers from the same "multiple include" malady as did `sdb`. If you have a program consisting of a number of object files and each is built from source files that include header files, the symbolic information for the header files is replicated in each object file. Since about one debugger start-up is done for each link, having the linker (`ld`) re-organize the symbol information would not save much time, though it would reduce some of the disk space used.

This problem is an artifact of the unrestricted semantics of `#include`'s in C. For example, an include file can contain static declarations that are separate entities for each file in which they are included.

NAME

mmap – map an open file into the process's address space

SYNOPSIS

```
#include <sys/types.h>
#include <sys/mman.h>

mmap(addr, len, prot, share, fd, pos)
caddr_t  addr;     /* starting virt-addr */
int      len;      /* length (bytes) to map */
int      prot;     /* RO, RW encoding */
int      share;    /* private/shared modifications */
int      fd;       /* open file to be mapped */
off_t    pos;      /* where in file to begin map */
```

DESCRIPTION

Mmap causes the file referenced by fd, starting at byte pos for len bytes in the file, to be mapped into the calling process's address space, starting at virtual address addr for len bytes, using protection specified by prot; modifications to the mapped memory are either private to the process or shared, as specified by share. Mmap can be used to allocate regions of shared memory, to map files into memory, and to access special regions of the physical address space.

Fd must reference an open regular (IFREG) or character special (IFCHR) file. The device driver that implements the IFCHR special file must support mapping for this to succeed. Typically, a regular file is used to map shared memory.

The share argument specifies whether modifications to a mapped file are to be kept private to the calling process or shared with other processes accessing the file. If share is MAP_SHARED, all modifications to the file are shared with others who have it concurrently mapped. If share is MAP_PRIVATE, all modifications are local to the calling process; this doesn't restrict other processes from mapping the file. MAP_SHARED and MAP_PRIVATE have no relation to flock(2) and do not restrict read and write system-calls. If share is MAP_ZEROFILL, the space indicated from addr for len bytes is replaced by private pages that are zero-filled when referenced. MAP_ZEROFILL ignores the fd argument, and pos is ignored other than being checked for alignment (specifying fd and pos = 0 is recommended). (Note: MAP_PRIVATE is not supported in this implementation.)

The prot argument should be PROT_WRITE for write access to the mapped region, PROT_READ for read access, PROT_EXEC for executable access. These values can be ORed to obtain read-write access, etc. For programming convenience, PROT_RDWR is defined as (PROT_READ|PROT_WRITE). The file access permissions on fd must allow the requested access. The prot argument affects only the calling process; other processes mapping the same file may have different access.

The `addr`, `len`, and `pos` arguments must be integral multiples of the system page size, as defined by getpagesize(2). It is possible to map over previously mapped pages. If `addr` and `len` specify a nonexistent part of the process's address space, the process's data segment is grown to accommodate the request, and the process "break" (see brk(2)) is set to the high end of the mapped region. Reference to any "holes" between the mapped region and the rest of the data segment result in a segmentation fault (`SIGSEGV`). `Mmap` does not allow mapping over text or stack pages.

When memory is mapped to a regular file, the file acts like a paging area for the mapped memory region. `Read` and `write` operations to mapped regions of the file also affect the corresponding memory. The memory contents are copied out to the file when the process is swapped or exits, or when the region is otherwise unmapped by the last process that has it mapped. For programs that use shared memory but do not need a permanent disk image of the memory, the file associated with `fd` can be `unlinked` (see unlink(2)) even before the call to `mmap`: if the file is `unlinked` when the region is unmapped, the disk space will not be updated.

Regular files have their size rounded up to a file system block boundary. Any non-existent space in the file at the time of the `mmap` request (for example, in a sparse file) is allocated and filled with zeroes when referenced. Both of these operations require write access to the file.

The type of file referenced may impose further restrictions on the `pos`, `offset`, or other parameters. Refer to the manual entry of the relevant device driver (for example, pmap(4)) for details.

Closing a file descriptor previously used in an `mmap` operation unmaps all pages mapped by that file descriptor (see also munmap(2)). If the file-descriptor has been `duped` prior to being closed, no unmap takes place.

`Mmap` can be called multiple times with the same file descriptor, resulting in several (possibly overlapping) mapped regions. A process can have up to 8 regions mapped simultaneously; mappings that are completely overlapped by subsequent mappings are not counted in this total. Mappings which use the same file descriptor, and `addr` and `pos` arguments that align virtually with a previous mapping, also don't count in this total; the simplest case is mapping more of a file, starting from the end of a previous mapping.

All mapped files remain mapped in both the parent and child process after a `fork`. All flavors of the `exit` system call, when successful, remove all maps the calling process had established. If a process has any maps, `vfork` behaves exactly like `fork`.

There are three types of mapping: paged, physical, and non-paged memory. The type of mapping is determined by the type of file being mapped. Paged maps support shared memories and mapped regular files. Physical maps deal with hardware that has restrictive access capability (for example, the MULTIBUS address space, including Atomic Lock Memory). Non-paged memory maps are typically used for special reserved areas of system memory; they are assumed to behave exactly like memory, supporting accesses of arbitrary size and alignment, DMA, etc.

System services (raw IO, read/write, stat, etc.) are supported in paged and non-paged memory maps; attempts at such services in physically mapped address space result in an error, typically EFAULT. Core dumps include a copy of any mapped address space; however, physically mapped addresses read as zero.

Regular files (IFREG) are always page-mapped. Character special files (IFCHR) can support paged, physical, or non-paged maps, depending on the underlying hardware. Physical and non-paged maps are always valid in the process address space; references won't cause a page fault.

RETURN VALUE

Mmap returns zero when successful. Otherwise it returns −1 and places the error number in the global variable errno.

EXAMPLES

The following code sets up a 1-Mbyte region of shared memory at the first page boundary above the current program "break". This region will be shared with the process's children and with any other process that maps the file "shmem".

```
pgsz = getpagesize();
shm_base = (char *) ( ((int)sbrk(0) + (pgsz-1)) & ~(pgsz-1) );
fd = open ("shmem", O_CREAT | O_RDWR, 0666);
mmap (shm_base, 0x100000, PROT_RDWR, MAP_SHARED, fd, 0);
```

The following code maps the first page of Atomic Lock Memory into the process's virtual address space at address 0x200000. This region will be shared with the process's children and with any other process that maps the file "/dev/alm/alm00".

```
pgsz = getpagesize();
fd = open ("/dev/alm/alm00", O_RDWR, 0);
mmap (0x200000, pgsz, PROT_RDWR, MAP_SHARED, fd, 0);
```

ERRORS

[EINVAL]   Addr, pos, or len is not a multiple of the system page size.

[EINVAL]   Prot did not specify at least one of PROT_WRITE or PROT_READ, share did not specify MAP_SHARED or MAP_ZEROFILL, or share specified MAP_ZEROFILL, but prot did not contain PROT_RDWR. (MAP_PRIVATE is currently unsupported).

[EINVAL]   Fd does not represent a regular or character special file.

[EINVAL]   The process is the child of a vfork.

[EINVAL]   The area defined by the `addr` and `len` arguments overlaps text or stack pages of the process.

[ENODEV]   The device driver indicated by `fd` does not support mapping.

[ENOMEM]   There is no swap space for the page table of a mapped regular file, or you are trying to create too large a process.

[EMFILE]   The system-defined per-process limit on the number of `mmap`ed files (currently 8) was exceeded.

[ENFILE]   The system-wide limit on the number of mapped regular files was exceeded. This limit is defined by the variable `nmfile` in `/sys/conf/param.c`.

[EACCES]   `Fd` does not allow the desired access (read or write), or a write-only file descriptor was used.

[EACCES]   A mapped regular file must be extended to a file system block boundary, or the file must have space allocated, and the file descriptor is read-only.

[ENOSPC]   A mapped regular file was sparse, and there was insufficient space in the file system to satisfy the request.

[EFBIG]   The `pos` and `len` arguments would create too large a file.

[others]   Other error values may be returned by some device drivers when requested to map. See the relevant driver manual entry for details.

SEE ALSO
fork(2), getpagesize(2), munmap(2), pmap(4), vm_ctl(2)
Balance Guide to Parallel Programming

BUGS
A mapped file may not be truncated.

If a file is extended to a file system block boundary, its original size is lost.

Current restrictions on what parts of the address space can be re-mapped should be lifted.

NOTES
Due to a hardware restriction, PROT_WRITE implies PROT_READ also. PROT_EXEC is ignored.

To minimize overhead, mapped regions should be kept as close as possible to the low end of process memory.

Address space holes under the process "break" read as zeroes in core files.

H4. Compiler directives

To parallelize a Fortran DO loop by partitioning on data, the variables as used within the loop must be classified and the appropriate compiler directives added to the code.

The possible variable classifications are:

- *Shared*—scalar or array that is read-only, or array where each element is referenced by only one loop iteration.

- *Local*—scalar initialized in each loop iteration before it is used (i.e., the variable could be renamed in each iteration without affecting the result).

- *Reduction*—scalar or array used (perhaps more than once) in only one associative, commutative operation within the loop, which is of the form *var = var op expr*.

- *Shared ordered*—scalar or array that is not *shared*, *local*, or *reduction*, and execution of the loop iterations one at a time in random order would produce incorrect results.

- *Shared locked*—scalar or array that is none of the above (i.e., the variable can be read and written by more than one loop iteration, and execution of the iterations one at a time in random order would produce correct results).

The available compiler directives are:

- C$DOACROSS—identify DO loop for parallel execution.

- C$ORDER—start loop section containing a shared ordered variable.

- C$ENDORDER—end loop section containing a shared ordered variable.

- C$—add Fortran statement for conditional compilation.

- C$&—continue parallel programming directive.

In addition, the DYNIX Parallel Programming Library routines m_lock and m_unlock are used to mark loop sections containing shared locked variables.

The C$DOACROSS directive is inserted on the line immediately preceding the DO statement. The directive has the form:

C$DOACROSS *option* [, *option* . . .]

The options are SHARE, LOCAL, REDUCTION, ORDER, UNROLL, and CHUNK. The variables associated with each option are listed after the option, in parentheses and separated by commas.

The SHARE option is used to list all *shared*, *shared ordered*, and *shared locked* variables. The LOCAL option is followed by all *local* variables, and the REDUCTION option is followed by all *reduction* variables.

If the loop includes any *shared ordered* variables, the loop section containing each of them must be named and delimited with the C$ORDER and C$ENDORDER directives:

C$ORDER *section_name*
C$ENDORDER *section_name*

The *section_name* parameter can be any valid Fortran name. The C$ORDER directive is placed on the line immediately preceding the first reference to the variable, and the C$ENDORDER directive is placed on the line immediately following the last reference to the variable. In addition, the *section_name* must be listed in the C$DOACROSS directive using the ORDER option. A long C$DOACROSS directive can be continued to a new line using the C$& directive.

A *shared locked* variable must be protected by calls to the DYNIX Parallel Programming Library routines m_lock and m_unlock. The call to m_lock is placed on the line immediately preceding the first reference to the variable, and the call to m_unlock is placed on the line immediately following the last reference to the variable. The C$ directive can be used with these calls (or any valid Fortran statement) so that they are compiled only when the preprocessor is invoked.

The C$DOACROSS options UNROLL and CHUNK are described in the *Balance 8000/21000 Fortran Compiler User's Manual*.

H5.   The DYNIX Parallel Programming Library

The DYNIX Parallel Programming Library contains routines for creation, synchronization, and termination of parallel processes, and for management of shared memory.

A loop to be executed in parallel is placed in a subprogram and called using the `m_fork` function. This function forks a set of child processes and assigns an identical copy of the subprogram (and any non-shared data) to each process for parallel execution. The parent process also gets a copy to execute. The default number of child processes forked is half the number of CPUs online. The number of child processes can be set explicitly by first calling `m_set_procs`. If desired, the number given to `m_set_procs` can be dependent on the number of actual CPUs available, which is determined by the function `cpus_online`.

After execution of the loop, the default action is to let the child processes spin until the next `m_fork` call. `M_fork` will then reuse the existing processes, saving the overhead of process creation. Alternatively, the child processes can be suspended via a call to `m_park_procs` and later resumed via `m_rele_procs`. This saves the overhead of spinning processes at a minimal cost. After the last call to `m_fork`, all child processes should be terminated using `m_kill_procs`.

Loop iterations within the subprogram can be allocated statically or dynamically. Library routines available to set up scheduling are `m_get_myid`, which returns the process identification number assigned by `m_fork`, `m_get_numprocs`, which returns the total number of child processes, and `m_next`, which increments a global counter.

Static scheduling assigns each process an equal number of iterations and is appropriate if each iteration involves the same amount of computation. A typical algorithm for this is to get `n`, the total number of child processes, and execute every `n`th iteration starting with the process id.

Dynamic scheduling allows each process to obtain one or more loop iterations, execute them, and return to an iteration queue for more work. This type of scheduling is appropriate when the amount of computation in each iteration varies. If the loop iterations are sufficiently computationally intense, dynamic scheduling can be implemented easily and efficiently by using the global counter as the iteration queue. Otherwise, the queue can be implemented by creating a shared loop index protected by a lock. Lock overhead and contention can be minimized by allowing a process to grab a large number of iterations at each visit to the queue.

The Parallel Programming Library contains lock and barrier functions for use in synchronization. Lock routines `m_lock` and `m_unlock` interface to a single lock. `S_init_lock`, `s_lock`, `s_clock`, and `s_unlock` are used when multiple active locks are needed. `M_sync` sets up a single barrier for all active processes, while `s_init_barrier` and `s_wait_barrier` can be used to set multiple barriers and synchronize subsets of the processes.

A single-process section can be set up using `m_single` and `m_multi`. `M_single` halts the execution of child processes, allowing the parent process to perform some function such as I/O. Child process execution is resumed by calling `m_multi`.

    `Shmalloc` and `shfree` are used for dynamic memory allocation in C. `Shbrk` and `shsbrk` change the size of a process's shared data segment, and `brk` and `sbrk` change the size of the private data segment.

NAME

intro – introduction to Parallel Programming Library

DESCRIPTION

These routines constitute the Parallel Programming Library, which supports microtasking and multitasking in C, Pascal, and Fortran programs. (For information on microtasking and multitasking programming models, refer to the *Balance Guide to Parallel Programming*.) The Parallel Programming Library is not supported under System V (att universe).

The routines described here include the current Parallel Programming Library, /usr/lib/libpps.a, and the previous version, /usr/lib/libpp.a. The older version is retained for compatibility with earlier DYNIX releases. The routines from the current library are linked into a program by including the -lpps option in the cc or ld command line, or by including the -lpps or -mp option in the fortran or pascal command line. The routines from the old library are linked by including the -lpp option. You must not link both libraries with the same program.

For an overview of how the current Parallel Programming Library routines are used, and for sample programs and related information, refer to the *Balance Guide to Parallel Programming*.

LIST OF FUNCTIONS

The following routines support microtasking:

Name	Appears on Page	Description
m_fork	m_fork(3P)	execute a subprogram in parallel
m_get_myid	m_get_myid(3P)	return process identification
m_get_numprocs	m_get_numprocs(3P)	get number of child processes
m_kill_procs	m_kill_procs(3P)	kill child processes
m_lock	m_lock(3P)	initialize and lock a lock
m_multi	m_single(3P)	end single-process section
m_next	m_next(3P)	increment global counter
m_park_procs	m_park_procs(3P)	suspend child process execution
m_rele_procs	m_park_procs(3P)	resume child process execution
m_set_procs	m_set_procs(3P)	set number of child processes
m_single	m_single(3P)	start single-process section
m_sync	m_sync(3P)	check in at barrier
m_unlock	m_lock(3P)	unlock a lock

The following routines support multitasking:

Name	Appears on Page	Description
cpus_online	cpus_online(3P)	return number of CPUs on-line
s_clock	s_lock(3P)	lock a lock, return if unsuccessful
s_init_barrier	s_wait_barrier(3P)	initialize a barrier

s_init_lock	s_lock(3P)	initialize a lock
s_lock	s_lock(3P)	lock a lock
S_LOCK	s_lock(3P)	lock a lock (C macro)
s_unlock	s_lock(3P)	unlock a lock
S_UNLOCK	s_lock(3P)	unlock a lock (C macro)
s_wait_barrier	s_wait_barrier(3P)	wait at a barrier

The following routines support memory allocation for parallel programming. The brk and sbrk routines are available without loading the Parallel Programming Library (see brk(2)), but the versions in the Parallel Programming Library are necessary for compatibility with the rest of the library.

Name	Appears on Page	Description
brk	brk(3P)	change private data segment size
sbrk	brk(3P)	change private data segment size
shbrk	shbrk(3P)	change shared data segment size

The following routines constitute the previous version of the Parallel Programming Library /usr/lib/libpp.a, and are retained for compatibility with earlier releases:

Name	Appears on Page	Description
p_cpus_online	p_cpus_online(3P)	get number of processors in system
p_finit_barrier	p_wait_barrier(3P)	initialize a barrier (Fortran)
p_init	p_init(3P)	initialize shared memory and Atomic Lock Memory
p_init_barrier	p_wait_barrier(3P)	initialize a barrier
p_init_lock	p_lock(3P)	initialize a lock
p_lock	p_lock(3P)	lock a lock
p_shmalloc	p_shmalloc(3P)	allocate shared memory
p_unlock	p_lock(3P)	unlock a lock
p_wait_barrier	p_wait_barrier(3P)	wait at a barrier

The following routines are retained in the old Parallel Programming Library for compatibility with earlier releases, but are not described elsewhere in these man pages:

p_exit   is equivalent to exit(3)

p_fexit   is equivalent to the standard Fortran routine fhalt

p_finit   has no effect

NAME

      brk, sbrk – change private data segment size

SYNOPSIS

    C syntax:

```
#include <parallel/parallel.h>
caddr_t brk(addr)
caddr_t addr;
caddr_t sbrk(incr)
int incr;
```

    Pascal syntax:

      none

    Fortran syntax:

      none

DESCRIPTION

    These routines are identical to the standard `brk` and `sbrk` (see `brk(2)`) routines except that these routines verify that the private data segment does not overlap the shared data segment which follows it. If the `brk` or `sbrk` call will cause the segments to overlap, the routine issues an error.

ERRORS

    If an error occurs, the return value is −1 and the variable `errno` contains the error code. `Brk` and `sbrk` can return the following error codes:

    [ENOMEM]   The requested private data segment will overlap the shared data segment.

    [ENOMEM]   The routine cannot allocate file system space to expand the file which has been memory mapped to the shared data segment (see `mmap(2)`). The routine tries to allocate file system space from directories in the following order:

        1. The directory indicated by the `$TMPPATH` environment variable
        2. The current directory
        3. The user's home directory
        4. The directory `/usr/tmp`
        5. The directory `/tmp`

    [ENOMEM]   The limit, as set by `setrlimit`, was exceeded.

SEE ALSO

    execve(2), getrlimit(2), malloc(3), end(3)
    Balance Guide to Parallel Programming

NOTES

The gap between the private data segment and the shared data segment can be adjusted by using the −Z linker option (see ld(1)).

NAME

      cpus_online – returns the number of CPUs on-line

SYNOPSIS

    C syntax:

```
int cpus_online ();
```

    Pascal syntax:

```
function cpus_online : integer;
cexternal;
```

    Fortran syntax:

```
integer*4 function cpus_online
```

DESCRIPTION

      The `cpus_online` routine returns the number of processors currently configured and on-line.

SEE ALSO

      tmp_ctl(2), p_cpus_online(3P)

      Balance Guide to Parallel Programming

NAME
        shbrk, shsbrk – change shared data segment size

SYNOPSIS
    C syntax:

```
#include  <parallel/parallel.h>
caddr_t  shbrk(addr)
caddr_t  addr;

caddr_t  shsbrk(incr)
int  incr;
```

    Pascal syntax:

```
none
```

    Fortran syntax:

```
none
```

DESCRIPTION
        For a set of parallel processes executing a single application, shbrk sets the system's idea of
        the lowest shared data segment location not used by the program (called the shared break) to
        addr (rounded up to the next multiple of the system's page size). Locations greater than addr
        and below the stack pointer or another memory mapped region (see mmap(2)) are not in the
        address space and will thus cause a memory violation if accessed.

        In the alternate function, shsbrk, incr more bytes are added to the program's shared data
        space and a pointer to the start of the new area is returned.

        When a program begins execution via exec, the shared break is set at the highest location
        defined by the program. Ordinarily, therefore, only programs with growing shared data areas
        need to use shsbrk.

RETURN VALUE
        Zero is returned if the shared break could be set; −1 if the program requests more memory than
        the system limit. Shsbrk returns −1 if the break could not be set.

ERRORS
        Shbrk and shsbrk will fail, and no additional memory will be allocated if any of the fol-
        lowing error conditions occur:

        [EINVAL]   The shared break address would be lowered.

[ENOMEM]   The routine cannot allocate file system space to expand the file which has been memory mapped to the shared data segment (see mmap(2)). The routine tries to allocate file system space from directories in the following order:

1. The directory indicated by the $TMPPATH environment variable
2. The current directory
3. The user's home directory
4. The directory /usr/tmp
5. The directory /tmp

[ENOMEM]   The limit, as set by setrlimit, was exceeded.

[ENOMEM]   The new shared data segment would overlap the stack segment.

SEE ALSO

exec(2), getrlimit(2), shmalloc(3), end(3), mmap(2)
Balance Guide to Parallel Programming

BUGS

At this time, the size of the shared data segment can only be increased.

The shared break cannot be set above the stack segment limit for any of the processes in the program. (Remember that each process can have a different stack size.) If a process sets the shared break above the bottom of any process's stack, any reference to the overlapping area of that stack causes a core dump and aborts the program with a status of SIGSEV.

Shbrk and shsbrk use the SIGSEGV signal and signal handler for internal purposes. Users who declare their own SIGSEGV handler cannot expect reliable results from these routines.

If a shbrk or shsbrk call causes the shared data segment to overlap a memory mapped region, the shared data segment replaces the mapped region.

NAME
     shmalloc, shfree – shared memory allocator

SYNOPSIS
     C syntax:

```
char *shmalloc(size)
unsigned size;
shfree(ptr)
char *ptr;
```

     Pascal syntax:

```
none
```

     Fortran syntax:

```
none
```

DESCRIPTION
     Shmalloc and shfree provide a simple general-purpose shared memory allocation package
     for a set of processes executing a single application. To use these routines, the program must
     have been linked with the Parallel Programming Library. Shmalloc returns a pointer to a
     block of at least size bytes beginning on a 4-byte word boundary.

     The argument to shfree is a pointer to a block previously allocated by shmalloc; this
     space is made available for further allocation, but its contents are left undisturbed.

     Clearly, grave disorder will result if the space assigned by shmalloc is overrun or if some
     random number is handed to shfree.

     Shmalloc maintains multiple lists of free blocks according to size, allocating space from the
     appropriate list. It calls shsbrk (see shbrk(3P)) to get more memory from the system when
     there is no suitable space already free. Shmalloc and shfree coordinate the allocation of
     shared memory among the processes in the task. They maintain a consistent list of free blocks
     even when several processes are allocating shared memory concurrently. Concurrent requests for
     shared memory blocks always return unique blocks from the program's shared data segment.

DIAGNOSTICS
     Shmalloc returns a null pointer (0) if there is no available shared memory or if the region has
     been detectably corrupted by storing data outside the bounds of a block. Shmalloc may be
     recompiled to check the arena very stringently on every transaction; those sites with a source
     code license may check the source code to see how this can be done.

SEE ALSO
     shbrk(3P)
     Balance Guide to Parallel Programming

NAME

m_fork – execute a subprogram in parallel

SYNOPSIS

C syntax:

```
#include <parallel/microtask.h>
m_fork(func[,arg,...]);
void (*func)();
sometype args;
```

Pascal syntax:

```
function mfork: integer;
cexternal;
{$E+}
procedure func(arg,...);
(code)
{$E-}
m_fork(func[,arg,...]);
args : sometype;
```

Fortran syntax:

```
external func
integer*4 m_fork
i=m_fork(func[,arg,...])
subroutine func(arg,...)
```

DESCRIPTION

The `m_fork` routine assigns a subprogram to child processes, which then cooperate in executing the subprogram in parallel. The number of child processes used by the `m_fork` call can be set with a previous call to `m_set_procs`. If `m_set_procs` has not been called, the number of child processes defaults to:

```
(number of CPUs on-line)/2
```

If the program has no child processes from previous `m_fork` calls, the call creates the child processes. If there are already child processes from a previous call, `m_fork` re-uses the existing processes.

When an `m_fork` call creates child processes, each child process is given a private integer variable called `m_myid` , which identifies it within the set of child processes being created. The parent process's identification number is always zero. The first child process's identification is

1, the second's is 2, and so on. You can call the routine `m_getmyid` to find out the identification number of a child process (see m_getmyid(3P)).

For C programs, the header file `/parallel/microtask.h` contains an external declaration of the variable `m_myid` and the variable `m_numprocs`, which indicates the total number of processes executing the subprogram (including all the child processes and the parent process).

Once child processes are available, `m_fork` starts them executing the subprogram `func` with the given arguments. The child processes execute the subprogram until they all return from it. At this point, the program returns from the `m_fork` call, and the child processes spin, waiting for more work. The program can either kill the child processes with a call to the routine `m_kill`, suspend them with a call to `m_park_procs`, or let the child processes spin until they are re-used by another `m_fork` call. If the child processes are to be re-used, the `m_park_procs` offers the most efficient use of the Balance, because it saves the CPU usage of having the processes spin, and it saves the overhead of having to recreate processes on the next `m_fork` call.

You must ensure that arguments passed to the subprogram `func` are either call-by-value arguments or addresses of data in shared memory. They must not be addresses in the parent's private data segment.

ERRORS

The `m_fork` call fails, and no child processes are created if one of the following error conditions occurs:

[EINVAL]   This call to `m_fork` is nested within a previous call.

[EAGAIN]   The `m_fork` call would exceed `nproc`, the system's limit on the total number of executing processes.

[EAGAIN]   The `m_fork` call would exceed `maxuprc`, the system's limit on executing processes for a single user.

NOTES

Each call to `m_fork` resets the global counter (see m_next(3P)).

SEE ALSO

getrlimit(2), shmalloc(3), brk(3P), m_set_procs(3P), m_kill_procs(3P), m_next(3P)
Balance Guide to Parallel Programming

NAME

m_get_myid – return process identification

SYNOPSIS

C syntax:

```
#include <parallel/microtask.h>
int  m_get_myid();
int  i;
i=m_get_myid();
```

Pascal syntax:

```
function  m_get_myid : integer ;
cexternal  ;
```

Fortran syntax:

```
integer*4  function  m_get_myid
```

DESCRIPTION

The `m_get_myid` routine returns the value of the variable `m_myid`, the process's
identification number. For the parent process, this variable has the value zero. Child processes
are assigned identification numbers in the order of their creation: the first child process has
identification number 1, the second has 2, and so on. The C header file:

```
/usr/include/parallel/microtask.h
```

contains an external declaration of the variable.

SEE ALSO

fortran(1), m_fork(3P)
Balance Guide to Parallel Programming

NAME

m_get_numprocs – return number of child processes

SYNOPSIS

C syntax:

```
#include <parallel/microtask.h>
int m_get_numprocs();
```

Pascal syntax:

```
function m_get_numprocs : integer ;
cexternal ;
```

Fortran syntax:

```
integer*4 function m_get_numprocs
```

DESCRIPTION

The `m_get_numprocs` routine returns the value of the variable `m_numprocs`, the current number of processes in the program. This value reflects the number of child processes plus one, the parent process.

SEE ALSO

fortran(1), m_set_procs(3P)
Balance Guide to Parallel Programming

NAME

　　m_kill_procs – kill child processes

SYNOPSIS

　C syntax:

```
#include <parallel/microtask.h>
m_kill_procs();
```

　Pascal syntax:

```
procedure m_kill_procs ;
cexternal ;
```

　Fortran syntax:

```
subroutine m_kill_procs
```

DESCRIPTION

　　The m_kill_procs routine terminates the child processes created by a previous call to m_fork.

　　The m_kill_procs routine fails if it is called from a subprogram invoked by an m_fork call.

ERRORS

　　The m_kill_procs call fails if the following error condition occurs:

　　[EINVAL]　　Some child processes are still executing within an m_fork call.

SEE ALSO

　　m_fork(3P)

　　Balance Guide to Parallel Programming

NAME
          m_lock, m_unlock – lock, unlock locks

SYNOPSIS
     C syntax:

```
#include <parallel/microtask.h>
m_lock ();
m_unlock ();
```

     Pascal syntax:

```
procedure m_lock ;
cexternal ;
procedure m_unlock ;
cexternal ;
```

     Fortran syntax:

```
subroutine m_lock()
subroutine m_unlock()
```

DESCRIPTION
          The m_lock and m_unlock routines are microtasking interfaces to a single slock_t-type
          lock. For a single lock, they are easier to use than the s_init_lock, s_lock, and
          s_unlock routines because they don't require you to declare or initialize the lock before using
          it. They are also faster than the other routines because they do not pass the lock address as an
          argument.

          M_lock locks the lock. M_lock is always successful; it spins as long as is necessary to
          acquire the lock.

          M_unlock unlocks the lock.

SEE ALSO
          intro(3P), s_lock(3P), m_shmalloc(3P)
          Balance Guide to Parallel Programming

NAME

   m_next – increment global counter

SYNOPSIS

   C syntax:

```
#include <parallel/microtask.h>
int  m_next();
```

   Pascal syntax:

```
function  m_next  :  longint  ;
cexternal  ;
```

   Fortran syntax:

```
integer*4  function  m_next
```

DESCRIPTION

   The `m_next` routine atomically increments a global counter. The program's first call to `m_next` returns the value 1, the second returns 2, and so on. Calls to the `m_fork`, `m_sync`, or `m_single` routines reset the global counter to zero.

SEE ALSO

   m_fork(3P), m_sync(3P), m_single(3P)
   Balance Guide to Parallel Programming

NAME
       m_park_procs, m_rele_procs
              – suspend and resume child process execution

SYNOPSIS
   C syntax:

```
#include <parallel/microtask.h>
m_park_procs();
(serial code)
m_rele_procs();
```

   Pascal syntax:

```
procedure  m_park_procs  ;
cexternal  ;
procedure  m_rele_procs  ;
cexternal  ;
```

   Fortran syntax:

```
subroutine  m_park_procs
subroutine  m_rele_procs
```

DESCRIPTION
       The m_park_procs routine suspends execution of child processes created by an m_fork
       call. Typically, you would suspend child processes while the parent process is doing extensive
       I/O or setting up another phase of the program. The m_rele_procs routine resumes child
       process execution when the child processes are again required.

       Do not call   m_park_procs   when   m_fork   is executing.   Likewise, do not call
       m_park_procs when the child processes are already suspended. To suspend child process
       execution within an m_fork call, use m_single and m_next.

ERRORS
       These routines can return the following error:

       [EINVAL]   The routine was called in an inappropriate context. For example, the routine was
                   called from a subprogram executing in an m_fork call, or the processes were
                   already suspended.

SEE ALSO
       m_single(3P)
       Balance Guide to Parallel Programming

NAME

m_set_procs – set number of child processes

SYNOPSIS

C syntax:

```
#include <parallel/microtask.h>
int  m_set_procs(nprocs);
int  nprocs;
```

Pascal syntax:

```
function m_set_procs (numprocs : longint) : longint;
cexternal;
```

Fortran syntax:

```
integer*4 function m_set_procs(nprocs)
integer*4 nprocs
```

DESCRIPTION

The `m_set_procs` routine declares the number of processes to execute subprograms in parallel on subsequent calls to `m_fork`. The argument `nprocs` declares the total number of processes that will run in parallel, including the parent process and the child processes. If `nprocs` is zero, the program creates no child processes, but all barriers and locks are initialized as if the program were going to create child processes.

The `m_set_procs` routine initializes a shared variable called `m_numprocs`, which controls the number of processes created by subsequent calls to `m_fork`. The C header file:

```
/usr/include/parallel/microtask.h
```

contains an external declaration of `m_numprocs`, as well as the constant `MAXPROCS` which determines the maximum number of processes that the system will allow the program to create. The other limiting factor is the number of CPUs on-line: `m_nprocs` can be no more than the number of CPUs on-line minus one.

The `m_set_procs` routine is optional; if the program does not call this routine before calling `m_fork`, the number of processes defaults to:

```
(number of CPUs on-line)/2
```

The program must not call `m_set_procs` while the child processes from an `m_fork` call are still alive (that is, before an `m_kill_procs` call to kill the child processes).

ERRORS

If an `m_set_procs` call is successful, the return value is zero. If the call fails, the return value is `-1`, and the variable `errno` holds the error code.

The m_set_procs call fails if one of the following error conditions occurs:

[EINVAL]   The argument nprocs is greater than MAXPROCS, or it is greater than or equal to the number of on-line CPUs.

[EINVAL]   Children from an m_fork call are already running. In this case, call m_kill_procs to kill the existing child processes before calling m_set_procs.

SEE ALSO

m_fork(3P), m_kill_procs(3P)
Balance Guide to Parallel Programming

NAME

m_single, m_multi – mark single-process code section

SYNOPSIS

C syntax:

```
#include <parallel/microtask.h>
m_single();
(CODE)
m_multi();
```

Pascal syntax:

```
procedure m_single;
cexternal;
procedure m_multi;
cexternal;
```

Fortran syntax:

```
subroutine m_single
subroutine m_multi
```

DESCRIPTION

The `m_single` routine causes child processes to spin at a barrier until the parent process has executed the code following the `m_single` call and called the `m_multi` routine. The child processes then resume execution at the source line after the `m_multi` call. These routines are typically used to allow the parent process to perform I/O or other serial operations during an `m_fork` call.

NOTES

Calls to `m_single` are allowed only during `m_fork` calls. To suspend child processes after an `m_fork` call, use `m_park_procs` and `m_rele_procs`.

Do not call `m_multi` without calling `m_single` first.

Nested `m_single` calls are not allowed. Neither are `m_single` calls nested between calls to other lock routines, such as `s_lock` and `s_unlock`.

ERRORS

These routines can return the following error:

[EINVAL]   The routine was called in an inappropriate context. For example, `m_fork` had never been called, or the processes were already suspended with a call to `m_park_procs`.

371

SEE ALSO

    m_park_procs(3P)

    Balance Guide to Parallel Programming

NAME

m_sync – check in at barrier

SYNOPSIS

C syntax:

```
#include <parallel/microtask.h>
m_sync();
```

Pascal syntax:

```
procedure m_sync;
cexternal;
```

Fortran syntax:

```
subroutine m_sync
```

DESCRIPTION

The m_sync routine causes a process to spin until all cooperating processes have reached the same point and called m_sync. The program must not call the m_sync routine unless there are multiple processes executing; that is, unless the program is executing a subprogram during an m_fork call and is not between a pair of m_single/m_multi, m_lock/m_unlock, or s_lock/s_unlock calls.

NOTES

Calls to m_sync reset the global counter (see m_next(3P)).

ERRORS

These routines can return the following error:

[EINVAL]   There are no child processes executing.

SEE ALSO

m_set_procs(3P), m_fork(3P), m_single(3P), m_park_procs(3P), m_kill_procs(3P), m_next(3P)
Balance Guide to Parallel Programming

NAME

s_init_lock, s_lock, s_clock, s_unlock – initialize, lock, unlock locks

SYNOPSIS

C syntax:

```
#include <parallel/parallel.h>
slock_t *lp;
s_init_lock (lp);
s_lock (lp);
S_LOCK (lp);
s_clock (lp);
s_unlock (lp);
S_UNLOCK (lp);
```

Pascal syntax:

```
procedure s_init_lock(var lp : integer);
cexternal;
procedure s_lock(var lp : integer);
cexternal;
procedure s_clock(var lp : integer);
cexternal;
procedure s_unlock(var lp : integer);
cexternal;
```

Fortran syntax:

```
subroutine s_init_lock(lp)
subroutine s_lock(lp)
subroutine s_clock(lp)
subroutine s_unlock(lp)
integer*1 lp
```

DESCRIPTION

`S_init_lock` initializes a memory-based lock. After the lock is initialized, it can be locked with the `s_lock` or `s_clock` routine and unlocked with the `s_unlock` routine. There is no practical limit to the number of locks that can be used by a process.

In the C language, a lock is a shared data structure of type `slock_t`, as shown in the following declaration statement:

```
shared slock_t lock;
```

In Pascal, a lock is a global integer variable. In Fortran, a lock is an `INTEGER*1` variable. A Fortran lock must be placed in shared memory either by declaring it in a common block and using the loader `-F` option or by using the Fortran compiler `-mp` option, which places all variables into shared memory.

`S_lock` and `s_clock` lock the lock whose address is `lp`. The lock must previously have been initialized using `s_init_lock`. `S_lock` is always successful; it spins as long as is necessary to acquire the lock. `S_clock` is successful only if the lock is free; if the lock is held by another process, `s_clock` returns the value `S_FAILED`. `S_clock` can be used when a process does not need to acquire a particular lock (for instance, when another lock could be used instead).

`S_unlock` unlocks the lock whose address is `lp`.

`S_LOCK` and `S_UNLOCK` are available as C-preprocessor macro versions of `s_lock` and `s_unlock`. These macros are found in the header file:

`/usr/include/parallel/parallel.h`

The macros are faster than the normal function calls, but they can add to the code size. See the source code in:

`<parallel/parallel.h>`

for more information on the macros.

SEE ALSO

intro(3P), shmalloc(3P), fortran(1), ld(1)
Balance Guide to Parallel Programming

NOTES

The function names `s_init_lock`, `s_lock`, `s_clock`, and `s_unlock` are used in C, Pascal, and Fortran. In C, the `lp` argument is passed as a pointer to the lock, while in Pascal and Fortran, the argument is the address of the lock itself.

NAME

s_init_barrier, s_wait_barrier – initialize barrier, wait at barrier

SYNOPSIS

C syntax:

```
#include <parallel/parallel.h>
s_init_barrier (bp, nprocs);
sbarrier_t *bp;
int nprocs;

s_wait_barrier (bp);
sbarrier_t *bp;
```

Pascal syntax:

```
procedure s_init_barrier (var barrier : longint;
                                       nprocs : longint);
cexternal;
procedure s_wait_barrier (var barrier : longint);
cexternal;
```

Fortran syntax:

```
integer*4 barrier, nprocs
subroutine s_init_barrier (barrier, nprocs)
subroutine s_wait_barrier (barrier)
```

DESCRIPTION

S_init_barrier initializes a barrier as a rendezvous point for exactly nprocs processes. This barrier can be used subsequently with s_wait_barrier.

In C, a barrier is a shared data structure of type sbarrier_t as in:

```
shared sbarrier_t barrier;
```

In Pascal, a barrier is a global integer variable. In Fortran, a barrier is an INTEGER*4 variable. A Fortran barrier must be placed in shared memory either by declaring it in a common block and using the loader -F option or by using the Fortran -mp option, which places all variables into shared memory.

S_wait_barrier delays the process in a busy wait until exactly nprocs processes have called s_wait_barrier. At that point, all processes exit the busy wait simultaneously. The barrier must have been previously initialized using s_init_barrier.

Results are undefined if more than `nprocs` processes call `s_wait_barrier`. A barrier can be used any number of times without being re-initialized. A barrier should not be re-initialized while processes are waiting at the barrier.

SEE ALSO

intro(3P), s_shmalloc(3P)

Balance Guide to Parallel Programming

Index